WEB DATABASE

PRIMER PLUS

CONNECT YOUR DATABASE TO THE
WORLD WIDE WEB USING
HTML, CGI, AND JAVA™

PIROZ MOHSENI

WAITE GROUP PRESS™
A Division of
Sams Publishing
Corte Madera, CA

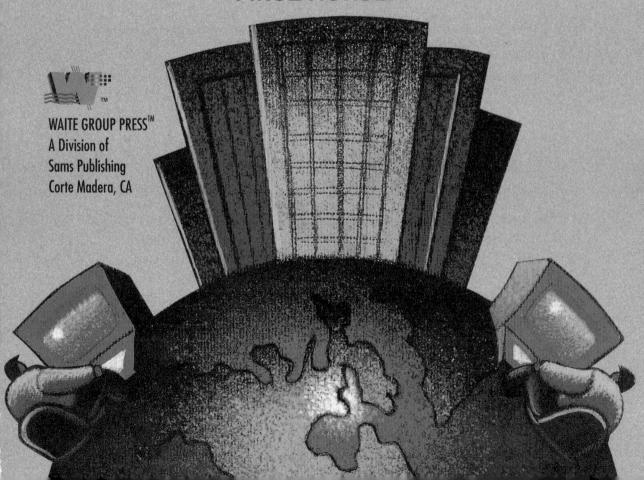

PUBLISHER: Mitchell Waite
ASSOCIATE PUBLISHER: Charles Drucker

ACQUISITIONS MANAGER: Jill Pisoni
ACQUISITIONS EDITOR: Joanne Miller

EDITORIAL DIRECTOR: John Crudo
PROJECT EDITOR: Lisa Goldstein
CONTENT EDITOR: Scott Rhoades
COPY EDITOR: Michelle Goodman/Creative Solutions
TECHNICAL REVIEWER: Alan Richmond

PRODUCTION DIRECTOR: Julianne Ososke
PRODUCTION MANAGER: Cecile Kaufman
SENIOR DESIGNER: Sestina Quarequio
DESIGNERS: Karen Johnston, Jil Weil
COVER ILLUSTRATION: David Tillinghast
PRODUCTION: Charlotte Clapp, Michael Henry, Ayanna Lacey, Paula Lowell, Andrew Stone

Printed in the United States of America
96 97 98 99 • 10 9 8 7 6 5 4 3 2 1

Library of Congress Cataloging-in-Publication Data
Mohseni, Piroz, 1972-
    Web database primer plus: connect your database to the world wide web using HTML, CGI, and Java™ / Piroz Mohseni.
        p.   cm.
    Includes index.
    ISBN 1-57169-070-0
    1. Database design.   2. World Wide Web (Information retrieval system) I. Title.
QA76.9.D26M66   1996
005.75'8--dc20

96-26988
CIP

Dedication

To Paria

Message from the
Publisher

WELCOME TO OUR NERVOUS SYSTEM

Some people say that the World Wide Web is a graphical extension of the information superhighway, just a network of humans and machines sending each other long lists of the equivalent of digital junk mail.

I think it is much more than that. To me, the Web is nothing less than the nervous system of the entire planet—not just a collection of computer brains connected together, but more like a billion silicon neurons entangled and recirculating electrochemical signals of information and data, each contributing to the birth of another CPU and another Web site.

Think of each person's hard disk connected at once to every other hard disk on earth, driven by human navigators searching like Columbus for the New World. Seen this way the Web is more of a super entity, a growing, living thing, controlled by the universal human will to expand, to be more. Yet, unlike a purposeful business plan with rigid rules, the Web expands in a nonlinear, unpredictable, creative way that echoes natural evolution.

We created our Web site not just to extend the reach of our computer book products but to be part of this synaptic neural network, to experience, like a nerve in the body, the flow of ideas and then to pass those ideas up the food chain of the mind. Your mind. Even more, we wanted to pump some of our own creative juices into this rich wine of technology.

TASTE OUR DIGITAL WINE

And so we ask you to taste our wine by visiting the body of our business. Begin by understanding the metaphor we have created for our Web site—a universal learning center, situated in outer space in the form of a space station. A place where you can journey to study any topic from the convenience of your own screen. Right now we are focusing on computer topics, but the stars are the limit on the Web.

If you are interested in discussing this Web site or finding out more about the Waite Group, please send me e-mail with your comments, and I will be happy to respond. Being a programmer myself, I love to talk about technology and find out what our readers are looking for.

200 Tamal Plaza
Corte Madera, CA 94925
415-924-2575
415-924-2576 fax

Sincerely,

Mitchell Waite

Web site:
http://www.waite.com/waite

CREATING THE HIGHEST QUALITY COMPUTER BOOKS IN THE INDUSTRY

Waite Group Press

Come Visit

WAITE.COM

Waite Group Press
World Wide Web Site

Now find all the latest information on Waite Group books at our new Web site, **http://www.waite.com/waite**. You'll find an online catalog where you can examine and order any title, review upcoming books, and send e-mail to our authors and editors. Our FTP site has all you need to update your book: the latest program listings, errata sheets, most recent versions of Fractint, POV Ray, Polyray, DMorph, and all the programs featured in our books. So download, talk to us, ask questions, on **http://www.waite.com/waite**.

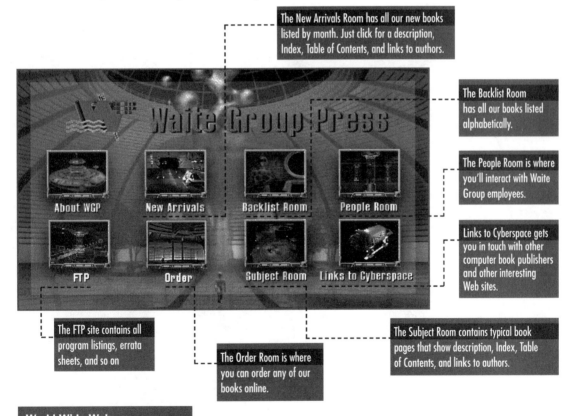

The New Arrivals Room has all our new books listed by month. Just click for a description, Index, Table of Contents, and links to authors.

The Backlist Room has all our books listed alphabetically.

The People Room is where you'll interact with Waite Group employees.

Links to Cyberspace gets you in touch with other computer book publishers and other interesting Web sites.

The FTP site contains all program listings, errata sheets, and so on

The Order Room is where you can order any of our books online.

The Subject Room contains typical book pages that show description, Index, Table of Contents, and links to authors.

About the Author

Piroz Mohseni works at Lucent Technologies as a software consultant. He is involved in a variety of Web and database projects. Prior to that, he was an assistant scientist at Ames Laboratory in Iowa. He received a B.S. in computer engineering from Iowa State University in May of 1995. His professional interests include the Internet, Java, and databases. Outside of computers, he enjoys reading, walking by the beach, and watching 49er football.

Table of Contents

Contents

Acknowledgments

Completion of this project would not have been possible without the support of many individuals. I'd like to thank my parents, Ali and Shirin, for their support and encouragement. Special thanks go to Dr. Reza Ehtessabian and his wife Arlene for their kind support throughout the past years. I am grateful to my uncle, Said Mohseni, for introducing me to the world of computers and for his continued guidance. I would like to also acknowledge all the members of the Applied Mathematical Sciences group at Ames Laboratory for creating the best working environment. In particular, I'd like to thank Dr. James Corones, Barbara Helland, Nazanin Imani, Ronald Winther, and James Lees.

A final appreciation to everyone at Waite Group Press for giving me this opportunity. Special thanks go to Lisa Goldstein for being a great project editor and Alan Richmond for reviewing all the technical details.

Introduction

The World Wide Web has revolutionized the computing world. Suddenly, there is open access to a vast amount of information to anyone who wants it anywhere around the world. New and innovative technology is being created daily. Yet, there is a powerful component of the Web that has yet to flourish. It is database publishing on the Web, and it is accomplished through a combination of Hypertext Markup Language (HTML), the Web authoring language, Common Gateway Interface (CGI), and database programming.

Whether you just want to make your favorite recipes available to the Web community or your company needs to provide an on-line ordering system to millions of potential customers, *Web Database Primer Plus* can help.

Web database publishing is becoming increasingly popular for several reasons. With soaring development costs, it is key to develop a graphical user interface for the database that will stay consistent across different platforms. The cost of commercial products that claim to create platform-independent applications is prohibitive for most organizations. However, such an interface can be built using inexpensive software and the World Wide Web, as *Web Database Primer Plus* will show you. Imagine the power of millions of users, all working on different systems, yet all accessing your database in a consistent and user-friendly manner.

With the popularity of the Web, individuals and companies have recognized the potential of setting up a database, linking it to the WWW, and thus reaching an already huge and still expanding potential customer base. This is much more valuable than a static HTML file because it allows for two-way interaction between the database owner and the user. For example, a company could have a one-page advertisement on their home page about their latest product (an informative home page), or they could publish an ad with an option for the readers to enter their address to receive more information about the product (an informative home page with links to a customer database). Clearly, the second option is preferable, and that is the focus of *Web Database Primer Plus*. Whether you're starting from scratch or already have a database, the information you need to connect it to the WWW is covered in this book.

Due to the open architecture of CGI and some databases, several configurations are possible to achieve the same objective. There is also an abundance of related tools and resources available on the Internet. This is all good, but at the same time can be confusing. This book puts this maze of information in perspective and provides step-by-step instructions that will save time, money, and resources. *Web Database Primer Plus* is a complete reference and how-to book for Web database publishing.

Web Database Primer Plus provides the information necessary to set up a database and link it to the World Wide Web. It is general enough to apply to a wide audience using different browsers and software on different computer platforms (PC, Mac, UNIX, and so on). At the same time, detailed information is provided when necessary. For example, we start with basic concepts about Web database publishing, the World Wide Web, and HTML. Then, to differentiate between what existing database systems are capable of, detailed explanations are provided to help you decide what you need.

To set up a database on the Web, a working knowledge of HTML, CGI, and the database itself is needed. This book covers all three areas and describes how they are connected.

Java™, one of the hottest Internet topics today, is also covered—how to create database connectivity using Java applets and the JDBC standard. The casual user can stick to the easy-to-implement CGI connectivity, while the more sophisticated user can explore more complex applications written in Java.

Chapter Outline

Here is how the material in the book is structured.

Part I: The Basics

Part I starts with a complete discussion of the Internet, the Web, and HTML. It also includes plenty of information on CGI, the programming standard for external applications for the Web.

Chapter 1: Why Web Database Publishing?

An introductory chapter designed to bring users from different backgrounds to the same starting point. This chapter talks about the advantages of a database published on the WWW over plain HTML text-based pages. Some of the useful applications that can be created using databases are also described.

Chapter 2: The Internet and the World Wide Web

A theoretical discussion of the World Wide Web and its underlying engine, the Internet. By understanding the theory behind the technology, you will be able to better use the technology itself.

Chapter 3: An Overview of HTML

A tutorial of HTML with examples. This material is necessary to develop the interface of a database application. Some of the latest HTML enhancements, such as frames, are discussed.

Chapter 4: User Input

Let the users run the show. This chapter concentrates on the interactive nature of HTML. Thus far you have learned to make static documents available over the Web. In this chapter, we explore how you can receive input from the user. A variety of input methods, including text boxes and menus, are discussed, and sample forms are presented.

Chapter 5: Common Gateway Interface (CGI) Basics

The missing link between your database and the Web. We can provide output and receive input. Now what? CGI is defined and explored in detail. We will discuss CGI implementation in specific platforms and show how the World Wide Web communicates to the external world via CGI.

Chapter 6: Database Basics

An overview of simple database concepts as they relate to the WWW setup. We will discuss SQL and individual database APIs. These are the two main components of linking a database to the WWW. Finally, we discuss the networking nature of databases.

Part II: Creating the Application

Part II looks at database applications and what to consider when deciding which one to work with. The book covers the entire application development process from design to testing within the World Wide Web programming paradigm. To cover the loose ends, one chapter is devoted to security issues, which are certainly a concern to any system administrator. We also discuss issues regarding maintenance of the application and its expansion.

Chapter 7: Application Design

The first and most important phase of coding. We now have all the tools. How do we go about creating an application? Different environments and configurations are discussed and what (if anything) needs to be changed before the user can communicate with a database and the WWW. The requirements of an application developed for the WWW are discussed and separated into the server and client sides to provide an overall perspective of how they work.

Chapter 8: Choosing a Programming Language

A walk through the maze of programming languages. Several programming languages are discussed in the context of CGI application development. References are made to CGI toolkits written specifically for some of the languages.

Chapter 9: Choosing the Right Tool

A summary of many of the application development tools available. Several tools reduce the amount of code necessary to connect a database to the Web and, therefore, can save hours of programming. A number of these tools along with their capabilities and sources for further information are described in this chapter.

Chapter 10: The Final Application

Final touches on the application. Now that we have everything in perspective, how does the overall system work? Can we enhance it in any way? What are the bottlenecks?

Chapter 11: Security Issues

If a Web database is going to work, it has to be secure. Security is a hot topic, and every Web publisher should be aware of its implications. It is also a rapidly changing issue as new technologies emerge. Several technologies are discussed as they relate to security. You will learn how to make your CGI scripts more secure, and special considerations for Java security are discussed.

Chapter 12: Maintaining Your Application

Not off the hook yet. You have developed an application, but it has to be maintained, debugged, and continually enhanced to keep your users interested. These issues are discussed and special considerations for the WWW are provided.

Part III: Sample Applications

In Part III, three real-life applications are presented: a conference registration system, a trouble reporting system, and an on-line shipping rate system (developed in Java). Each chapter follows a similar format with a different application developed from scratch.

Chapter 13: Conference Registration System

A simple application that takes registration information from the user and stores it in a database for further processing.

Chapter 14: Trouble Reporting System

An interactive system allowing users to report software and hardware problems. An interface is provided for system administrators to respond to the trouble via e-mail. Finally, a third interface allows users to browse through the reported problems and proposed solutions.

Chapter 15: Using the JDBC

Let Java do the dirty work. The application demonstrates how to connect a Java applet to a database to achieve real-time interaction with the user.

Chapter 16: Real World Applications

A look at some finished applications currently used on the WWW. Several applications in the production phase are discussed and analyzed. By relating the technology used in these applications to material covered in previous chapters of this book, you'll obtain the global perspective necessary to develop your own applications.

Chapter 17: New Technologies

Welcome to a world of change. The computer industry has been dynamic since its start, and there are no signs of it slowing down. This chapter takes a look at some of the new technologies that are related to the Web and databases.

Appendix A: HTML Quick Reference

A quick guide to HTML. As you decide how your application should look, this appendix will serve as a handy reference to the HTML tags you need.

Appendix B: HTML Style Guide

Suggestions for writing effective HTML code. This appendix lists some pointers for writing good HTML code and suggests how to avoid some of the pitfalls of Web page development.

Appendix C: Java™ Quick Reference

A brief overview of the Java programming language. This reference serves as a quick guide to the Java language, its components, and how they work. If you are new to Java, this is a great place to start.

Appendix D: SQL Quick Reference

Your ticket to conversation with your database. SQL is the standard database language. While several implementations exist, basic SQL commands and syntax are discussed in this chapter. We will show you how to search your database, add data to it, and modify existing data.

Appendix E: Perl Quick Reference

A general overview of the language. Perl's simple but very powerful characteristics have made it the language of choice for developing CGI applications. This appendix gives you the basics and serves as a quick reference to your Perl needs. The language itself, data types, control structures, and several classes of built-in functions are discussed.

Appendix F: On-Line Resources

No book can match the vast resources available on the Web. This appendix lists a number of sites to which you can refer for additional information or updates to technologies discussed in the book. Bookmark these sites, and you'll have instant access to the latest technology and information available for connecting your database to the WWW.

Appendix G: GNU GPL and LGPL

The GNU General Public License and Library General Public License covers the Comprehensive Perl Archive Network (CPAN), which is included on the CD. This license allows redistribution of the binaries, source code, and documentation free of charge.

About the CD-ROM

The CD-ROM contains all of the source code in the book as well as several powerful utility programs and the Java and Perl binaries. The actual contents and the directory structure of the CD are shown in Table CD-1.

   This table can be used as a guide as you read the following descriptions of each of the items.

Table CD-1 Content and directory structure of *Web Database Primer Plus* CD

Location		Description
Chapters		Example code from the book
	Ch01	
	Ch02	
	Ch03	
	Ch05	
	Ch06	
	Ch07	
	Ch08	
	Ch09	
	Ch10	
	Ch11	
	Ch12	
	Ch13	
	Ch14	
	Ch15	
Utilities		
	CGIhtml	A C implementation for CGI programming
	CGI-LIB	A Perl implementation for CGI programming
	GSQL	A tool for linking databases and the Web using CGI
	CGIpp	A C++ implementation for CGI programming
	SybPerl	A Perl interface for the Sybase database engine
	WebForms	An HTML authoring tool with support for forms
	HTMLAsst	A powerful and easy-to-use HTML authoring tool
Servers		
	Alibaba	Web Server for Windows 95
	InfoServ	MS Internet Information Server for Windows NT

Location	Description
Binaries	
JDK	Java Developer's Kit for Windows 95/NT
Perl	Binaries for Perl Development

The following describes each item on the CD. Special installation notes are also discussed.

Source Code

All the examples in the book are placed under the CHAPTERS directory on the CD. Examples from each chapter are included in their own subdirectory, specified by the chapter number. Subdirectories are not included for chapters that don't include source code. Within each of the subdirectories, the examples are identified by their listing number. For example, LIST04_3.txt is the file containing Listing 3 from Chapter 4.

To use the examples, copy them to your hard drive. To use the Perl and Java code, you'll need their respective interpreters installed on your machine. You can view the HTML code using any Web browser.

CGIHTML (\CGIHTML)

CGIHTML is a set of CGI and HTML routines written by Eugene Kim (`eekim@fas.harvard.edu`). It provides a nice interface to the CGI specification when you are using the C language to develop your CGI programs. The author has created a mailing list for users of CGIHTML. You can subscribe to the list by sending an e-mail message to `majordomo@hcs.harvard.edu` with the message body: subscribe cgihtml.

Details about this library, along with an example of how it is used, can be found in Chapter 8, "Choosing a Programming Language."

CGI-LIB (\CGI-LIB)

One of the most widely used packages for Perl programmers is CGI-LIB by Steven Brenner. Many revisions of the library exist. New features in version 2 include support for file uploading, improved robustness, and debugging. Version 1.14 is simpler to understand than the 2.x series and is used in this book. You can find the latest copy at `http://www.bio.cam.ac.uk/cgi-lib.` The library is a Perl file that needs to be included in your code.

GSQL (\GSQL)

GSQL is a gateway program that provides a forms interface to SQL databases. It creates forms based on commands found in a **proc** file. The syntax of a **proc** file along with other documentation can be found at `http://www.ncsa.uiuc.edu/SDG/People/jason/pub/gsql/starthere.html`. GSQL then creates an SQL query based on user input and sends that query to the database.

The gateway consists of two programs, GSQL and SQLMAIN. GSQL creates the form after processing the proc file. SQLMAIN is responsible for handing SQL statements and database communication. Jason NG (likkai@ncsa.uiuc.edu) developed the program while working at the National Center of Supercomputing Applications (NCSA) at the University of Illinois, Urbana-Champaign.

LibCGI++ (\LIBCGI++)

LibCGI++ is a class library intended for CGI programming using C++. The source is copyrighted by Dragos Manolescu, who is a Ph.D. student at University of Illinois, Urbana-Champaign and a member of the National Center of Supercomputing Applications (NCSA).

You will need a C++ compiler and the Standard Template Library (STL) to use the library. The author suggests g++2.7.2 as a suitable compiler. A detailed explanation of the library is provided in Chapter 8 and on the Web page http://sweetbay.will.uiuc.edu/cgi++/.

Sybperl (\SYBPERL)

Sybperl is a partial implementation of Sybase's DB-LIBRARY in Perl. It is a powerful and easy-to-use library when you need to interface Perl and a Sybase server. Since its introduction, Sybase has added WEB.SQL to its line of products, which supports embedded SQL and Perl statements in an HTML file. Several examples in the book use this technique. The author, Michael Peppler, generously gave his permission to include the library on the CD. Later versions of SybPerl add support for the CT-LIBRARY functions that superseded the DB-LIBRARY.

WebForms (\WebForms)

WebForms from Q&D Software Development (http://www.q-d.com) lets you create HTML forms that you can link to your home page. HTML forms are, of course, a main component of any Web database application. The program consists of two modules. The first module allows you to design your form, which can contain any HTML form object such as text input boxes, menus, and radio buttons. The second module reads input entered by the user and generates an e-mail message containing that information. You will need Visual Basic run-time to use this program.

HTML Assistant Pro (\HTMLAsst)

This software is from Brooklyn North Software Works (http://www.mlink.ca/brooklyn/). It is a Windows-based HTML authoring tool. This evaluation version lacks some of the advanced HTML features such as tables and frames, but it gives you a good feel of HTML authoring. The program contains a number of features including

- Automatic Page Creator, which allows you to create HTML pages by simply filling in the blanks
- Full support for forms and tables
- Page preview with any browser
- Spell-checker

- URL organizing tool that tracks your links
- Picture preview, which lets you check your inline images before you create an image link

Under the `HTMLASST` directory, you will get the file called `HTMLASST.EXE`. This is a self-extracting executable file. Double-click on the filename, and it will guide you through the installation process.

Microsoft Internet Information Server (\InfoServ)

The serious and heavy-duty World Wide Web server for Windows NT. It's powerful enough for the world's biggest Web sites and simple enough for small departments and individuals to set up in minutes and instantly improve their information sharing over the Web. It also supports CGI and MSAPI for Web database development. As for its future, it promises to integrate nicely into the operating system, further closing the gap between the desktop and network worlds. For more information, go to Microsoft's Web page at `http://www.microsoft.com/infoserv/tourstart.htm`.

Alibaba (\Alibaba)

A World Wide Web server for Windows 95 by Computer Software Manufaktur (CSM) in Austria. This is a demonstration version that has all the features of the full product so you can experiment with this multithreaded, high performance server. It expires after 30 days. This server is ideal for small applications and a great learning tool. It supports CGI, so you can develop Web database applications using Alibaba. The server can access large and small databases through ODBC and CGI. For more information, refer to CSM's Web page at `http://alibaba.austria.eu.net/`.

Java Developer's Kit (\JDK)

This is the key to the world of Java programming. The JDK helps you to develop applets that conform to the Java applet API, make sure your applets will run in all Java-enabled browsers, and develop Java applications. Aside from the Java run-time environment, the JDK includes a Java compiler, debugger, applet viewer, and a few other useful tools. You also have access to the source for some of the higher level classes used in the Java environment, giving you a deep understanding of how it works. For more information, refer to Sun's Web page at `http://java.sun.com`.

Perl (\Perl)

Perl is one of the most popular languages for developing simple Web applications such as data input forms. Its syntax is similar to the C language, but it is friendlier for novice users. Perl is an interpreted language, and as a result you can interactively write and debug your code. Also, Perl has powerful string manipulation capabilities that are very useful for writing CGI applications that deal with data from Web forms. With full network capabilities, Perl scripts can communicate with almost any back-end database. Finally, you will find an abundance of Perl source code samples on the Web, from simple form manipulations to sophisticated shopping carts.

PART I:
The Basics

1
Why Web Database Publishing?

Phrases such as "information is power," "information super-highway," and "information explosion" have become computer-age buzzwords. Information is nothing more than a meaningful way of looking at raw data. A bunch of numbers that seem meaningless to one person can be valuable to another. So information and data are in a way related, but at the same time, different from one another. We have come to an age where information and the ability to manage it have become extremely important, and we are overwhelmed by it.

Information management has become both a science and a business. Whether you are writing the national budget or choosing holiday gifts, you demand useful information at your fingertips on which you can base your decision.

So how do we handle this vast amount of information? Databases are the most common tool for collecting, manipulating, and utilizing information. Although database technology has been evolving for a long time, it was missing a critical element: There was no standard way to share the information and make it available to others on a global scale. Technology bailed us out with another revolutionary idea: the World Wide Web.

Given the incredible popularity of the World Wide Web, it makes sense to combine its power with databases and create a powerful tool to handle and share information.

This book brings together two of the most exciting tools of this century: databases and the World Wide Web. We will see how they complement one another and pave the way to exciting developments in the future.

Popularity of the World Wide Web

The network of networks, commonly called the Internet, has existed for more than a decade. Government and research institutions were enjoying its amazing power for some time, while the rest of the world looked at the Internet as another high-tech toy for die-hard computer nerds.

Many consider the Internet and the World Wide Web synonymous. The Internet actually refers to the collection of computer networks connected to one another around the world. In casual terms, the World Wide Web (WWW) is a protocol that runs on top of the Internet. The Web is only one of the many services available to computers that are connected to the Internet. We will discuss the ideas behind the Internet and WWW in Chapter 2,"The Internet and the World Wide Web."

The World Wide Web was revolutionary because it made the Internet user-friendly. Once the public could use Web browsers and explore the Internet, it became clear how powerful this technology was. That is why computer experts are calling the World Wide Web one of the greatest innovations in the computer world. The Web literally connects the globe through computer networks and has redefined how we share information.

At first, the World Wide Web was limited to the same institutions that were using the Internet, but quickly it spread to personal computer users. Figure 1-1 shows the state of Internet connectivity around the globe.

The emergence of on-line services and Internet service providers made it easier for average computer users to get connected. With innovations such as Point-to-Point Protocol (PPP), all a user needs to hop on the information super-highway is a modem and a personal computer. The growth of the Internet and the World Wide Web is phenomenal. Although there is no way to get an exact count of the number of connected computers (that number changes hourly), Figure 1-2 shows an approximation of how the Internet has grown over the past several years.

So why would you want to link a database to the World Wide Web? Remember that databases are our tool for managing information, and the World Wide Web provides us with the means for sharing the information. Therefore, it makes good sense to link the two. You can find a number of sites on the Internet that are already combining the powers of these two tools. Examples of actual implementations include

- Registration for conferences, workshops, and so on
- Software registration (http://www.microsoft.com /windows/pr/regwiz.htm)
- On-line shopping (http://www.shop.com/shops.html)
- Surveys and marketing analysis (http://galileo.resultsdirect.com /surveys/royal/royal.htm)

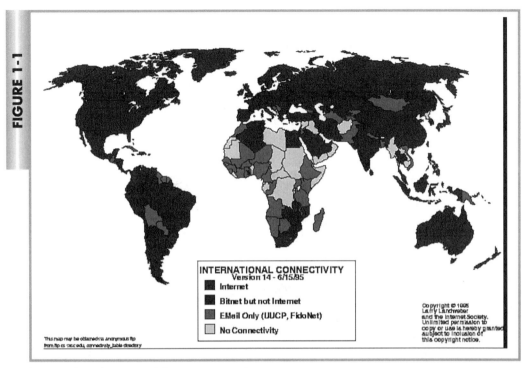

International connectivity

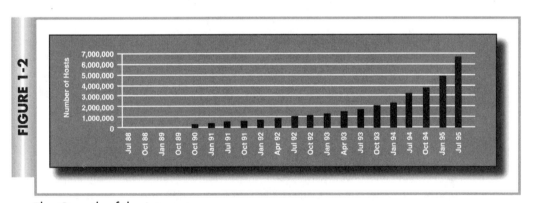

The Growth of the Internet
Source: Network Wizards
Updated data is available at `http://www.nw.com/`

- Employment databases (http://www.careermag.com/careermag/)
- Document retrieval systems (http://techreports.larc.nasa.gov/cgi-bin/NTRS)
- Online library systems (http://hathorne.libarary.cmu.edu)

The text in parentheses is the Uniform Resource Locator (URL) for the Web sites in the list. Think of URLs as the addresses for the millions of locations on the Net, much like our postal address system.

Save Yourself the Headache

URLs are case-sensitive (except for the domain name) and some of them can get very long. It is common for beginners to mistype the URL and get an error message. Carefully check the spelling before you decide that the address is invalid.

Start Surfing!

Throughout this book we make reference to on-line resources. Many browsers offer "bookmark" capabilities which allow you to organize useful sites into categories for future reference. You might want to start a new category for sites related to this book. Also, note that due to the dynamic nature of the Internet, some of these addresses might no longer be valid or their contents might have changed by the time this book is published.

Whether you have an existing database and want to share it with the World Wide Web community or you want to start an on-line database from scratch, you will face a number of issues during implementation. This book serves as a guide to help you create the application that best meets your needs. With endless possibilities, your imagination is the only barrier to what your database applications can accomplish over the Net.

Static Versus Interactive Pages

The World Wide Web is more than a "point-and-click" tool; it has the capability to be an interactive communication tool. In other words, you can both provide and receive information using the World Wide Web. Consider Figure 1-3. It shows the home page for Sybase corporation. This is an example of a static home page. The user clicks on an item that takes him or her to another page containing the requested information. The only input from the user is a mouse click. This obviously is not enough to implement a database interface. At a minimum, such an interface must provide the user with a means of data entry and validation of search criteria.

FIGURE 1-3

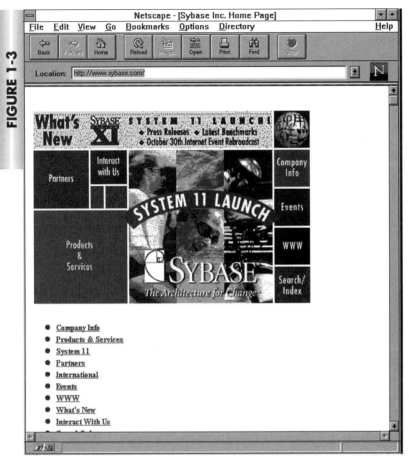

An example of a static page

In contrast to static pages, consider the home page shown in Figure 1-4. In this page, the user can enter information in the boxes provided, which most likely will be stored in a database or will help form the query to search the database. This ability opens the door to a two-way communication interface, very much like other computer programs. This aspect of the World Wide Web is the main focus of this book, although we will spend a great deal of time on static pages as well. As you will see, it is very common to find both types of pages at one site. In fact, most database applications require both types of pages. For example, if users need help on a certain item, a link can take them to a static page containing the help information.

Interactive pages, also referred to as forms, are the heart of the database user interface. You can use forms to accept input from the user and pass it to the database. Forms make linking databases and the World Wide Web possible and desirable. We will learn about forms in Chapter 4, "User Input." An obvious advantage of using forms is their graphical user interface, discussed in the next section.

FIGURE 1-4

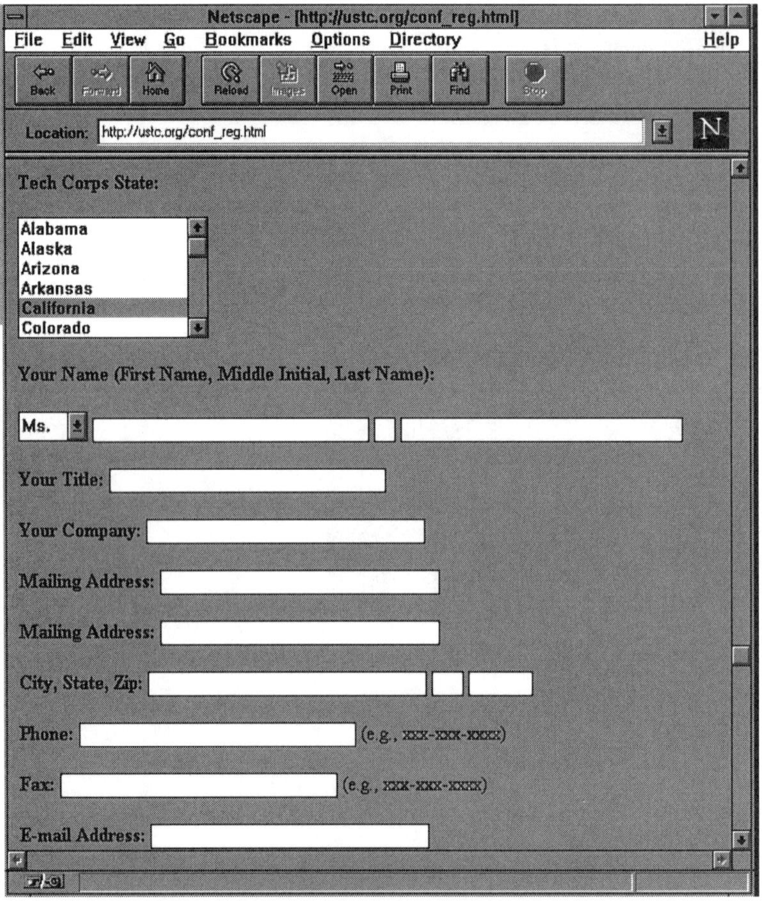

An example of an interactive page

Graphical User Interface

By nature, computers are machine-like. As humans, we view these tools as any other machines. However, unlike other machines that can perform mechanical functions better than we can, computers can perform certain intellectual functions better! For example, they have a good memory and can do arithmetic much faster than humans. This is probably the reason behind the years of research and work on user interfaces for computer programs.

The movement towards graphical user interfaces (GUI) really picked up in late 1980s with the emergence of several graphical operating systems for personal computers, including early versions of Microsoft Windows. What You See Is What You Get (WYSIWYG) became the industry slogan. The argument was that a graphical user interface makes the computer easier to use increases productivity. Although text-based interfaces still exist and many users are happy with them, graphical interfaces clearly dominate the market. The computer industry is coming to a point where it has to deal with users who have not worked with anything but a graphical interface. So it makes sense to use graphical user interfaces to develop new applications (and even change existing ones).

The World Wide Web protocol does not specify a user interface, but most browsers (the tool used to navigate the Web) support a graphical interface. Browsers provide a number of popular graphical elements such as pop-up menus, scroll bars, and radio buttons, allowing the developer to create effective, user-friendly applications. These graphical elements come at a price, though. Browsers that support forms require more memory than those that do not; however, more computers now are equipped with larger memory capacities. Figures 1-4 and 1-5 show some of the graphical elements, such as menus, text boxes, and pull-down menus. As you can see, they have the look and feel of a normal desktop program. This makes changing a conventional program to a WWW program easier. It also remains consistent with the industry norm of graphical user interfaces as an application's front-end.

FIGURE 1-5

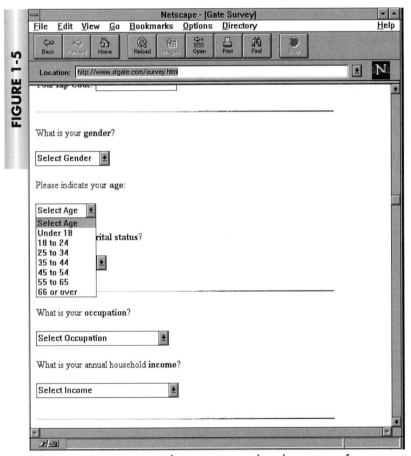

Menus are a common element in graphical user interfaces

Platform Independence

Graphical user interfaces would be an ideal solution if we had only one type of computer and one type of operating system. The computer industry had enough trouble taking text-based applications from one computer platform to another. With the emergence of graphical interfaces, the problems have been aggravated. As new computer systems entered the market, each developed a look and feel a little different from the others, and most developed a different language to create its user interface. From the development point of view, this was a lose-lose situation. Software companies invested a lot of money to develop their applications in a particular platform. Later, they found another market for their software and faced the problem of translating their program to the new platform. Even software companies that support multiple platforms constantly face incompatibility problems. If you have ever tried to move a document from a Macintosh computer to a DOS-based machine or vice versa, then you understand the difficulties associated with multiple-platform support. With the emergence of the World Wide Web, this problem seems to have been partially solved. Although WWW applications do have some limitations (there is not a word processing program written using the World Wide Web), for the most part they offer a platform-independent user interface. Currently, there are WWW browsers for almost any computer platform, including

- Macintosh
- DOS-based PCs
- Windows-based PCs
- Silicon Graphics (IRIX)
- Hewlett-Packard (HP-UX)
- Sun Microsystems (Solaris)
- Digital Equipment Corporation (OSF and Ultrix)
- NeXT (NeXTSTEP)
- IBM RISC System/6000 (AIX)

This is an amazing list considering that many of these systems run different operating systems. Netscape browsers are a leading example of multiple-platform support. Netscape looks very much the same regardless of the type of computer it is running on. If we develop an application based on the World Wide Web, we can be sure that at least the user interface portion of the application will run on different platforms without any extra coding effort on our part (although it might look a little different from browser to browser). With some care in choosing a standard language for the interface with the database, we can be sure that the database portion of the application will run on different platforms with little or no code modification. The convenience of platform independence, however simple it might seem, is extraordinary and potentially valuable. Such applications are easy to maintain and less costly than applications for which we must maintain a separate version for each computer type. Database applications are no exception to this rule. That is another reason why you should consider Web databases.

Network Access

Since the World Wide Web is a networking application, it expects users to have some form of network connection. It does not, however, care about the form of connection. Users can access the Web through an office Local Area Network (LAN), a direct line to an Internet provider, or even through a phone line (using a modem). As long as the communication means conform to the Internet protocols, WWW applications work fine.

By requiring a network connection, you might limit the number of your potential users. However, many personal computers are now shipped with modems or network cards pre-installed, and more people consider being on-line a necessity. Increasing membership in on-line services such as CompuServe and America Online, along with greater competition among Internet service providers, is supporting evidence of this trend.

World Wide Web and Library System

Let's consider an example of what network support can mean to a database and its users. Like all libraries, the Iowa State University library used card catalogs as its database for the thousands of books that it stored. If you were looking for a book and the drawer containing the card was in use by another person, your only choice was to wait. In a way, card catalogs were true "single-user" databases. More recently, the library implemented a computerized card catalog system. Terminals were scattered throughout the library. Then, multiple users could search the database. However, to use the database, they had to go to the library building. Later, with improved network connections on campus, the library system was connected to the campus network. Computers around the campus were able to access the library. As the campus was connected to the Internet, this capability was expanded globally, with certain restrictions. Today, the library offers a World Wide Web link to the database system (Figure 1-6) that provides users with a simple graphical interface to search the library system regardless of their location. This is so fast and convenient that few people still use the old card catalogs.

Before the World Wide Web, it was up to the developer to make sure each user of the database application was properly connected to the network. The developer also had to make special considerations in the code for different types of network connections. There was no good standard for networked applications. The World Wide Web and its protocol have virtually eliminated this problem.

As we will discover in this book, nearly all databases can provide network connectivity through the Web. If you have a database application which requires accessibility from remote areas, then you should seriously consider connecting to the Web.

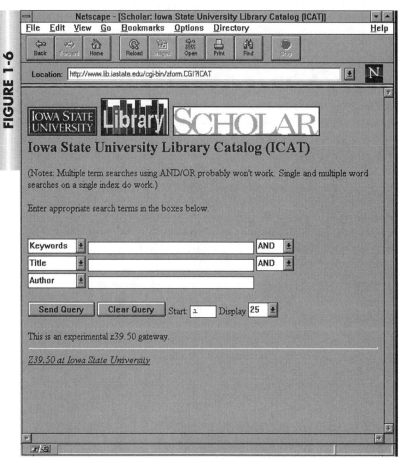

Iowa State University Library Catalog on the World Wide Web

Granted, in today's world of client/server computing, many databases support networking; however, their cost is considerably higher than databases designed for stand-alone workstations. SQL Server from Sybase is an example of a database server with full network support. Smaller packages such as FoxPro or MS Access were meant for smaller-scale applications, but they can be linked to the World Wide Web to provide a pseudo-global network support with ease.

Network access to a database has its advantages and disadvantages. While it allows the convenience of accessing the information from remote locations, it opens the door for intruders and snoopers. Chapter 11, "Security Issues," considers some of the security issues related to the World Wide Web.

Standard Interface

Another advantage of using the World Wide Web as your database interface is consistency. The standards are rigid enough to provide a smooth interface regardless of the computer platform. This has several advantages. Your users must learn only one user interface and can expect to find the same interface no matter where and when they run your application. From the developer's point of view, this can mean reduced costs in training and documentation.

Standards do not apply only to the user interface. Many of the interactions that occur in the World Wide Web follow very strict standards. As you will see in Chapter 5, Common Gateway Interface (CGI) provides a consistent channel for Web servers to communicate with databases. This brings us back to the fact that World Wide Web applications are, for the most part, independent of the platform they run on. This is mainly because the Web standards cover a great amount of detail, allowing us to concentrate on the aspects of the system that are related to our application.

The HTTP protocol (the foundation of the World Wide Web) is, for the most part, standardized, so you can expect consistency. Because of these standards and the requirements set by the client/server model, the World Wide Web offers an open interface to many of its functions. Figure 1-7 shows a very broad picture of the World Wide Web operation. It shows that Web browsers connect to Web servers through the Internet. The Web server is then responsible for making a connection to the database server using a standard known as CGI. Consider the distinct components (for example, database server, WWW browsers, and so on) in the picture and the arrows connecting them. The standards apply to the individual components and to all the connections, as discussed in detail in Chapter 2.

Easily Expanded

The Web standards and open interfaces lead to another advantage: expandability. Suppose you have developed a catalog ordering application using the World Wide Web and a FoxPro database. After a while, you decide to accept orders for a sister company which uses Access as its database. As shown in Figure 1-8, this addition can be accomplished by simply writing a CGI interface to the new database. No changes are necessary to the remainder of the application. Next, suppose management wants to allow customers to check the status of an order on-line. This requires only one more page to serve as the interface to the new functionality you want to offer. The rest of the application remains intact.

FIGURE 1-7

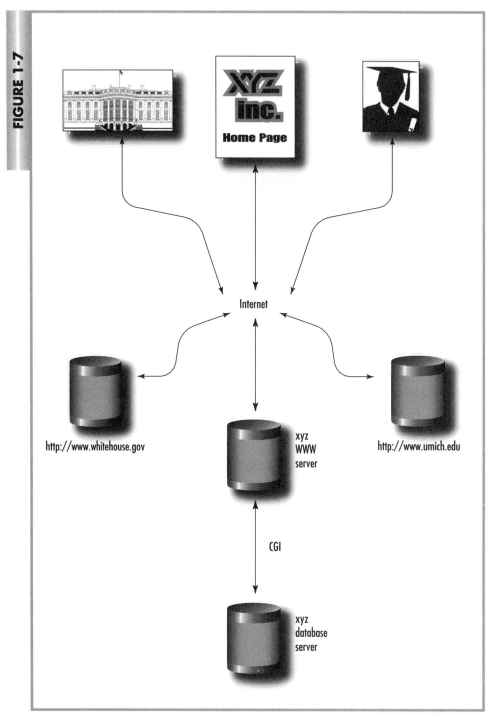

The Web database environment

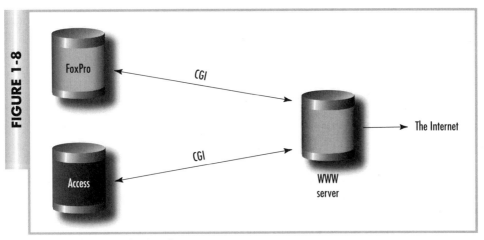

FIGURE 1-8

Expanding a Web database

By drawing boundaries among the different portions of an application and offering standard interfaces for the interactions among these components, the World Wide Web is able to offer an application development environment that is consistent, reliable, user-friendly, and easy to maintain.

Summary

Information management and information sharing play important roles in today's environment. Databases and the World Wide Web are two tools that can help us improve our abilities in these areas, respectively. With increasing global popularity, the World Wide Web is able to provide a graphical user interface to databases by way of interactive pages. Because browsers exist for almost any computer platform, we can be sure that the front-end of the database will work on multiple platforms without any extra effort on our part. The standard and open interface provided by the WWW leads the way for consistent and easily maintained applications. Network accessibility increases the number of people who can potentially benefit from your database application.

Questions

1. Distinguish between data and information.

2. What are some of the applications of a Web database in your organization?

3. What are forms and what ability do they provide?

4. What is platform independence and why is it important?

5. Do some Net surfing and consider how a database might be used in sites you visit.

Answers

1. Information is a meaningful way of looking at raw data.

2. Think of ways you interact with the databases in your organization and consider how a Web interface can enhance these interactions.

3. Forms are the graphical user interface elements which collect input from the user and provide the necessary information to enter into the database or search the database.

4. Platform independence refers to the ability of a program or language to run on different computers with minimal modifications by the programmer.

5. The URLs provided in this chapter are a good starting point.

2

The Internet and the World Wide Web

The World Wide Web is a part of the Internet. Therefore, in order to understand WWW, we should have some knowledge of how the Internet operates. Some of this discussion is technical and might seem unrelated, but an understanding of the material in this chapter will help you better appreciate the World Wide Web environment. With this in mind, let us begin our exploration of the network of networks, commonly called the Internet.

The Internet

The Internet is a by-product of ARPANET, an experimental project carried out by the U.S. Department of Defense Advanced Research Projects Agency (DARPA) during the early 1970s. The purpose of the project was to explore computer networking innovations that enabled researchers to link to expensive computing resources such as supercomputers and large databases. Originally, it was limited to military and universities conducting defense-related research, but slowly it grew and, after a few years, evolved into the massive computer network known as the Internet.

One of the first things people want to know about the Internet is who runs it. You might be surprised to learn that nobody is really "running" the Internet; it is a self-running entity. Its open architecture and its ability to run itself are probably the main reasons for its success and popularity. That is not to say that no intervention is necessary. Certainly, someone must lay out the wire to connect the networks and assign addresses to the millions of computers connected to the Internet. Also, there are several organizations that oversee the operation of the network and plan ahead for future expansion by making modifications to the protocols and standards.

Internet Addresses

To uniquely identify hosts on the Internet, an addressing scheme is required. The hosts are identified by an IP number. Since remembering a 12-digit number is not easy, most machines have a name associated with them. There are name servers that hold tables relating machine names and IP numbers.

Although it is possible to pick a number out of the sky for your machine, it is best that a number be assigned to your machine by a central organization. Depending on the size of the organization, you might get a bunch of numbers. It is up to you to distribute those numbers and assure their uniqueness within your organization. The following URLs point to organizations responsible for assigning Internet addresses in different regions of the world.

`http://www.internic.net` (American Region and the rest of the world)

`http://www.ripe.net` (Europe)

`http://www.apnic.net` (Asian-Pacific Region)

Usually, your Internet service provider will take care of your registration as part of your service agreement.

Computer networks have been around for a long time. Although computers in a single network could communicate with each other, internetwork communication was very difficult and in some cases impossible. Each vendor had its own network protocol. There was very little cooperative effort to make sure the protocols were compatible.

In network terminology, a *protocol* is a set of rules that governs the communication among computers. You can think of it as a language. People communicate well with others speaking their language, but when they travel to a foreign country, they experience communication problems because they don't know the native language. What do you suppose is a way of solving the language barrier problem? How about a universal language that everyone understands? As Figure 2-1 shows, this is precisely what the Internet uses.

The Internet made internetworking possible by specifying a universal protocol called TCP/IP (Transmission Control Protocol/Internet Protocol). At first, the protocol was implemented for several flavors of the UNIX operating system, but now it is available for almost any machine. The obvious implication of having a universal protocol is that as a user, you do not need to worry about the type of computer to which you are trying to connect. As long as your machine and the destination machine are connected to the Internet, you can be sure both support all the functionalities of the TCP/IP protocol and can communicate with each other as if they were speaking the same language.

TCP/IP

At a very general level, computer networks perform two tasks:

- Transfer of data
- Transfer of commands indicating what to do with the data

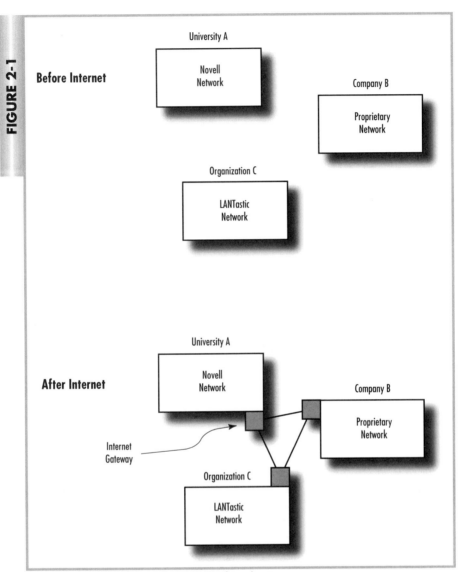

FIGURE 2-1

Before Internet

University A
Novell Network

Company B
Proprietary Network

Organization C
LANTastic Network

After Internet

University A
Novell Network

Company B
Proprietary Network

Internet Gateway

Organization C
LANTastic Network

Computer networks before and after the Internet

Consider Figure 2-2. This is an example of how an electronic mail message might make its way through the Internet. First the e-mail message is put in a *packet*. If the e-mail message is large, then it is broken up into several chunks, each going into a separate packet. Each packet includes its source address (where it came from) and a destination address (where

FIGURE 2-2

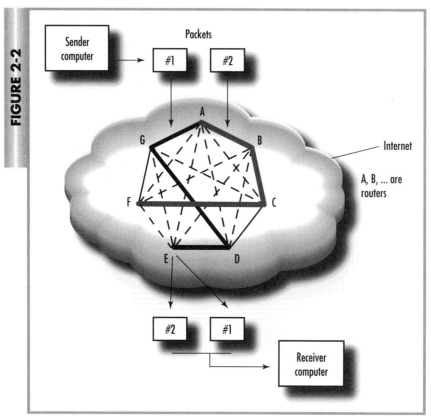

Electronic mail journey map

it is going). It is also stamped with a sequence number. With this information, the packet is sent on its way. Each packet is a complete, independent unit and can be transferred separately. In fact, in our example, the two packets take different routes. During their journeys, they pass through machines known as *routers*. The function of a router is to direct the packet to its next stop. After several *hops* from gateway to gateway, the packet reaches the destination machine. After reading the first packet, the machine knows that there are two packets in this transfer and waits for the second packet to arrive. Once it arrives, the machine uses the sequence numbers to determine how to put the packets together and form the original e-mail message.

Tracing the Path

Most UNIX operating systems include the traceroute program. Given a destination host, this command will show you the path that a packet will take to reach its destination. You might have to get root access to the machine before you can issue this command. Try the command with a site you access frequently, and you might be surprised as to how many hops your packets will take to reach their destination.

With this general description of Internet data transfer in mind, you can visualize how World Wide Web documents are transferred. All the pictures and texts get stuffed into packets and are sent to your browser. Your browser sorts them out. If it encounters an error, the browser asks the server for a retransmission.

Suppose there are two *hot spots*, or hyperlinks, on a Web page you are browsing. The first hot spot takes you to a page almost immediately, but the second one takes a while. Now you know why. The packet containing the information for the second link might be taking a completely different route, causing the delay.

It is very possible for a packet to get completely lost and never arrive at the destination. The most common cause is a physical problem such as a power outage or a disconnected wire. Depending on the application, this scenario can be treated in different ways. In most cases, the destination machine sends an acknowledgment packet when all the data is received. If a packet is missing, then the machine retransmits the missing packet identified by its sequence number, reducing traffic on the Net.

OSI Model

No networking discussion is complete without mentioning the Open Systems Interconnection (OSI) model. The goal of this model is to break down the task of transferring a packet based on the type of operations performed. The model defines seven layers as shown in Figure 2-3. Each layer fulfills the communication needs of the level directly above it. As a packet travels through each layer, the information related to that layer is appended to the packet. The protocols for each layer are specified independently from others. The only link needed is a way for a layer to receive information from the layer directly below it and send some information to the layer directly above it.

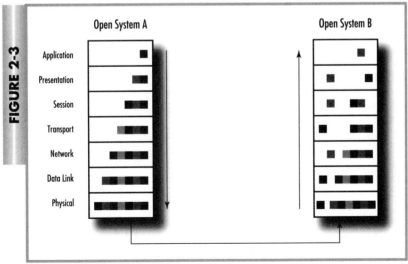

FIGURE 2-3

The OSI model

The following is an explanation of what each layer does:

Application Layer

The *application* layer deals with standards specific to the application. The HTTP protocol, which is how the World Wide Web operates, is contained in the application layer. Any user interface implementation will most likely fall into this layer. The application layer is responsible for giving the user the tools and means to use the program.

Presentation Layer

The *presentation* layer deals with representation of data that application layer components use or refer to in their communications. For example, if someone is running a WWW browser in text mode, this layer decides how to handle images, since they can't be displayed in a text terminal.

Session Layer

The *session* layer provides mechanisms to organize and synchronize data exchanges by higher layers. Different computers store data in different ways at the bits and bytes level. In order to transfer the data between two computers which use different storage mechanisms, a translation must be performed. Usually, this is done by the session layer.

Transport Layer

The *transport* layer deals with data transfer. It assures higher layers that a data transfer is performed in a reliable, cost-effective manner. This is the TCP part of the Internet protocol. Your program might make function calls to open a socket connection to a particular IP address. The task of making that connection is partially fulfilled by the transport layer.

Network Layer

The *network* layer takes care of routing and relay considerations. This is the IP part of the Internet protocol. This is the layer that interprets IP numbers, addresses, and other low level networking tasks.

Data Link Layer

The *data link* layer provides for transfer of data on a point-to-point basis. It also detects and sometimes corrects errors from the physical layer.

Physical Layer

The *physical* layer takes care of the electrical and mechanical means to start, maintain, and stop physical connections between data-link entities. The software dealing directly with the networking hardware such as your network card is considered part of the physical layer.

A packet starts at the top layer (application layer). As it goes through the underlying layers, each layer attaches information pertaining to its own protocol to the packet. The reverse process occurs at the destination machine. By the time the packet reaches the application layer of the destination machine, it has the same form as when it was first generated. In the World Wide Web, all you see is the application layer. You should be aware, however, that the final result must pass through all these layers at both ends. We can assume that the underlying layers will do their job correctly. For example, we assume that the transport layer will transfer packets sent to it. This is the basic principle of our programming environment and most networking environments. Each layer will do its job before passing the information to the next layer.

Network Tower

You might run into the term TCP/IP *stack* in the literature. This terminology refers to structures in which layers are stacked on top of each other.

Client/Server Model

Like many other networking applications, the World Wide Web conforms to the *client/server* model. The term client/server has been broadly used over the past few years to describe a variety of different systems. This section will provide a base definition for the term and concentrate on its impact on the World Wide Web.

In our client/server model (shown in Figure 2-4), there are two distinct programs residing on separate machines. Communication between the client and server occurs over the network, which, in the case of the World Wide Web, is the Internet. The client and server programs can be running on different operating systems, making our model platform independent.

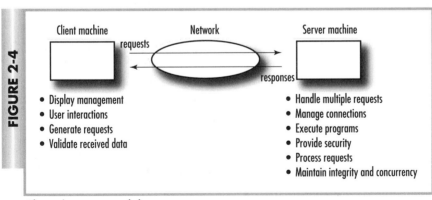

FIGURE 2-4

Client/server model

If you consider a program running on your PC, you will see that one program takes care of everything, including user input, accessing data files, and displaying results. In the client/server model, the tasks are divided. The server program usually takes care of processing, disk management, and integrity maintenance. The client usually takes care of user interactions and data validations.

Java and the Client/Server Model

The new programming environment, Java, has added a new twist to the client/server model. In the Java environment, the processing burden is mostly on the client's shoulders. The client requests a program from the server. The server sends that program in a platform-independent form (called byte-code). The client then runs that code on the client machine and displays the results. Also, the server not only serves data, it also serves the application itself, something that servers did not do in the traditional client/server model.

In the World Wide Web, the client is the browser you use. It takes a given URL, finds the server to which the URL points, requests information from the server, and displays the result. The server, on the other hand, receives requests from many different clients. It responds to the requests by either sending a file (HTML document, picture, movie, and so on) to the client or by executing a program and sending the results to the client. Note that the latter is what we are interested in. As shown in Figure 2-5, to link the World Wide Web

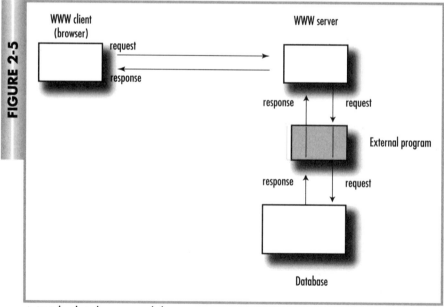

FIGURE 2-5

A Web database model

to a database, we write a program that communicates with the Web server. The client makes a request to the server. The server, in turn, invokes our program and usually provides some data to it. Then, our program performs the necessary database operation and sends the results to the server program. The server then sends that result back to the client.

The Client

You do not have much control over the client. When you make a public Web server, people from all around the world can access it. They could be using a Netscape browser, Mosaic, or any one of the hundreds of browsers available. Your hope is that their browser conforms to the standards set for HTML and HTTP. If you use specific extensions of a particular browser (for example, JavaScript in Netscape), you run the risk of limiting your audience.

The Server

Before you can link a database to the World Wide Web, you must first have a Web server. The Web server does all the things a server must do in a client/server environment, such as managing files, responding to client's requests, and sending the clients the requested information. The server also has a link to programs which are not HTTP clients. This link is created by a mechanism called Common Gateway Interface (CGI), discussed in Chapter 5, "Common Gateway Interface (GCI) Basics." The Web server is an important part of any database application we might develop. Its configuration and functionality are very important. A slow Web server makes the entire application lag. A limited Web server restricts our ability to communicate with the database program.

There are a number of servers on the market. Almost all of them conform to the latest HTTP standard. What distinguishes each server from the others is the extra functionalities it offers. Some manage multiple requests better than others. Some manage their resources better. Some offer security features. Some even offer a direct connection to a database server by bypassing the CGI link (the Oracle Web server falls into this category). If you already have a server, then you need to learn as much as possible about its capabilities and performance issues, because these factors will play an important role when you develop an application. If you need to start from scratch, then you have to make a choice about the server. Consider what your application is and envision where it might be a few years from now. Here are some questions you might ask.

- How many people (clients) will communicate with the server?
- What platform and operating system will the server run on?
- How important is security in the application you are developing?
- What additions and enhancements does the server have over standard HTTP?
- How much do you plan to spend on the server?
- Does the server support CGI? How efficient is its mechanism?

⬤ What logging mechanisms does the server offer? How can you measure the server load?

⬤ Does the server offer its own set of API functions to replace CGI?

⬤ Does the server have built-in database connectivity?

Server Comparison

A good comprehensive comparison of most common Web servers is available at `http://www.proper.com/www/servers-chart.html`. This page is updated periodically to reflect new versions.

Table 2-1 shows a listing of some more popular Web servers and gives a URL for each vendor.

Table 2-1   Listing of some Web servers and their URLs

Server Name	Server URL
Apache HTTP from the Apache Project	`http://www.apache.org`
httpd from CERN	`http://www.w3.org/hypertext/WWW/Daemon/Status.html`
FolkWeb Server from ILAR Concepts	`http://www.ilar.com/folkweb.htm`
GoServe for OS/2	`http://www2.hursley.ibm.com/goserve/`
MacHTTP from BIAP Systems	`http://www.biap.com`
NCSA httpd	`http://hoohoo.ncsa.uiuc.edu/docs`
Netscape Communications Server	`http://www.netscape.com/comprod/netscape_commun.html`
Open Market WebServer	`http://www.openmarket.com/omi/products/webserver.html`
WebSite from O'Reilly and Associates	`http://website.ora.com`
Oracle Web Server	`http://www.oracle.com`

Summary

The Internet is a network of networks. It is the infrastructure behind the World Wide Web. The Internet is too complex to be managed by a single authority. IP numbers are used to uniquely identify a computer that is connected to the Internet, and these numbers are assigned by an organization based on a user's geographical location. The networking protocol that makes the Internet run is TCP/IP. The protocol is simple and was originally designed to connect defense computers during a crisis. Emphasis was on the ability of the network to reroute packets if a particular machine went down.

The OSI model is used frequently to describe networking protocols. Although the layers of the Internet protocol do not have a one-to-one correspondence with the OSI layers, they do follow the general structure. A packet starts at the top layer, or the application layer, and works its way down to the bottom layer, or the physical layer. At that point, it is sent over the physical network and the reverse process occurs on the receiving end. By the time the packet is undone, it has been restored to its original form at the application layer of the destination machine.

The client/server model has been used extensively in the past decade to move away from centralized processing architecture of mainframe computers. The Web is inherently a client/server application. New technologies such as Java have added a new twist to the traditional client/server architecture.

Questions

1. What is an IP number?

2. What are the two main tasks of computer networks?

3. What is TCP/IP?

4. What is the function of the application layer?

5. What does the physical layer do?

6. What are the general expectations of the server in the client/server model?

7. Is your Netscape browser a client or a server?

Answers

1. An IP number is a 12-digit number which uniquely identifies a computer on the Internet.

2. Computer networks transfer data and commands that indicate what to do with the data.

3. TCP/IP is a networking protocol that allows the Internet to operate as it does today.

4. The application layer deals with standards specific to the application, such as its user interface, menu system, and so on.

5. The physical layer takes care of the electrical and mechanical means to transfer data on the network.

6. A server does most of the processing, serves data, and accepts requests from multiple clients.

7. A Web browser is a client that makes requests to the HTTP server by specifying a URL.

3

An Overview of HTML

HTML, which stands for HyperText Markup Language, is the language used to create WWW pages. If you have some experience with other programming languages, you will soon notice that HTML is a different kind of a language. For example, it does not include loops or other elements of a structured language such as C. HTML is a markup language, similar to LaTeX. It is a plain text document, but specific HTML items are denoted using tags and enclosed in a pair of <>. A parser reads an HTML document, identifies the tags, and performs the action or formatting specified by the tags. Tags can be used in three ways:

- <tag>
- <tag> text </tag>
- <tag attribute=argument> text </tag>

In this section, you will learn about the different tags that make up the HTML language. You are strongly encouraged to try out the examples and modify them to get a feel for the language. The remainder of this book deals with HTML, so it is important that you have a good grasp of the language. You will use documents created using the HTML language as the front-end of your database applications.

Tip

HTML tags are not case-sensitive. <title> is equivalent to <TITLE> or <TiTlE>.

State of HTML

HTML has a written standard, like other computer languages. The current standard is HTML 2.0, with HTML 3.0 expected to be out soon. HTML 3.0 will have full table support, limited support for mathematical symbols, plus some other features. Meanwhile, many vendors have been eager to jump ahead of the standard committee and include their own enhancements with their browsers. For example, Netscape browsers support tables even though the official specifications are not out yet. Chances are the official standard will adopt most of the current implementations, but you should be aware of non-standard enhancements in your HTML documents since some of them might change once HTML 3.0 is out, and because some might not be recognized by other browsers.

General Format

The beginning and end of an HTML document is marked by the *<html>* and *</html>* tags, respectively. While almost all browsers will work without these tags, you should include them since they are part of the standard.

Any HTML document can be divided into two parts: the header and the body. As you might suspect, each part is designated with a pair of tags. We use the *<head> </head>* pair for the header and *<body> </body>* for the main body of the document. The basic outline for an HTML document is

```
<html>
    <head>
    </head>

    <body>
    </body>
</html>
```

If you try to view an HTML document consisting of the above six lines, you will get a blank page since the document contains no text. The entire document consists of tags that make sense only to the HTML browser. None of these tags display any visual effects. Most browsers have a menu item that displays the source code for the displayed document. This is the only way you can see these tags on-line. Another way is to save the HTML document in a file and then use a text editor to view the file.

FIGURE 3-1

Text enclosed in the <title> tag is shown on the window bar

Header Tags

There are several tags that are restricted to the header. The most common one is the *<title>* tag. This tag is used to specify the document title. Most browsers display this title when showing the document. The title should say something meaningful about the document since many keyword search engines look at the content of this tag. Here is an example:

```
<title> How to write a good HTML document </title>
```

The text enclosed in the *<title> </title>* tags usually is not seen on the page along with the rest of the document. It is usually shown on a window bar, as in Figure 3-1.

Body Tags

Body tags are used within the main body of an HTML document. We divide them into the following categories:

- Headings
- Block elements
- Lists
- Character formatting
- Anchors
- Images

● HTML codes

● Tables

Headings

HTML offers six levels of headings, identified by H1-H6. Most browsers differentiate them by using a distinctive font or visual effect (such as boldface or italic). To indicate a particular text string as a level one heading, enclose it within the <H1> and </H1> tags. The following example contains all six heading levels. Figure 3-2 shows how they might look in the browser (some browsers might display headings differently than others).

```
<H1>This is an example of a level 1 heading</H1>
<H2>This is an example of a level 2 heading</H2>
<H3>This is an example of a level 3 heading</H3>
<H4>This is an example of a level 4 heading</H4>
<H5>This is an example of a level 5 heading</H5>
<H6>This is an example of a level 6 heading</H6>
```

Although the specifications do not mandate a particular format for displaying headings, the following is recommended:

H1: Bold, very large font, centered. One or two blank lines above and below.

H2: Bold, large font, flush-left. One or two blank lines above and below.

H3: Italic, large font, slightly indented from the left margin. One or two blank lines above and below.

H4: Bold, normal font, indented more than H3. One blank line above and below.

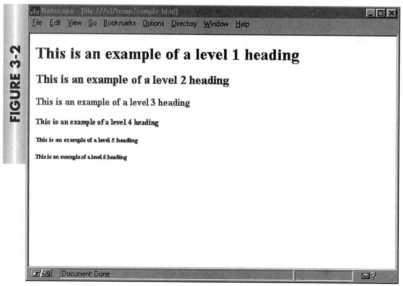

FIGURE 3-2

An example of different heading levels

H5: Italic, normal font, indented as H4. One blank line above.

H6: Bold, indented same as normal text, more than H5. One blank line above.

Note that *headings* are different from the *header* for the entire HTML document (identified by the *<head></head>* tag pair). Unlike the header, the text enclosed in the heading tags displays on the Web page. Also note that the way headings are displayed is controlled by the browser and not the author of the document.

Block Elements

In HTML, textual information is divided into paragraphs. A paragraph is separated from other paragraphs by a blank line; however, consecutive paragraph markers do not cause consecutive blank lines. The paragraph tags are *<p>* and *</p>*. For example:

```
<P>This is the text of a third paragraph.</P>
```

It is not required to enter the ending paragraph tag *</p>*. Each *<p>* starts a new paragraph. Indentations and white spaces within a paragraph are not recognized by the browser, so don't try to format the text and expect it to display your format on the Web page.

If you have some text that is in a special format and needs its indentations and white spaces preserved, then you must enclose it with the preformatted text tags. The tags are *<pre>* and *</pre>*. Text enclosed within these tags retains its formatting. You shouldn't use paragraph tags and headings within preformatted text, but anchor tags are allowed. An example along with the output is shown in Figure 3-3. Note that text enclosed within the *<pre></pre>* tags is displayed in a typewriter font.

```
<PRE>
You can begin a new line without the use of a paragraph tag.
This is a new line. Here is something
 Here is nothing
Note that something is aligned with nothing!
</PRE>
```

Another heavily used tag is the line break tag *
*. This tag starts a new line. Unlike *<p>*, multiple line breaks can be inserted using this tag. Here is an example with its output shown in Figure 3-4.

```
This is a line break demo. We break the line here <br>
and here<br>
and twice here <br><br>
This is the end.
```

Two other useful tags are the address tag and the block quote tag. The address tag contains information such as address, authorship, and signature, often at the beginning or end of the body of a document. The block quote tag is similar to the long quotes as they appear in literary documents. Here is an example of both. The result is shown in Figure 3-5.

```
This is what he said at the end
<BLOCKQUOTE>
This is a block quote example.
</BLOCKQUOTE>
```

```
And that is how it ended.<p>

<ADDRESS>
The author<BR>
John Doe<BR>
some city, ST, 12345<BR>
</ADDRESS>
```

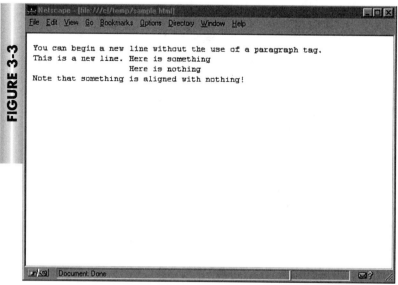

An example of the preformatted text tag

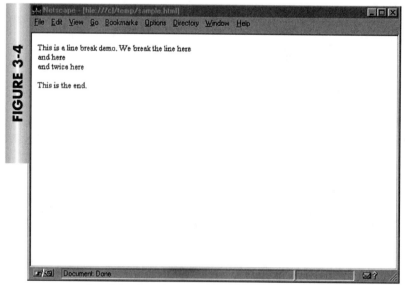

An example of the line break tag

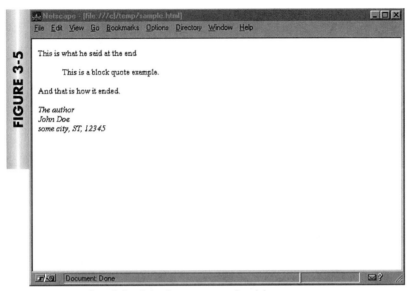

FIGURE 3-5

An example of the block quote and address tags

As with any computer language, there is a comment tag in HTML for documenting your pages. The syntax is

```
<!-- your comments -->
```

For better visual appearance you might want to separate your document using a horizontal line. The tag for a horizontal line uses the syntax of *<hr>*. Simply include the tag in your HTML document where you want to place the horizontal line.

Lists

The following list types are supported in HTML:

- Unordered list (UL)
- Ordered list (OL)
- Directory list (DIR)

The unordered list typically shows a number of items as in a bullet list. Each element is preceded with the tag *<li>*. The entire list is enclosed in a pair of *<ul> </ul>* tags. Figure 3-6 is the result of the sample unordered list shown below.

```
<ul>
<li>First list item
<li>Second list item
<li>Third list item
</ul>
```

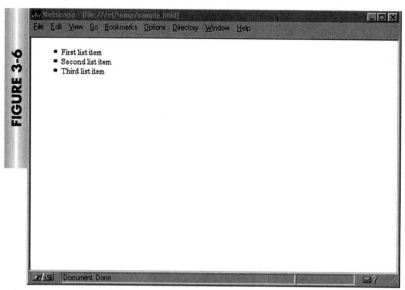

FIGURE 3-6

An example of the unordered list

An ordered list is used to show an ordered set of items sorted by sequence or order of importance. It is typically rendered as a numbered list and can have multiple levels of indentation. Again, the individual items are preceded with the *<li>* tag. The entire list is enclosed in a pair of *<ol> </ol>* tags. Listed below is a sample ordered list with two levels of indentation. The output is shown in Figure 3-7.

```
<ol>
<li>Chapter 1
<li>Chapter 2
<ol>
<li>Section 2.1
<li>Section 2.2
</ol>
<li>Chapter 3
</ol>
```

The MENU listing is similar to the unordered list. It does not allow for nested levels. It is usually more compact than the unordered list, but many browsers treat both types of lists the same way. Here is an example:

```
<menu>
<li>First menu item
<li>Second menu item
<li>Third menu item
</menu>
```

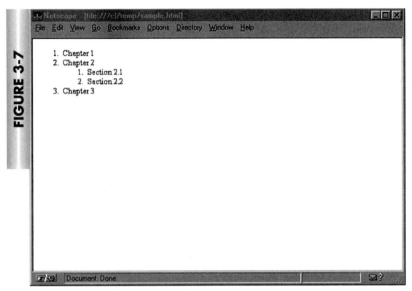

FIGURE 3-7

An example of the ordered list

Definition lists are useful when you need to separate a word and its definition in a consistent manner. The list is surrounded with the *<dl>* and *</dl>* tags. Each term is preceded with the *<dt>* tag and each definition is started with the *<dd>* tag. The result of the following example is shown in Figure 3-8.

```
<DL>
<DT>Term 1<DD>Definition for term 1.
<DT>Term 2<DD>Definition for term 2.
</DL>
```

For smaller definitions, you can use the COMPACT attribute. The result is shown in Figure 3-9.

```
<DL COMPACT>
<DT>Term<DD> Definition for term 1 in compact form.
<DT>Term<DD> Definition for term 2 in compact form.
</DL>
```

Character Formatting

In HTML, you can make text boldface or italic. For boldface, enclose the text within the *<b> </b>* tags. For italicized text, use the *<i> </i>* tag pairs. There are two other tags that usually have the same effect, but their intent is content-driven. These tags are *<em> </em>* (emphasized text) and *<strong> </strong>* (strong text). Most browsers display emphasized text in italics and strong text in boldface. Some browsers also support underlines using the tags *<u> </u>*.

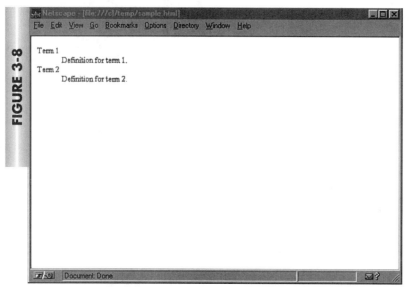

FIGURE 3-8

An example of a definition list

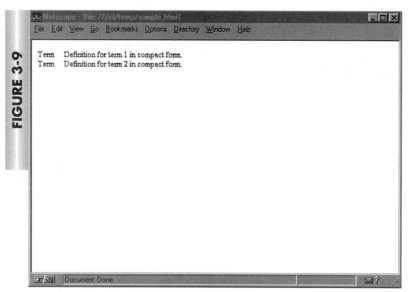

FIGURE 3-9

An example of a definition list with the COMPACT attribute

Anchors

Anchors are used to create links to other Web documents. The anchor tag is *<a></a>*. Unlike the tags we have seen so far, the anchor tag requires some attributes. You can think of attributes as arguments that you pass to a function. To use them, you specify the attribute name,

followed by an equal sign, followed by its value. Depending on the attribute, you might need to enclose its value in quotation marks. Here is an anchor tag example with the HREF attribute:

```
<a HREF="http://sun.java.com">Java</a>
```

Here, we create a link to the Web page referenced by the URL address `http://sun.java.com`. The word *Java* appears as a hot spot in our Web page, allowing the user to click on it.

There is a mechanism to reference (create links to) a specific portion of a document. This is useful if you have a long document and want to let the user go to a specific section quickly. To create these links, you need to use the anchor tag twice. First, mark the section of the document to which you want to create a link. Then, create the actual link to it. Let us use an example for demonstration. Suppose you want to create a link to Part 3 of your document. Mark Part 3 as shown below:

```
<a NAME="part3">Part 3</a>
```

This displays Part 3 on the Web page. You can include the entire anchor in a heading tag for visual effects.

```
<h2><a NAME="part3">Part 3</a></h2>
```

The NAME attribute gives a reference name to this section of the document. You can then make a link to Part 3 of your document by specifying the reference name as an argument to the HREF tag:

```
<a HREF="#part3">Part 3</a>
```

This anchor makes the words *Part 3* a hot spot. When you click on the link, the browser jumps to the part of the document marked by the reference name Part 3. Note the use of the # to indicate the argument to HREF is a reference name and not a filename. Figure 3-10 shows the linking mechanism. In our example above we restricted ourselves to links within a single document. You can create links to specific sections of documents on other machines if you know the reference name that was used to mark the particular section. In the following example, we provide HREF with a complete URL (rather than just a filename) and indicate the specific section of the document.

```
<a HREF="http://www.xyz.com/paper.html#part3">Part 3</a>
```

Another useful attribute for the anchor tag is TITLE. This attribute is merely a suggestion for a title the client can show while accessing the document. The TITLE attribute can display a title prior to accessing the actual document. The suggested title can appear while the mouse is over the anchor or while the document is being loaded. The title is also used to include a title for resources that do not have one, such as pictures or plain text.

Images

One of the key features of the World Wide Web is its multimedia nature. It is very common to see pictures embedded in an HTML document. Similar to other elements, there is a special tag for inclusion of images. The image tag has several attributes that give us flexibility as to how and where the picture is shown. The general format for the image tag is

```
<img src="filename / URL">
```

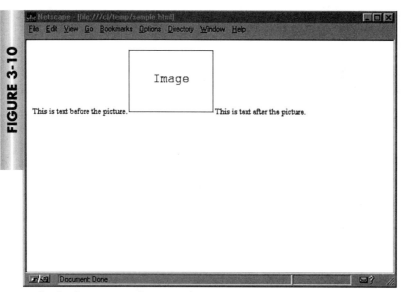

FIGURE 3-10

Default alignment of text and image

The tag by itself displays the specified image on the upper left corner of the screen. The SRC attribute specifies the image to be displayed. If the image is on another machine, then the full URL needs to be specified. Most likely, you will have some text to go with the image. Here is an example, with the result displayed in Figure 3-10.

```
This is text before the picture.<img src="image.gif">This is text after the
picture.
```

The ALIGN attribute specifies the type of alignment of the image and the text. The format is

```
<img src="image.gif" align=alignment type>
```

where *alignment type* is one of the following:

- TOP specifies that the top of the image aligns with the tallest item on the line containing the image.

- MIDDLE specifies that the center of the image aligns with the line containing the image.

- BOTTOM specifies that the bottom of the image aligns with the line containing the image. (default)

Figures 3-11 and 3-12 show the TOP and MIDDLE alignments, respectively.

Compared with text information, images take considerably longer to display. Many browsers give the user the option of loading the images on demand. That is, the user can look at the document and see a place holder where the image(s) would be. To view the image, the user asks the browser to retrieve it from the server. You can specify some text to be shown with

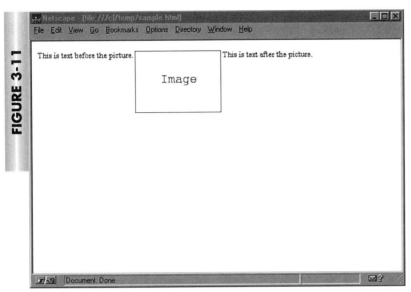

Top alignment of text and image

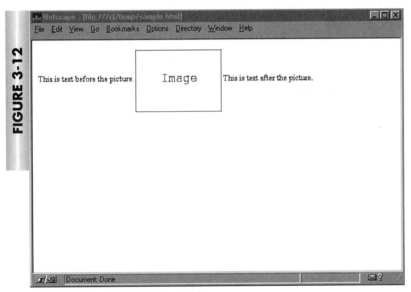

Middle alignment of text and image

the image place holder. This is usually information about the image that should give the user a good idea of what the image is and whether it is worth the wait to load it. This informative text is specified by the ALT attribute.

```
<img src="http://www.xyz.com/images/pres.gif" align=TOP alt="photo of the
president">
```

A popular tool on the World Wide Web is the imagemap facility. It allows you to specify a document link for certain locations on an image. It is like a visual anchor. You can learn more about imagemaps from http://hoohoo.ncsa.uiuc.edu/docs/tutorials/imagemapping.html. There is also a discussion on imagemaps in the next chapter.

If the image you are displaying will be used as an imagemap, then you must specify this with the ISMAP attribute.

```
<img src="image.gif" ISMAP>
```

Netscape Extensions to the IMG Tag

Netscape browsers have added a number of additional attributes to the image tag, giving you more control over how the images display. Although these are not part of the standard yet, it is very likely that they will be included in future versions of HTML.

Aside from the TOP, BOTTOM, and MIDDLE values, the alignment attribute can be set to LEFT or RIGHT. Figures 3-13 and 3-14 show such alignments, respectively.

Netscape extensions also allow you to specify a WIDTH and HEIGHT for the image. This way the browser knows the size of the image before receiving it from the network. The syntax is

```
<IMG WIDTH=value HEIGHT=value>
```

When you specify an alignment value of LEFT or RIGHT for an image, you create a floating image. To control how far apart other elements will be in relation to the image, two new attributes are introduced — VSPACE and HSPACE — which give you control over the vertical space and horizontal space around the image, respectively. The syntax is

```
<IMG VSPACE=value HSPACE=value>
```

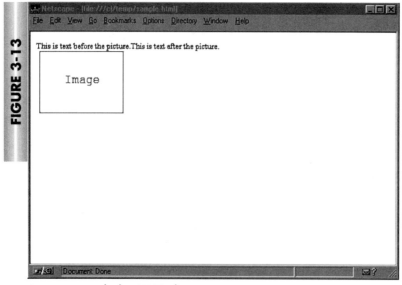

FIGURE 3-13

An image with the LEFT alignment

FIGURE 3-14

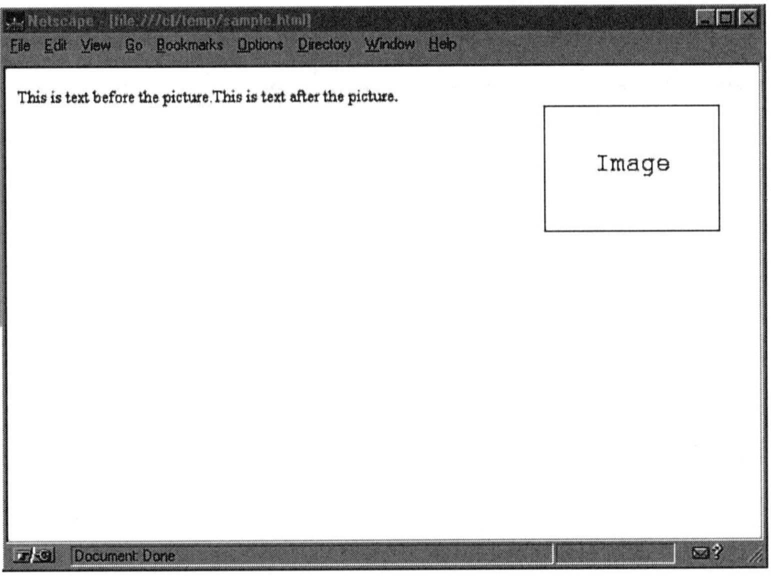

An image with the RIGHT alignment

HTML Codes

As we have seen, HTML tags mark the document and enhance the way it appears to the user. Sooner or later we will come across text that has one of the special characters used to mark the tags, so we need to find a way to display that character. We have to tell the browser that we want this character to actually be displayed and not interpreted as a tag. HTML has provided the following syntax to do just that:

- *<* displays <
- *>* displays for >
- *&* displays &

Actually, you can display any ASCII character by preceding its ASCII code with an ampersand (for example, &65; to display A). HTML supports the ISO-8859 character set. Table 3-1 shows a listing of the characters and the names used to display them.

ISO-8859

ISO-8859 is a standardized series of 8-bit character sets for writing in Western alphabetic languages. It was designed by the European Computer Manufacturer's Association (ECMA). ISO-8859 is a major improvement over the 7-bit US-ASCII code since it supports a larger number of characters. You can learn more about the ISO-8859 character sets from `http://www.cs.tu-berlin.de/user/czyborra/charsets/`.

Table 3-1 Extended characters and their display codes

Character	Display name	Character	Display name	Character	Display name
Æ	&AElig	Ø	&Oslash	ë	&euml
Á	&Aacute	Õ	&Otilde	í	&iacute
Â	&Acirc	Ö	&Ouml	î	&icirc
À	&Agrave	Þ	&THORN	ì	&igrave
Å	&Aring	Ú	&Uacute	ï	&iuml
Ã	&Atilde	Û	&Ucirc	ñ	&ntilde
Ä	&Auml	Ù	&Ugrave	ó	&oacute
Ç	&Ccedil	Ü	&Uuml	ô	&ocirc
Ð	&ETH	Y	&Yacute	ò	&ograve
É	&Eacute	á	&aacute	ø	&oslash
Ê	&Ecirc	â	&acirc	õ	&otilde
È	&Egrave	æ	&aelig	ö	&ouml
Ë	&Euml	à	&agrave	ß	&szlig
Í	&Iacute	å	&aring	þ	&thorn
Î	&Icirc	ã	&atilde	ú	&uacute
Ì	&Igrave	ä	&auml	û	&ucirc
Ï	&Iuml	ç	&ccedil	ù	&ugrave
Ñ	&Ntilde	é	&eacute	ü	&uuml
Ó	&Oacute	ê	&ecirc	y	&yacute
Ô	&Ocirc	è	&egrave	ÿ	&yuml
Ò	&Ograve	ð	&eth		

Tables

HTML 3.0 promises to have complete support for tables. Several vendors, including Netscape, have already added table support to their browsers. Tables are a useful way to organize information. Because we will use HTML to access database information, the ability to display information in a tabular format is important. Therefore, even though tables are not yet part of standard HTML, this section is devoted to their implementation based on the specifications for Netscape browsers.

The beginning and ending of a table is marked similarly to lists and other HTML objects. The contents of the table, including all table-related tags, are enclosed within the *<table>* *</table>* tags. Currently, a table is placed on the page with a line break before and after it. You do not have the positioning flexibility of images with tables.

We specify the contents of a table one row at a time by enclosing it within the *<tr>* *</tr>* tags. As a result, the number of *<tr>* tags can quickly tell us how many rows are included in a table. This feature is also handy when a script is used to create the table and it is not known in advance how many rows the table contains. The script can print one row at a time and just before it is finished, it can print the *</table>* tag to indicate the end of the table. The contents of each row (individual data elements) are specified using the *<td>* *</td>* tags. There is no requirement that all rows have the same number of data elements. Shorter rows will be padded with blank data elements on the right side. There are no restrictions on what the data elements must consist of. They can be plain text, HTML tags, or even images. The following is an example of a simple table with the output shown in Figure 3-15.

```
<TABLE BORDER>
<TR>
        <TD>R1C1</TD>  <TD>R1C2</TD>  <TD>R1C3</TD>
</TR>
<TR>
        <TD>R1C1</TD>  <TD>R2C2</TD>  <TD>R2C3</TD>
</TR>
</TABLE>
```

You can designate one or more rows in the table as the table header by enclosing the header within the *<th>* *</th>* tag. The content of the header is automatically displayed using

FIGURE 3-15

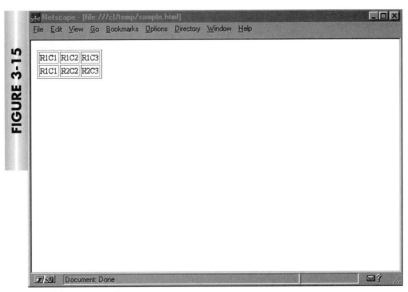

A table example

a boldface font. The *<caption> </caption>* tags let you specify a table caption. Captions have the same maximum width as the table.

There are several attributes that apply to the entire table. The BORDER attribute is specified within the table tag. It draws borders around all data elements of a table.

The ALIGN attribute's behavior depends on where it is placed. The *<tr>*, *<th>*, or *<td>* tag specifies the alignment for the data elements. The *<caption>* tag has values of TOP or BOTTOM and specifies where the caption should be placed in relation to the table. The VALIGN attribute is similar to ALIGN but controls the vertical alignment of data elements. It can only be specified within the *<tr>*, *<th>*, and *<td>* tags.

The NOWRAP attribute controls whether text wrapping is allowed within the data elements or table headers. Finally, COLSPAN and ROWSPAN specify how many column or rows a given data element should span. The default value for both is 1. Here is an example that uses some of these attributes. Its output is shown in Figure 3-16.

```
<TABLE BORDER>
<TR>
        <TH>Head 1</TH>
        <TH>Head 2 </TH>
        <TH>Head 3</TH>
</TR>
<TR VALIGN=top>
        <TD>element 1</TD>
        <TD>element 2 is <br> brokn</TD>
        <TD>element 3</TD>
</TR>
<TR>
        <TD VALIGN=top >top alignment</TD>
        <TD default alignment of center</TD>
        <TD>VALIGN=bottom>bottom alignment </TD>
</TR>
</TABLE>
```

You can find the table specifications for Netscape browsers and other table-related information at:

- http://www.netscape.com/assist/net_sites/tables.html

- http://www.ncsa.uiuc.edu/SDG/Software/Mosaic/Tables/tutorial.html

- http://www.w3.org/pub/www/TR/WD-tables.html

Frames

Another popular enhancement from Netscape browsers is the introduction of *frames* in HTML. By using frames you can divide a home page into several parts, each capable of displaying a separate Web page. Frames can also be used in a manner similar to freezing panes in spreadsheets. You can divide a page into two parts or more. The first part can hold a menu-like page where the user can click on a number of different links. The other parts can display the Web page corresponding to the user's choice. This eliminates some of the forward-backward browsing and creates a nice user interface for our applications. Figure 3-17 shows an example of a Web page using frames.

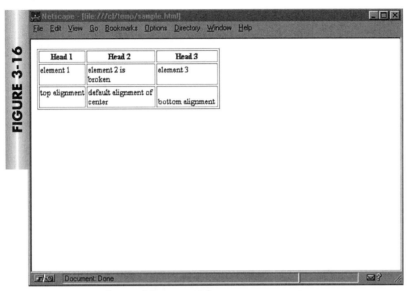

A more complete table example

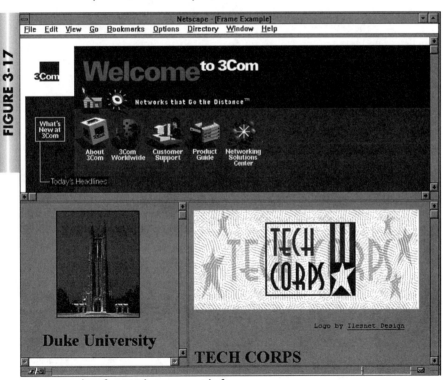

An example of a Web page with frames

Despite their usefulness, frames are very easy to create and maintain. Recall that an HTML document has the following structure:

```
<html>
       <head>
       </head>

       <body>
       </body>
</html>
```

When using frames, we will have to use a slightly different structure:

```
<html>
       <head>
       </head>

       <frameset>
       </frameset>
</html>
```

The *<frameset>* tag identifies an HTML document that uses frames. Note that a frame document cannot have a *<body>* tag. Inclusion of a *<body>* tag causes the browser to ignore the *<frameset>* tag. The basic approach is that you define your page layout using one or more *<frameset>* tags, then identify a URL to display within each frame. We divide the page into sections using the ROWS and COLS attributes. The value of each of these attributes is a comma-separated list of numbers. The number of elements in the list indicates the number of rows or columns (depending on the attribute). Let us look at some examples.

Example 1:

```
<frameset rows="100, 200">
```

In this example, we specify a frameset that has two rows (since there are two numbers in the list). The height of each row is specified by an absolute pixel value. That is, the first row has a height of 100 pixels and the second row has a height of 200 pixels. This method of specifying heights and widths is not recommended because it removes the inherent flexibility within frames. If the size of the browser window is smaller than the specified values, then the client ignores the numbers and determines its own compromise values. We call this method of specification *absolute pixel values*.

Example 2:

```
<frameset rows="40%, 60%">
```

In this example, we again specify a frameset with two rows; however, the height for each row is specified as a percentage of the total browser window size. This is much more flexible than absolute pixel values since the browser can split the window based on our specification, no matter how small the browser window is. In any case, the first row has a smaller height compared to the second row, based on a 40-60 split. We call this method the *percentage values*.

Example 3:

```
<frameset rows="20, *">
```

The last example utilizes relative scaling values and can be a bit confusing. Here, we are making a frameset with two rows. The first row has a height of 20 pixels and the second row occupies the *remaining* space. If you want to specify absolute pixel values, this is the preferred method since you are leaving some room for error. Another useful variation is when the frameset includes three rows, as shown here:

```
<frameset rows="80,*,80">
```

In this case, we specify the height for the top and bottom rows, but we leave the middle row to use the *remaining* space.

Depending on the number of rows and columns we specified in the *<frameset>* tag, we must provide a number of *<frame>* tags to fill the frames. The *<frame>* tag is our way of telling the browser what to display in each frame box. The required attribute is SRC, which indicates a URL or a local filename to be used as the source for the frame box. Several other attributes are supported as follows:

- SCROLLING—This attribute can have the values *yes, no,* or *auto.* It specifies whether scroll bars should be attached to the frame box.

- NORESIZE—The presence of this flag prohibits the user from resizing the frame box.

- NAME—The value for this attribute is a unique name which can be used to create a link to the frame from other documents or the same document. This is similar to the NAME attribute in the *<href>* tag.

The last tag related to frames is the *<noframes>* tag. This tag is used to show a message or a non-frames version of Web pages to users whose browser is not capable of supporting frames. The message is enclosed within the *<noframes> </noframes>* tag pair.

To end this section, we will present a few examples. Figure 3-18 shows a 2x2 frame. Here is the code to generate it.

```
<HTML>
<FRAMESET rows="50%,50%">
   <FRAMESET cols="50%,50%">
       <FRAME src="sample.htm" scrolling="yes">
       <FRAME src="sample.htm" scrolling="yes">
   </FRAMESET>

   <FRAMESET cols="50%,50%">
       <FRAME src="sample.htm" scrolling="yes">
       <FRAME src="sample.htm" scrolling="yes">
   </FRAMESET>
</FRAMESET>
</HTML>
```

FIGURE 3-18

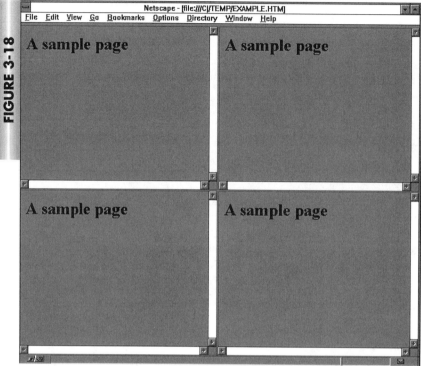

A 2x2 frame

Next, we try to create a frame as shown in Figure 3-19. Here is the code for it.

```
<HTML>
<FRAMESET rows="20%,30%,50%">
   <FRAME src="sample.htm" scrolling="yes">
   <FRAMESET cols="50%,50%">
      <FRAME src="sample.htm">
      <FRAME src="sample.htm">
   </FRAMESET>
   <FRAMESET cols="300,*,300">
      <FRAME src="sample.htm">
      <FRAME src="sample.htm" scrolling="yes">
      <FRAME src="sample.htm">
   </FRAMESET>
</FRAMESET>
</HTML>
```

You can learn more about frames and their specifications from http://home.netscape.com/comprod/products/navigator/version_2.0/frames/index.html.

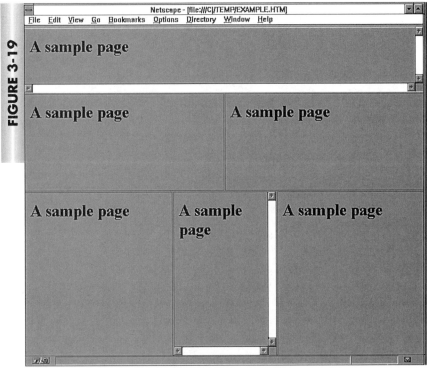

A multilevel frame

URL

URLs (Uniform Resource Locators) are the equivalent of our postal addresses. A URL is supposed to be able to uniquely identify an Internet service such as a News server or a Web server. A URL address is composed of six parts:

1. Service identifier followed by a colon

2. The characters "//"

3. Path to the resource's filename (optional)

4. The type of the resource (optional)

5. An internal marker within the resource (optional)

6. The search/selection specification (optional)

The service identifier is your indication of what type of service to which the URL is pointing. The most common ones are

- `file` - a file residing on the host machine
- `ftp` - File Transfer protocol
- `gopher` - the Gopher protocol
- `http` - Hypertext Transfer Protocol
- `mailto` - electronic mail address which can be processed either by your browser or sent to a Mail server
- `news` - USENET news
- `telnet` - allows you to log in to another machine; usually requires an account on that machine
- `wais` - Wide Area Information Servers

The characters "//" are used only if you are referencing an absolute address. They are usually followed by the hostname of the machine offering the service. Internet services have well-known port numbers. For example, the http protocol uses port 80 as its default communication port number. In some cases, the service is offered through another non-standard port number. If this is the case, the port number must be explicitly stated in the URL, as in `http://www.xyz.com:8000/part1.html`.

Here are some valid URL examples.

- `file:///C|/MYSTUFF/HELLO.HTM`—points to the file HELLO.HTM which resides in the MYSTUFF directory on drive C:\>
- `ftp://ftp.xyz.com/pub/some_document.ps`—points to a file named some_document.ps, which is available from a machine named ftp.xyz.com
- `mailto:bgingery@Wyoming.com`—indicates mail should be sent to the specified address
- `http://www.uiuc.edu`—links to the welcome page on the WWW server on the machine, www.uiuc.edu

You can learn more about URLs from `http://turnpike.net/metro/bagingry/URLs.html`.

Summary

The HTML language is a markup language used to create static pages on the World Wide Web. It uses tags to identify different sections of the document and create links to others. Several vendors have added their own extensions to the HTML language, such as tables and floating images. Different parts of the document are marked with special tags enclosed in a pair of <>. These tags instruct the browser how to display the information. For example, the items of an unordered list are enclosed within the *<ul></ul>* tags. This causes the browser to display the items in a list-like format. If the browser encounters a tag that it does not understand, it should ignore the tag.

Common HTML tags include tables, frames, lists, menus, images, hyperlinks, and paragraph marks. There are also tags that have no visual effects but are essential in the construction of the page, since they indicate the header and body part of the document.

In order to uniquely address the different resources available on the Internet, we use a Uniform Resource Locator (URL). A URL follows a standard format and is the addressing scheme used to identify a resource in a Web application.

Questions

1. What is HTTP? How does it differ from HTML?

2. How does HTML mark its commands?

3. How do you reference other Web documents in HTML?

4. What character set does HTML support?

5. What is a URL?

Answers

1. HTTP is the network protocol for the World Wide Web. It sits at the application layer in the OSI model. HTML is a markup language used to make static pages on the World Wide Web. Both are necessary to make the Web work.

2. All HTML-related commands are marked with a unique tag enclosed between the characters < and >.

3. The anchor tag is used to reference other documents on the same or different servers.

4. ISO-8859

5. A URL is an address for a resource on the Internet. The URL identifies the type of resource (for example, ftp or http) and its address, including the port number if a well-known port is not being used.

4
User Input

So far we have discussed elements of a *static* Web page. We now turn to *interactive* Web pages. These pages, which enable us to receive input from the user, are an absolute necessity when developing a database front-end using the World Wide Web. We start with a brief overview of the Web programming environment. Next, we discuss the different elements of an interactive Web page. All of this is done through HTML without Java or JavaScripts. A popular addition to Web pages is the imagemap, which we will explore in this chapter. We end this chapter by discussing some of the tools that can help you create and maintain Web pages.

The Basics

The fill-out forms interface was an addition to the HTML and HTTP standard. With the explosive popularity of the World Wide Web, there was a great push to create an open interface between the World Wide Web and external programs. As you have seen, none of the elements of a static Web page allow for user input. The only selection a user can make is what link to follow, which is insufficient for most applications, including database applications.

Forms and Common Gateway Interface (CGI) are responsible for collecting information from the user, putting it in a standard format, and sending it to an external program. The external program can process the information it receives, perform some tasks (for example, query a database), and output its result in HTML format. We discuss forms in this chapter and CGI in Chapter 5, "Common Gateway Interface (CGI) Basics."

A key aspect of the Web programming environment is the interface between the external program and its input. While conventional programming environments allow the program to have some control over the input phase, such control is non-existent in a Web program. The external program will not see *any* input until the user *submits* the form. It is very common to alter the choices in a list based on what the user has entered in another part of the

55

data entry form. Such interaction is simply not possible in the Web programming environment because all input is submitted to the external program at once. As we will see later in the chapter, one way to get around this is to use multiple forms. Figures 4-1 and 4-2 show this difference. In Figure 4-1, we have a simple login form that was created using Visual Basic. Almost any user interaction generates a message that gets sent to the program. Such interactions include mouse movement, menu selection, text entry, and clicking on buttons. The program might or might not make a response to all of the messages, but the important fact is that such information is available to it. Figure 4-2 shows the same login screen generated by a Web form. Note that this screen displays on a browser (client). As the user interacts with the form, no information is sent to the server until the submit button is clicked.

Event-Based Programming

If you have programmed in any window-based environment (such as Motif or MS Windows), then you are familiar with event-based programming. In such an environment, the program spends most of its time in an event loop. Based on user interaction, the program comes out of this mode, executes a certain function, then goes back to the event loop. Objects on the screen have different attributes and can send messages to the main program or to other objects. For example, when the user clicks on the OK button, a *click* message is generated. The program processes it by executing a series of designated commands. Message generation and message processing is instantaneous and continuous. In the Web programming environment, such interaction is not possible. The program which must act on user inputs resides on the server. The user input, however, is entered on the client. Since the server and client do not have a continuous connection, the server program does not define what the user has entered until the form's contents are sent to it explicitly. This distinction between event-based programming and Web programming is very important and must be given constant consideration as we develop our applications. Of course, Java and JavaScripts make an attempt to address this shortcoming of the Web environment by taking an object-oriented approach to application development, treating the different elements on the screen as objects and associating events with those objects. The fact remains that unless such applications open and maintain their own connection to the server, the HTTP connection will not be continuous.

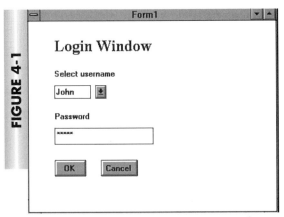

User input processing in conventional programming environment

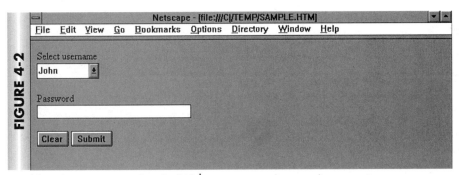

User input processing in Web programming environment

Fill-Out Forms Using the FORM Tag

Forms are marked with a special tag in an HTML document. Between the tag pairs, there are usually a number of elements which allow the user to enter some input. These elements are simple text input, menus, and multiple-line text input. Each form has an external program associated with it which is responsible for receiving the input from the form and processing it. Finally, the last element of a form is a submit button, which tells the HTTP client (browser) to request the server to run the external program using the collected input. The details of how the external program works, how user input is transferred to it, and how it is executed are covered in the Common Gateway Interface (CGI) specifications and discussed in detail in Chapter 5. For now, let us concentrate on the client side of the interaction.

The *<form>* tag within an HTML document identifies the boundaries for a fill-out form. Although you can have multiple forms within a single HTML document, these forms cannot be nested within one another. It is very common to separate a form from the rest of the Web page via the horizontal line tag. The basic syntax for forms is

```
<form ACTION="url">
form elements
</form>
```

The *<form>* tag has a number of attributes associated with it. The ACTION attribute specifies the URL for the external program. This is the program which executes once the form is submitted. This program interacts directly with the Web server and must comply with the CGI standard. If the ACTION attribute is not specified, the URL for the current document is the default value.

The second attribute is METHOD. The valid values for this attribute are *get* and *post*. The METHOD attribute specifies the way the input data is sent to the external program via the server. In almost all cases, you should specify the *post* method. The *get* method was originally part of the standard, but due to its limitations it is being discouraged and will probably be removed from the standard in the near future. We will now discuss the elements which make up the user interface and reside inside a form.

INPUT Tag

The *<input>* tag is used to receive one input item from the user. It is the most basic of input elements inside a form and follows the syntax shown below:

```
<input NAME="name" TYPE=type>
```

This tag must include at least the NAME attribute which is used by the CGI program to get the information typed in the box. If the *<type>* tag is omitted, it defaults to *text*. Other values allow us to create a variety of input elements, as discussed below.

Text Box

With a value of *text* for the TYPE attribute, we can create simple text boxes to accept user input. Such boxes are the most basic element in user interfaces. They allow for input of such items as names, addresses, and ID numbers. The SIZE attribute specifies the length of the text box in characters, with a default of 20. The MAXLENGTH attribute specifies the actual number of characters that is acceptable as input for the text box. Note that this number can be larger than the value specified by the SIZE attribute. See the following examples and the result shown in Figure 4-3.

```
<p>Name: <input NAME="name" TYPE=text>
<p>Address: <input NAME="address" TYPE=text SIZE="30">
<p>City: <input NAME="city" TYPE=text SIZE="15" MAXLENGTH="30">
```

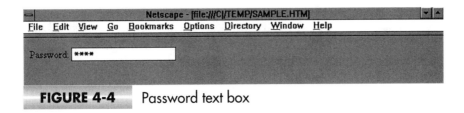

FIGURE 4-3

Text box examples

Password Text Box

This type of input is identical to a text input with one exception: All characters entered in a password text box are echoed back as an asterisk as shown in Figure 4-4.

```
<p>Password: <input NAME="password" TYPE=password>
```

Checkbox

A *checkbox* is a single toggle button with possible values of *on* or *off*. A checkbox is useful when you need to ask the user to select from two mutually exclusive alternatives. For example, to determine whether a date stamp should be printed in a report, you can use a checkbox as shown in Figure 4-5. A group of checkboxes can be used collectively to allow for a *many of many* selection behavior as shown in Figure 4-6. The presence of the attribute CHECKED indicates that the checkbox is checked by default.

```
<input TYPE="checkbox" NAME="prt_date" VALUE="print"> Print the date on each
page

Select all that apply:
<uL>
<li><input TYPE="checkbox" NAME="computer" VALUE="ibm_comp"> IBM compatible
<li><input TYPE="checkbox" NAME="computer" VALUE="mac"> Macintosh
<li><input TYPE="checkbox" NAME="computer" VALUE="unix"> Unix
</ul>
```

FIGURE 4-4   Password text box

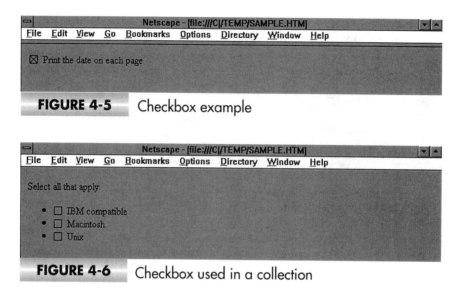

FIGURE 4-5   Checkbox example

FIGURE 4-6   Checkbox used in a collection

Radio Button

A *radio button* is a collection of checkboxes and allows for a *one of many* selection behavior. Radio buttons are useful when you want to let the user see all the options and select *only* one, thus excluding others. An example is shown in Figure 4-7. Similar to a checkbox, the presence of the CHECKED attribute indicates that the radio button is armed by default.

```
Select machine type:
<uL>
<Li> <input TYPE="radio" NAME="tr_mach_type" VALUE="SGI" CHECKED> SGI
<Li> <input TYPE="radio" NAME="tr_mach_type" VALUE="Alpha"> Alpha
<Li> <input TYPE="radio" NAME="tr_mach_type" VALUE="Mac"> Macintosh
<Li> <input TYPE="radio" NAME="tr_mach_type" VALUE="PC"> PC
<Li> <input TYPE="radio" NAME="tr_mach_type" VALUE="Other"> Other
</uL>
```

There are two attributes that are common to all input types. The first is the VALUE attribute, which specifies the default content of a text input or a password field. This value is displayed when the user sees the box. In the case of checkboxes or radio buttons, the VALUE attribute indicates the value of the item when it is *checked*. The second common attribute is NAME. This is a unique name identifying the value of this field and is required for all types. It is very much like a variable name whose value is the content of the input field. As we will see later, the value of the NAME attribute is used to identify the user input when it is transferred to an external program.

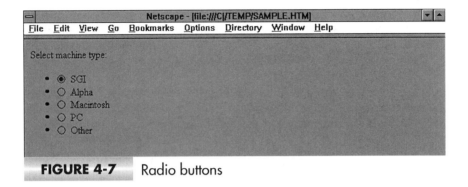

FIGURE 4-7   Radio buttons

Submit Button

A *submit button* sends the content of the current form to the Web server. You can have more than one submit button in a form if you want to send the content of the form to different back-end programs. Each form requires at least one submit button. The syntax is like other input elements.

```
<input VALUE="Submit" TYPE="submit">
```

The text associated with the VALUE attribute is what is displayed inside the push button.

Reset

The *clear button* can be used to clear or reset the content of the current form. Here is an example:

```
<input VALUE="Clear" TYPE="reset">
```

Similar to the submit button, the text associated with the VALUE attribute is what is displayed inside the push button.

Menus

A common element of all graphical user interfaces is the *menu*. Menus offer the user an easy way to select from a given set of choices. They reduce user input to a single mouse click and eliminate mistakes which might occur if the user had to type the selection in a text box. In HTML you can create menu-like structures by using the *<select> </select>* tag pair. Each tag must have a NAME attribute which again acts as a variable name and holds the value of the selected item(s). The menu choices are specified using the *<option>* tag inside the *<select>* tag. Unless a VALUE attribute is explicitly stated, the value of each menu option is the text that follows the *<option>* tag. An attribute of SELECTED inside the *<option>* tag preselects the item.

Based on the value of the SIZE attribute, two menu types can be generated. If the size is not specified or is equal to 1, then the menu is presented as a drop-down list box as shown in Figure 4-8. This menu type always shows the selected item. By clicking on the item, the user can see the remaining choices and select another one.

```
Select machine type:
<select name="machine_menu">
<option> SGI
<option> Alpha
<option> Macintosh
<option> PC
<option> Other
</select>
```

The drop-down list box is known as the option menu in Motif and is shown in Figure 4-9. Its behavior is exactly the same, but its appearance is somewhat different.

If the SIZE attribute is 2 or more, then the menu is presented as a list and the user can select only one item from the menu as shown in Figure 4-10. If the MULTIPLE attribute is present, the menu is always shown as a list regardless the value of SIZE, and the user can make more than one selection as shown in Figure 4-11.

```
<strong>Select State:</strong><p>
<SELECT NAME="rstate" SIZE="6">
<OPTION> Alabama
<OPTION> Alaska
<OPTION> Arizona
<OPTION> Arkansas
<OPTION> California
<OPTION> Colorado
<OPTION> Connecticut
<OPTION> Delaware
<OPTION> Florida
<OPTION> Georgia
<OPTION> Hawaii
<OPTION> Idaho
<OPTION> Illinois
</SELECT><p>
```

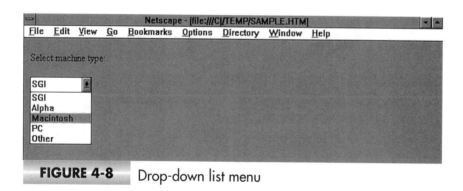

FIGURE 4-8   Drop-down list menu

Your Name (First Name, Middle Initial, Last Name):

Ms. ▭ [   ] [ ] [   ]

FIGURE 4-9   Option menu in Motif

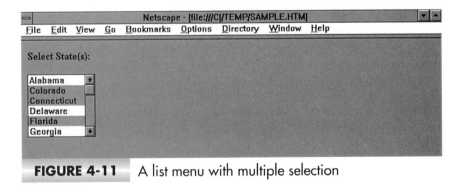

FIGURE 4-10   A list menu with single selection

```
<strong>Select State(s):</strong><p>
<SELECT NAME="rstate" SIZE="6" MULTIPLE>
<OPTION SELECTED> Alabama
<OPTION> Colorado
<OPTION> Connecticut
<OPTION> Delaware
<OPTION> Florida
<OPTION> Georgia
<OPTION> Hawaii
<OPTION> Idaho
<OPTION> Illinois
</SELECT><p>
```

FIGURE 4-11   A list menu with multiple selection

Multiline Text Input

The last tag considered is the *<textarea>* tag, which allows us to collect multiple lines of text from the user. We don't have much control over the text itself, but we can influence the appearance of the multiline text box by specifying its width and height. Many database applications include an area where notes and comments are stored. A multiline text box works very well in this context. The syntax is shown here:

```
<textarea name="memo" rows=5 cols=50> some default text </textarea>
```

Any text entered between the tag pairs is considered default text and is displayed in the box. The user can edit that text. The *<textarea>* tag automatically adds vertical and horizontal scroll bars as shown in Figure 4-12. Any amount of text can be entered in a multiline text element. Our program will not know about the length of the textual data until the form is submitted. As we shall see in Chapter 5, this presents an interesting programming challenge.

```
<textarea name="somename" rows=5 cols=50>
Any text entered between the tag pairs is considered as default text and
is displayed in the box. The user can edit that text. The <textarea> tag
automatically adds vertical and horizontal scrollbars. Any amount of text
can be entered in a multiline text element and our program will not know
about the length of the textual data until the form is submitted. As we
shall see in Chapter this presents an interesting programming challenge.
</textarea>
```

So far we have presented a variety of elements that allow us to create a graphical user interface and collect data from the user. Recall that the World Wide Web is a client/server environment. Once the user is finished filling out the form, the data is still residing at the client. We must transfer this data in a standard manner to the server and have the server perform a task based on the data. This process, called *submitting a form*, is discussed in Chapter 5 along with the tags and attributes contained in that chapter.

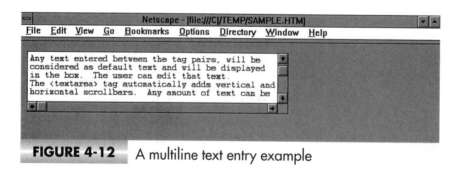

FIGURE 4-12   A multiline text entry example

Sample Forms

To get a feel for how form elements mix together, we will look at two examples. The first, a simple fill-out form collecting information about the user, is shown in Listing 4-1 and Figure 4-13. Note how the different elements (menus, text entry, and so on) are mixed together. Also pay attention to the alignment of the different elements. Form elements do not have support for edit masks; therefore, the user can enter phone and fax numbers in any format they choose. Your program must be prepared to accept anything. Remember, your program will not see any of the inputs until they are all submitted.

FIGURE 4-13

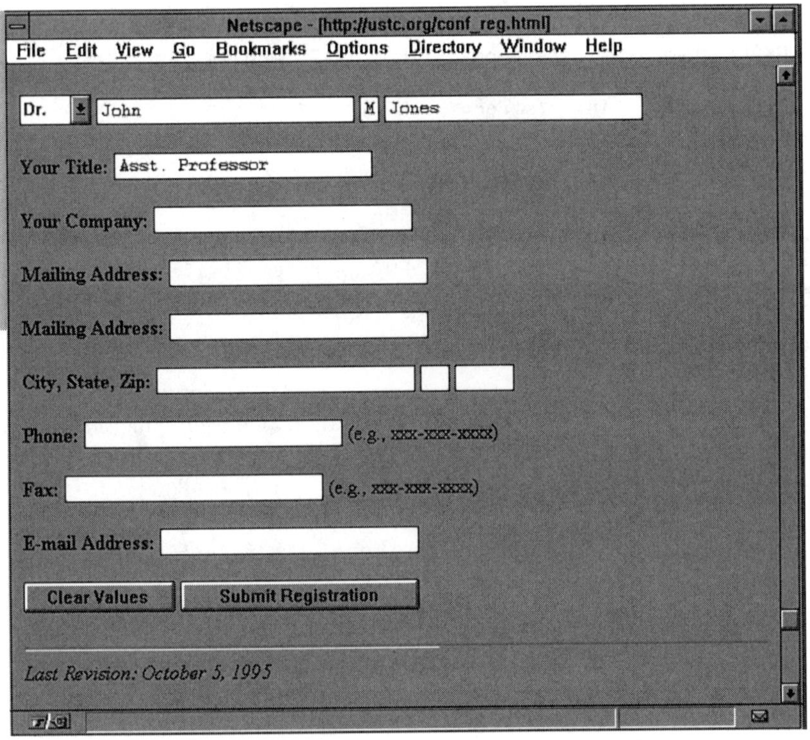

Address entry form

Listing 4-1 Code for the address entry form

```
<FORM method=POST action="http://XXXXX/cgi-bin/register.cgi">
<strong>Your Name (First Name, Middle Initial, Last Name):</strong><p>
<SELECT NAME="prefix">
 <OPTION SELECTED> Ms.
 <OPTION> Mr.
 <OPTION> Dr.
</SELECT>

<INPUT NAME="fname"size="25">
<INPUT NAME="mname" size="1">
<INPUT NAME="lname"size="25"><p>
<strong> Your Title: </strong> <INPUT NAME="title"size="25"><p>
<strong> Your Company: </strong> <INPUT NAME="company"size="25"><p>
<strong> Mailing Address: </strong> <INPUT NAME="add1"size="25"><p>
<strong> Mailing Address: </strong> <INPUT NAME="add2"size="25"><p>
<strong> City, State, Zip: </strong> <INPUT NAME="city"size="25">
<INPUT NAME="state" size="2">
<INPUT NAME="zip" size="5"><p>
<strong> Phone: </strong> <INPUT NAME="phone"size="25"> (e.g., xxx-xxx-
xxxx)<p>
<strong> Fax:  </strong> <INPUT NAME="fax"size="25"> (e.g., xxx-xxx-xxxx)<p>
<strong> E-mail Address:  </strong> <INPUT NAME="email"size="25"><p>
<input type="reset" value="Clear Values"> <input type="submit" value="Submit
Registration"> <p>
<hr> <i>Last Revision: October 5, 1995</i><br> <p>
</FORM>
```

The next example (see Listing 4-2) comes from a hardware trouble reporting facility. The fill-out form is presented to users who want to report a problem. Consider the NAME attribute in the elements. Note that all names begin with the prefix *tr*. This choice allows us to uniquely identify variables from this form in our external program. Also note that the browser has automatically put scroll bars around the text entry boxes as shown in Figure 4-14.

Listing 4-2 Trouble reporting facility

```
<FORM METHOD="POST" ACTION="http://XXXXXX/cgi-bin/trget.pl">

Your Name: <INPUT TYPE="text" NAME="tr_reporter" SIZE=30 MAXLENGTH=30>
<P>
Your Email address: <INPUT TYPE="text" NAME="tr_email" SIZE=30 MAXLENGTH=30>
<P>
Date of problem (e.g., 9-8-95): <INPUT TYPE="date" NAME="tr_date"
MAXLENGTH=10>
<P>
Time of problem (e.g., 10:30pm): <INPUT TYPE="text" NAME="tr_time" SIZE=8
MAXLENGTH=8>
<P>
Machine name (if any): <INPUT TYPE="text" NAME="tr_mach_name" SIZE=20
MAXLENGTH=20>
<P>
```

```
Machine type:
<uL>
<LI> <INPUT TYPE="radio" NAME="tr_mach_type" VALUE="SGI"> SGI
<LI> <INPUT TYPE="radio" NAME="tr_mach_type" VALUE="Alpha"> Alpha
<LI> <INPUT TYPE="radio" NAME="tr_mach_type" VALUE="Mac"> Macintosh
<LI> <INPUT TYPE="radio" NAME="tr_mach_type" VALUE="PC"> PC
<LI> <INPUT TYPE="radio" NAME="tr_mach_type" VALUE="Other"> Other
</uL>
<P>
Enter a <STRONG>brief</STRONG> description of the problem: <TEXTAREA
NAME="tr_b_desc" ROWS=2 COLS=50></TEXTAREA>
<P>
Enter a <STRONG>complete</STRONG> description here: <TEXTAREA NAME="tr_f_desc"
ROWS=4 COLS=60></TEXTAREA>
<P>
<input type="reset" value="Clear Values"> <input type="submit" value="Submit
Report"> <p>
</FORM>
```

FIGURE 4-14

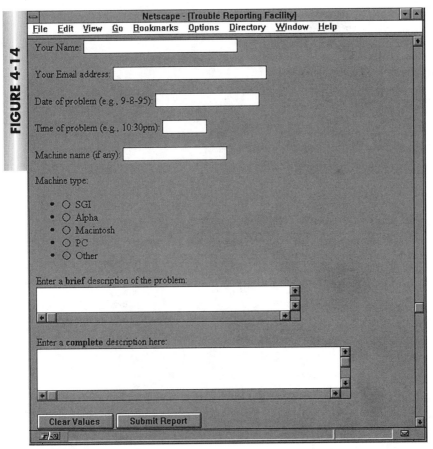

Trouble reporting form

Imagemaps

Imagemaps are becoming a popular addition to user interfaces. The imagemap facility allows you to define certain portions of an image as hyperlinks to other Web pages. With such a simple and open definition, Web authors have used imagemaps in a variety of ways. For example, US Techcorps has created a map of the United States which allows the user to jump to the state of his interest (see Figure 4-15). Powersoft has used imagemaps to create a graphical interface to the different parts of its World Wide Web server (see Figure 4-16). Keep in mind that imagemaps can slow down your users if they do not enjoy a high-speed connection. Before making a selection, the entire image must be downloaded to the

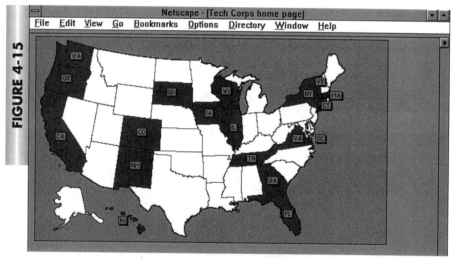

FIGURE 4-15

An imagemap used to create links to different states

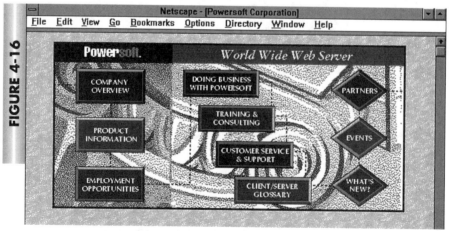

FIGURE 4-16

An imagemap used to provide graphical links

client. As with any image, this can take a while. Also, not all browsers support imagemaps. You should always have a text alternative for such clients.

Imagemaps can add some visual touches to our applications. Imagemaps are divided into two broad categories:

- Server-side imagemaps
- Client-side imagemaps

Server-Side Imagemaps

Server-side imagemaps are processed by the server and have the following components:

- The image itself
- An imagemap script
- Web pages to which the imagemap will point

The first thing you should check is whether your server supports imagemaps. Most popular servers do. There is no standard for imagemaps. Therefore, there are subtle differences in the way each server handles imagemaps. In the following example, we use a UNIX machine running the NCSA HTTP server (version 1.4.2) with default configuration.

Once you have determined that your server supports imagemaps, you need to decide on the image. You can either create your own or use an existing image. What is important is the graphics format. Since an imagemap is meant to be shown on the Web page, it must be in one of the supported formats for inline images. For most browsers, the inline image format is GIF and JPEG. For demonstration purposes, we have created the image shown in Figure 4-17 to be used in our imagemap.

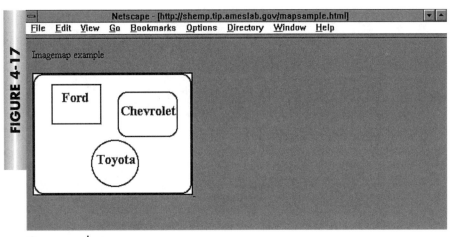

FIGURE 4-17

Our sample image

The next step is to divide your image into distinct parts and decide on the hyperlinks for each part. Your specifications are expressed in a map script file. The format of the script file is as follows:

```
method URL coordinate 1 coordinate 2 ... coordinate n
```

The method is the geometric shape of the region for which you want to assign a link. Valid values are

- *circle:* Maps a circular region based on the coordinates for the center of the circle and a point on the circle itself.

- *poly:* Maps a polygon with a maximum number of vertices less than 100. Each specified coordinate is a vertex.

- *rect:* Maps a rectangular region based on coordinates showing the upper-left and lower-right corners.

- *point:* Maps to the closest point specified by the coordinate.

- *default:* If the user clicks on an area of the image not specified by any of the above methods, then the URL shown by the default method is used. This URL can be either a local or a full one.

The coordinates are all in the form of *x,y* with a pixel as the unit of measurement. Listing 4-3 is the map script used in our example:

Listing 4-3 The map script used in our example

```
default /mapsample.html
rect http://www.ford.com 29,16 108,79
rect http://www.chevrolet.com 140,33 226,93
circle http://www.toyota.com 131,141 130,103
```

Imagemap Utilities

As you might guess, creating map scripts can become very tedious as the complexity of the image increases. Fortunately, there are a number of utility programs which can help you create accurate and effective imagemaps. In most cases, you should use such programs rather than creating the scripts by hand. Examples include

Mac-ImageMap (*http://weyl.zib-berlin.de/imagemap/Mac-ImageMap.html*)

Map THIS! (*http://galadriel.ecaetc.ohio-state.edu/tc/mt/*)

mapedit (*http://sunsite.unc.edu/boutell/mapedit/mapedit.html*)

After we create the script, we need to put the image on the page and mark it as an imagemap image. This is done using a *<href >* tag and one of the attributes of the *<img>* tag.

```
Imagemap example
<P>
<A HREF="/cgi-bin/imagemap/mymaps/carmap.map">
<IMG SRC="carmap.gif" ISMAP>
</A>
```

In this example, we have placed the map file (carmap.map) in a directory called mymaps. Note the usage of the imagemap program which resides in the cgi-bin directory as most external programs do. This program is responsible for parsing the map script file. By clicking on the different areas of the image, you should jump to the corresponding page. Try it and see for yourself.

Client-Side Imagemaps

Current imagemap implementations require the client to make a connection to the server each time the user clicks on part of the image. This connection allows the client to retrieve the corresponding URL for the clicked portion of the image. It seems that processing the map script is not such a complicated process and can be done by the browser itself. This observation has led to a new standard called client-side imagemaps. Such imagemaps reduce the load on the server, since they can extract the corresponding URL for the different parts of an image from the enhanced HTML tags in the document.

To use client-side imagemaps, you simply replace the imagemap script with special HTML commands. The *<map></map>* tag is used to enclose commands related to an imagemap. Each *<map>* tag has a NAME attribute which uniquely identifies it and associates it with a picture displayed using the *<img>* tag. Here is the imagemap script from the previous example, translated to the client-side imagemap format:

```
<map name="sample_map">
<area shape="rect" coords="29, 16, 108, 79" href="http://www.ford.com">
<area shape="rect" coords="140, 33, 226, 93" href="http://www.chevrolet.com">
<area shape="circle" coords="131, 141, 130, 103" href="http://www.toyota.com">
<area shape="rect" coords="0, 0, 226, 103" href="/mapsample.html">
</map>
```

Note that there is no need for a default tag. If the clicked coordinates do not fall on a specified boundary, the last *<area>* tag is used as the default.

To use the above imagemap, you must associate it with an actual image. This is done in the following statement:

```
<img src="carmap.gif" USEMAP="#sample_map">
```

You can learn more about this standard at `http://www.hway.com/ihip/cside.html`.

HTML Editors

At times, creating complex Web pages with forms and imagemaps might seem like a formidable task. For serious application development, you should plan on using one or more utility programs. There are many such programs available, both commercial and freeware. Most of these programs allow you to create effective Web pages by giving you a graphical user interface for placing the different HTML tags. They also eliminate the need to remember the syntax for all the different tags and their attributes. Most provide import/export support from/to your favorite word processor. One such program is HTML Assistant (see Figure 4-18). It supports all major features of HTML and enhanced standards such as tables. You can see how your Web page will look instantly as the result of your code displays on your browser. More information about this program is available at `http://fox.nstn.ca/~harawitz/index.html`.

A second program is WebForms (see Figure 4-19). This program is more geared for forms generation and processing. It uses a fill-in-the-blank format to specify the different elements in a form and then creates the HTML code. The latest version of WebForms is available at `http://www.q-d.com/wf.htm`. Both of these programs run under MS Windows. There are many more similar programs. An inquiry on one of the Web search engines leads to more than 100 such utility programs; it is beyond the scope of this book to cover them all.

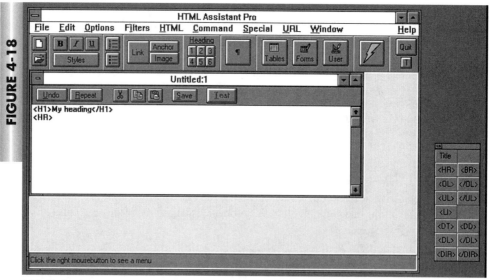

FIGURE 4-18

HTML Assistant

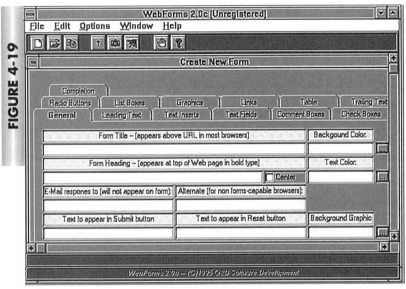

FIGURE 4-19

WebForms

Summary

Any database application must be able to accept input from the user. HTML supports a number of user input elements, including text boxes, menus, checkboxes, radio buttons, and multiline text entry boxes. Such elements give us the needed functionality to interact with the user in a high-level manner. The elements follow the standard of window environments and should seem familiar to the casual user. Once the form is filled out, it is submitted to the server, and an external program responsible for accepting and processing its content is executed.

Imagemaps are a popular way to add graphics to a Web page. They make an image hot and let us link URLs to different portions of an image. We can divide the image based on certain geometrical figures, namely circles, rectangles, polygons, and points. This division process is usually done by a utility program because the process can become tedious as the image grows in complexity. The divisions are specified in a map script file which resides on the server. Since not all browsers support images, you should always have a text version which provides the same function as the imagemap links.

HTML documents can be developed using a variety of utility programs. These programs let you create a HTML element with a graphical interface, freeing you from remembering all the syntax.

Questions

1. What is meant by submitting a form?

2. What is the difference between checkboxes and radio boxes?

3. How does one present menus using *forms*?

4. What is the purpose of the NAME attribute in form elements?

5. What is special about an image tagged as an imagemap?

6. When should you use the point method in your image script?

7. What is the unit used in specifying coordinates in an image script?

8. What are client-side imagemaps?

Answers

1. The data entered by the user resides on the client machine. In order to notify the server and the external program about the data, you must send the data in a standard manner to the server. This sending process is known as *submitting* forms.

2. Checkboxes are used to distinguish between two mutually exclusive options. In a group they can present a *many of many* selection behavior. Radio boxes in a group present a *one of many* selection behavior.

3. The menu is enclosed within the *<select></select>* tags. Each menu element is marked with the *<option>* tag.

4. The NAME attribute uniquely identifies the different data elements when they are submitted to the server.

5. An imagemap is an ordinary image which has been made hot. The user can expect to jump to a different Web page by clicking on different portions of the imagemap.

6. A point method specifies a coordinate and is activated when the user clicks on the point closest to it. By its careful placement, you can gain more control over parts of the image that ordinary geometric shapes will not cover.

7. Pixels.

8. Client-side imagemaps are an extension to HTML. They specify the hotspots of an image within the HTML document, instead of an image script. This allows the client (browser) to process such information and eliminates the need for an extra connection to the server.

5

Common Gateway Interface (CGI) Basics

In this chapter, we will discuss the Common Gateway Interface (CGI) and its role in Web database application development. CGI is the link that connects the Web to programs like databases. Because the CGI plays such a critical role in Web database design, we need to understand its function. This chapter describes the CGI standard and discusses its implementation under the UNIX operating system. We will then explore the differences in implementation under the Mac OS and Windows environment. Simple programs demonstrate CGI capabilities to give you a feel for the development environment. We will end the chapter with a look at MIME types and how they are used in the Web environment. By the end of this chapter, we will have completed our discussion about two of the three main components of a Web database: the Web itself and its link to the database (CGI).

Overview

Although the client interacts with external applications, CGI serves as a link between the Web and external programs. The World Wide Web is a client/server application which runs on top of the Internet protocol. The client (commonly referred to as a *browser*) and the server communicate with each other using the HTTP protocol over a network. The HTTP server (Web server) is a well-defined program. Its job is to listen for requests from Web clients

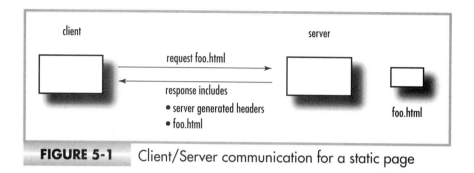

FIGURE 5-1   Client/Server communication for a static page

and respond to them. Some of these requests are for HTML documents as shown in Figure 5-1. The user has clicked on a link and the client asks the server to *serve* that particular page. The server has access to a portion of the file system on the machine on which it runs. It looks for the requested file in the file system, and if it finds the file, it generates some header information about the file and sends the HTML document over the network back to the client. This is typically the interaction that occurs for static pages.

For interactive pages (for example, pages that include forms or imagemaps), the process is somewhat different. By submitting a form to the server, the client asks the server to *execute* an external program. This is a program that is completely independent of the server program (hence the name *external program*), but it resides on the same machine as the HTTP server. This process is shown in Figure 5-2. The external program is either a native executable program or a script that can be executed by the operating system. Also, the server has the appropriate permissions to execute this program. The external program is executed and its output is sent directly to the client. It is up to the external program to include the necessary headers in its output.

Actually, we used such a program when we created imagemaps. The imagemap program is a special external program invoked by a request from the client when the user clicks on part of the imagemap. This program compares the coordinates sent to it by the client to the corresponding map file and decides which URL to send back to the client.

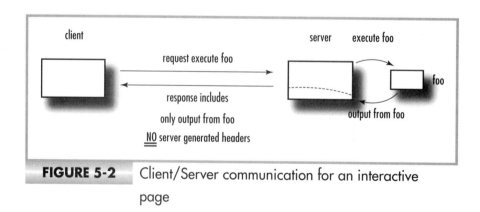

FIGURE 5-2   Client/Server communication for an interactive page

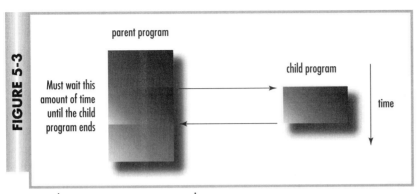

Synchronous execution mode

The concept of one program executing another is nothing new. It is used frequently in computer applications. For example, when you launch Equation Editor from Microsoft Word, you are actually executing an external application. All operating systems have means for this type of execution. Of course, the implementations are very different.

Two types of external execution are possible:

- Synchronous
- Asynchronous

In a *synchronous* execution, the parent program issues the command to execute an external program. It must then wait until the execution of the external program is completed before proceeding. This process is shown in Figure 5-3.

In an *asynchronous* execution mode, the parent program can launch several external programs and continue its own operations while the external programs are executing. This method is illustrated in Figure 5-4.

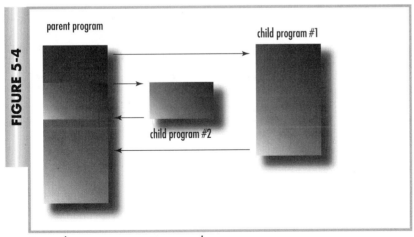

Asynchronous execution mode

A good HTTP server should support asynchronous execution, since this mode allows the server to continually respond to clients' requests. While such operations are natural for operating systems like UNIX, their implementation under an OS like DOS can be cumbersome and tricky. Due to these low-level differences, several implementations of CGI exist under different operating systems. We begin our discussion with an HTTP server on a UNIX machine. Specifically, we will use NCSA HTTPD (version 1.5) running on a Silicon Graphics workstation using IRIX 5.3. We will then discuss the implementations under Windows 3.x, Windows 95, and the Mac OS.

 The HTTP Server

Internet packets including HTTP packets head for a destination machine and a destination *port*. A machine has a large number of ports which allow it to send and receive multiple packets simultaneously, provided that the packets use different port numbers. A server program is written to listen to one or more ports for requests from clients. All standard applications such as the World Wide Web, telnet, and ftp have well-known ports. This means that particular port numbers are reserved for those specific applications. For example, the Web's port number is 80. By default, all clients send their requests to port 80 and all servers listen to port 80. By virtue of its function, which is to constantly wait for requests, the HTTP server program must run at all times. As a result, multitasking operating systems run the HTTP server in the background. This means the server constantly occupies memory and resources. It also serves as a parent to all external programs that might be executed due to client requests. If your server must execute many external programs or your external programs are resource-intensive, be sure the machine running the server is fast and has sufficient memory and resources. Depending on the load, it might be a good idea to dedicate an entire machine to the Web server.

CGI in UNIX

Based on Figure 5-5, we break down the process of executing an external program into four distinct phases:

1. Client to server

2. Server to external program

3. External program to server

4. Server to client

Each phase is discussed separately in the following sections.

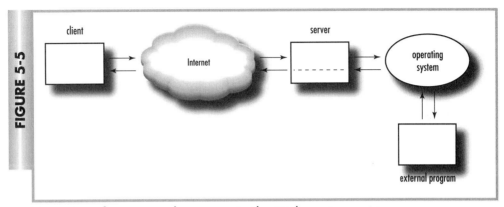

Execution of an external program in the Web environment

Client to Server

This phase of the data transfer is transparent to the programmer. The HTTP protocol takes care of it. Therefore, if you have a client and a server that understand forms, the data transfer is done behind the scenes for you. You really should not be concerned with this phase of the data transfer unless you are writing an HTTP server or client. There are some Web clients and servers that have enhanced security features that handle this phase of the data transfer in a secure manner. For our purposes, we can assume that the data is packed in an HTTP packet and sent to the server via the Internet. We will deal with the data after it has been received by the server.

Server to External Program

At this stage, the server has received the HTTP packet and parsed it. The server determines what external program the packet needs to run and what data should be passed to it. This phase involves the specifications set by CGI. CGI specifies how the data should be transferred, what its format should be, and what additional information should be passed along with the data. First, let us examine the format of the data as it is passed to the external program.

Recall that each element in a form includes a *name* option which behaves similarly to a variable name. Consider the following:

```
<input type=TEXT name=FIRST_NAME>
```

This simple form element generates a text input box. What the user enters into this box is captured by the client and associated with the name FIRST_NAME, creating a pair. This pair is commonly referred to as the *name=value* pair and is the basis of how data is organized and passed to an external program. All the data in the form is organized into the *name=value* pair and separated by the ampersand character (&). Consider the following form:

```
<form>
First name: <input type=TEXT name=FIRST_NAME>
<br>
Last name: <input type=TEXT name=LAST_NAME>
<p>
<input type=SUBMIT>
</form>
```

Figure 5-6 shows the result of this form.

If the user enters *John* as the first name and *Jones* as the last name, then the external program receives the data in the following format:

```
FIRST_NAME=John&LAST_NAME=Jones
```

It is up to the external program to parse this line and extract the different *name=value* pairs. Depending on the language you choose, there are a number of library routines available to help you in parsing the data. Many of these tools are included on the CD-ROM and discussed in Chapter 8. It should be mentioned that the data (names and values) go through a transformation called URL encoding before being sent to the external program. This transformation changes all spaces to the plus character (+) and replaces special URL characters (such as /, :, &) with a percent character followed by their hexadecimal value. Let us look at an example. We use the same form as above, but we enter different values. For the first name, we use *Mary Ann*. The result is

```
FIRST_NAME=Mary+Ann&LAST_NAME=Jones
```

The reason URL encoding is performed on the data is that forms are not the only way to send data to an external program. You can invoke an external program directly and pass some data to it. Here is an example URL:

```
http://servername/cgi-bin/form_test?name=john
```

This URL is asking the server to execute a program called form_test and pass to it the data name=john. Note that the name of the program and the data are separated by a question mark.

You can see why it is important to choose meaningful names when we design our forms. With different types of input elements (for example, menus, text boxes, and checkboxes) it is imperative that we can identify each *name=value* pair and make sense of it within the

FIGURE 5-6   A simple form

external program. Recall that if the *action* option is not specified within a form tag, then the content of the form is sent to the current document. While this does not accomplish anything useful, we can use it to see what the external program would have received as data if the *action* option had been specified. If the current document is itself a program, then the data is sent to it and the program is executed. You might use this feature in some of your applications. Let us consider examples of each input element.

Text Box

We have already seen some examples for text boxes. The following example shows some of the URL encoding that takes place. Figure 5-7 shows the form.

```
<form>
Enter something: <input type=text>
<br>
Enter something else: <input type=text name=something>
<p>
<input type=submit>
</form>
```

The following data is generated:

```
something=%3F+%25
```

Note that the first input box does not contribute to the data since it includes no name option. Also note that the characters in the second input box have been replaced by their hexadecimal values, and the space in between has been translated to a plus character.

The following is a form with a password entry box. Note that although the password cannot be seen as it is entered, it is stored in the *name=value* pair as plain text. Figure 5-8 shows the password entry form.

```
<form>
Enter your password:<input type=text name=passwd>
<p>
<input type=submit>
</form>
```

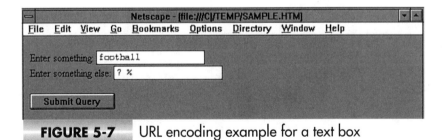

FIGURE 5-7   URL encoding example for a text box

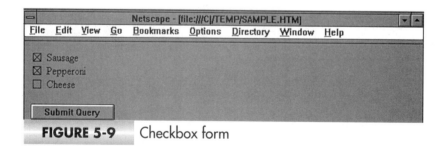

FIGURE 5-8   Password entry form

The generated output is

```
passwd=abc123
```

Checkbox

The following demonstrates how checkbox values are passed to the external program. The form is shown in Figure 5-9.

```
<form>
<input type=checkbox name=sausage> Sausage
<br>
<input type=checkbox name=pepperoni> Pepperoni
<br>
<input type=checkbox name=cheese> Cheese
<br>
<p>
<input type=submit>
</form>
```

If no box is checked, no result is generated. If one or more boxes are checked, the name of the box followed by the string *on* is returned. Here is the result for the selection shown in Figure 5-9:

```
sausage=on&pepperoni=on
```

FIGURE 5-9   Checkbox form

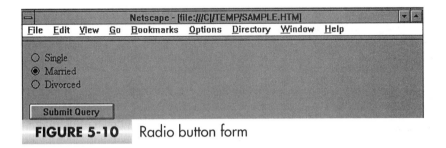

FIGURE 5-10   Radio button form

Radio Button

Recall that radio buttons resemble a *one-of-many* selection behavior. Here is a sample form with its output shown in Figure 5-10.

```
<form>
<input type=radio name=status value=single> Single
<br>
<input type=radio name=status value=married> Married
<br>
<input type=radio name=status value=divorced> Divorced
<p>
<input type=submit>
</form>
```

Only one button can be selected. The result includes the *name=value* pair for the selected button:

```
status=married
```

Single Selection Menu

Figure 5-11 shows a single selection menu. The code is

```
<form>
<select name=age>
<option>under 21
<option>22-25
<option>26-30
<option>31-40
<option>41-?
<p>
</select>
<input type=submit>
</form>
```

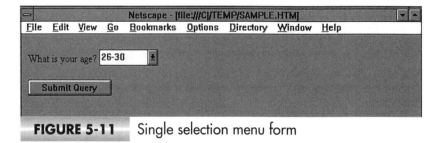

FIGURE 5-11 Single selection menu form

Only one selection is possible. The *name=value* pair includes the name option specified in the *<select>* tag and the text following the selected *<option>* tag. The result is

age=26-30

Multiple Selection Menu

```
<form>
Select all that apply:
<select name=lang MULTIPLE>
<option>English
<option>French
<option>Spanish
<option>German
<option>Russian
<option>Arabic
</select>
<p>
<input type=submit>
</form>
```

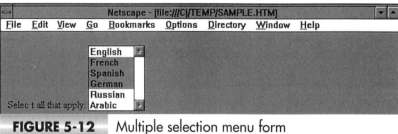

FIGURE 5-12 Multiple selection menu form

With multiple selection menus, there is only one name but one or more selection(s). It is strictly up to the external program to recognize this fact and parse the data passed to it accordingly. Here is the result generated by the selection shown in Figure 5-12:

```
lang=French&lang=Spanish&lang=German
```

Multiline Text Input

The following is the HTML code for a form with a multiline text input element. The form is shown in Figure 5-13.

```
<form>
<textarea name=memo rows=3 cols=30>
</textarea>
<p>
<input type=submit>
</form>
```

The result is similar to that of a text input box. The end of a line is denoted by including the line feed and carriage return characters.

```
memo=This+is+a+sample+for+a+%0D%0Amultiline+text+input+element.
```

Now that we have a grasp of how the data is represented in a consistent format, we must find a way to transfer it to the external program. It turns out that the transfer method depends on the *method* option specified in the *<form>* tag. Recall that valid values for this option are GET and POST. When using the POST method, the content of the form is passed to the external program via its standard input (stdin). This is the preferred method, due to its flexibility and the fact that most programmers are used to receiving input from stdin. If the GET method is used, then the data is passed by an environmental variable called QUERY_STRING. The obvious drawback of this method is the limitation on the size of environmental variables. In some operating systems, the maximum size of the value of an environmental variable is 256 characters. You can see that even a simple form with a multiline edit box can exhaust this limited space. For this reason, the GET method is not used frequently and will probably be phased out in the upcoming standard specification.

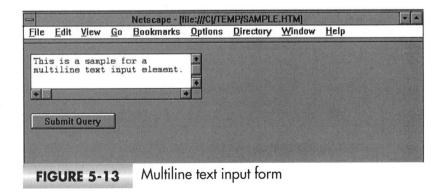

FIGURE 5-13   Multiline text input form

Aside from the data, the server also passes some additional information to the external program through a number of predefined environmental variables. Depending on the application, you might or might not be interested in the values of these variables. They are there if you need them. Let us look at these variables and their meanings.

- REMOTE_ADDR: The IP address of the client making a request to execute an external program. This can be used to guard against unauthorized clients accessing your application.

- REMOTE_HOST: The name of the machine on which the client is running. In cases where this information is not available, the server sets this variable to a blank value.

- REMOTE_USER: If the server is capable of authenticating the users and the external program is protected, this variable is set to the name of the user who was authenticated.

- AUTH_TYPE: This variable specifies the authentication method, if any, that is being used.

- SERVER_PROTOCOL: The protocol and version number through which the request for execution of the external program has been received. This variable follows the format protocol name/version number.

- SERVER_PORT: The port number on the server machine which received the request. In almost all cases this is port 80, which is the default port for the World Wide Web. Checking the port number is one way to defend against attacks by unauthorized individuals.

- PATH_INFO: The client can pass some extra information to the server and the external program. This information is specified by embedding it in the URL pointing to the external program. You might have a script that takes the data from a form, but can process it differently based on a parameter that you pass to it. The PATH_INFO variable is used to pass such information. Another useful application of this variable is to specify the path to a file that you want the external program to process.

- PATH_TRANSLATED: The server performs a translation on the PATH_INFO variable and stores the result in the PATH_TRANSLATED variable. PATH_INFO refers to files using their *virtual* path, that is, their path compared to a base path specified in the server's configuration file. Assume that the server is installed in the directory /usr/local/etc/httpd. The directory /usr/local/etc/httpd/cgi-bin is designated as the document root directory for the server. A URL of the form http://*servername*/cgi-bin/welcome.cgi causes PATH_INFO to be set to welcome.html and PATH_TRANSLATED to contain /usr/local/etc/httpd/cgi-bin/welcome.cgi.

- SCRIPT_NAME: The external program and its virtual path are stored here.

- QUERY_STRING: Contains the data passed to the server when the form uses the GET method.

- REQUEST_METHOD: The method specified in the request, which, for our purposes is either GET or POST.

- CONTENT_LENGTH: The length of the data passed to the server by the client. Recall that the server passes the data to the external program by way of the program's stdin. The program must use this variable to know how much data it should read from its standard input. This only applies when the POST method is used.

- CONTENT_TYPE: This specifies the type of data passed to the server by the client. Sometimes you might need to write an external program that performs when called from different servers. If that is the case, you might need to know what server is calling the script and perform certain functions differently. The following variables can help you with this task.

  - SERVER_SOFTWARE: The is the name and the version number for the server software. The format is name/version. For example, version 1.5 of the NCSA HTTP server would produce the following: NCSA httpd/1.5.

  - SERVER_NAME: This is the name of the machine on which the server is running. Because, in most cases, the external program and the server are running on the same machine, your program can get this information directly from the operating system. In case the machine does not have a name, the variable contains the IP number.

  - GATEWAY_INTERFACE: This variable specifies the revision of the CGI specification under which the server is operating. This variable is important when CGI undergoes a major revision and stops its full backward compatibility.

External Program to Server

Once the external program has finished its execution, it will likely produce some output for the client to view. The output can have many different formats. For example, it could be an image, a simple text message, another form, or perhaps a video or audio clip. Anytime the server sends something to the client, it must specify the type of document so the client knows how to present it. When the server receives a request for an HTML page or a picture, it automatically includes the data type information in the packet that it sends to the client. However, when the result is generated by an external program, the server has no idea what the data type is. It is the responsibility of the external program to include that information in its output. The server blindly sends the input it receives to the client. If that input does not include a data type header, the client does not display it.

The external program can produce two types of output:

- A self-contained document

- A reference to another document

In both cases, the type of the document is specified via a simple header in ASCII text. This header specifies the type of the document by using a MIME type. MIME types are discussed later in this chapter. If the output is text, then the header looks like this:

```
Content-type: text/plain
```

This header is then followed by a blank line and then the actual text. Similarly, for an HTML output, the header is

```
Content-type: text/html
```

In the second output type, the header is followed by a second line indicating the location of another document (rather than including the document itself, as in the first case). Here is an example:

```
Content-type: text/html
Location: http://servername/welcome.html
```

If the referenced document resides on the same server machine, you can specify its *virtual* path rather than its URL:

```
Content-type: text/html
Location: intro/welcome.html
```

Servers compatible with CGI 1.1 understand some additional headers.

- The Content-encoding header specifies the encoding type used for secure transmission of data when the server and client both support this type of transmission.

- The Expires header informs the client whether the requested document has reached its expiration date.

Finally, there is a status code that the server sends to the client. If appropriate, your external program can also send a status code that the server relays to the client. Here is a listing of the valid status codes with a brief description of each. For detailed explanation, look at the HTTP specifications at `http://www.w3.org/hypertext/WWW/Protocols/HTTP/HTTP2.html`.

Success 2xx

The server uses these codes to indicate success in granting the client's request. If the request required a document, that document is sent to the client in MIME format.

- **OK 200**—The request was fulfilled.

- **Created 201**—If the request method was a POST command and the external program generated some output, you can specify a new URL for that output. You send that URL with this status code to the client.

- **Accepted 202**—This code means that the request has been accepted for processing, but the processing has not been completed.

Partial Information 203—This indicates that the data is not complete. It usually accompanies additional information about the data.

No Response 204—The server has received the client's request, but for some reason it cannot send any information back to the client. This causes the client to stay in the same document view.

Redirection 3xx

These codes ask the client to perform some action before the server can complete the request.

Moved 301—This code is returned when the data requested by the client has been assigned a new URL and the server is aware of it. Along with the code, header lines for the form

```
URI<url> String CrLf
```

are sent back to the client which specify alternative addresses for the requested data. *<url>* is replaced with the new addresses, String is an optional comment field, and CrLf represents the Carriage Return and Linefeed characters.

Found 302—This code is similar to Moved 301, but the requested data has not permanently moved to a new location. Similar header lines are returned back to the client.

Error 4xx

These codes are intended for cases in which the server blames the client for an error. In other words, the server tells the client that an invalid request was made.

Bad Request 400—This is the most generic of all 4xx codes. It states that the request could not be understood by the server, due either to a syntax error or some other fundamental problem.

Unauthorized 401—Although there are several authorization schemes available, servers do not support them all. If the authorization mechanism used by the client does not match one the server understands, this status code is returned by the server along with a list of authorization mechanisms that the server does understand.

Payment Required 402—Similar to the previous code, except here the payment method is not understood by the server. The client should retry with a payment mechanism accepted by the server.

Forbidden 403—This code is generated when the client has made a request for a forbidden document or action. Note that authorization does not help in this case.

● **Not Found 404**—The server cannot find any file matching the given URL in the request. This can be due to the fact that filenames or directory structures have changed.

Error 5xx

These codes are intended for cases in which the server knows the error has occurred on its side.

● **Internal Error 500**—When the server encounters an internal error, this status code is returned. It is also returned when the external program generates an error or does not create an appropriate output.

● **Not Implemented 501**—The request is understood by the server, but cannot be fulfilled because the server software does not support it. This is mostly to keep servers functioning as new standards come out.

Server to Client

This stage of data transfer is handled by the HTTP protocol. Your external program does not have any effect on it. You can safely assume that the server will transfer the data to the client as you have specified.

Sample Program

Listing 5-1 shows a simple form that uses radio boxes for its selection method. The result is shown in Figure 5-14.

Listing 5-1 A form with radio buttons

```
<form method=POST action=http://server_name/cgi-bin/entry.pl>
What party do you belong to:
<br>
<input type=radio name=party value=Democrat> Democratic
<br>
<input type=radio name=party value=Republican> Republican
<br>
<input type=radio name=party value=Independent> Independent
<p>
<input type=submit value=Submit>
</form>
```

An external program, entry.pl, receives the content of the form once it is submitted and displays what the user selected. Listing 5-2 shows this program, which is written in Perl. Figure 5-15 shows the result of the external program as seen by the client.

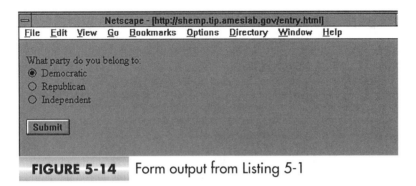

FIGURE 5-14   Form output from Listing 5-1

Listing 5-2 An external program to process a form

```perl
#!/usr/local/bin/perl

require "cgi-lib.pl";

MAIN:
{
# Read in all the variables set by the form
   &ReadParse(*input);
   $mparty = $input{'party'};
   print &PrintHeader;

   print "<b> You have selected the following political party:<b>\n";
   print "<br>\n";
   print "<h2> $mparty </h2> \n";
}
```

This program uses a set of routines included in the cgi-lib.pl file. This file is available on the CD-ROM accompanying this book. The data passed to the external program by its stdin is read and processed with the line

```perl
&ReadParse(*input);
```

Next, the *name=value* pair with name=party is found and its value is stored in a variable. The rest of the program prints the necessary headers and the data forming the page. The entire page is then sent to the server.

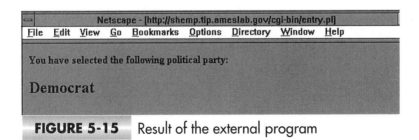

FIGURE 5-15   Result of the external program

Server Configuration

HTTP is a flexible, yet complex protocol. Servers' behavior is based on some default settings, but their actions can be altered by special configuration files. NCSA HTTP servers use the following configuration files:

- ACCESS.CONF: Configuration parameters related to access control are stored here. Limitations can be placed on the server as to which clients it should serve and what files it can send to clients.

- HTTP.CONF: This is the general configuration file for the server. Port numbers, method of invocation, and directory structures are some of the items specified in this file.

- MIME.TYPES: The server looks at this file to find out the MIME type of a document before sending it to the client. It can then generate an appropriate header for the packet in which the document is enclosed.

- SRM.CONF: This configuration file defines the portion of your file system which is visible to the HTTP server.

Most of the configuration parameters will be discussed as we develop our database applications in later chapters. CGI's behavior does partly depend on some of the configuration file parameters. To ensure that you get the same results as the examples in the book, the content of the configuration files are listed here.

ACCESS.CONF

```
# access.conf: Global access configuration
# Online docs at http://hoohoo.ncsa.uiuc.edu/

# /usr/local/etc/httpd/ should be changed to whatever you set ServerRoot to.
<Directory /usr/local/etc/httpd/cgi-bin>
Options Indexes FollowSymLinks

<Limit GET>
order deny,allow
allow from all
</Limit>

</Directory>

# This should be changed to whatever you set DocumentRoot to.

<Directory /usr/local/etc/httpd/htdocs>

# This may also be "None," "All," or any combination of "Indexes,"
# "Includes," or "FollowSymLinks"

Options Indexes FollowSymLinks
```

```
# This controls which options the .htaccess files in directories can
# override. Can also be "None," or any combination of "Options," "FileInfo,"
# "AuthConfig," and "Limit"

AllowOverride All

# Controls who can get stuff from this server.

<Limit GET>
order deny,allow
allow from all
</Limit>

</Directory>

# You may place any other directories you wish to have access
# information for after this one.
```

HTTP.CONF

```
# This is the main server configuration file. It is best to
# leave the directives in this file in the order they are listed in, or
# things may not go the way you'd like. See URL http://hoohoo.ncsa.uiuc.edu/
# for instructions.

# NCSA httpd

# ServerType is either inetd, or standalone.

ServerType standalone

# If you are running from inetd, go to "ServerAdmin."

# Port: The port the standalone listens to. For ports < 1023, you will
# need httpd to be run as root initially.

Port 80

# StartServers: The number of servers to launch at startup. Must be
# compiled without the NO_PASS compile option

StartServers 5

# MaxServers: The number of servers to launch until mimic'ing the 1.3
# scheme (new server for each connection). These servers will stay around
# until the server is restarted. They will be reused as needed, however.
# See the documentation on hoohoo.ncsa.uiuc.edu for more information.

MaxServers 20
```

continued on next page

continued from previous page

```
# If you wish httpd to run as a different user or group, you must run
# httpd as root initially and it will switch.

# User/Group: The name (or #number) of the user/group to run httpd as.

User mohseni
Group #-0

# ServerAdmin: Your address, where problems with the server should be
# e-mailed.

ServerAdmin mohseni@xxxxxx.xxx

# ServerRoot: The directory the server's config, error, and log files
# are kept in

ServerRoot /usr/local/etc/httpd

# ErrorLog: The location of the error log file. If this does not start
# with /, ServerRoot is prepended to it.

ErrorLog logs/error_log

# TransferLog: The location of the transfer log file. If this does not
# start with /, ServerRoot is prepended to it.

TransferLog logs/access_log

# AgentLog: The location of the agent log file. If this does not start
# with /, ServerRoot is prepended to it.

AgentLog logs/agent_log

# RefererLog: The location of the referer log file. If this does not
# start with /, ServerRoot is prepended to it.

RefererLog logs/referer_log

# RefererIgnore: If you don't want to keep track of links from certain
# servers (like your own), place it here. If you want to log them all,
# keep this line commented.

#RefererIgnore servername

# PidFile: The file the server should log its pid to
PidFile logs/httpd.pid

# ServerName allows you to set a host name which is sent back to clients for
# your server if it's different than the one the program would get (i.e. use
# "www" instead of the host's real name).
#
```

```
# Note: You cannot just invent host names and hope they work. The name you
# define here must be a valid DNS name for your host. If you don't understand
# this, ask your network administrator.

#ServerName new.host.name
```

MIME.TYPES

```
# This is a comment


application/activemessage
application/andrew-inset
application/applefile
application/atomicmail
application/dca-rft
application/dec-dx
application/mac-binhex40
application/macwriteii
application/msword
application/news-message-id
application/news-transmission
application/octet-stream        bin
application/oda                 oda
application/pdf                 pdf
application/postscript          ai eps ps
application/remote-printing
application/rtf                 rtf
application/slate
application/x-mif               mif
application/wita
application/wordperfect5.1
application/x-csh               csh
application/x-dvi               dvi
application/x-hdf               hdf
application/x-latex             latex
application/x-netcdf            nc cdf
application/x-sh                sh
application/x-tcl               tcl
application/x-tex               tex
application/x-texinfo           texinfo texi
application/x-troff             t tr roff
application/x-troff-man         man
application/x-troff-me          me
application/x-troff-ms          ms
application/x-wais-source       src
application/zip                 zip
application/x-bcpio             bcpio
```

continued on next page

continued from previous page

```
application/x-cpio            cpio
application/x-gtar            gtar
application/x-shar            shar
application/x-sv4cpio         sv4cpio
application/x-sv4crc          sv4crc
application/x-tar             tar
application/x-ustar          ustar
audio/basic                  au snd
audio/x-aiff                 aif aiff aifc
audio/x-wav                  wav
image/gif                    gif
image/ief                    ief
image/jpeg                   jpeg jpg jpe
image/tiff                   tiff tif
image/x-cmu-raster           ras
image/x-portable-anymap      pnm
image/x-portable-bitmap      pbm
image/x-portable-graymap     pgm
image/x-portable-pixmap      ppm
image/x-rgb                  rgb
image/x-xbitmap              xbm
image/x-xpixmap              xpm
image/x-xwindowdump          xwd
message/external-body
message/news
message/partial
message/rfc822
multipart/alternative
multipart/appledouble
multipart/digest
multipart/mixed
multipart/parallel
text/html                    html htm
text/x-sgml                  sgml sgm
text/plain                   txt
text/richtext                rtx
text/tab-separated-values    tsv
text/x-setext                etx
video/mpeg                   mpeg mpg mpe
video/quicktime              qt mov
video/x-msvideo              avi
video/x-sgi-movie            movie
```

SRM.CONF

```
# With this document, you define the name space that users see of your http
# server.

# See the tutorials at http://hoohoo.ncsa.uiuc.edu/docs/tutorials/ for
# more information.

# NCSA httpd (httpd@ncsa.uiuc.edu)
```

```
# DocumentRoot: The directory out of which you will serve your
# documents. By default, all requests are taken from this directory, but
# symbolic links and aliases may be used to point to other locations.

DocumentRoot /usr/local/etc/httpd/htdocs

# UserDir: The name of the directory which is appended onto a user's home
# directory if a ~user request is received.

UserDir public_html

# DirectoryIndex: Name of the file to use as a pre-written HTML
# directory index

DirectoryIndex index.html

# FancyIndexing is whether you want fancy directory indexing or standard

FancyIndexing on

# AddIcon tells the server which icon to show for different files or filename
# extensions

AddIconByType (TXT,/icons/text.xbm) text/*
AddIconByType (IMG,/icons/image.xbm) image/*
AddIconByType (SND,/icons/sound.xbm) audio/*
AddIcon /icons/movie.xbm .mpg .qt
AddIcon /icons/binary.xbm .bin
AddIcon /icons/back.xbm ..
AddIcon /icons/menu.xbm ^^DIRECTORY^^
AddIcon /icons/blank.xbm ^^BLANKICON^^

# DefaultIcon is which icon to show for files which do not have an icon
# explicitly set.

DefaultIcon /icons/unknown.xbm

# AddDescription allows you to place a short description after a file in
# server-generated indexes.
# Format: AddDescription "description" filename

# ReadmeName is the name of the README file the server will look for by
# default. Format: ReadmeName name
#
# The server will first look for name.html, include it if found, and it will
# then look for name and include it as plaintext if found.
#
# HeaderName is the name of a file which should be prepended to
# directory indexes.

ReadmeName README
HeaderName HEADER
```

continued on next page

continued from previous page

```
# IndexIgnore is a set of filenames which directory indexing should ignore
# Format: IndexIgnore name1 name2...

IndexIgnore */.??* *~ *# */HEADER* */README*

# AccessFileName: The name of the file to look for in each directory
# for access control information.

AccessFileName .htaccess

# DefaultType is the default MIME type for documents for which the server
# cannot determine the type by the filename extensions.

DefaultType text/plain

# AddType allows you to tweak mime.types without actually editing it, or to
# make certain files to be certain types.
# Format: AddType type/subtype ext1

# AddEncoding allows you to have certain browsers (Mosaic/X 2.1+) uncompress
# information on the fly. Note: Not all browsers support this.

#AddEncoding x-compress Z
#AddEncoding x-gzip gz

# Redirect allows you to tell clients about documents which used to exist in
# your server's namespace, but do not anymore. This allows you to tell the
# clients where to look for the relocated document.
# Format: Redirect fakename url


# Aliases: Add here as many aliases as you need, up to 20. The format is
# Alias fakename realname

Alias /icons/ /usr/local/etc/httpd/icons/

# ScriptAlias: This controls which directories contain server scripts.
# Format: ScriptAlias fakename realname

ScriptAlias /cgi-bin/ /usr/local/etc/httpd/cgi-bin/

# If you want to use server side includes, or CGI outside
# ScriptAliased directories, uncomment the following lines.

#AddType text/x-server-parsed-html .shtml
#AddType application/x-httpd-cgi .cgi

# If you want to have files/scripts sent instead of the built-in version
# in case of errors, uncomment the following lines and set them as you
# will.  Note: scripts must be able to be run as if they were called
# directly (in ScriptAlias directory, for instance)
```

```
# 302 - REDIRECT
# 400 - BAD_REQUEST
# 401 - AUTH_REQUIRED
# 403 - FORBIDDEN
# 404 - NOT_FOUND
# 500 - SERVER_ERROR
# 501 - NOT_IMPLEMENTED

#ErrorDocument 302 /cgi-bin/redirect.cgi
#ErrorDocument 500 /errors/server.html
#ErrorDocument 403 /errors/forbidden.html
```

CGI in Windows

Despite the overall simplicity of the CGI specification, its implementation depends on the platform it uses. In the Microsoft Windows environment, concepts such as environmental variables and standard input are nonexistent. Unfortunately, there is no standardized CGI specification for MS Windows. Most servers implement CGI by way of a proprietary library. As a programmer, you write your code and establish communication to the server with a set of API calls specific to the server. The most popular languages are C and C++, although servers are beginning to support other languages.

Although this approach is efficient, it sacrifices one of the important elements of CGI: its openness. If you write your external program using the API for a particular server, your program will not readily execute under a different server. Keep this in mind as you choose a server and a programming environment. For example, if you plan on using Perl for your CGI programs, then be sure the server API supports Perl.

Another approach is to use a DOS program as the external program. Similar to their UNIX counterparts, DOS programs can take advantage of environmental variables and parameters passed to them via the standard input. Because of the inefficiencies associated with executing DOS programs within the Windows environment, this approach should be avoided if at all possible. Check out **http://www.achilles.net/~john/cgi-dos/** for more information.

A popular HTTP server for the Microsoft Windows environment is Windows HTTPD. This program is included on the accompanying CD-ROM or can be downloaded from **http://www.city.net/win-httpd/**. Rather than using a set of API calls, Windows HTTPD supports an open interface implementation of CGI specifications. We discuss this implementation in this section.

Launching the External Program

The external program must be a standard Windows application. The data is transferred between the server and the external program through a file-based interface. Although file operations are expensive compared to memory operations, a file-based interface simplifies the requirements and allows for an open interface. Figure 5-16 shows this interface.

FIGURE 5-16

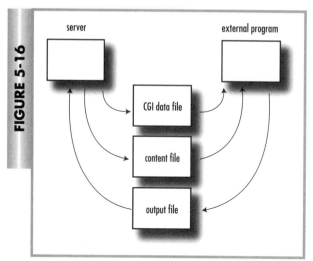

File-based CGI interface

Once the server receives a CGI request, its first task is to execute the external program. This is done with the WinExec() function. By including the parameters SW_SHOWMIN-NOACTIVE, the external program window does not become active and is iconized. This is the ideal mode of execution for a CGI program.

Here are the parameters passed to the WinExec() function:

- **external program:** The full path to the gateway program. Unlike the UNIX environment, the server does not look at any environmental variables or server configurations to determine the path. Therefore, you must supply the complete path to the program. Also, note that this file does not necessarily need to be an executable file. It is common to establish associations between file extensions and executables in the WIN.INI or the Registration Database in the Microsoft Windows environment. Therefore, the file can be one of these associations.

- **data file:** The data file transfers data between the server and the external program. The parameters should include the full path to the file.

- **content file:** If the client's request to execute a CGI program included any content, then it is placed in this file. If no content was received, a zero-length file is created. Once again, this parameter should include the full path to the filename.

- **output file:** This is the full path to the file in which the external program places its output. This output must conform to the CGI specifications; that is, the first line should indicate the type of output.

- **url-args:** This string contains the enhanced portion of the URL. This is the part appearing after the "?", which can include extra parameters sent to the external program from the client.

With these specifications, Windows CGI conforms to the standard CGI. It provides a method for the server to launch an external program, send data to it, and receive data from it.

The CGI Data File

The server places data in a private profile file. Such files are commonly used by applications to save program options and customization parameters. Perhaps the most famous profile file is WIN.INI. A profile file usually consists of one or more sections. Each section is denoted by a distinct name enclosed in brackets. Within each section, there are a number of *key=value* pairs. Here is an excerpt from WIN.INI:

```
[Desktop]
Pattern=(None)
Wallpaper=(None)
TileWallPaper=1
GridGranularity=0
IconSpacing=80

[Extensions]
MNY=C:\MSMONEY\MSMONEY.EXE ^.MNY
crd=cardfile.exe ^.crd
trm=terminal.exe ^.trm
```

The Windows API includes a set of routines, namely GetProfileString() and PutProfileString(), to read and write items to these files. With such structure and accessibility to any Windows program, a private profile file becomes a good candidate for passing data parameters from the server to the client. Here are the different sections in the CGI data file:

- [CGI]
- [Accept]
- [System]
- [Extra Headers]
- [Form Literal]
- [Form External]
- [Form Huge]

Each section is followed by a series of *key=value* pairs specifiying a particular parameter related to the section. In your CGI program you will use Windows API calls to read values from these files. These values are the content of the HTML form that your CGI program needs to process. In principle, this is very similar to environmental variables in UNIX in function.

[CGI]

This section contains most of the CGI-related items. In the UNIX environment, an environmental variable conveys the value of each item. In the Windows environment, such items are expressed as a keyword, followed by an equal sign, followed by its value. In cases where the value is not provided by the server or does not apply, the entire entry is left out of the file. These keywords were discussed at length when we described the CGI implementation under UNIX. Under Microsoft Windows, the keyword names are slightly different, but it should be easy to match each one with the corresponding environmental variable. Table 5-1 shows this relationship.

Table 5-1 Windows CGI arguments and their UNIX counterparts

Win CGI	UNIX CGI
Request Protocol	SERVER_PROTOCOL
Request Method	REQUEST_METHOD
Executable Path	SCRIPT_NAME
Logical Path	PATH_INFO
Physical Path	PATH_TRANSLATED
Query String	QUERY_STRING
Content Type	CONTENT_TYPE
Content Length	CONTENT_LENGTH
Content File	N/A
Server Software	SERVER_SOFTWARE
Server Name	SERVER_NAME
Server Port	SERVER_PORT
Server Admin	N/A
CGI Version	GATEWAY_INTERFACE
Remote Host	REMOTE_HOST
Remote Address	REMOTE_ADDR
Authentication Method	AUTH_TYPE
Authenticated Username	REMOTE_USER

[Accept]

This section contains the data types the client would accept. For example, if the client is a text-only browser, then it would be inappropriate to send an image to it. Many programmers tend to ignore the values in this section and simply assume that the client is a graphical one and is capable of accepting most simple data types (for example, HTML documents and pictures). The server knows what data types the client can accept because each request from the client includes the accepted data types in its header. If your application sends files with unusual data types, then you should check the keys in this section to be sure the client understands what you send.

[System]

This section contains items that are specific to the Windows implementation of CGI. The following keys are accompanied by their values:

- **Output File**: The full path and filename of the file, which includes the output generated by the external program.

- **Content File**: If the request included attached data, this key is set to the full path and filename of the file that stores this data.

[Extra Headers]

Any extra parameters that were sent to the server are included in this section. Recall that these are parameters included in the URL following the "?". Similar to the contents of a form, the *key=value* format is used to include these parameters.

[Form Literal]

If the client request is using the POST option in a form, then the content of the form is placed in this section as a *key=value* pair.

[Form External]

If one or more of the *key=value* pairs include a value string longer than 254 characters (for example, multiline text edit), or if they contain any control characters, then the server places such values in a temporary file rather than including them in the Form Literal section. The Form External section includes the following line for such keys:

```
key=pathname length
```

where pathname is the full path and name for the temporary file containing the string associated with the key. The length indicates the number of bytes in that string, essentially the size of the temporary file.

[Form Huge]

If the value associated with a key exceeds 65,535 bytes, the location and size of the value in the Content File is marked in this section. An entry in the Form Huge section looks like this:

```
key=offset length
```

Here, *offset* is the offset from the beginning of the Content File where the value string for this key is located, and *length* is the length of the value string in bytes.

Sample Program

Consider the form shown in Listing 5-3. Its output is shown in Figure 5-17.

Listing 5-3 Sample entry form

```
<html>
<head>
<title>Sample Form
</title>
</head>

<body>
<FORM METHOD="POST" ACTION="/cgi-win/entry.exe">

Please fill out this form:
<p>

<pre>
     Name: <input SIZE=30 NAME="name">
 Phone number: <input SIZE=15 NAME="phone">
</pre>

What database do you use <br>
<OL>
<LI> <INPUT TYPE="radio" NAME="dbase" VALUE="sybase"> Sybase
<LI> <INPUT TYPE="radio" NAME="dbase" VALUE="oracle"> Oracle
</OL>

<INPUT TYPE="submit" VALUE="Submit form">

</FORM>
```

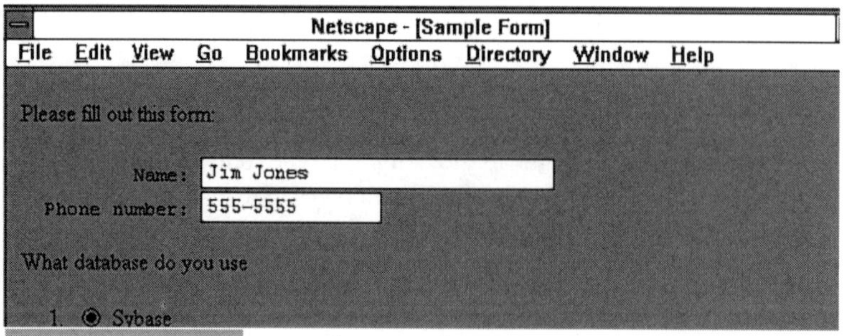

FIGURE 5-17   Sample entry form

Listing 5-4 is a Visual Basic subroutine to process this form. Note that you are not restricted to Visual Basic. Any development language which supports Windows API can be used. This program was compiled and the executable file (ENTRY.EXE) was placed in the CGI/WIN directory.

Listing 5-4 CGI_Main()

```
Sub CGI_Main ()
    Dim buf As String
    Dim fname As String
    Dim fphone As String
    Dim fdbase As String

' Put the form information into our local vars
    fname = GetSmallField("name")
    fphone = GetSmallField("phone")
    fdbase = GetSmallField("dbase")

    Send ("Content-type: text/html")
    Send ("")
    Send ("<HTML>")
    Send ("<BODY>")

    If fname = "" Or fphone = "" Then
        Send ("Please fill out all the fields")
        Send ("</BODY>")
        Send ("</HTML>")
        Exit Sub
    End If

    Send ("<H1>Program reply</H1>")
    Send ("<p> Your name is:  " & fname)
    Send ("<p> Your phone is: " & fphone)
    Send ("<p> Your database is: " & fdbase)
    Send ("</BODY>")
    Send ("</HTML>")

End Sub
```

Listing 5-5 is the Main() routine which marks the starting point of the program.

Listing 5-5 Main() routine

```
Sub Main ()
    On Error GoTo ErrorHandler
InitializeCGI      ' Create the CGI environment
CGI_Main           ' Execute the cgi script
Cleanup:
    Close #CGI_ContentFN
    Close #CGI_OutputFN
    Exit Sub                      ' End the program
```

continued on next page

continued from previous page

```
    '------------
ErrorHandler:
    ErrorString = Error$          ' Save the error
    On Error GoTo 0               ' Prevent recursion
    ErrorHandler (Err)            ' Generate appropriate HTTP error result
    Resume Cleanup
    '------------
End Sub
```

Windows HTTPD includes a file called CGI.BAS which has nearly all the routines related to the CGI implementation of the server. Listing 5-5 shows the general skeleton of CGI applications written in Visual Basic. You must write the CGI_Main routine, which performs actions particular to your application. In the example shown, the data is placed into several variables. Then, a message is created that prints out the data as it was received by the external program. The function GetSmallField() is included in the CGI.BAS module. Given a name in the *name=value* pair, it returns the value. The Send() function is also defined in the CGI.BAS module. It adds its argument to the page being sent to the server. Figure 5-18 shows the output of the program as viewed by the client.

Server Configuration

The configuration files are similar to those listed for the NCSA HTTP server.

Windows 95 and Windows NT

The CGI implementation under Windows 95 and Windows NT is almost identical to the Windows 3.x implementation discussed in the previous section. However, the new environment does offer some useful options taken advantage of in Windows CGI 1.3 specifications. In this section, we highlight these differences. A popular HTTP server under these environments is WebSite, available from `http://website.ora.com/`.

Under the Windows CGI 1.3 specification, the HTTP server executes the external program by calling the CreateProcess() function. This system call executes the program as a separate process, similar to how the UNIX operating system handles external program execution. The CreateProcess() function is called with the following parameters:

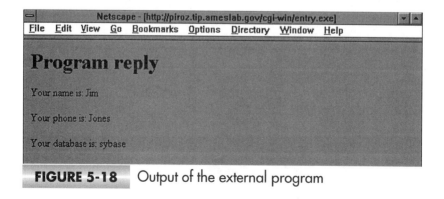

FIGURE 5-18   Output of the external program

- external_program: the full path to the program being executed

- cgi-data-file: the full path to the CGI data file

Note that since the [System] section includes the paths for the files named content-file and output-file, it is not necessary to repeat these paths as parameters to the CreateProcess() function.

The CGI data file has the same format as the Windows 3.x CGI specification with some minor differences. In the [System] section, the following keys are added:

- **GMT Offset:** The number of seconds added to GMT time to reach local time. To get Pacific Standard time, the number should be -28,800.

- **Debug Mode:** This option is set to "No" as the default. If the server is put in debug mode by enabling its CGI/script tracing mode, this option is set to "Yes."

CGI in the Mac OS

This section discusses an implementation of CGI under the Mac OS operating system. The server used is the popular Mac OS HTTP server, available from `http://www.star-nine.com/machttp/machttpsoft.html`. As with other servers, we need to know how the server executes an external application and how data transfer between the two is accomplished.

Invocation of the External Program

The Mac HTTP server launches the external program by a system call. The specifics of this event are not relevant to our purpose. You can assume that the server will launch the external program, wait for it to finish execution, and return some results. The data transfer technique used in Mac HTTP is very different from what we have seen in other servers. In the Mac OS, there is an internal communication mechanism called an Apple event. Apple events allow two Macintosh programs to communicate with each other, exchange data, and even request execution of a certain function from one another. For example, your word processing program can use Apple events to send some text to your e-mail program and ask the e-mail program to send it to a particular address.

 Apple Script

A thorough understanding of Apple Script is necessary in order to develop effective applications using the Web. Most examples in this book use C and Perl. Therefore, if you plan to develop your applications using Apple Script,

continued on next page

continued from previous page

you should consult one or more of the references listed below for Apple Script–specific issues and syntax. The concepts described in this book, such as CGI, are application independent and can be used under any operating system. Apple Script references include:

The Tao of Apple Script (second edition) by Derrick Schneider. Publisher: Hayden Books, 11711 N. College Ave., Carmel, IN 46032. (800) 776-BMUG.

Applied Mac Scripting by Tom Trinko. Publisher: M&T Books.

Ultimate Mac Programming: Methods of the Macintosh Masters by Dave Mark. Publisher: IDG Books Worldwide, Inc.

Apple Script Software Development Toolkit from Apple Computer, Inc. Available from Apple (part # RO175Z/B).

Useful scripts, demos, and other scripting-related files can be found at
`ftp://gaea.kgs.ukans.edu/applescript`

More reference material is available from
`http://www.scriptweb.com/scriptweb/books/books_new.html`

Apple events are a very powerful mechanism. Since an application is implemented at the operating system level, you can assume its reliability and efficiency. The Mac HTTP server uses this mechanism to communicate with the external applications. Like any other server, it receives a CGI request from a client. It executes the program specified in the request and creates an appropriate Apple event that includes the data to be sent to the program. It then waits for an Apple event reply from the external program, which includes the data to be sent to the client. As with other CGI implementation, the return data can either be a self-contained document (for example, an HTML file) or a reference to another document.

The only requirement for an external application under the Mac OS is that it be capable of accepting and sending Apple events. Most programming languages have this capability, so the external program can be written in a variety of languages including C, MacPerl (a flavor of Perl specific to Macintosh), Hypercard, and Apple Script.

Due to its relative simplicity and availability, Apple Script is commonly used in Macintosh CGI applications. The examples in this book are written in Apple Script, but the method of approach is identical, regardless of the programming language used.

Data Transfer

Consider the simple form shown below. Its result is shown in Figure 5-19. Note that the method used is POST and the action refers to an Apple Script which is shown in Listing 5-6.

```
<form method=POST action="http://server_name/entry.script">
First name: <input type =TEXT name=FNAME>
<br>
```

```
Last name: <input type =TEXT name=LNAME>
<p>
<input type =SUBMIT>
</form>
```

Listing 5-6 External program in Apple Script

```
property crlf : (ASCII character 13) & (ASCII character 10)
property http_10_header : "HTTP/1.0 200 OK" & crlf & "Server: MacHTTP" & ⇐
  crlf & "MIME-Version: 1.0" & crlf & "Content-type: text/html" & crlf & crlf

set my_page to http_10_header ⇐
  & "<HTML><BODY><H2>Result from entry form</H2>" & return
set my_page to my_page & "<pre>" & return

set oldDelim to AppleScript's text item delimiters
set AppleScript's text item delimiters to {"&"}
set postarglist to text items of post_args
set AppleScript's text item delimiters to oldDelim

set postargtext to ""
repeat with curritem in postarglist
  set postargtext to postargtext & curritem & return
end repeat

set my_page to my_page ⇐
  & postargtext & "</PRE>" & return
set my_page to my_page ⇐
  & "</BODY></HTML>"
return my_page
```

The script sets the variables crlf and http_10_header to appropriate values. It then constructs the data that will end up in the variable my_page. This is the data that is sent back to the server. Similar to other implementations of CGI, a set of parameters is sent to each external program. We have already discussed these items in the CGI in UNIX section. Here we just list them and match them to their corresponding environmental variable used in UNIX CGI.

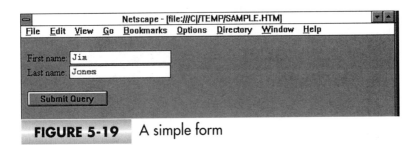

FIGURE 5-19   A simple form

Table 5-2 Mac CGI arguments and their UNIX counterparts

Mac OS CGI	UNIX CGI
method	REQUEST_METHOD
script_name	SCRIPT_NAME
http_search_args	PATH_INFO
Physical Path	PATH_TRANSLATED
post_args	QUERY_STRING
content_type	CONTENT_TYPE
server_name	SERVER_NAME
server_port	SERVER_PORT
client_address	REMOTE_HOST
client_ip	REMOTE_ADDR
username	REMOTE_USER

In addition, Mac CGI stores the name of the client software in the parameter user_agent. Also, the complete text of the client request is stored in the parameter full_request.

The most important parameter is post_args, which contains the form data from the client in the URL encoded format. The next few lines parse this argument using the ampersand character as the delimiter. Each *name=value* pair is appended to the output data. Finally, the data is returned to the server, which creates the result shown in Figure 5-20.

Server Configuration

Once again, to ensure that you get the same results as the examples in the book, the configuration file for Mac HTTP is shown here.

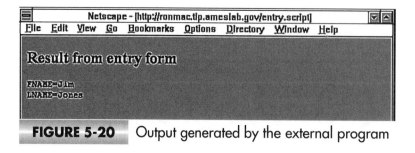

FIGURE 5-20   Output generated by the external program

Mac HTTP Configuration File

```
#Mac HTTP Configuration file, v. 2.2

# The version number below must match Mac HTTP's version number
VERSION 2.2

######################################################
# "Special" Files
#
#The following line defines the default file type if a suffix match isn't⇐
found.
#The syntax is: DEFAULT <default transfer type> <default MIME type>
DEFAULT TEXT text/html

INDEX    Default.html
ERROR    :Error.html
NOACCESS :NoAccess.html

#If the LOG file directive is missing or commented out, no logging will occur.
LOG      :MacHTTP.log

######################################################
# The following commands can be used to adjust Mac HTTP's behavior and
# performance. Most of them can be adjusted via Apple Script and Apple events
# as well.

#Sets the timeout for inactive connections to 60 seconds
TIMEOUT 60

#Sets the max number of simultaneous users.
MAXUSERS 10

#Sets the number of "listens" Mac HTTP performs simultaneously.
MAXLISTENS 6

PORT 80

PIG_DELAY 30

# This is the chunk size that Mac HTTP will divide file transfers into.
DUMP_BUF_SIZE 4096

# Mac HTTP can be configured to eliminate DNS accesses.
#NO_DNS

######################################################
#These lines define the suffix and file type mappings for MIME types.
#The syntax is <type> <suffix> <mac file type> <mac creator> <mime type>
#                                                  continued on next page
```

continued on next page

continued from previous page

```
#Unspecified parameters should be replaced with "*". Mac HTTP tries to match
#a file suffix first. Failing that, it tries to match Mac file type info, and
#if it can, Mac creator info as well. Matching either suffix or type/creator
#determines the transfer type and MIME type.

TEXT    .HTML TEXT * text/html
BINARY  .GIF  GIF * image/gif
CGI .CGI APPL * text/html
ACGI .ACGI APPL * text/html
SCRIPT  .SCRIPT TEXT * text/html
SCRIPT  * TEXT ToyS text/html
APPL    .EXE APPL * text/html
TEXT    .TEXT TEXT * text/plain
TEXT    .TXT TEXT * text/plain
TEXT    .HQX TEXT * application/mac-binhex40
BINARY  .JPG JPEG * image/jpeg
BINARY  .JPEG JPEG * image/jpeg
BINARY  .PICT PICT * image/pict
BINARY .AU * * audio/basic
BINARY .AIFF * * audio/x-aiff
BINARY .XBM * * image/x-xbm
BINARY  .MOV MOOV * video/quicktime
BINARY .MPEG MPEG * video/mpeg
BINARY .WORD WDBN MSWD application/msword
BINARY .XL XLS3 * application/excel
BINARY .SIT SITD * application/x-stuffit
BINARY .PDF PDF%20 * application/pdf


#####################################################
# Security configuration

# Security realms
#REALM workers Co-Workers
#REALM cust Customers

ALLOW *
```

Additional information about Mac HTTP and CGI programming under the Mac OS can be found from the following resources:

- Macintosh WWW Resources: http://www.comvista.com/net/www/WWWDirectory.html

- Ian's Mac Web Tools: http://trinculo.educ.sfu.ca/tools.html

- ACS Mac Pages: http://www.ualr.edu/doc/mac/mac_home.html

- The Well Connected Mac: http://www.macfaq.com/

MIME

If you have ever used attachments in your e-mail communications, then you have used MIME. The original e-mail protocol was restricted to text messages. In an effort to break that barrier, several standards were introduced to convert the binary contents of non-text information (for example, pictures and sound clips) to text so that the e-mail protocol could handle it. On the receiving end, another conversion process was performed to extract the original binary information.

MIME, the Multipurpose Internet Mail Extensions, is a specification that standardized the process described above. MIME offers a way to interchange text in languages with different character sets and multimedia e-mail among many different computer systems that use Internet mail standards. Some of the types of information which can be exchanged via MIME include:

- character sets other than ASCII
- enriched text
- images
- sounds
- PostScript
- movie clips

MIME not only supports several predefined types of non-textual formats, it also allows you to define your own message formats, making it a very powerful and extendible standard. Actually, the MIME specification is not limited to e-mail messages. The HTTP protocol uses Internet Media Types derived from MIME to serve data in a variety of different formats. Usually a configuration file is used to specify the different MIME types and how they should be treated. The MIME types must be specified both by the server and the client to allow for a smooth exchange of information.

When a message is sent from the server to the client or vice versa, it includes a *content-type* parameter which is actually a MIME type. There are a large of number of MIME types available and many of them, such as text, are well standardized. Many HTTP clients and servers are programmed to recognize the most common MIME types without any configuration files, but an understanding of MIME can help you create more robust applications.

Table 5-3 lists the most common MIME types. They are specified in a Type/Subtype format. The types (content types) are more established and more general than the subtypes. If you want to generate your own MIME type to handle a specific data format, you should find the type most appropriate and add your extension as a subtype.

Table 5-3 Sample MIME types/subtypes

type/subtype	meaning
text/plain	unformatted text
text/richtext	Microsoft's RTF (rich text format)
text/tab-separated-values	tab-delimited fields stored in a text file
text/html	text file containing valid HTML tags
audio/basic	AU format audio
audio/x-aiff	AIFF format audio message
video/mpeg	MPEG movie
video/quicktime	QuickTime movie
image/jpeg	JPEG format
image/gif	GIF (Graphics Interchange Format) image
image/tiff	TIFF (Tagged Image File Format) image
image/x-pict	PICT image (Macintosh-only format)
image/x-xbm	X bitmap image
application/octet-stream	uninterpreted binary data
application/postscript	Adobe PostScript format
application/mac-binhex40	file encoded in the BinHexed format
application/zip	file compressed with PKZip
application/macwriteii	MacWrite II document
application/msword	Microsoft Word document

More information about the MIME specifications and standard MIME types can be found at the following resources:

- MIME Frequently Asked Questions:
  http://www.cis.ohio-state.edu/hypertext/
  faq/usenet/mail/mime-faq/top.html

- Representation of Non-ASCII Text in Internet Message Headers:
  http://www.cis.ohio-state.edu:82/rfc/rfc1342.html

MIME in Web Applications

Let us consider how MIME types are used in the World Wide Web. Anytime the server must send a message to the client, it needs to include the MIME type associated with the message. This is specified in a header field called *content-type*. How does the server know the content type for a given file? Most servers have a configuration file which links file extensions to a MIME type. In an NCSA HTTP server, this file is stored as mime.types. When the server receives a request for the file thesis.ps, it attempts to find the extension .ps in its configuration file. It can then determine the content type associated with the file.

On the client side, the reverse process occurs. Once the client receives a response from the server, it looks at the header to see what the content type is. It then looks at a configuration file commonly called the Mailcap file. This file has a listing of content types along with the appropriate command to view a particular content type. Here is an excerpt from a Mailcap file:

```
audio/basic; showaudio %s
image/*; xv %s
application/postscript; ghostview %s
```

When the subtype portion of a content type is replaced by an asterisk (as image/*), it means: Treat all documents with a certain type the same. That is, the same program (xv) is used to display any file which has an image type specified as its content type. The %s is replaced by the name of the file to be displayed or processed.

In non-UNIX environments, each browser has its own method for dealing with MIME types and Mailcap files. Consult the documentation for your browser to see how it is done.

This ends our discussion of the link between the Web server and external programs. At this time, you should familiarize yourself with CGI implementation particular to the operating system and the Web server you are using. Make sure the examples presented in this chapter work in your environment. We have now completed our discussion of two of the three elements of a Web database. The next step is to discuss databases. Then we can start developing applications.

Summary

The CGI standard allows the Web server to communicate with an external program which performs a specific task. Due to internal differences among operating systems, the CGI implementation varies greatly. In the UNIX environment, the form data is passed to the external program via its standard input. In addition, several useful parameters about the request are passed to the program by way of environmental variables. The server directs the output of the external program directly to the client. Therefore, it is imperative that the external program generate the necessary headers for the client. The most important element of the header is the content-type, which lets the client know how to display the data.

In the Windows environment, a file-based mechanism passes data to the external program. Similarly, the output of the program is placed in a file for the server to read. All the data is stored in a private profile file in the *name=value* format.

Under the Mac OS, Apple events are the means of communication between the server and the external program. This method is very efficient. External applications can be developed in any language, including Apple Script, as long as the language supports Apple events.

The MIME specification is a mechanism to transfer non-ASCII data in a standard manner. A number of MIME types have been standardized to represent common data types such as HTML, PostScript, and so on. In the HTTP protocol, the MIME type of a document is specified by the content-type header. The HTTP server normally has a configuration file that links different file extensions with a MIME type. On the client side, a configuration file links a content type to a program used to display files with that content type.

Questions

1. What are the four phases of communication between the client and the server when an external program is launched?

2. Of the four phases specified in Question 1, which ones involve the CGI standard?

3. What is the function of the *name* option inside a form element tag?

4. Why is it not a good idea to use the GET method in a form?

5. What does URL encoding mean?

6. What is the difference between a virtual path and a full path?

7. Can the external program and the Web server reside on two different machines?

8. What are MIME types?

Answers

1. The four phases are client to server, server to external program, external program to server, and server to client.

2. CGI specifies the communication that takes place between the server and the external program (phases 2 and 3).

3. The *name* option is used to form a *name=value* pair which indicates the value the user has entered for a certain form element.

4. If the GET method is used, then the form content is returned using an environmental variable. Most operating systems place a limit on the size of an environmental variable. This limit is usually very small. As a result, contents of relatively large forms cannot be processed.

5. URL encoding means that the content of the form is placed in *name=value* pairs, with each pair separated from the next one by an ampersand character. The entire

string is separated from the URL by a question mark. Also, special characters are replaced by their hexadecimal values.

6. A virtual path is how files are referenced in a URL. A virtual path is relative to a specified document root directory, which is usually set in a configuration file. A full path is the complete path to the file starting from the root level.

7. No. CGI does not specify any mechanism to establish communication between the external program and the server if they reside on different machines. There is no restriction, however, on the external program communicating with another program on a different machine.

8. MIME types are an attempt to standardize the transfer of non-text documents across the Net. Once a file is identified as having a particular MIME type, the client can launch an appropriate application to view it. The server specifies the MIME type of the documents it serves by way of the content-type header.

6
Database Basics

So far, we have discussed the World Wide Web and its gateway to external programs. We now change gears and concentrate on database systems. After all, our main goal is achieving a Web-interfaced database. Databases have been around much longer than the Web, so naturally their technology is more mature and established. This chapter discusses databases and their general properties, emphasizing Web-related issues.

The client/server model is revisited as it applies to database systems. Structured Query Language (SQL) is introduced and discussed. By the end of this chapter, you will have covered the three main components of a Web database and will be ready to begin designing applications.

What Is a Database?

The word database is used in two different contexts. It refers to the abstract notion of an organized collection of information. A customer database refers to a collection of specific information about customers, such as names, addresses, and perhaps customer identification numbers. In a more general sense, the word database refers to the computer program which manages a collection of information. (For example, Company XYZ uses a Sybase database to run its daily operations.) In this section, we use the term database to mean an organized collection of information.

There are several methods to organize a set of information. They have been thoroughly explained in the literature using different models. Most of these models are the fruits of mathematical work in set theory and information theory. The most common model used is the *relational* model. You can refer to texts on database design and theory for an in-depth discussion of such models.

Collection and organization of information is a very difficult task. Both stages—sometimes individually, sometimes collectively—are the main bottlenecks in database application development.

Data Collection

Data collection seems to take two different forms, best expressed by examples.

Case 1. Suppose Association XYZ has just started its first year. Its success heavily depends on how effectively it can acquire members whose dues will support the association. Once the association has set up a database, it starts *populating* it (putting information into it) by accepting members. The database started empty but is gradually filled with valuable information. In other words, the task of information collection is gradual and directly related to the growth of the database. Figure 6-1 shows this.

Case 2. The second form of information collection deals with an existing set of information. Company XYZ wants to offer an on-line employment service. It sets up a database that includes employers' profiles and needs. Rather than taking the gradual approach, it decides to populate its database with information already available. Many newspapers already

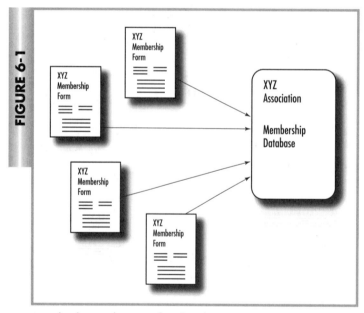

FIGURE 6-1

Gradual population of a database

collect and present employment information. Company XYZ's approach is to collect all the information from newspapers across the country and place this information in its database, where it will be available to its users. The company must decide what information is relevant and how to collect and enter it into the database. The database populates in a hurry, but the value of the information depends upon how well the screening process occurs. Figure 6-2 illustrates this idea.

As you plan your new database, decide which approach is most appropriate for you. If the information you want is already out there, don't reinvent the wheel. Perhaps a combination of these approaches works best for you. Your database system and its ability to import information from external sources plays an important role in how you proceed. In any case, your information collection decisions are important. Give them some thought.

FIGURE 6-2

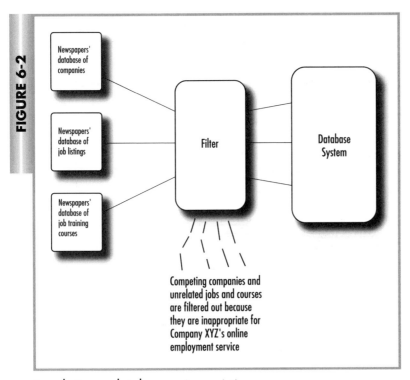

Newspapers' database of companies

Newspapers' database of job listings

Newspapers' database of job training courses

Filter

Database System

Competing companies and unrelated jobs and courses are filtered out because they are inappropriate for Company XYZ's online employment service

Populating a database using existing sources

Data Organization

After resolving your data collection issues, you need to concentrate on your data organization. Computers can deal with vast amounts of information if that information is organized in a logical and consistent manner. Don't worry about the computer. Your primary goal should be to organize the data in a way that makes the most sense to you. Chances are that your method of organization can be expressed in terms acceptable to the computer. Organization depends on several factors:

- **The content of data:** What the data actually consists of plays a key role on how it is organized. You organize 500 images differently than 500 names and addresses.

- **Usage of data:** You need to have an idea of how the data will be used. Some of the data will be presented directly to the user. Some other data is used to keep the integrity of the system and is not normally shown to the user. Your organization somewhat depends on what the data is being used for.

- **Security of data:** There could be some aspects of the data that are classified or should not be readily accessible to normal users. You might have to split your data and hide a certain part in order to address security concerns.

Flat Layout

The simplest data organization is a flat layout in which data is placed in a grid of columns and rows (see Figure 6-3). The grid is commonly referred to as a table. A typical phone and address book fits this organizational scheme. Each row is a set of related data called a record.

In our example, each row holds the information related to an individual, such as name, address, and so on. Each column is an indicator of a distinct property from the record. These properties are called *fields*. The question "What is Jack Smith's phone number?" translated into the database terminology just discussed becomes: "What is the value of the phone

FIGURE 6-3

First name	Last name	Address	City	State	Zip
John Lisa - - - -	Mitchell Miles	555 1st Street 235 Oak Ave.	New York Chicago	NY IL	10002

An address book typically uses a flat layout

number field for the record which has its first name field set to *Jack* and its last name field set to *Smith*?"

Each row in the table must be distinctly identifiable from the rest. This disconnection is achieved by using one or more fields as *key field(s)*. Integrity of the table depends on the fact that no two rows contain the same key field(s). In the phone and address book example, designating the combination of first and last name fields as the key fields is probably sufficient, but it is possible to have two different individuals with the same first and last name. We might want to include another field (such as the phone number) in our combination of fields to make sure each record has a unique key.

The short discussion above is the basis of some of the most sophisticated databases used today. It is very important that you understand the terminology presented above. A good exercise is to think of a collection of information (for example, your baseball cards or your recipes) and decide how to organize that data in a table format. What are the different columns (fields)? How would you make each record unique?

A collection of tables makes up a database. Your "friends" database might include a table with an address and phone number for each of your friends. A second table might include their names along with their birthdays. Finally, a third table might include your friends' names and their anniversary dates (if they are married). The three tables make up your friends database, which provides you with an organized method of searching for specific information about your friends. Although the flat organizational model meets the requirements for many applications, it has an important shortcoming which the following example illustrates.

Let's consider a time-sheet tracking system. The system needs to identify each employee with an ID number. It also needs to store the employees' first and last names. Employees are required to fill out a weekly time-sheet indicating their total hours for each day of the week. Figure 6-4 shows how the time-sheet looks. The date of the time-sheet is the date for the Monday of the working week.

Here are the fields that need to be specified in the table(s) for the time-sheet database:

- Employee first name (fname)
- Employee last name (lname)
- Employee ID (emp_id)
- Time-sheet date (ts_date)
- Total hours for Monday (m_hrs)
- Total hours for Tuesday (t_hrs)
- Total hours for Wednesday (w_hrs)
- Total hours for Thursday (r_hrs)
- Total hours for Friday (f_hrs)

FIGURE 6-4

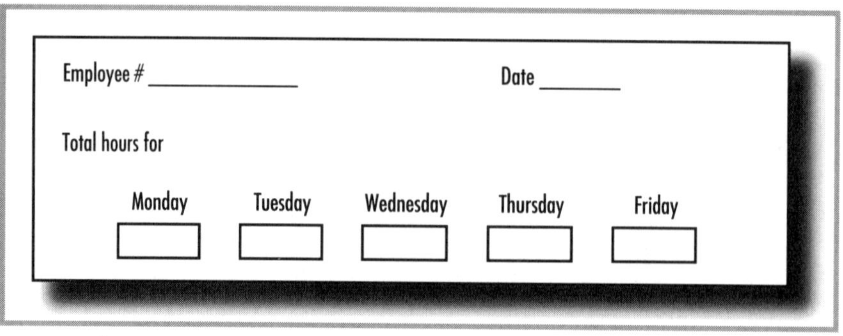

Employee # _____   Date _____

Total hours for

| Monday | Tuesday | Wednesday | Thursday | Friday |

A typical time-sheet

First we try the flat organizational method. A typical row (record) in the table would look like Table 6-1.

Table 6-1 A flat layout for the time-sheet table

fname	lname	emp_id	ts_date	m_hrs	t_hrs	w_hrs	r_hrs	f_hrs
Marc	Jones	345	1-15-96	8	9	8	7	9

Marc Jones with employee number 345 is submitting his time-sheet for the week of 1-15-96. He worked 8, 9, 8, 7, and 9 hours on days Monday through Friday respectively. Table 6-2 shows the time-sheet table after the second week.

Table 6-2 Time-sheet table after two weeks

fname	lname	emp_id	ts_date	m_hrs	t_hrs	w_hrs	r_hrs	f_hrs
Marc	Jones	345	1-15-96	8	9	8	7	9
Marc	Jones	345	1-22-96	7	0	8	9	6

Note the three fields which are repeated, namely fname, lname, and emp_id. Although repetition of three fields might not seem significant, chances are that the table requires other information, such as employee's address, phone number, hourly rate, and so on. No advantage is gained by repeating the same information over and over in the table. In fact, storage space is wasted by repetition of identical information. This problem is the main drawback of the flat organization model. Its solution is the relational model.

Without going into much detail, the *relational* model calls for creation of two or more tables linked via a common key. This is best shown with an example. The time-sheet table is split into two tables: employee table and time table. The employee table (see

Table 6-3) includes the following fields: fname, lname, emp_id. The time table (see Table 6-4) includes the emp_id, ts_date, m_hrs, t_hrs, w_hrs, r_hrs, and f_hrs fields.

Table 6-3 Employee table

fname	lname	emp_id
Marc	Jones	345

Table 6-4 Time table

emp_id	ts_date	m_hrs	t_hrs	w_hrs	r_hrs	f_hrs
345	1-15-96	8	9	8	7	9
345	1-22-96	7	0	8	9	6

The employee information is kept in the employee table and needs to be stored only once. The emp_id field connects the two tables. Given a certain time-sheet, one table can find its owner by tracing the emp_id field from the time table back to the employee name in the employee table as shown in Figure 6-5.

Almost all database applications can be expressed in a relational model similar to what is described above. Of course, more complex applications will have more tables and perhaps more key fields. Not all tables need to be connected by the same key. Also, the key does not need to be a single field; it can be a combination of two or more fields. There are some rules and guidelines for deriving a relational model for a given set of information, but for the most part, the solution to this design problem is an art. Depending on the complexity of your problem, there are some tools which can help you design a relational model for your information. But even those require you to understand your data and how different segments fit together. Unfortunately, the computer cannot do this thinking for you. As for any project, the final product will be a better one if sufficient time is spent during the design stage.

The time-sheet database can be split even further to demonstrate the use of a combination key. We split the time table into two tables: the date table and the time-sheet table. The date table includes the following fields:

emp_id, ts_date

The time-sheet table includes the following fields:

emp_id, ts_date, m_hrs, t_hrs, w_hrs, r_hrs, f_hrs

For a given employee number, we can determine all the weeks for which he or she submitted a timesheet. If further detail is needed, then a combination of emp_id and ts_date can be used to find the hours reported for each day of the week in the time-sheet table. Figure 6-6 shows this relationship.

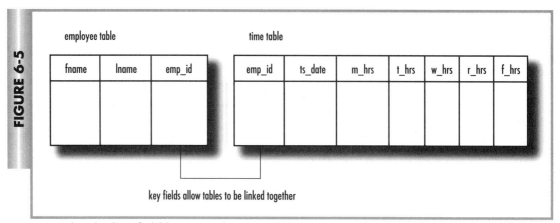

FIGURE 6-5

emp_id is the key field between the two tables

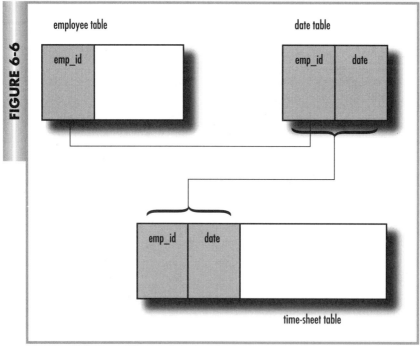

FIGURE 6-6

Using all three tables in the database

By splitting the time table further, we have added another level of detail and another relationship to the database. A well-designed database creates a hierarchy of information using relationships among the different components. The hierarchy allows for a modular design of the application, with each piece covering a specific part of the database. In the above example, the operator entering the time-sheet information does not need to know the owner of each time-sheet. The employee is identified via an ID number only. Similarly, when a new employee is hired, the operator at the personnel office only needs to enter the employee's name and assign an ID number to that name.

No matter how complicated your data might seem at first, careful thinking and under-standing of the data can help you create a well-organized database with useful relationships to enable you create a hierarchical view of your information. Your database application heav-ily depends on the structure of your database. Spend some time organizing your database. It pays in the long run.

Tables and Databases

Some of the older database systems stored a table in a file and referred to it as a database. In those systems, a database contained other databases. FoxPro is one of the systems that utilized this notation. Each table was stored as a separate file with the extension .DBF. Most applications stored related tables in the same directory, emulating a database (collection of tables). Today, such programs include an additional object called the data-base, but the terminology still is misused by some. Remember, a database is a collection of groups of tables, but a collection of tables is not necessarily a database.

Database Client/Server Model

Databases were one of the first applications of computer systems. The ability to store, man-age, and retrieve vast amounts of information has been instrumental in the information revolution, and the main workhorse for this process is the database system. With the growth of net-worked computers, databases gradually conformed to the client/server model. In fact, database systems are a classic example for the client/server model since they very distinctively pos-sess the properties of this model.

The Server

The database server is the main engine of the database. Typically, data is stored in a pro-prietary format on disk. The way the data is physically stored plays an important role in the overall efficiency of the database and how quickly it retrieves selection information. The server must be able to manage the physical layout of the data. In many cases, it accom-plishes this task by careful coordination with the operating system as shown in Figure 6-7.

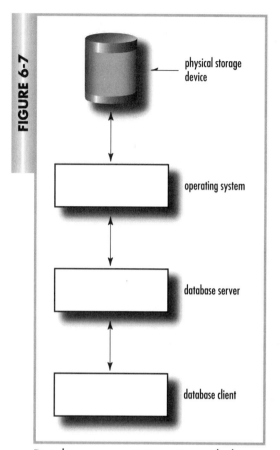

FIGURE 6-7

Database server interaction with the
storage device using the operating system

In other cases, it solely takes care of accessing and manipulating the storage device (see Figure 6-8).

The server also provides an interface to retrieve selected information from the database. Recall that the function of a Web server is to listen to a port for requests from clients and, after verification, respond to each request. Its response could be sending a Web page back to the client or executing an external program and directing its output to the client. A database server functions in a similar way. It accepts commands from a client and executes those commands.

Unlike Web servers, which universally use HTTP as their communication protocol, each database uses its own protocol for communicating with its clients. In other words, the commands understood by each database are different from one another. The closest thing to a standard is the Structured Query Language (SQL) which this chapter discusses at

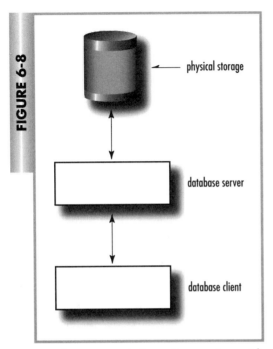

FIGURE 6-8

← physical storage

database server

database client

Database server direct interaction with
the storage device

length. SQL is the client's means of making requests to a server. SQL commands can generate different forms of output. A command to insert some data into the database merely
yields a success/failure output. On the other hand, a command to find all customers residing within a certain zip code can lead to a more sophisticated form of output.

Depending on the complexity of the database server, it might offer additional functions
such as data security, data recovery, and integrity. In short, all direct contacts with data are
made by the server based on requests from the client.

The Client

After the previous discussion about the functions of a database server, the work of the client
should be clear. There are several types of database clients. Administrative clients provide
an interface for a database administrator to accomplish his or her tasks. Some of these tasks
are

- Issuing user accounts
- Granting and revoking permissions
- Database backup and recovery
- Monitoring the performance of the database

Applications clients are another class of clients. Although both types of client can be implemented using a Web interface, this book focuses on application clients. An electronic address book, employee time-sheet tracking system, and a catalog ordering system are examples of database applications.

Generally, applications are written for a specific purpose and work with a specific set of data. They provide a high level of abstraction for the underlying data to the user. In other words, they allow the user to take a task-oriented approach to accomplishing his or her work. For example, a sales manager might want to know total sales amounts for each store in a given district. The database application should provide a mechanism (through menus, lists, and so on) to retrieve this data from the database. The application should translate this high-level request to a low-level language such as SQL, receive the result from the server, and present it to the user in a meaningful way (for example, a bar graph). This process is illustrated in Figure 6-9.

How the data is stored on the server and its format should be transparent to the application user. Because of its high abstraction level, a portable database application is often desired. In other words, the application code should be able to run on different machines. The application is composed of two main parts: the user interface and its communication link to the database. Portability comes into play in both parts. As you might have guessed, the World Wide Web is a good solution to the portability problem at the user interface level. Using forms and other HTML elements, a consistent user interface can be created. This interface will stay the same regardless of the user platform. Java offers the same advantage, but it goes a step further. With an open database connectivity class, Java makes the way you access a database uniform among different platforms.

FIGURE 6-9

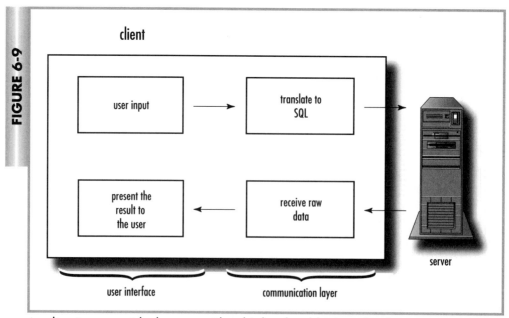

Applications provide the user with a higher level look at the data

The communication link to the database is a more difficult problem; its implementation differs from database to database. For a long time, the database industry had no solution to this problem. In recent years, major steps have been taken to address the problem; however, it still remains a challenge. The most successful approach is to create a standard that acts as a middle layer between the client and the server. Clients are written to communicate with this middle layer. Each database server also offers a link between its own functions and the middle layer using software known as *drivers*. As a result, a "standard" communication method is established between the client and the server. This approach is shown in Figure 6-10. An example of such an approach is ODBC (Open Database Connectivity), which is a widely used standard in the MS Windows environment. The Java Database Connectivity (JDBC) is another example.

The obvious drawbacks of such an approach are twofold. First, the middle layer adds extra overhead to the communication path. It must intercept the data, parse it, and then pass it on to the next level. No matter how fast the implementation is, this step consumes valuable time. The second drawback is an inherent criticism of the middle-layer approach. The existence of a middle layer depends on a *common denominator* among the different databases. To find a common denominator, you must overlook the special features offered by each database system. In other words, you must ignore distinctive features of a database system in order to use it within the middle-layer paradigm. This is more of a philosophical argument: You give up the special features for the sake of portability, or vice versa.

With this overview of the database client/server model, we now turn to a discussion of the relational database model.

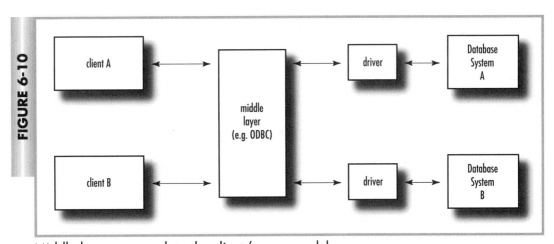

FIGURE 6-10

Middle-layer approach to the client/server model

Which Group Do You Belong To?

If you are planning to set up a database on the Web, you probably belong to one of the following two groups: 1. You might already be using a database and have developed client applications for it. In other words, you are looking for the global audience and the portability benefits that the Web can bring to your database application. 2. The other group is composed of users who are starting from scratch. They want to develop a database and put it on the Web. Regardless of which group you belong to, a good understanding of the relational database model and your database system is a must in the development of solid applications. The discussion in the book should be sufficient for basic application design, but for more complex situations, you should consult a text dedicated to the topic of database and information science.

SQL

Database systems utilize a variety of languages to manipulate their data. In recent years, Structured Query Language (SQL) has become the standard database language, and almost all database systems support it. As with HTML, vendors have enhanced SQL and added additional functions to the language. Microsoft Access uses a flavor of SQL called Access SQL. Sybase uses another flavor called Transact-SQL (pronounced *transact sequel*). The examples in this chapter use Sybase as the database engine. They should work with little or no modification under other database systems.

SQL Standard

SQL was a product of IBM research labs in the late 1960s. The primary inventor was Dr. E. F. Codd, who published the classical paper that laid the foundation for relational database systems. A dialect of SQL was adopted by the American National Standard Institute (ANSI) in 1986 and by the International Organization for Standardization (ISO) in 1987. Refer to http://www.jcc.com/sql_stnd.html for more information.

As a programmer, SQL is your tool to talk to the database. As shown in Figure 6-11, the database is like a black box. When you issue SQL commands, you can expect the black box to return some results to you. If your query is erroneous or does not match any part of the data, you can expect an appropriate message.

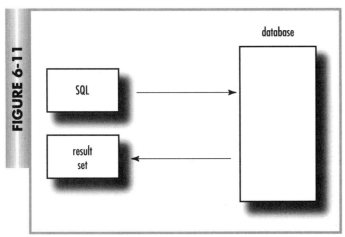

FIGURE 6-11

The role of SQL in a database system

Depending on the database system, there are usually three methods for using SQL in your communication with the database:

1. **Interactive terminal.** In this method, you have a terminal session with the database server. You type some commands, and the database sends the appropriate result to the terminal. This method is useful for debugging your application. It is also useful for learning purposes since no extra programming is required and the results are almost instantaneous.

2. **Embedded SQL.** Some database systems support embedded SQL. With this method, the SQL statements are embedded in the program. A pre-processor translates the embedded SQL into compilable code. There is support for a variety of languages such as C and COBOL.

3. **Database API.** This is the most popular method for programmers. Your program communicates with the database using a set of function calls. Each database system tends to have its own set of functions, so portability becomes an issue. These functions can be categorized as follows:

   - **Initialization, login, and establishment of a server connection:** These functions allow your program to establish communication with the database and begin a transaction.

   - **Building and executing an SQL command batch:** These commands let you build SQL commands and send them to the database for execution.

   - **Result processing:** These commands allow you to manipulate the result set returned from an SQL command.

   - **Error handling:** These functions provide the capability to trap errors and resolve them.

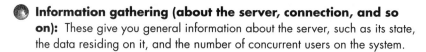 **Information gathering (about the server, connection, and so on):** These give you general information about the server, such as its state, the data residing on it, and the number of concurrent users on the system.

Of the three methods mentioned above, the last one is used almost universally in Web databases. The CGI program must be written in a language for which your database API is supported. We will discuss database API later in this chapter. In the next sections, we concentrate on SQL and its syntax.

Creating a Table

Before data is entered in a database, there must be a place to store the data. Some systems require that a database be explicitly created. Others use the loose interpretation of a database and require that only tables be created. They leave it up to the user to decide which tables form a database. Before creating a table you need to decide what its name will be, what the names for its fields will be, and what data type the fields will be declared as. This is the minimum information required to create a table. Depending on your database system, you might be able to specify additional information about the table or its fields. For example, in Sybase you can specify whether a field can hold a NULL value. The following creates the employee table discussed earlier in the chapter. The accompanying CD-ROM contains a file called ts.sql which includes all the SQL code to create the time-sheet tables and populate them with sample data. You should be able to use this code on any database supporting SQL with little or no modification.

```
create table employee
(fname      char(15)     not null,
 lname      char(30)     not null,
 emp_id     integer      not null)
```

Each field name must be unique within the table. The fields for the first and last name have been declared as a string type. Note that the size of the string is also specified. The employee identification number is declared as an integer. Finally, all the fields are required to have values. Null values will not be accepted. The following code generates the date table:

```
create table date
(emp_id     integer      not null,
 ts_date    datetime     not null)
```

The only new thing in the date table is the use of the datetime data type. In Sybase, this data type is used to store both date and time. Of course, in the sample application, only the date portion is used.

Finally, here is the code to create the time-sheet table:

```
create table timesheet
(emp_id        integer        not null,
 ts_date       datetime       not null,
 m_hrs         decimal(3,1)   not null,
 t_hrs         decimal(3,1)   not null,
```

```
w_hrs        decimal(3,1)     not null,
r_hrs        decimal(3,1)     not null,
f_hrs        decimal(3,1)     not null)
```

In order to store the number of hours an employee has worked on a given day, the decimal data type is used. Unlike the integer data type, the decimal data type lets you store fractional values needed to store fractions of hours worked. The first value inside the parentheses is the total size of the number, and the second value is the number of decimals allowed. Examples of valid values for the *hour* fields are 5, 7.5, and 10.5. Values such as 11.25 are not acceptable.

Although it is possible to create tables within an application program, usually they are created outside the program. The tables and their structures are the main building blocks for your database, so you will probably create them before writing any code. If your database system allows it, write scripts containing the necessary code to create your tables. Save these scripts in case you need to re-create the tables or create them on another machine.

Data Insertion

After tables are created, they must be filled with data. This can be done using the insert command as shown below:

```
insert [into] table [(column(s))]
values ( expression(s))
```

The command takes as its arguments the names of the columns in which you want to insert data. It then takes the values for those columns from the *values* clause and enters them into the database. For example, to add a new employee named Marc Jones whose employee identification number is 432, use the following:

```
insert into employee (fname, lname, emp_id)
values ('Marc', 'Jones', 432)
```

Since the above insert command uses all the available columns in the employee table, it is not necessary to explicitly name each one. The following would suffice:

```
insert into employee
values ('Marc', 'Jones', 432)
```

Most database programs allow for an alternate method of insertion in which the data is not explicitly stated but is the result of a query. The syntax is shown below:

```
insert [into] table [(column(s))]
query
```

Queries

Perhaps the most common database operation is a *query*. Queries allow the user to retrieve information from the database based on some criterion. Even when you know that the required information is stored in the database, coming up with an appropriate criterion to produce the desired result can be challenging.

The idea behind queries is similar to ordering items over the telephone. When you call your favorite mail order company, you ask for an item by its item number or perhaps by its name (the operator will most likely use the name to find an item number). You do not, for example, ask for all the items which have a certain color or weigh within a certain range. The database was not meant to be used that way. It was meant to be queried using an item number.

The purpose of the database and the way it will be used dictate how it should be structured and queried. Queries in SQL are very flexible. It is possible that different queries can produce similar results. The distinguishing mark is how efficient their performance is. Coming up with an efficient query requires a thorough understanding of the design of the database.

Queries are performed using the select statement whose syntax is shown below:

```
select [all | distinct] field list
[into table name]
[from table name]
[where predicate]
[group by expression]
[order by column(s)]
```

The actual syntax for the SELECT statement in Sybase (and other database systems) is more complex than what is shown above. We encourage you to consult your database manual for the complete syntax supported by your software. The query returns its result in a table-like structure called the *result set*. It includes rows containing the fields specified in the field list. The select statement is broken down into pieces. Each piece is described below:

[all | distinct]

If *all* is specified, then all the items in the result set are accepted. If *distinct* is specified, then duplicate rows in the result set are reduced to a single row.

Field List

This list includes the field names containing the data we want. It is a good idea to precede a field name by the name of its table. For example, to refer to the emp_id field from the employee table, we write employee.emp_id. The items in the list are separated by a comma.

[into table name]

This clause causes the result set to be stored in the specified table. This is helpful for storing intermediate results when issuing complex queries.

[from table name]

This clause specifies the table(s) on which the query is being performed. The list is again *comma delimited,* which means individual items in the list are separated by a comma.

[where predicate]

The *where* clause is the place the selection criterion is specified. A variety of formats are used for the predicate, but they all follow one of these forms:

- Field name operation expression
- Field name operation field name

In the first form, the criterion checks the value of a field and compares it to an expression (for example, emp_id = 235). In the second form, the values of two fields are compared (for example, employee.emp_id = timesheet.emp_id). Depending on the data types of the values being compared, several operations can be performed. They include:

- = checks for equality
- != checks for inequality
- > checks for the left-hand side to be greater than the right-hand side
- < checks for the left-hand side to be less than the right-hand side
- [not] between—checks for the left-hand side to be (not to be) within a certain range
- [not] in—checks for the left-hand side to be (not to be) a member of a specified set
- [not] like—checks for the left-hand side to be (not to be) a substring of the right hand side
- is [not] null—checks for the left-hand side to be (not to be) a NULL value

The underscore character stands for any single character, and the % character stands for any combination of characters. For example, an employee.lname like "Jo%" would match Jones and Johnson.

Complex predicates can be created using keywords AND, OR, and NOT. They allow for checking multiple criteria sets using Boolean expressions. For example, to check for timecards in a range of dates, we can use timesheet.ts_date > "1/1/96" and timesheet.ts_date < "1/3/96" as the predicate.

[group by expression]

Often it is desirable to have the result set expressed in groups. For example, a total sales query gathers data from each store around the nation. When grouped by state, the total sales for each state are returned as a result set.

[order by column(s)]

This clause controls how the result set is sorted. The result is sorted based on the columns specified in this clause.

For demonstration purposes, the three tables from the time-tracking database are populated with some data, as shown in Tables 6-5, 6-6, and 6-7.

Table 6-5 Employee table

fname	lname	emp_id
Marc	Jones	345
Jim	Johnson	234
Linda	Smith	126
Kim	Krause	986
Jason	Fox	498

Table 6-6 Date table

emp_id	ts_date
345	1/8/96
234	1/8/96
126	1/8/96
986	1/8/96
498	1/15/96
986	1/15/96
234	1/15/96

Table 6-7 Time-sheet table

emp_id	ts_date	m_hrs	t_hrs	w_hrs	r_hrs	f_hrs
345	1/8/96	4	5	8	5	0
234	1/8/96	5	5	5	5	5
126	1/8/96	8	2	3	8	3
986	1/8/96	0	0	2	5	3
498	1/15/96	3	5	5	0	6

emp_id	ts_date	m_hrs	t_hrs	w_hrs	r_hrs	f_hrs
986	1/15/96	2	3	7	4	2
234	1/15/96	4	4	5	5	5

The following query picks the last name of the employee with identification number 234.

```
select lname
from employee
where emp_id = 234
```

Result:

```
lname
-----------------------------
Johnson
```

This query selects both the first and last name of the employee with identification number 234.

```
select fname, lname
from employee
where emp_id = 234
```

Result:

```
fname            lname
---------------- -----------------------------
Jim              Johnson
```

The following query selects all the values from the ts_date field of the data table, sorting them in ascending order and removing any duplicates from the result set. Note that since the ts_date field was declared as a datetime type, it includes both date and time information. For this application, we ignore the time component.

```
select distinct ts_date
from date
order by ts_date
```

Result:

```
ts_date
-----------------------------
Jan  8 1996 12:00:00:000AM
Jan 15 1996 12:00:00:000AM
```

The next query selects everything from the time-sheet table.

```
select * from timesheet
```

Result:

```
emp_id          ts_date                        m_hrs  t_hrs  w_hrs  r_hrs  f_hrs
--------  ----------------------------------   -------  -----  -------  ------  ------
345       Jan  8 1996 12:00:00:000AM           4.0    5.0    8.0    5.0    0.0
234       Jan  8 1996 12:00:00:000AM           5.0    5.0    5.0    5.0    5.0
126       Jan  8 1996 12:00:00:000AM           8.0    2.0    3.0    8.0    3.0
986       Jan  8 1996 12:00:00:000AM           0.0    0.0    2.0    5.0    3.0
498       Jan 15 1996 12:00:00:000AM           3.0    5.0    5.0    0.0    6.0
986       Jan 15 1996 12:00:00:000AM           2.0    3.0    7.0    4.0    2.0
234       Jan 15 1996 12:00:00:000AM           4.0    4.0    5.0    5.0    5.0
```

The following query demonstrates the usage of complex predicates using the AND operator.

```
select m_hrs, t_hrs, w_hrs, r_hrs, f_hrs
from timesheet
where emp_id = 986 and ts_date = "1/8/96"
```

Result:

```
m_hrs         t_hrs         w_hrs         r_hrs         f_hrs
----------    --------    -------------    -------------    -----------------
0.0           0.0           2.0           5.0           3.0
```

Here, the aggregate function SUM is used to get the total number of hours employee 986 has worked on Mondays.

```
select sum(m_hrs)
from timesheet
where emp_id = 986
```

Result:

```
-----------------------------------------------------------
2.0
```

This query shows each employee number followed by the total number of hours worked each day.

```
select emp_id, sum(m_hrs), sum(t_hrs), sum(w_hrs), sum(r_hrs), sum(f_hrs)
from timesheet
group by emp_id
order by emp_id
```

Result:

```
emp_id
------------------------------------------------------------------------
126       8.0     2.0     3.0     8.0     3.0
234       9.0     9.0     10.0    10.0    10.0
345       4.0     5.0     8.0     5.0     0.0
498       3.0     5.0     5.0     0.0     6.0
986       2.0     3.0     9.0     9.0     5.0
```

The BETWEEN operator is demonstrated below.

```
select emp_id
from timesheet
where m_hrs between 5 and 7
```

Result:

```
emp_id
----------
234
```

String comparisons can be made as part of the where clause as shown below, using the % characters as a wild card.

```
select lname, fname
from employee
where lname like "Jo%"
```

Result:

```
lname       fname
------------------------------- ----------------
Jones       Marc
Johnson     Jim
```

Joins

Perhaps the most powerful feature of relational databases is the ability to join two or more tables, combining the information contained in each one. *Joins* are usually considered an expensive operation, and their efficiency is a direct result of how well a database structure is designed and thought out. Consider the following join which uses the employee and date table:

```
select employee.emp_id, employee.lname, date.emp_id
from employee, date
where date.emp_id = employee.emp_id
```

Result:

```
emp_id     lname                          emp_id
---------- ------------------------------ ----------
345        Jones                          345
986        Krause                         986
986        Krause                         986
234        Johnson                        234
234        Johnson                        234
126        Smith                          126
986        Krause                         986
986        Krause                         986
498        Fox                            498
```

When a join query between two tables is performed, it is often necessary to first find the cross-product of the two tables. The cross-product will contain all the combinations between the rows of the two tables. For the above example, 35 (5x7) combinations are possible, some of which are shown below:

```
Marc       Jones         345        345        1/8/96
Marc       Jones         345        234        1/8/96
Marc       Jones         345        126        1/8/96
Marc       Jones         345        986        1/8/96
Marc       Jones         345        498        1/15/96
Marc       Jones         345        986        1/15/96
Marc       Jones         345        234        1/15/96
Jim        Johnson       234        345        1/8/96
Jim        Johnson       234        234        1/8/96
Jim        Johnson       234        126        1/8/96
.
.
.
```

The *where* clause need not have an *equality* predicate. It can contain any of the standard operators supported by the database, including > and < operators. Additionally, the *where* clause is not limited to simple predicates. It can be a combination of predicates joined with AND and OR operators. The following query finds the last name of employees who have worked more than five hours on a Friday. Note that the *where* clause contains two predicates. One is the join condition for the two tables (employee and timesheet). The other limits the result set to only those employees who worked more than five hours.

```
select employee.emp_id, employee.lname
from employee, timesheet
where employee.emp_id = timesheet.emp_id
and timesheet.f_hrs > 5
```

Result:

```
emp_id     lname
---------- ------------------------------
498        Fox
```

Joins are an integral part of relational databases. It is beyond the scope of this book to consider all the varieties of joins, such as three-way joins, four-way joins, and joins of a table with itself. You are encouraged to consult many of the texts available on the subject.

Because of their importance, joins also have a significant impact on how fast your queries are performed. This can be analyzed at two levels. First, the types of joins needed to retrieve information are usually dictated by the way a database is designed. So when you design your database, always keep in mind how you are going to retrieve information from it. If you find a query that requires a four-way join of large tables, then you need to reconsider the database design.

The second level of analysis is within the database program. Database systems offer a variety of optimization techniques that speed up queries and joins. Indexes are the most common method. In the timesheet tracking example, the emp_id field should be indexed for faster access to its contents. As a result, joins based on the emp_id field will be faster. Some databases might require creation of an intermediate temporary table as they perform complicated joins. By storing such tables on fast disks or virtual disks, you can greatly enhance speed. Make an effort to familiarize yourself with your database system and see what tools it offers you for optimization of queries.

Sub-queries

Sub-queries and joins are very similar. Sub-queries allow you to include a query as the *where* clause instead of a simple expression. Multiple nesting levels are allowed, but depending on the database some restrictions apply. Sometimes, it is easier to visualize a query intuitively as a sub-query rather than a join query. Most databases are smart enough to internally translate the sub-query to a join query for optimized performance. The following shows a query expressed both as a join query and a sub-query. The result is the same in both cases.

Join Query:

```
select employee.emp_id, employee.lname
from employee, timesheet
where employee.emp_id = timesheet.emp_id
and timesheet.f_hrs > 5
```

Result:

emp_id	lname
498	Fox

Sub-Query:

```
select emp_id, lname
from employee
where employee.emp_id in
   (select emp_id
    from timesheet
    where timesheet.f_hrs > 5)
```

Result:

emp_id	lname
498	Fox

Union

Sometimes the information you seek is included in two or more tables. Suppose you have three tables, each including the subscription information to a particular magazine. In such an environment your routine operations involve only one of the three tables; however, it is possible to query each table and combine your results into a single result set. Of course, this is only possible if the tables have one or more common fields with the same field names. The UNION operation is your tool for making such a query. Here is an example:

```
select name, address
from magazine_a
where zipcode = "12345"
union
select name, address
from magazine_b
where zipcode = "12345"
```

The above query removes any redundant rows in its result set. That is, if an individual whose zip code is 12345 has subscribed to both magazines, then his or her name will be included in the result set only once. If you need the duplicates, then you can use the UNION ALL operation.

It is possible to perform a UNION operation on a single table. The result is the same as using the OR operator in the *where* clause. Consider the following:

```
select lname
from employee
where emp_id = 123 OR emp_id = 345
```

Result:

```
lname
-----------------------------
Jones
```

The above query can be expressed with a UNION operation.

```
select lname
from employee
where emp_id = 123
union
select lname
from employee
where emp_id = 345
```

Result:

```
lname
-----------------------------
Jones
```

Modifying Data

So far you have learned how to put your data into a database and how to retrieve selected subsets of data. It is very common for data to change over periods of time. Some information, such as the share price for a company, can change by the minute. Other information, such as the annual gross revenue, takes longer to change. In either case, data changes, meaning the database must be able to modify its data. SQL offers two commands for this purpose: UPDATE and DELETE. Note that in our discussion we consider deletion a form of modification. The syntax is similar to the SELECT statement, but the results of the commands are different. While the SELECT statement outputs its result to the terminal (or sends it to the client), the UPDATE and DELETE operations make modifications to the result set. Here is the syntax for the UPDATE statement:

```
UPDATE table_name
SET col_name1 = expression,
    col_name2 = expression, ...
where search_condition
```

For example, the following would change the first name of employee number 234 to James.

```
UPDATE employee
SET fname = 'James'
WHERE emp_no = 234
```

You can also delete an entire row from a table using the DELETE command. The syntax is

```
DELETE from table_name
where search_condition
```

To delete the record for employee number 234, you would issue the following command:

```
DELETE from employee
where emp_no = 234
```

Pay close attention to the *where* clause of these statements. Note that the *where* clause is how we specify which records need to be changed. It is very important to uniquely identify a record; that is why key columns and their uniqueness are imperative in database operations.

Modifications of information in a relational database can be tricky at times. Because of the relational model and the interdependence of tables, modifications usually affect more than one table. It is up to the designer to assure that a modification is made in the proper manner. For example, emp_id is a key used in all three tables. By removing an employee from the employee table, you violate the referential integrity of the database since there are records in the other two tables using the employee number you just removed. You must design your UPDATE and DELETE statements so that they take care of all affected tables.

Changing non-key columns is not as complicated. For example, you need to change the last name of an employee in only one table. Because the employee is identified throughout the rest of the database by his or her number, the name change automatically affects the entire database. This is a very attractive feature of the relational model.

Functions

SQL implementations offer a number of built-in functions that can be used in expressions of SQL statements. These functions perform an operation in their argument before that argument is sent to the server for processing. For example:

```
select substring(employee.lname, 1, 3)
from employee
where upper(employee.lname) = "JONES"
```

Result:

```
---
Jon
```

The above example is using two functions. The first is SUBSTR(), which extracts a substring from a string, and the second is UPPER(), which converts its string argument to uppercase. Most SQL implementations offer functions in the following areas:

- Character and string manipulation
- Mathematical functions
- Date and time functions
- System function

Functions can be both useful and harmful. In certain cases, you might be able to avoid performing an expensive join operation by using one or two functions. In others, you might be performing a function when it really is not needed. For example, if the last names of employees were stored as uppercase letters, then there is no need to call the UPPER() function in the query. That is, the UPPER() function does not need to be performed on every row as the select command tries to find a matching result set. Study the functions offered by your database. Chances are you can avoid several lines of code by using one of the built-in functions from your database. In cases where you need information about the database itself or the system, built-in functions might be your only method.

Backup and Recovery

Depending on the size of your database and the operation of your organization, you might have a designated database administrator. This person is responsible for keeping the database system operational at all times. One of the most important duties of a database administrator is backup and recovery of the database. If such a position is absent from your organization, then you might have to perform backup and recovery on your own. While some databases count on the user to backup the data files, others offer extensive backup and recovery tools. In any case, you should be aware of how your database treats this very important issue. You should make a log of when backups were created and what data they contain. You should also have a plan for how to recover the data if disaster strikes. Develop several scenarios in which different portions of your database are damaged and decide what steps should be taken to recover the lost information.

Locks

Recall that the HTTP server listens to a designated port for requests from clients. Once a client has requested execution of an external program, that program is run. In the UNIX environment, multiple requests can be handled by launching multiple copies of the external program. As shown in Figure 6-12, it is possible that each external program needs to modify the same portion of the data. The question is which program gets priority.

As with any network access to a database, locking mechanisms are used to accomplish conflict resolution. Some databases perform this action automatically, while others require the programmer to lock the data he or she plans to modify. Issues related to locking and its performance implications are too extensive to be covered in this book. We mention it as a reminder that a Web database does need locking since it is possible to have multiple instances of the external program running simultaneously.

A Word on Data Integrity

As discussed before, multiple tables used by the same program are a popular way to design complicated applications. This design allows the programmer to group the data into several tables, each containing a set of logically related information. Such a division simplifies the overall task, since each module deals with only one table in a somewhat independent way. It also helps better define the problem in a more structured and modular way. Each table holds information that is coherent and related in a logical manner. One requirement arising from this design is that such tables must have a common *key* field to *link* them together.

FIGURE 6-12

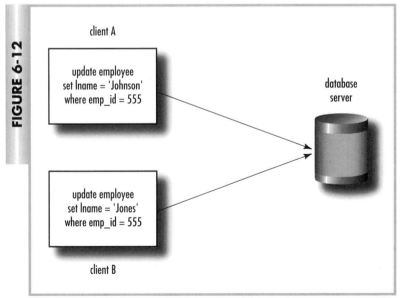

Two instances of an application modifying the same data

Due to its nature, the key field(s) must be unique. If two employees have the same identification number, then retrieval of their hours will become impossible, since there is no way to distinguish which record belongs to which person. There are many ways to create unique keys. The simplest approach is to use a number that is known to be unique, such as a social security number. Another approach is to generate your own unique keys. For example, you can use a hash function that takes several keys, chops them up, and mixes them together to obtain a key. The following hash function creates a key based on four different pieces of information. Note that the choice of what information is used in the hash function and how the different parts are mixed together is somewhat arbitrary.

1. Last name (characters 2-11);

2. First name (characters 1-2);

3. Number of seconds elapsed since the beginning of the current year;

4. The last two digits of the current year (for example, 93 for 1993).

The data is concatenated to form a string of characters. For example, suppose there is an employee by the name of *Kelli Blaire*. The above algorithm is applied as shown:

1. Characters 2 to 11 of the last name are taken. In cases where the last name is smaller than 11 characters, the remaining slots are filled with asterisks. By performing this operation the string "laire******" is obtained.

2. The first and second characters from the first name are taken to form the string "Ke."

3. The number of seconds elapsed since the beginning of the current year can be obtained using one of the database functions.

4. Similarly, the last two digits of the current year can be obtained from a database function. The resulting key will be something similar to the following: "laire******Ke543678596." Due to its structure, uniqueness of such a field is almost guaranteed, since the probability of entering two people with the same first and last name, at the same exact time, is very remote. And so the uniqueness criterion for the common field is met.

Database Systems

As mentioned before, SQL is merely a standard. For it to be useful, it needs to be implemented in a database system. There are a number of database systems on the market, ranging from packages written for mainframe machines to smaller ones targeted for desktop computers. The most common method of communication between an application and a database is through a set of function calls. Each vendor has its own set of function calls for database communication. We refer to these functions as the database API (Application Programmer Interface). Using the API, an application programmer can connect to a database, perform a query, and retrieve the result set.

Generally, database systems can be grouped into two categories: local and network systems. An example of a local database is shown in Figure 6-13. Here the database resides on the same machine as the client program. The client makes direct calls to the database back-end.

Network databases follow a different structure, as shown in Figure 6-14. These systems make a call to a network library which then transfers the request to the database back-end which, in most cases, resides on another machine. The result is sent back by the network library and passed onto the client program.

The choice of a database system is an important one that usually involves more than its Web applications. Database systems usually comprise an integral part of the operations of an organization, so the decision process takes a long time. Table 6-8 shows a listing of some of the more popular database systems along with a URL for more information. Chapter 9, "Choosing the Right Tool," discusses some of the issues involved with using each database in a Web environment.

FIGURE 6-13

Local database system

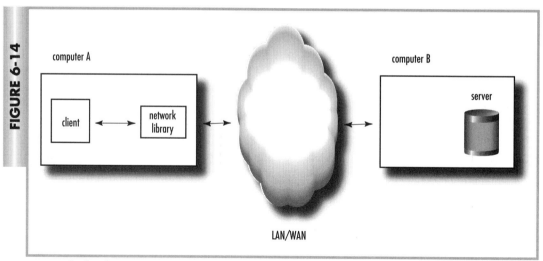

FIGURE 6-14

Network database system

Table 6-8 Some popular database systems

Database system	URL for more information
Oracle	http://www.oracle.com
Sybase	http://www.sybase.com
MS SQL Server	http://www.microsoft.com/SQL/default.htm
Informix	http://www.informix.com
FoxPro	http://www.microsoft.com/FoxPro/
MS Access	http://www.microsoft.com/MSAccess/
FileMaker PRO	http://www.claris.com/
Paradox	http://www.borland.com

Summary

Database systems are the main tools for managing information. As with the World Wide Web, databases follow a client/server model. The server is responsible for management of the data in a physical sense, and it responds to requests made by its authorized clients. The client program provides the graphical user interface and should give the user a high-level view of the database. The client is responsible for making queries to the database, usually in SQL, and presenting the results sent back by the server.

A database is a collection of information arranged in units called tables. Tables organize the data in a row/column format. Each row is called a record, and each column is referred to as a field. If a single table is used to organize the data, then the approach is called a flat data layout. If multiple tables with links are used to organize the data, then the relational model is used.

SQL offers a standardized and consistent interface to data manipulation. It incorporates all the functions a database system must perform into a single language. Examples of such functions include creation of data objects, insertion of data, querying the data, and data modification. Queries are the most common task performed by a database system. Careful design of the database and its organization will lead to better performance. Join queries, sub-queries, and unions are special types of queries that exploit the true potential of the relational data model.

Questions

1. What is the role of a database server?

2. What does a database client do?

3. T/F: Tables are composed of a collection of databases.

4. What is a record in a table?

5. T/F: A table can have two identical rows.

6. T/F: A table can have two identical columns.

7. What is a key column?

8. What is a join query?

Answers

1. Physical access to the data and physical modification of the data as requested by the client.

2. Present a user interface and establish communication with the server.

3. False. A database is a collection of groups tables.

4. A row in a table is also referred to as a record.

5. False. If the two rows are identical, then there is no way to distinguish between them. This goes against the relational data model.

6. False. Each attribute is stored as a column (field). You cannot have two fields with the same name which basically means you are keeping track of the same attribute twice.

7. A column that is guaranteed to be unique for each record is a key column.

8. A join query uses columns (usually key columns) from two or more tables to extract certain information contained in those tables.

PART II:
Creating the
Application

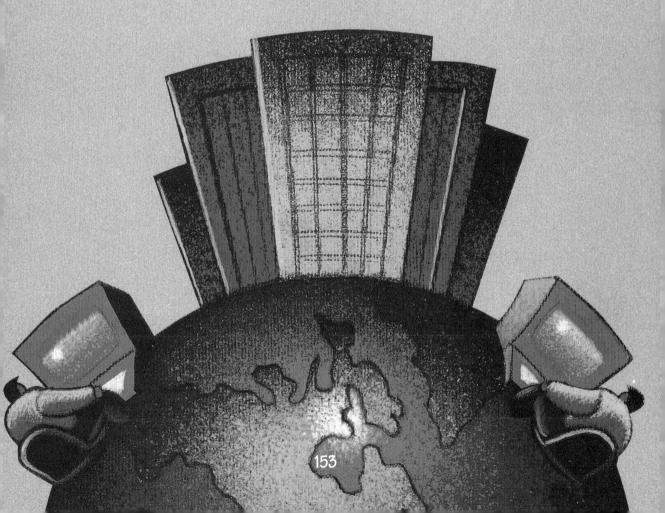

7
Application Design

In order to develop a front end for a database using the Web, you need to set up a development environment. You have a lot of flexibility in choosing your tools. New development products enter the market almost daily. The major components of your development environment are

- **HTTP server:** You will need to make a server available to users of your application. You will develop your CGI programs to work on this server.

- **HTTP client:** To test your server and your application as it is being developed, you will need an appropriate Web browser.

- **Compiler/interpreter:** Regardless of the language with which you choose to develop your CGI application, you will need either a compiler or an interpreter. If the Web server offers direct connectivity to the database server, you can ignore this component.

- **Database system:** Your CGI application needs a database system for its data manipulation operations. This can be a sophisticated system like Sybase or a simple tab delimited text file to store user input.

These requirements are discussed separately. This chapter also includes a discussion of the software methodology used for Web application development.

HTTP Server

You may or may not already have an HTTP server. If one already is installed, then you need to ask your system administrator for proper permissions so that you can develop your application. Otherwise, you need to set up the server from scratch. In either case, there are some questions with answers that are imperative for both setting up the server and designing the

155

application. The following sections describe each of these questions, why its answer is important, and how you can get the answer.

Windows and Macintosh Servers

These sections assume a UNIX development environment. Some of the specifics might be different on other platforms, but the general guidelines apply to all HTTP servers. In general, setting up servers on Windows or Macintosh systems is more straightforward than on their UNIX counterparts.

Machine's IP Number

The IP number is like a postal address. It is the address for a given machine on the Internet. Look at the file /etc/hosts. It should have the IP number of your machine along with some of the other machines in your network domain. Also, when you use telnet to connect to a machine, it usually outputs the IP number of the target machine. This is another way to find the IP number of a machine.

Machine's Name

IP numbers work well by uniquely identifying a computer, but a 12-digit number is hard to remember. Most machines also have a name associated with them. There is direct mapping between the name and the IP number. The hostname command gives you the name of the machine. This name, along with the domain name, is what is used to compose a URL to the HTTP server running on your machine. For example, if your machine's name is sarek and the network domain name for it is market.xyz.com, the URL would be `http://sarek.market.xyz.com`.

Superuser Password

Recall that the default port number for an HTTP server is 80. Clients send their requests to this port and assume that the server is listening to it. Under UNIX, normally port numbers less than 1,024 can only be used by processes which are started by the superuser. You need to know the superuser password for your machine in order to start the HTTP process with port 80 as its default port. Figure 7-1 shows the relationship between port numbers and HTTP.

Memory Size, Disk Space, and So On

You should have a general idea of how much memory your computer has, how much free disk space is contains, and other similar information. You will need this information as you optimize your application and consider ways to make it more efficient. In IRIX, the hinv command gives you hardware parameters, including the memory size as shown below:

```
Iris Audio Processor: version A2 revision 4.1.0
1 134 MHZ IP22 Processor
```

```
FPU: MIPS R4610 Floating Point Chip Revision: 2.0
CPU: MIPS R4600 Processor Chip Revision: 2.0
On-board serial ports: 2
On-board bi-directional parallel port
Data cache size: 16 Kbytes
Instruction cache size: 16 Kbytes
Main memory size: 64 Mbytes
Integral ISDN: Basic Rate Interface unit 0, revision 1.0
Integral Ethernet: ec0, version 1
Integral SCSI controller 0: Version WD33C93B, revision D
Disk drive: unit 1 on SCSI controller 0
Graphics board: Indy 8-bit
Vino video: unit 0, revision 0, IndyCam connected
```

Other UNIX flavors offer their own native command for hardware information. The df command gives you information about your hard drive and the percentage of free space as shown below:

```
Filesystem              Type  blocks      use     avail %use  Mounted on
/dev/root               efs 1869744 1611471  258273  86%  /
```

You should also check to see what other servers are running on your machine. You might have a database server or an anonymous ftp server running on your computer. Running too many servers on one machine can degrade the overall performance. The ps command lists the processes running on your machine which you started. To get a listing of all processes on the machine, including those started by the superuser (root), you will have to provide additional flags to the command. On IRIX, ps -elf produces the desired result, a subset of which is shown here. Note that each process name is listed along with its owner, its status, it process number, its parent's process number, how long it has been running, and some other information which depends on your UNIX implementation. The httpd processes are the Web server's and are shown in bold type.

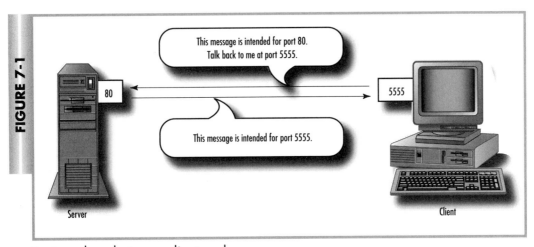

FIGURE 7-1

Port numbers between client and server

```
F S     UID   PID  PPID  C PRI NI  P   SZ:RSS   WCHAN    STIME TTY    TIME COMD
39 S    root    0    0   0  39 RT  *    0:0    8819a640 08:13:46 ?    0:01 sched
39 S    root    5    0   0  39 RT  *    0:0    881a1c80 08:13:46 ?    0:00 pdflush
30 S  user_a  467  463   0  26 20  * 477:80    88f0e7c8 08:14:21 ?    0:00
/usr/local/etc/httpd/httpd
30 S  user_a  468  463   0  26 20  * 475:78    88f0ea20 08:14:21 ?    0:00
/usr/local/etc/httpd/httpd
30 S  user_a  465  463   0  26 20  * 477:80    88f0e318 08:14:21 ?    0:00
/usr/local/etc/httpd/httpd
30 S  user_a  469  463   0  26 20  * 461:55    88f0ec78 08:14:21 ?    0:00
/usr/local/etc/httpd/httpd
30 S  user_a  544  540   1  39 20  * 488:208   88197d40 08:17:19 pts/1 0:02 -tcsh
30 S  user_a  545  543   0  28 20  * 506:243   881983c0 08:17:19 pts/2 0:27 -tcsh
30 R  user_a 1748  544  10  65 20  0 311:73             17:22:43 pts/1 0:00 ps -elf
```

You can also use the top command to get a listing of the top CPU-consuming applications on your machine. The listing is updated periodically to give you a continuous picture of what is happening on your machine. The information provided depends on your UNIX implementation. Usually the process name, its number, its group number, its owner, the percentage of CPU time it is consuming, and how long it has been running are shown. For a detailed explanation of UNIX processes, refer to your UNIX manual. Here is a sample output:

```
IRIX macine_name 5.3 11091812 IP22 Load[0.19,0.15,0.23] 17:23:15   56 procs
 user   pid  pgrp  %cpu  proc  pri  size   rss   time  command
 root   454   454 15.16    *    71  1989  1011   8:35  Xsgi
user_a  522   520  6.49    *    26  1753   814   0:31  ov
user_a  528   526  2.16    *    60   716   260   2:53  xeyes
user_a  508   486  1.59    *    26  1592   764   0:31  4Dwm
user_a  519   486  1.09    *    26  2260   799   0:11  desktopManager
user_a 1749  1749  0.80    0    61   422   123   0:00  top
user_a  540   538  0.24    *    26   761   307   0:14  xwsh
user_a 1750  1750  0.17    *    26   806   308   0:00  xedit
user_a  525   523  0.10    *    26   785   282   0:36  xclock
user_a  514   486  0.10    *    26  1205   472   0:01  toolchest
user_a  543   541  0.09    *    26   755   301   0:10  xwsh
 root     4     0  0.03    *   +39     0     0   0:01  vfs_sync
 root   473   473  0.02    *    26   744   133   0:00  xdm
 root   470   434  0.02    *    26 33467   466   0:01  objectserver
 root     3     0  0.01    *   +39     0     0   0:05  bdflush
```

Setting Up the HTTP Server

There are a number of servers you can use. As with any product, what distinguishes the different servers is the extra functionality they offer along with their efficiency. This section describes the installation of the NCSA HTTP server, version 1.5. You can download it from `http://hoohoo.ncsa.uiuc.edu/`.

Depending on your platform, you might be able to find a compiled version of the software. Otherwise, you will need to get the source code and compile it yourself. As of the writing of this book, binaries were provided for the following platforms

- IRIX 4.0.5 - SGI Indigo
- IRIX 5.3 - SGI Indy
- SunOS 4.1.3 / Solaris 1.x - SPARCserver 690MP
- SunOS 5.4 / Solaris 2.4 x86 - Pentium 90
- SunOS 5.4 / Solaris 2.4 SPARC - SPARCstation 20
- SunOS 5.3 / Solaris 2.3 SPARC - SPARCstation 20
- AIX 3.2.5 - IBM RS/6000 Model 550
- HP-UX 9.05 - HP 9000 Model 715
- OSF/1 3.0 - Dec Alpha
- Ultrix 4.0 - Dec Mips 3100
- Linux 1.2.13, libc 5.0.9 ELF - Pentium 120

Once you bring the file to your machine, you will need to uncompress it and then expand it. The following commands perform these functions, respectively:

```
uncompress filename
tar -xvf filename
```

The recommended place to put all the files is under the following directory path:

```
/usr/local/etc/httpd
```

This path is normally owned by the root. You need the superuser password before you can write to this directory. After the expansion, the above directory path should contain the following:

```
BUGS
CHANGES
COPYRIGHT
```

```
CREDITS
Makefile
README
cgi-bin/
cgi-src/
conf/
htdocs/
httpd*
icons/
logs/
src/
support/
```

Here is a brief description of a few of the entries:

cgi-bin

This directory will include any CGI script or program that you write. By default, any URL pointing to this directory will be executed rather than served. Due to its sensitive nature, you need to disable any unnecessary file and directory permissions in the cgi-bin directory. All files here should have execution permission. The directory generally should not have any write permissions by users other than root (superuser). Chapter 11, "Security Issues," discusses some of the security issues arising from the way the cgi-bin directory is set up.

cgi-src

This is a convenient directory for placing the source files of the programs which reside under the cgi-bin directory. Ideally, you want to keep a one-to-one correspondence between the contents of the cgi-bin directory and the entries in the cgi-src directory.

conf

This directory contains all the configuration files for the server. Some of the configuration parameters can be changed while the server is running, yet others require you to restart the server for them to take effect. The configuration files are well-commented so that you can see what each option does and how you can change it. Take a moment to read through the configuration files. For most cases, you do not need to make any changes.

 Development Port

Some servers allow you to map a port number to a particular directory. This is convenient when trying to maintain a development and a production version of your application. In such a case, the URL http://www.xyz.com/welcome.cgi would run the production version of the script called welcome.cgi. Similarly, the URL http://www.xyz.com:7000/welcome.cgi would run the development version of the script welcome.cgi which resides in a different directory than the production version. Check your server's documentation for availability of this option.

htdocs

By default, this is the directory from which documents are served. A URL of the form `http://sarek.xyc.com` points to this directory. The HTTP server does not allow the client to access files outside of the htdocs directory unless symbolic links are specifically set up. This directory is also referred to as the document root directory. On a normal file system, a / symbol denotes the root directory or parent of all other directories. Under the Web, the htdocs subdirectory has a similar role for Web documents.

httpd

This is the actual server. It is an executable program. After you become a superuser, you can simply type httpd & to run the server. You can then check and see that the server is running by using the ps command.

Running httpd as a Normal User

You can set up the HTTP server to listen to a port number greater than 1,024 and run it as any user. Simply modify the httpd.conf file and specify a different port number. If you do this, remember to include the port number in any URL you construct to connect to this server. For example, if your server is running on port 5,435 on a host sarek.market.xyz.com, then the URL would become `http://sarek.market.xyz.com:5435`.

Logs

The HTTP server keeps a number of log files about its usage. One of the files is access_log, which records information about all the requests made to the server. There are a number of programs that analyze the log files and produce detailed reports about how your server is being used. Using such programs can help you determine what pages are most frequently served from your server. A number of these programs are available over the Internet. A few are listed here.

- ● Getstats (`http://www.eit.com/software/getstats/getstats.html`) is a C language program that takes the log file from your CERN, NCSA, Plexus, GN, Mac HTTP, or UNIX Gopher server and produces a number of useful statistics.

- ● WWWstat (`http://www.ics.uci.edu/WebSoft/wwwstat/`) is a Perl script program, but it can analyze only NCSA httpd log files.

- ● Wusage (`http://siva.cshl.org/wusage.html`) maintains usage statistics for a WWW server and works with both NCSA and CERN httpd servers.

- Webstat (`http://arpp1.carleton.ca/machttp/doc/util/stats/webstat.html`) analyzes your logs and produces reports about the usage of the Web server.

- WebReporter (`http://www.openmarket.com/products/webreport.html`) analyzes your logs and produces reports about the usage of the Web server.

Another important log file is httpd.pid. This file contains the process number of the server. To shut down the server, you need to supply this number to the kill command. This kills the httpd process, which is equivalent to shutting down the server. Some servers might provide a separate shutdown command.

HTTP Client

To establish communication with the server, you need a client (browser). There are a number of Web browsers available. You should use a browser that your users will most likely use (if you can determine that). The browser should support standard HTML and forms. If you plan on using HTML enhancements, then choose an appropriate browser that supports those enhancements. Most browsers support standard HTML and forms and therefore make good candidates. Throughout this book, the Netscape browser is used. This browser is available from `http://www.netscape.com`.

After installing the browser, put a simple HTML file in your htdocs directory. Assuming that you have named it test.html, the following URL should display this file on your browser:

```
http://server_name/test.html
```

where server_name is the full name of the machine running your HTTP server (for example, frog.xyz.org).

Once you have successfully performed this test, try running one of the CGI programs in the cgi-bin directory. The NCSA server comes with a few programs in the cgi-bin directory. Try the date program, which outputs today's date as known by the server machine. Use the following URL for your test:

```
http://server_name/cgi-bin/date
```

Some machines do not have an entry in the name server. It is perfectly acceptable from a technical point of view to construct a URL based on the machine's IP number rather than its name. A URL of the form `http://129.123.156.23/test.html` is acceptable, but hard to remember.

Compiler/Interpreter

Your development environment must include a compiler or an interpreter, depending on the language in which you choose to develop your CGI programs. Chapter 8, "Choosing a Programming Language," is devoted entirely to a discussion of several languages and their implications in a Web environment. Your goal is to develop optimized CGI programs, since a server could be executing several CGI scripts at once. You want to stay away from huge executables generated by some client/server development programs. Efficiency is one of your top goals.

Database System

You need a database system to support the database operations of your applications. The choice of a database depends on several factors, some of which are beyond the scope of this book. Depending on your platform, you might be limited to what database you can use. Other factors include the language you choose for CGI programs, the expected size of your database, and the expected number of users.

Most UNIX flavors provide a simple database system called DBM. It allows for a collection of *key=value* pairs to be stored in files. The file sizes can grow dramatically as you add more data. For some very simple Web applications, this might be all you need in terms of a database system. Other applications require access to a true database system such as Oracle, Sybase, or Informix. In such cases, you must install the appropriate database client libraries on the machine running your HTTP server. Your CGI programs communicate with the database by making library calls provided in the database client. Most of these libraries are provided for languages written in C. Some databases offer either a direct connection to a Web server or automate the process by allowing you to include SQL statements directly in your HTML documents. Oracle offers such a product. Depending on your application, you might want to consider this class of database products.

You can use the above configuration on a DOS or Windows system. However, such systems have traditionally used simpler database systems. For example, Visual Basic can read and write to database files stored in Microsoft Access format. Similarly, a number of libraries exist for accessing the popular DBF format from a variety of languages, including C. In such cases, your application directly accesses the data files, and there is no database server involved. This reduces the overhead on the machine.

Whatever format you choose, you should purchase a database program such as Microsoft Access, FoxPro, or dBASE. Throughout your development, you will need to make changes to the structure of the database, look at the contents of the different tables, and perform other database-related tasks. While you can perform all of these using the same libraries you use for your CGI programs, having an application specifically designed to interact with the database is a must.

You will not use any of the user interface design functions of the database program you purchase. Remember, the Web is your user interface. Most programs on the market today give you the ability to create complete applications by providing a scripting language, such as Access BASIC. These features are useful when your user runs MS Access as a client, not as a Web application. Similarly, there are a number of tools such as PowerBuilder and Delphi which offer no database function of their own and whose primary purpose is user-interface design. Although such programs can be used to examine the data in a Web development environment, they are not used directly in a Web application.

Application Design

The design of your application is a delicate process. It is best to think about your application from three distinct viewpoints:

- Function
- User interface
- Implementation

This triangular approach is shown in Figure 7-2. The following is a discussion of how each point of view is used to enhance your application.

Function

You need to define the function of your application in high-level terms. It is best to categorize the functions into groups since it makes implementation somewhat easier. For example, you can describe a conference registration application as follows:

FIGURE 7-2

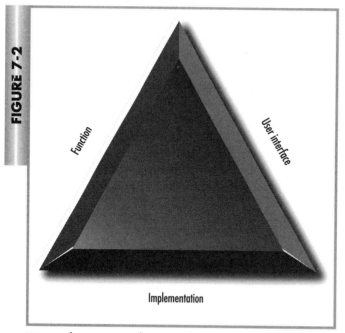

Triangular approach to application design

1. The system will be accessible to all users.

2. It should then check to see if the entry already exists in the database.

3. The program should prompt the user for name, address, phone number, fax number, and e-mail address.

4. If it does not, it should be stored; otherwise, the user should see an appropriate message.

Typically, you would draw a functional diagram of the application similar to a flow chart. The functional diagram should give a visual view of what the program does, not how it does it. The simple functional diagram for the conference registration system is shown in Figure 7-3.

FIGURE 7-3

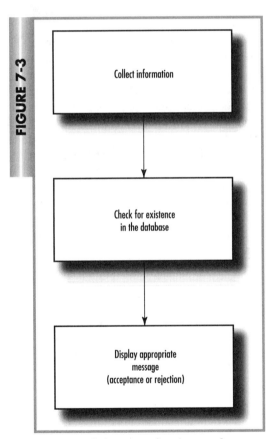

Functional diagram for the conference registration system

If you need to discuss the requirements of the application with management or end users, this should be the level of your discussion. Do not think about the implementation details, nor the user interface at this level. Those details come later. With a solid understanding of the function of your program, you can begin designing the user interface.

User Interface

The user interface of a program is the middle ground between the functional viewpoint of the application and the actual implementation. Normally, it is better to start from the functional end of the spectrum and work your way toward implementation, skewing the user interface toward the functional viewpoint. There are instances, however, where the implementation dictates how the user interface should look. For example, there is no construct in HTML for a graphical scale. Many programs use a scale (similar to a scroll bar) to show the progress of an operation. This is an instance in which the implementation dictates how the user interface should look.

With a detailed functional diagram, it is easy to design a user interface. For the conference registration system, you will most likely use simple text boxes for the necessary input. Since all state abbreviations are two letters, you might decide to provide only enough space for two characters in the state text box. Similarly, you can limit the number of characters in the ZIP CODE text box to five. There are some books that discuss psychological aspects of user interfaces. Issues such as when to use a list instead of a pop-up menu or how you should place the different components of the interface on the screen are analyzed in those texts. Another source of information is a style guide which your company might already have developed.

In most cases, the look of your interface has a great impact on how effective it is. Consider the two user interfaces for the conference registration system shown in Figures 7-4 and 7-5. They both perform the same function; that is, they accept a set amount of information from the user. But one seems more effective than the other simply because of its layout and visual appeal.

FIGURE 7-4

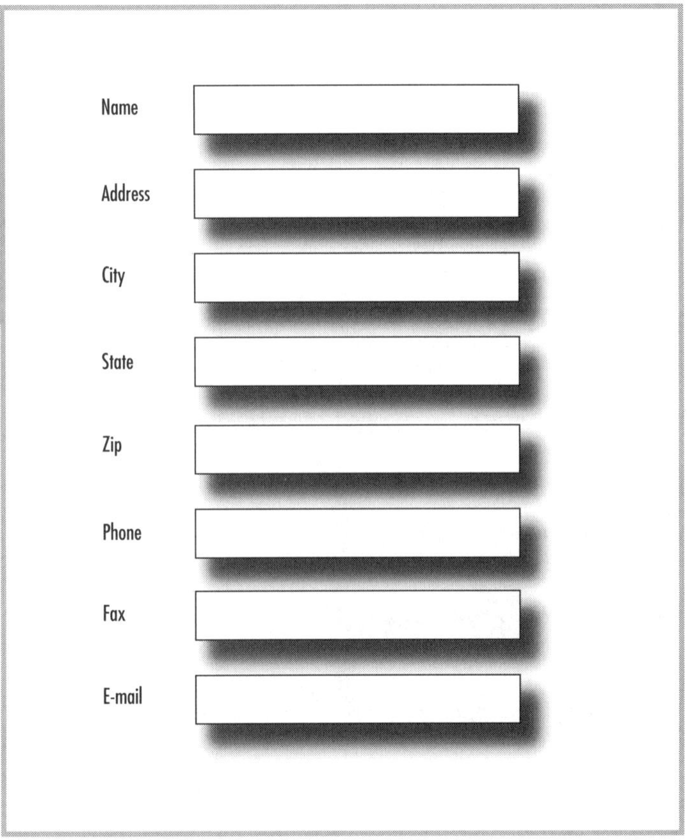

Name

Address

City

State

Zip

Phone

Fax

E-mail

Bad user interface

FIGURE 7-5

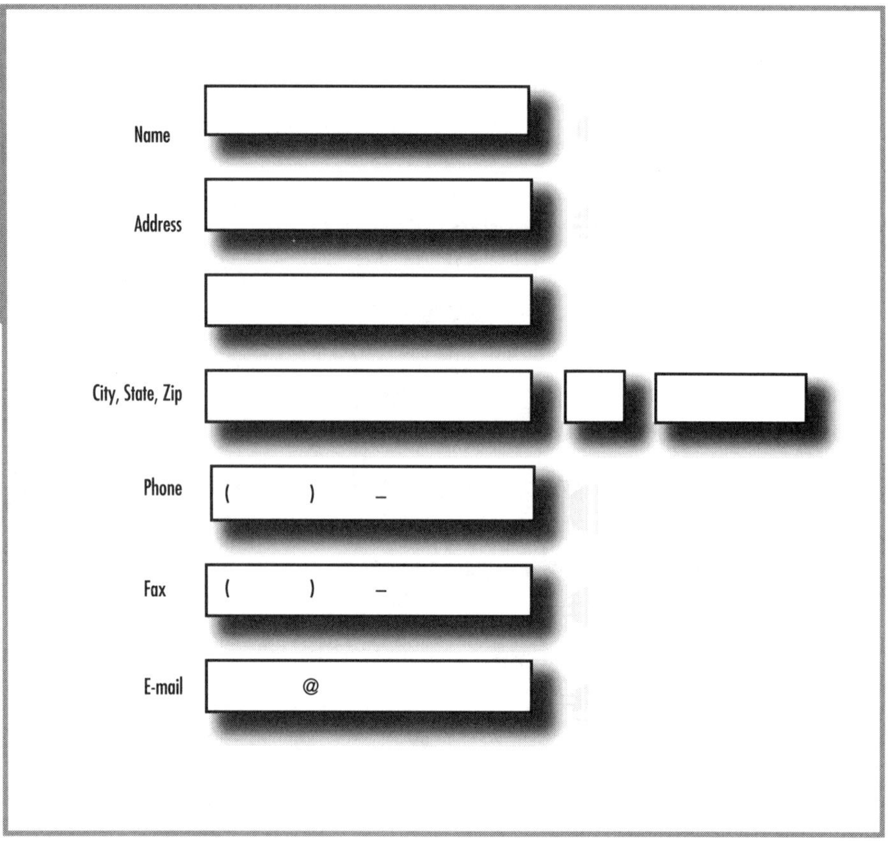

Name	
Address	
City, State, Zip	
Phone	( ) –
Fax	( ) –
E-mail	@

Attractive user interface

Implementation

Implementation is strictly a programming issue. It dictates what happens beneath the user interface level. Obviously, the programming language has a direct influence on the implementation details. This is the level in which you define the variables you need for your program, any subroutine or function calls or any external libraries you need, and other similar specifications. Just like any development environment, the Web application environment takes some time to get used to. All the usual software engineering principles and application development principles apply. However, the Web environment has some features which are specific to itself, and any developer should become familiar with these points.

Open Architecture

Perhaps the most important difference from other client/server development environments is the Web's truly open architecture. In traditional client/server systems, you have a very good idea of what is available on the server side and on the client side. After all, you are developing the client application and probably will help in its installation and support. By providing a Web database, you are dealing with a global audience, unless you implement password protection and other security measures to intentionally limit your audience, or unless you intend to run your application on your intranet. You really don't have much control over the client side. Your main interaction is with the Web server, the CGI programs, and the database system. This distinction is shown in Figure 7-6.

By changing any of the these components, you can affect the application and its performance. Of course, your goal is to hide as many implementation details as possible from the users. For example, if you change your database system, your users should not feel any changes in the application.

With such global impact, it is imperative that you maintain a development and production version of all the software involved. You simply do not want to change a CGI program and inadvertently introduce a bug. The result becomes apparent to your users instantaneously. Also, it might be a good idea to use two different machines, each dedicated to either development or production.

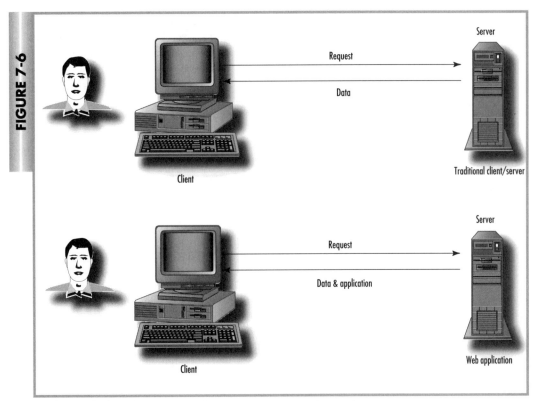

FIGURE 7-6

Traditional client/server applications versus Web applications

Running Two Servers on the Same Machine

If your system resources allow it, you can run more than one HTTP server on the same machine. You employ the same procedure used to set up the original server, but you place the second server under a different directory and configure it so that it listens to a nonstandard port. Also, you can maintain two source code directories: one for the development version and one for the production version.

You also need to keep the production and development versions of the data separate. The best approach is to extract a subset of your production database, store it in its own database, and use it as the development version.

It is a good idea to protect your development version with passwords and other access control mechanisms. For example, it is possible to protect a given Web page with a password. When a client requests that the page be served, the HTTP server asks the client to provide a user name and a password. It then compares the information to what it has stored in its database and decides whether the page should be served or not. This process is shown in Figure 7-7. Your application usually has a main page which is the initial entry point to the application. You should protect this page with a password.

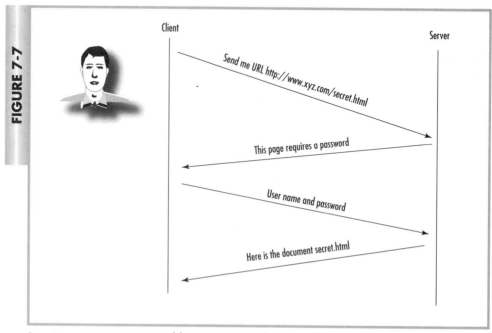

FIGURE 7-7

Serving a page protected by a password

If your operating system has access control features, change the permissions of the files and directories containing the source code to your CGI programs so that only you and other programmers in your development team can change them. You might also want to discuss the possibility of using source revision control systems such as RCS with your system administrator. Protection of the data itself is also important. If your database allows it, limit the permissions on the development version of the data. By creating a controlled environment, you decrease the number of ways bugs can be introduced into your application, and you increase your chances of finding and solving problems.

Code Execution on the Client

From an implementation point of view, there is another huge difference between Web database applications and ordinary client/server applications. Suppose you have a customer look-up application written in Visual Basic. Figure 7-8 shows the main user interface screen for this application.

You fill in at least one of the given fields, and the application creates an appropriate SQL to search the customer database. The same user interface can be implemented using HTML commands. However, there remains a major difference between the two applications. The Visual Basic application has processing power. It can read the user input and perform some function on it before it is sent to the database server. For example, if an alphabetic character is entered in the Zip code field, the application can generate an error message *before* any contact is made to the server.

A Web application has no processing power until the content of the form reaches the CGI program. That is when your application becomes aware of what the user has entered and can generate an error message or perform other actions as necessary. From the time

FIGURE 7-8

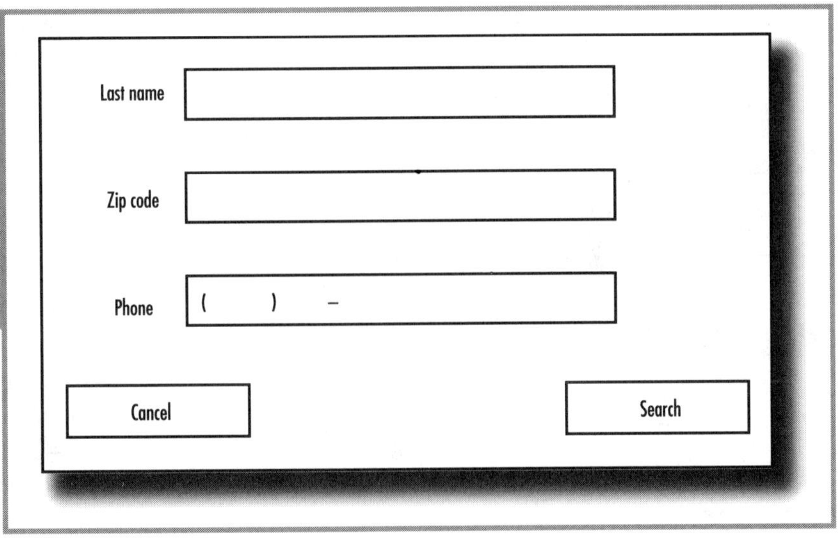

Customer look-up application

the user fills in a field, a complete round-trip communication has to be made to the HTTP server before the user is notified about an error in the entry. This difference is depicted in Figure 7-9. This limitation (if it can be called a limitation) brings about simplicity to Web applications, but programmers should be aware of it as they develop their applications.

In an effort to address this problem, Netscape browsers support JavaScripts (formerly known as LiveScripts). JavaScripts are code segments executed on the HTTP client machine. Using JavaScripts, you can perform data validation before the data is sent to the HTTP server. The CGI application will not know what the user has entered until the data is sent to the server, but at least some verification is done on the data, and in case of error, a round-trip communication between the client and the server can be avoided. Of course, you can only use this approach if you know your clients are using a Netscape browser or another browser which supports JavaScripts.

A more elegant solution is using the Java language and Java applets to provide the user interface to your application. With Java applets, the entire picture changes. Now, your HTTP server not only serves the requested document to the client, but also serves your *application* in the form of a Java applet. The Java applet then establishes direct communication to the database if the database supports it and the database client is available on the machine

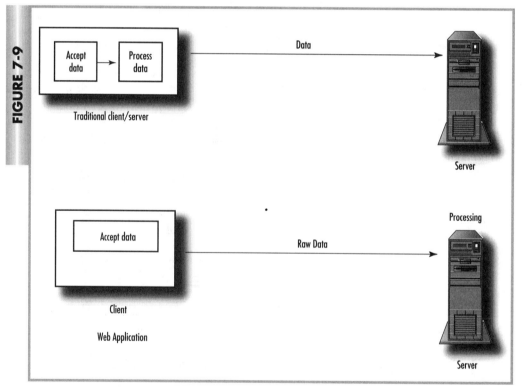

FIGURE 7-9

Processing is done at different points

running the HTTP client, or it establishes communication with a CGI program which in turn connects to the database. We discuss Java in the next chapter.

Stateless Environment

Another important characteristic of Web applications is that they run in a stateless environment. The HTTP protocol (on which Web applications are based) is stateless; that is, the application cannot keep track of its previous actions. Going back to the Visual Basic application, it can internally keep track of what it has done by using variables or a stack. Consider the transaction depicted in Figure 7-10.

The application sends a query to a database, requesting all customers whose address includes the 12345 Zip code. The server sends back a list. Seeing that there is more than one entry in the list, the application limits its search by specifying the last name of the customer and sends another query to the database. This time only one entry is returned from the database, and the operator can perform the necessary modification on this customer's record. Notice how the application keeps track of its interaction with the database and modifies its search query interactively.

What would happen if you developed this application using a Web database? Due to the stateless nature of the HTTP protocol, internal tracking needs to be implemented differently. Let's follow the steps. A user enters a URL to access the main form of your Web application. He or she then enters a Zip code and submits the form. Your CGI program receives the form, processes it, submits a query to the database, and returns the result to the client.

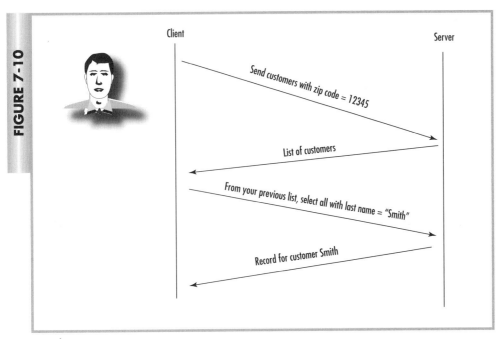

FIGURE 7-10

Client

Server

Send customers with zip code = 12345

List of customers

From your previous list, select all with last name = "Smith"

Record for customer Smith

Database transaction

When the user adds a last name to the search and submits the form, the CGI program treats the request as a *completely new* request. It has no sense of knowing that the request is coming from the same user. It blindly creates a query, sends it to the database, and returns the result to the client.

Most client/server applications—specifically database applications—perform transactions which consist of several steps. Implementation of transactions in Web applications requires careful considerations in the design stage. The most common method is to include a hidden text field in the form, which includes a transaction identification number. This field can be created using a construct similar to the following:

```
<input type = hidden name = tran_id value = tran_id>
```

With such a value, the CGI application can distinguish between the different form contents submitted to it and perform differently as required. Another approach to overcome the stateless mode of the HTTP protocol is to use Java applets which, like any programming language, can internally keep track of their transaction state.

Specifying the Program Flow

With an understanding of how applications work in a Web environment and how data flow occurs, you can begin designing effective user interfaces. Anything you want to show the user or any information you need from the user must be coded in an HTML document, which is then sent to the browser. These include error messages, acknowledgment messages, output from your program, and other components of your application. Initially, keeping track of the screens might seem simple, but as your application grows, you will need to spend more time organizing the user interface of your program.

The suggested method for designing the user interface is to separate the task into two levels. In the lower level, you design each individual screen and pay attention to the layout and design of the different components on that page. You have all the HTML tags available to create visually appealing pages. You can use frames to separate your page into meaningful functional parts. Also, tables can be used to place the different components in a tabular format. At this level, your focus is on each individual page. Concentrate on each component and decide whether it can be hard-coded or needs to be generated on the fly.

At a higher level, you consider all the pages together and create links between them. Most often, you will find out that you need a few more pages and will go back to the lower level where you design an individual page. At this stage, you have to choose the chain of events you want in your application. If the user is presented with a form, you need to write an external program to handle the CGI interface for that form. Sometimes different screens are presented to the user based on what he or she entered in the form. All such possibilities must be considered. When considering all the possible states, you end up with something similar to a flow chart that specifies the actions performed by your application. Figure 7-11 shows a simple flow chart for an application used to collect registration entries for a conference.

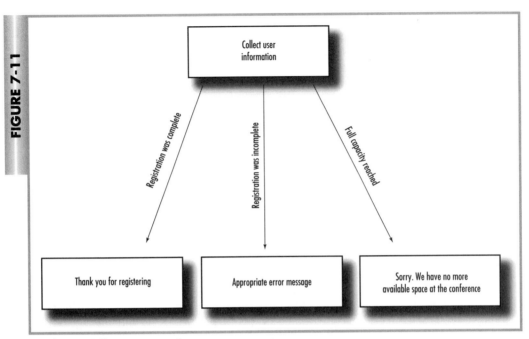

FIGURE 7-11

Application flow in a conference registration system

The main screen provides a form which includes the usual information about the conference attendee. Once that form is submitted, three things can happen:

1. If the form is complete, the information is entered into the database, and an acknowledgment screen is shown to the user.

2. If the form is incomplete or contains errors, then an appropriate error screen is presented.

3. If the deadline for registration has passed or the conference has reached its capacity, then an appropriate message is shown.

Creation of such diagrams also helps you code your CGI programs. Once the program receives the form input, it follows the logic you have documented in your flow chart to determine what HTML file it should generate and send to the client.

Summary

Your Web database development environment consists of an HTTP server, HTTP client, compiler/interpreter, and a database system. In order to set up the HTTP server, you need to gather some information about your machine such as its name, IP number, superuser password, memory size, and disk size. Once the server is up and running, you can use the ps command to check for its existence among the many other processes running on your machine. By default, the NCSA HTTP server serves HTML documents from the htdocs subdirectory, executes CGI scripts from the cgi-bin subdirectory, and maintains its configuration files in the conf subdirectory. It also keeps a number of log files in the logs subdirectory. There are several programs available which allow you to analyze these log files and get useful information about your server and its performance.

You can use any of the browsers on the market as long as they support forms and any HTML enhancements you plan on using in your applications, such as frames, tables, and JavaScripts. You can test your server by forming a URL that points to a document on it and examining the document.

Your development environment also needs a compiler or an interpreter, depending on the language you decide to use for programming your CGI scripts. You also need a database system on which to store your data. Many choices exist, ranging from enterprise systems such as Sybase to smaller systems such as MS Access or FoxPro.

In designing your application, you should consider three different viewpoints: function, user interface, and implementation. You should consider the global nature of your audience for your Web application and keep in mind that changes in your program will be noticed instantaneously by all the clients. You also need to consider the stateless nature of the HTTP protocol and how it plays a role in database transactions which consist of two or more phases.

Questions

1. What are the four main components of a Web development environment?

2. Why do you need the root password on a UNIX workstation in order to start the HTTP server?

3. What is the purpose of the htdocs directory?

4. What does the cgi-bin directory contain?

5. Where would you look to change the default port for your server?

6. What are the three areas of consideration for an application designer?

7. Why is HTTP a stateless protocol?

8. What are the two levels of consideration for a user-interface design?

Answers

1. HTTP server, HTTP client, compiler/interpreter, database system.

2. The default port number for the HTTP protocol is 80. On UNIX machines, port numbers less than 1,024 can be used only by the superuser (root).

3. The htdocs directory is the root directory from which documents are served. Clients can access the files only under this subdirectory unless you specifically grant them permission to look at other parts of your file system.

4. The cgi-bin directory contains executable CGI programs and scripts. Any URL pointing to this directory is executed by the server rather than served.

5. In the conf subdirectory there is a file called httpd.conf. The port number for the server is set in this file.

6. Function, user interface, and implementation.

7. The server treats each request from clients as a separate request. It has no way of knowing that, for example, two requests are coming from the same client.

8. At a lower level, you consider the individual screens and concentrate on each page's components. At a higher level, you consider all the screens and how they relate to each other.

8

Choosing a Programming Language

As with any development project, the choice of the programming language is an important one. Web application development is no different. However, due to the open architecture of the Web, you have a large pool of programming languages to choose from. This chapter discusses some of the more popular languages and how to use them in a Web environment. If the choice has a distinct advantage or disadvantage compared to other languages, it will be mentioned. The second half of the chapter discusses a relatively new idea: client-side programs. It also discusses the most common of all such programs: JavaScripts and Visual Basic Scripts.

Overview

Programming languages are an integral part of software engineering and its evolution. Early languages were tightly coupled with the hardware they ran on, so tight that they were referred to as *machine* language and *assembly* language. Today, languages are much more complex, and the ability to run the same program on a variety of platforms is heavily emphasized.

In any development project, one of the first questions is what programming language(s) will be used in the project. The answer, of course, depends on several factors, some of which are

- Proficiency of existing developers
- Size of the project
- Type of application

Emergence of New Languages

To show you how important the choice of a programming language can be in a project, consider the following: In a white paper published by Sun Microsystems about Java, the authors confess that during a project, the developers at Sun were unhappy with some of the features of C++ and decided to develop their own language, now known as Java.

In a Web development environment, a few other factors play specific roles in the choice of a language. The most important factor is the database engine you plan on using in your application. Recall that applications usually communicate with the database server using a series of API function calls that are database dependent. Even in cases where middleware such as ODBC is used, your program still must make certain function calls to the ODBC driver. When considering a programming language, you should ask yourself whether the database program supports that language. Almost all databases support C or C++, but some of the new languages such as Java, or languages such as Visual Basic which are platform dependent, do not yet enjoy wide acceptability. (Sun has proposed JDBC, which is similar to ODBC in function and intended for Java application development.) That is why it is important to know your application and where and how it will be used. For example, if you plan on using Visual Basic as your language, keep in mind that porting such an application to a UNIX platform might not be straightforward.

Another issue you should consider is the efficiency in communication between your application and your database. It is always better to have a native connection than to go through middleware. Of course, there are applications where such a configuration is not possible, but if you have a choice, you should opt for the native connection. For example, Visual Basic programs can access a Microsoft Access database both through native calls and through ODBC calls as shown in Figures 8-1 and 8-2, respectively. The preferred method is to make native calls without the extra overhead. So sometimes, the deciding choice is not the language that the database supports, but the language that the middleware program you plan on using supports.

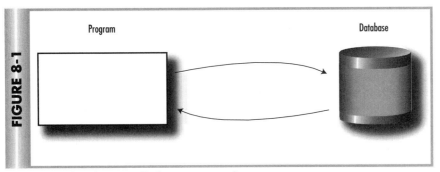

FIGURE 8-1

Direct database calls from a Visual Basic program

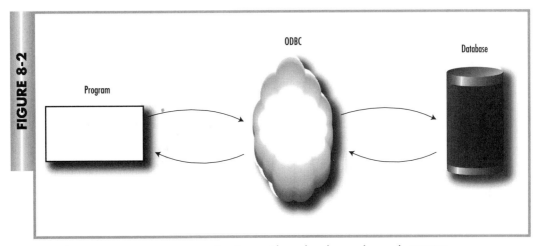

FIGURE 8-2

Visual Basic program communication with a database through ODBC

Legacy Systems

Often in large development projects, your goal is to make a legacy database available over the Web. These projects demand heavy planning and coordination with several groups in the organization. Since the systems are accessed through terminals and often do not support SQL, you have to look around for a product suitable for your project. There is no question that legacy systems are a thing of the past, but many organizations still use them and want the data available on the Web.

Recall that your CGI programs must establish communication with the HTTP server and the database server. Therefore, your choice of programming language might depend on what HTTP server you plan on using. We used the word *might* because CGI implementations differ among servers. Recall that on a UNIX platform, servers communicate with an external program via several channels, one of which is environmental variables. Almost all programming languages and even shell languages have the capability of processing environmental variables, therefore, the HTTP server does not play a great role in making a decision regarding the language you will use in your project. On the PC side (and even on some UNIX machines) another method of communication is through vendor-supplied API libraries. Your program communicates with the HTTP server in a similar manner as it does with the database program. In these situations, you need to be certain that the language you plan on using is supported by your HTTP server.

Based on the above discussion, you can expect a CGI program to include three distinct parts:

1. Code to decode and process form data submitted by the browser

2. Code to communicate with a database

3. Code to generate HTML output to be presented to the user

Consider the following code (Listing 8-1) which is written in Perl. It uses Sybperl (discussed in the next chapter) to establish communication with a Sybase database server. If you don't know Perl, just read along. The following discussion is not about the language, but about the structure of the program.

Listing 8-1 A sample CGI script written in Perl

```perl
#!/usr/local/bin/perl

require "cgi-lib.pl";
print &PrintHeader;

#read the variables passed to us from company form and save it to company

&ReadParse(*input);

$mcompany = $input{'company'};
$maddress1 = $input{'address'};
$mcity = $input{'city'};
$mstate = $input{'state'};
$mzip = $input{'zip'};
$mcountry = $input{'country'};
$mid = $input{'id'};
#=================================================================
use Sybase::DBlib;
$dbh = Sybase::DBlib->dblogin(_username , _password , _server_name , ⇐
_app_name );
$dbh->dbuse('database');
```

```
$sqlcmd = "update company ";
$sqlcmd = $sqlcmd . "address1 = \"$maddress\", ";
$sqlcmd = $sqlcmd . "city = \"$mcity\", ";
$sqlcmd = $sqlcmd . "state = \"$mstate\", ";
$sqlcmd = $sqlcmd . "zip = \"$mzip\", ";
$sqlcmd = $sqlcmd . "country = \"$mcountry\", ";
$sqlcmd = $sqlcmd . "where id = $mid";
$dbh->dbcmd($sqlcmd . "\n");
$dbh->dbsqlexec;
$dbh->dbresults;
#=====================================================================
# Next, search the database for the different products and display them
$sqlcmd = "select distinct product, rtrim(plid) \n";
$sqlcmd = $sqlcmd . "from products \n";
$sqlcmd = $sqlcmd . "where product.cid = $mid \n";

$dbh->dbcmd($sqlcmd . "\n");
$dbh->dbsqlexec;
$dbh->dbresults;

if ($status = $dbh->DBROWS)
{
  while (@data = $dbh->dbnextrow)
  {
    print "<a href=\"http://server_name/cgi-bin/company.pl?plid=" . $data[1] .⇐
"&id=$mid\">" . $data[0] . "</a><br>";
  }
}
```

 Perl Shortcut

SQL commands can be very lengthy for complex queries. The construct $sql-cmd = $sqlcmd . "*string*" is a handy way to break down the long SQL command into smaller parts. The same construct can be even further shortened using the following notation:

```
$sqlcmd .= "string"
```

which, as in the previous case, adds the *string* to the variable $sqlcmd.

The program is broken down into its three main components by a line of the equal sign character. The first portion simply reads the content of the submitted form and stores it in local variables that can be used throughout the Perl script. The next part performs a database operation and updates the existing data stored in the database with the data submitted by the form. Finally, the last part of the script queries the database for the products associated with a company and generates a list of hyperlinks which gets sent back to the browser.

Keeping in mind the previous breakdown, the following section discusses several popular programming languages and how they are used in a Web application development environment.

C

C is one of the most common languages and is used in a wide range of computer programming projects. Its popularity has made it a major player in CGI application development. You can find a C compiler on any platform that has a Web server. In fact, most Web servers and browsers are written in C. You might want to get the source code to the NCSA Web server and its Mosaic browser. There you will find plenty of C code. As you might suspect, a variety of tools exists for handling CGI standards using the C language. Three of these tools are discussed in this section. They are

- cgic
- LIBCGI
- CGIHTML

cgic: An ANSI C Library for CGI Programming

cgic is a library of routines which handle CGI programming tasks at a high level. The author of this library is Thomas Boutell. The latest version, along with complete documentation, can be found at `http://www.boutell.com/cgic/`.

According to the documentation, cgic performs the following tasks:

- Parses form data, correcting for defective and/or inconsistent browsers
- Transparently accepts both GET and POST form data
- Handles line breaks in form fields in a consistent manner
- Provides string, integer, floating-point, and single- and multiple-choice functions to retrieve form data
- Provides bounds checking for numeric fields
- Loads CGI environment variables into C strings which are always non-null
- Provides a way to capture CGI situations for replay in a debugging environment

The main() function of the program is actually defined in the cgic.c file, so your program needs to be linked to this file. Your program must include the cgiMain() function, which is called from main() in cgic. Listing 8-2 shows the general structure of the cgiMain() function.

Listing 8-2 Structure of cgiMain() function

```
int cgiMain() {
cgiHeaderContentType("text/html");
```

```
Company();
Address();                  function
NonExButtons();
RadioButtons();
return 0;
}
```

Note that the first task is to print the content-type for the document generated by the CGI program. In this case, the usual text/html type is used. After that, the CGI program performs various functions which deal with individual form elements. A series of functions is provided to retrieve the content of different form elements such as menus, radio buttons, and text boxes. For example, consider the function Company() shown in Listing 8-3.

It must retrieve the value of the text field company. The function declares a string called company. It then uses cgiFromStringNoNewlines(*parameters*) to actually retrieve the value of this text box. Note that this function takes three parameters:

- the NAME attribute specified in the HTML document

- the variable (actually a pointer) which will store the value

- maximum number of characters allowed

Finally, the program writes its output to cgiOut. Currently, cgiOut is the equivalent of standard output, but this might change in future versions.

Listing 8-3 Company() function

```
void Company() {
char company[81];
cgiFormStringNoNewlines("company", company, 81);
fprintf(cgiOut, "Name: %s<BR>\n", name);
}
```

As mentioned before, there are functions for different form elements. A complete listing can be found in the documentation for the software. A few samples are mentioned below:

- cgiFormCheckboxSingle("*name*") returns cgiFormSuccess or cgiFormNotFound depending on whether or not the checkbox with the specified name is marked.

- cgiFormDoubleBounded("*name*", &*variable_name*, *lower_bound*, *upper_bound*, *default value*) stores the numerical value in *variable_name* whose address is provided. This function eliminates the need for reading numerical fields as text and then converting them to the numeric type.

- cgiFormSelectSingle("*name*", *pointer to acceptable values*, *number of entries*, &*variable_name*, *index of default*) is used to process single-selection menus.

Recall that the CGI standard specifies a number of environmental variables which are set by the server. Depending on the server, it is sometimes unpredictable whether these variables will be null or point to empty strings if an environmental variable is not set. Instead of calling getenv() to determine the value of a variable such as HTTP_USER_AGENT (the browser software being used), it is recommended you use the internal copies of environmental variables held by cgic. They are always valid C strings; in other words, they are never null, although they may point to an empty string.

LIBCGI

LIBCGI is another tool you can use to link your program with the CGI specification. Its approach is more like cgi-lib.pl. The latest version, along with documentation, can be found at **http://wsk.eit.com/wsk/dist/doc/libcgi/libcgi.html**.

The programming interface is very simple. A dynamically allocated list is generated that stores the *name=value* pairs passed on from the server. Your program simply goes through a loop, looking for the different names, getting their values, and assigning the values to the variables declared in your program. Consider Listing 8-4 which demonstrates using LIBCGI.

Listing 8-4 Usage of LIBCGI

```
/*
 * This file is part of the LIBCGI library
 * Copyright 1994 by Enterprise Integration Technologies Corporation
 * This is freeware with commercialization rights reserved; see the
 * LICENSE included in the distribution for specifics.
 */

#include<stdio.h>
#include "cgi.h"

cgi_main(cgi_info *ci) {
 char *parmval(form_entry *, char *);
 form_entry *parms, *p;
 form_entry *get_form_entries(cgi_info *);
 char *name1, *name2;

 print_mimeheader("text/html");

/* get the name=value pairs */
 parms = get_form_entries(ci);
 if (parms) {
  /* extract specific form parameters */
  for(p=parms; p; p = p->next) {
   if (strcasecmp(p->name, "name1")) name1 = p->val;
   else if (strcasecmp(p->name, "name2")) name2 = p->val;
  }
 }
/* free up allocated memory */
 free_form_entries(parms);
}
```

LIBCGI is very simple and efficient, which means you probably will end up writing some of the more complex data handling routines yourself. For example, you have to consider how to process the value of a multiple selection list. Before using LIBCGI, be sure that you are comfortable with pointers and their operation and syntax in structures. LIBCGI is simple, powerful, and has minimum overhead, but if you are not comfortable with pointers, you can spend hours debugging your code.

CGIHTML

CGIHTML is yet another CGI implementation in C. The latest version, along with documentation, can be found at `http://hcs.harvard.edu/~eekim/web/cgihtml/`.

With CGIHTML, there is a structured skeleton that your program must follow. You must include two header files in your code. They are cgi-lib.h and html-lib.h. Next, you declare a list that stores the *name=value* pairs. You fill this list by calling the read_cgi_input() function. After this preliminary initialization, you can call the cgi_val() function with the name attribute of the field for which you want the value. This function returns a pointer to the value associated with that field. You can then assign the value to a variable declared in your program and use it in the database portion of your code.

The html_header() function will print the necessary Content-type = text/html header. You can also use a printf() statement to print this header yourself. html_begin(*string*) prints the appropriate header and the title tag for the generated HTML file. The rest of the HTML file is generated using printf() statements in your program. Finally, remember to call the list_clear() function to free the allocated memory. Listing 8-5 shows a typical CGI program using CGIHTML.

Listing 8-5 Typical CGIHTML program

```
#include <stdio.h>  /* standard io functions */
#include <signal.h>  /* this and unistd.h for signal trapping */
#include <unistd.h>
#include "cgi-lib.h" /* CGI-related routines */
#include "html-lib.h" /* HTML-related routines */

int main()
{
 llist entries; /* define a linked list; this is where the entries are ⇐
stored. */
 read_cgi_input(&entries); /* parse the form data and add it to the list */

 cgi_val(entries, "name")

 html_header(); /* print HTML MIME header */
 html_begin("Title");
printf("Your messages and HTML code goes here");
 html_end();
 list_clear(&entries);  /* free up the pointers in the linked list */
}
```

C++

C++ has gained wide popularity over the past few years. Its object-oriented nature makes it a powerful language for serious development work. Many database vendors provide an API library that can be called from a C++ program. Also, C++ is a natural language for GUI development since GUI elements and event-driven programming fit very well in an object-oriented paradigm. Since C++ is in a way a superset of the C language, usually you can use the C library that comes with your database. However, to take advantage of C++'s object-oriented features such as classes and inheritance, you would need a vendor-supplied library specifically for C++.

On the HTTP server side, you can develop your own set of tools or use one of the many existing ones. A popular C++ class library for handling CGI communication is cgi++ by Dragos Manolescu. cgi++ gives you a high level abstraction of the CGI and form elements, so you don't have to worry about details such as URL encoding/decoding. The latest version of this package and documentation is available from `http://sweetbay.will.uiuc.edu/cgi++`.

The top level class in cgi++ is cgi, which is derived from a general purpose class called TokenList. The Varval class stores the form data as a list of *name=value* pairs. Table 8-1 shows the methods you can use to retrieve the data.

Table 8-1 Data retrieval methods offered by cgi++

Method	Description
Exist	Check if a given variable is on the list
Fetch	Return the value corresponding to a given variable
Add	Append a new pair to the list
Replace	Replace the value corresponding to a given variable
Length	Return the number of elements (such as Varval objects) in the list
Dump	Dump the whole list as "var1=val1\nvar2=val2..." in a String

For most form elements such as text boxes and menus, you would use Fetch to retrieve the value associated with a particular name. For form elements such as checkboxes which have no value associated with them, you use the Exist method to see if the checkbox was checked or not.

Using the cgi++ library is very easy. After including the appropriate header file libcgi++.H, you need only make an instance of a CGI object. The constructor of that object decodes the form data passed to the script and stores it in the specified object. All of this happens with the following line of code:

```
Cgi myform; // myform gets everything
```

You can now use the previously mentioned methods to retrieve values from myform. Assuming you had a simple text field in your form with the name *occupation*, you can retrieve its value with the following line:

```
String Name=Input.Fetch("occupation");
```

We recommend using GNU libg++—in particular, g++ 2.7.2 and libg++-2.7.1.3—in order to compile cgi++.

The software is distributed under the terms of the GNU licensing agreement in a file called cgi++-2.2.tar.gz (the version number may vary). It contains the files briefly described below:

```
-r--r--r-- dam/users     3696 Jan 18 22:09 1996 Cgi.C
-r--r--r-- dam/users     1301 Jan 18 22:09 1996 Sprintf.C
-r--r--r-- dam/users     4011 Jan 18 22:09 1996 TokenList.C
-r--r--r-- dam/users     1656 Jan 18 22:09 1996 Varval.C
-r--r--r-- dam/users     3543 Jan 18 22:09 1996 libcgi++.H
-rw-rw-rw- dam/users     1154 Jan 18 22:15 1996 Makefile
```

- The Varval class is defined in Varval.C

- The TokenList class is defined in TokenList.C

- The Cgi class is defined in Cgi.C

- Sprintf.C is a simple function that mimics the standard C function sprintf.

- libcgi++.H is a common header file that contains the class declarations, and so on

- Makefile is a UNIX Makefile that will generate libcgi++.a

Perl

Perl stands for Practical Extraction and Reporting Language. It is a shell-like language intended to make the lives of system programmers easier by providing a C-like interface to shell programming. Today, Perl has greatly surpassed its original goal and has become a very popular programming language. Its simplicity and its open interface have made it a favorite among Web developers. Also, Perl has been ported to many different platforms. This means you can expect your Perl script to run smoothly on different machines. On the downside, Perl is an interpreted language. The script you write is read and interpreted line by line by the Perl executable program. As with any interpreted language, it does not have the efficiency and speed of a compiled language, but in many cases its simplicity far outweighs its speed. Appendix E is a quick reference of the Perl language. If you already know C or any other language for that matter, your transition to Perl should be smooth. There are a number of resources on the Web dedicated to Perl, some of which are

- Perl Home Page (http://perl.com/perl)

- Perl FAQ (http://www.cis.ohio-state.edu:80/text/faq/usenet/perl-faq/top.html)

- Perl 5 Documentation (http://www.metronet.com/0/perlinfo/perl5/manual/perl.html)

- Perl Newsgroup (news:comp.lang.perl)

- Perl Sources and Binaries (http://www.metronet.com/1/perlinfo/source)

- MacPerl (ftp://sra.co.jp/pub/lang/perl/MacPerl/)

- Perl 386 for DOS (ftp://ftp.ee.umanitoba.ca/pub/msdos/perl/)

- Perl Resources (http://www.stars.com/Seminars/CGI/Perl.html)

cgi-lib by Steve Brenner has become the standard tool to interface Perl with CGI. The latest version is available from **http://www.bio.cam.ac.uk/web/form.html**.

As you might suspect, the library offers functions which allow you to decode the input from a form and store it in a series of *name=value* pairs. This easy interface keeps the functionality simple and effective. Listing 8-6 is the cgi-lib.pl source.

Listing 8-6 cgi-lib.pl source code

```perl
#!/usr/local/bin/perl
# Perl Routines to Manipulate CGI input
# S.E.Brenner@bioc.cam.ac.uk
# Copyright 1994 Steven E. Brenner
# Unpublished work.
# Permission granted to use and modify this library so long as the
# copyright above is maintained, modifications are documented, and
# credit is given for any use of the library.
#
# Thanks are due to many people for reporting bugs and suggestions
# especially Meng Weng Wong, Maki Watanabe, Bo Frese Rasmussen,
# Andrew Dalke, Mark-Jason Dominus and Dave Dittrich.

# see http://www.seas.upenn.edu/~mengwong/forms/  or
#   http://www.bio.cam.ac.uk/web/for more information

# Minimalist http form and script (http://www.bio.cam.ac.uk/web/minimal.cgi):
# if (&MethGet) {
#   print &PrintHeader,
#     '<form method=POST><input type="submit">Data: <input name="myfield">';
# } else {
#   &ReadParse(*input);
#   print &PrintHeader, &PrintVariables(%input);
# }
```

```perl
# MethGet
# Return true if this cgi call was using the GET request, false otherwise
# Now that cgi scripts can be put in the normal file space, it is useful
# to combine both the form and the script in one place with GET used to
# retrieve the form, and POST used to get the result.

sub MethGet {
 return ($ENV{'REQUEST_METHOD'} eq "GET");
}


# ReadParse
# Reads in GET or POST data, converts it to unescaped text, and puts
# one key=value in each member of the list "@in"
# Also creates key/value pairs in %in, using '\0' to separate multiple
# selections

# If a variable-glob parameter (e.g., *cgi_input) is passed to ReadParse,
# information is stored there, rather than in $in, @in, and %in.

sub ReadParse {
  local (*in) = @_ if @_;


  local ($i, $loc, $key, $val);

  # Read in text
  if ($ENV{'REQUEST_METHOD'} eq "GET") {
   $in = $ENV{'QUERY_STRING'};
  } elsif ($ENV{'REQUEST_METHOD'} eq "POST") {
   read(STDIN,$in,$ENV{'CONTENT_LENGTH'});
  }

  @in = split(/&/,$in);

  foreach $i (0 .. $#in) {
   # Convert plus's to spaces
   $in[$i] =~ s/\+/ /g;

   # Split into key and value.
   ($key, $val) = split(/=/,$in[$i],2); # splits on the first =.

   # Convert %XX from hex numbers to alphanumeric
   $key =~ s/%(..)/pack("c",hex($1))/ge;
   $val =~ s/%(..)/pack("c",hex($1))/ge;

   # Associate key and value
   $in{$key} .= "\0" if (defined($in{$key})); # \0 is the multiple separator
   $in{$key} .= $val;

  }
```

continued on next page

continued from previous page

```
      return 1; # just for fun
    }

    # PrintHeader
    # Returns the magic line which tells WWW that we're an HTML document

    sub PrintHeader {
     return "Content-type: text/html\n\n";
    }

    # PrintVariables
    # Nicely formats variables in an associative array passed as a parameter
    # And returns the HTML string.

    sub PrintVariables {
     local (%in) = @_;
     local ($old, $out, $output);
     $old = $*; $* =1;
     $output .= "<DL COMPACT>";
     foreach $key (sort keys(%in)) {
      foreach (split("\0", $in{$key})) {
       ($out = $_) =~ s/\n/<BR>/g;
        $output .= "<DT><B>$key</B><DD><I>$out</I><BR>";
      }
     }
     $output .= "</DL>";
     $* = $old;

     return $output;
    }

    # PrintVariablesShort
    # Nicely formats variables in an associative array passed as a parameter
    # Using one line per pair (unless value is multiline)
    # And returns the HTML string.


    sub PrintVariablesShort {
     local (%in) = @_;
     local ($old, $out, $output);
     $old = $*; $* =1;
     foreach $key (sort keys(%in)) {
      foreach (split("\0", $in{$key})) {
       ($out = $_) =~ s/\n/<BR>/g;
        $output .= "<B>$key</B> is <I>$out</I><BR>";
      }
     }
     $* = $old;

     return $output;
    }

    1; #return true
```

Sample data collection form

Now let's consider how cgi-lib.pl can be used in a CGI script. Consider the form shown in Figure 8-3.

It is a simple data collection form. The submit button sends the content of the form to the CGI script, part of which is shown in Listing 8-7.

Listing 8-7 Perl script used to handle the content of a form

```
#!/usr/local/bin/perl
require "cgi-lib.pl";
print &PrintHeader;

&ReadParse(*input);

$mcompany = $input{'company'};
$maddress1 = $input{'address1'};
$maddress2 = $input{'address2'};
$mcity = $input{'city'};
$mstate = $input{'state'};
$mzip = $input{'zip'};
$mcountry = $input{'country'};
$mpoc = $input{'poc'};
$mphone = $input{'phone'};
$mfax = $input{'fax'};
$memail = $input{'email'};
```

Any Perl script starts with the standard shell declaration notation. In this case, the Perl executable program is located in the /usr/local/bin directory. Therefore, the notation becomes:

```
#!/usr/local/bin/perl
```

The next line is similar to a #include directive in C or C++ programs. It gets the content of the specified file and inserts it at the point the directive appears. The cgi-lib.pl includes all the necessary routines to perform CGI operations. Before any processing, the header Content=text/html is printed. Recall that this text header is necessary before the browser can display any other information.

The following single line reads the content of the form and stores it as *name=value* pairs in the array called input.

```
&ReadParse(*input);
```

Once this operation has been performed, you can access any form element by using the following notation:

```
$variable_name = $input{'name'};
```

For example, the company name was stored in a text field called *company*. The value of this text field can be retrieved by the following:

```
$mcompany = $input{'company'};
```

It is probably a good idea to use variable names which somehow relate to the NAME attribute in the HTML form. This way, you can correlate all variables in your program to the form elements they are processing. In the above script, the convention has been to name each variable the same as its form name preceded by the letter *m*.

What you do with the variables after getting their values depends on your application. Sybperl, which is a Perl interface to Sybase, will be discussed in the next chapter. There are other tools to link Perl with other popular databases. Perl also has a simple interface to rdbm, the UNIX internal database system. This database system implements a *key=value* data storage and retrieval system. It is not as powerful as a full relational database, but for some applications it might suffice.

CGI.pm

Users of cgi-lib.pl might consider using the newer version CGI.pm. This Perl 5 library has more functions and lets you create HTML forms on the fly. It has an added feature in which the previous query is used to create the new form, preserving the form's state from invocation to invocation.

TCL

TCL stands for Tool Command Language. It is a shell-like language similar to Perl, but it offers the additional capability of creating GUI applications. It supports all the usual widgets such as buttons, lists, radio buttons, and so on. TCL is an interpreted language, so it is not as fast as compiled languages such as C. As with any language used for CGI programming, you are concerned not about its GUI capabilities, but its ability to interface with CGI efficiently and link to your database system. TCL meets the above two requirements, and if you already have some experience in TCL programming, you might choose to use TCL for your CGI programs. TCL has been ported to almost all UNIX platforms and is freely distributed. There aren't many native libraries from database vendors designed specifically for TCL, but TCL has an open architecture that allows it to link to C libraries. The following

URL has some details about using TCL in CGI programming: `http://hplyot.obspm.fr/~dl/www-tools.html`. Information about TCL can be found from the following sites:

- The TCL/Tk Project At Sun Microsystems Laboratories (`http://www.sunlabs.com:80/research/tcl/`)

- The Santa Cruz Operation (`http://www.sco.com/Technology/tcl/Tcl.html`)

- An index of TCL resources, by Wade Holst (`http://web.cs.ualberta.ca/~wade/Auto/Tcl.html`)

- A brief introduction to TCL and Tk. (`http://http2.brunel.ac.uk:8080/~csstd-dm/TCL2/TCL2.html`)

- Teacher Hypertools for TCL and Tk, by David Svoboda (`http://www.ece.cmu.edu/afs/ece/usr/svoboda/www/th/homepage.html`)

Listing 8-8 shows a typical implementation using TCL. The code should be self-explanatory for readers familiar with TCL.

Listing 8-8 TCL used in a CGI script

```
#!/usr/local/bin/tclsh
# tcl-cgi.tcl
# robert.bagwill@nist.gov, no warranty, no rights reserved
## some fixes by dl@hplyot.obspm.fr - v1.2 - May 20 1995
## better get test-cgi2.tcl from http://hplyot.obspm.fr/~dl/wwwtools.html
#
set envvars {REQUEST_METHOD QUERY_STRING CONTENT_LENGTH}

puts "Content-type: text/html\n"

if {[string compare $env(REQUEST_METHOD) "POST"]==0} {
set message [split [read stdin $env(CONTENT_LENGTH)] &]
} else {
set message [split $env(QUERY_STRING) &]
}
foreach pair $message {
set name [lindex [split $pair =] 0]
set val [lindex [split $pair =] 1]
regsub -all {\+} $val { } val
# kludge to unescape some chars
regsub -all {\%0A} $val \n\t val
regsub -all {\%2C} $val {,} val
regsub -all {\%27} $val {'} val
puts "$name\t= $val"
}
```

Shell Script

UNIX shell scripts are one of the trademarks of the UNIX operating system. Complex tasks can be completed using scripts. Shell scripts became so popular that a variety of *shell interpreters* hit the market in the early UNIX days. Some of the more famous ones are tcsh, csh, sh, and ksh. All of them let you execute UNIX commands, but they also give you program-like structures such as loops and if-then-else elements. Because of their close integration with the operating system, UNIX shell scripts seem like an ideal choice for writing simple, quick CGI scripts. The problem arises on the other side of the spectrum: database interface. Aside from UNIX's internal database system (which is not a relational database), other interfaces are hard to find. If the purpose of your HTML form is to collect some information and save it in a text file, then shell scripts work just fine. If your application requires searching or modification of that data, you probably want to consider a higher-level language.

A popular package for using CGI in shell scripts is Un-CGI. It is available from `http://www.hyperion.com/~koreth/uncgi.html`. This site also includes documentation for using the package. Un-CGI is written by Steven Grimm (`koreth@hyperion.com`).

Un-CGI basically grabs the content of a submitted form, performs a URL-decoding on each *name=value* pair, and puts them in appropriate environmental variables. As a result, they become available to any process running within the shell including C programs or other shell scripts.

Suppose the submitted form included a text input box like this:

```
<input type=text name=sport size=20>
```

The *<form>* tag points to your script, which uses Un-CGI in its action attribute. The server will run Un-CGI, which in turn will set the environmental variable WWW_sport to the value entered by the user. After setting the environmental variables (it sets one for each form element), it executes your program (another shell script or any other program).

All the usual CGI environment variables (for example, PATH_INFO, QUERY_STRING) are also available to your program.

A simple shell script is shown in Listing 8-9. It basically prints the content-type of the generated document and a message which includes the value entered in the sport field in the form.

Listing 8-9 Sample shell script

```
#!/bin/sh
echo 'Content-type: text/html'
echo ''I got the following sport from the client: $WWW_sport"
```

If your form includes multiple selection menus, then individual selections are separated by the # character. It is up to you to parse the string to extract the individual selections in your program. In C, you would use the STRTOK() function. Most languages have a similar function for this purpose.

Visual Basic

If you plan on developing CGI applications on a Windows platform such as NT or Windows 95, you should seriously consider Visual Basic. Its powerful yet simple scripting language suits the CGI development environment very well. The language is concise, efficient, and can be easily maintained. Also, Visual Basic offers native support to the Microsoft Access database engine, which is a relational database. The Professional version fully supports the ODBC interface, which means you can gain access to a number of databases, both local and remote. The CGI interface in Visual Basic was described in detail in Chapter 5. You can find more information about using Visual Basic in CGI applications from `http://website.ora.com/devcorner/db-src/index.html`. Since Microsoft has a Web server, browser, and a database server in its product line, Visual Basic tends to interface nicely with any of them.

PowerBuilder

PowerBuilder has emerged as a leader for client/server development on Windows-based machines. It offers no database operations of its own but provides a powerful and consistent interface for linking with a number of popular back-end databases. With recent announcements about its availability on the Macintosh and UNIX platforms, PowerBuilder has come closer to multi-platform support. Although most people associate PowerBuilder with a GUI client/server application development tool, there is no need for a PowerBuilder application to display GUI output. You can use PowerBuilder's interface to Win CGI (or its ability to link to vendor-provided server libraries) and database connectivity to develop CGI programs. The main plus for PowerBuilder is, of course, its already proven capability to link to database systems in a consistent manner.

CGI application development using PowerBuilder is very similar to Visual Basic. You retrieve the content of an HTML form either through the Win CGI specification (described in Chapter 5) or through a proprietary vendor-supplied library that allows you to get the information directly from the HTTP server. Once that information is in place, you can perform your database operations as needed. PowerBuilder supports no output to standard output (for example, no print-like statement). This, however, is not necessary, since the Win CGI specification requires the CGI program to put its output in a text file. This is the output which will be sent to the browser and should conform to HTML standards. PowerBuilder does allow writing to a text file, which satisfies the output requirement. You can find some examples of CGI programs using PowerBuilder at the following sites:

- PowerCerv's Sampler Site: (`http://www.powercerv.com/index.html`)
- Ventana's Own Software Archive (`http://www.vmedia.com/alternate/vvc/`⇐ `onlcomp/PowerBuilder/software.html`)

Listing 8-10 is an example written by Frank Starsinic. The code is very much self-documented for readers familiar with PowerBuilder's scripting language PowerScript.

Listing 8-10 Example of PowerScript used as a CGI application

```
//CGI Example in PowerScript for PowerBuilder
//Function: To write the most basic possible CGI program for Website possible
usin PowerBuilder
//Author: Frank Starsinic
//Date: 7/29/95
//

string ls_cmd, ls_arg[]
integer i, li_argcnt
string CGI_OutputFile,CGI_InputFile,CGI_ProfileFile,s_buf,CGI_ContentFile
integer CGI_OutputFN


//When we run a cgi program from a server running WEBSITE, Website does a ⇐
couple of things
//It runs the executable with some command parameters...
//prog-name cgi-profile-file input-file output-file urs-args
//so lets see what the command parameters are...
ls_cmd = Trim(CommandParm( ))

li_argcnt = 1
DO WHILE Len(ls_cmd ) > 0

// Find the first blank
i = Pos( ls_cmd, " " )
// If no blanks (only one argument),
// set i to point to the hypothetical character
// after the end of the string
if i = 0 then i = Len(ls_cmd) + 1

// Assign the arg to the argument array.

// The number of chars copied is one less than the
// position of the space found with Pos
ls_arg[li_argcnt] = Left( ls_cmd, i - 1 )

// Increment the argument count for the next loop

li_argcnt = li_argcnt + 1

// Remove the argument from the string

// so the next argument becomes first
ls_cmd = Replace( ls_cmd, 1, i, "" )
LOOP
```

```
//get the necessary files from the command parameters
CGI_ProfileFile = ls_arg[1]
CGI_InputFile = ls_arg[2]
CGI_OutputFile = ls_arg[3]


//open the output file for the server
//PowerBuilder is nice enought to figure out which file we need to open.
//No FREEFILE necessary like in VB!!
//Notice we are opening the CGI_outputfile from above which was arg[3] in ⇐
the command line
CGI_OutputFN = FileOpen(CGI_OutputFile, &
Linemode!, Write!, LockWrite!, Replace!)

//Write out the stuff we always have to write out
FileWrite(CGI_OutputFN, "Content-type: text/html")
FileWrite(CGI_OutputFN, "")

//Now write out the text we want to display on the browser (in html of ⇐
course).
FileWrite(CGI_outputFN, "<h1>This is my first PowerBuilder CGI
application!</h1>")

//All Done. Close the Output File and done.
fileclose(CGI_OutputFN)
```

Java

Java, the revolutionary language from Sun Microsystems, has greatly boosted Internet application development. Java is an object-oriented language and is considered the first language to specifically target the Internet and Web environments. Java, as it stands now, is an interpreted language. Many make the analogy that Java is to C++ as Perl is to the C language. Its wide acceptance has made it a very popular language, and as development environments and tools are created, Java can be used in serious application development projects. A unique feature of Java is its two modes of operation: as a stand-alone program on a machine or as a program sent via the Web to a client machine with a built-in Java interpreter. A Java application can be executed as a stand-alone program on a machine if a Java interpreter is available. In this mode, Java is like any other language. The second mode of operation is achieved when a Java program is sent to a client machine with a Java interpreter via the Web, and the browser on the client machine accepts the Java program and executes it. This is how Java is used in Web environments.

Several measures are taken to assure that the Java program does not perform any harmful operations on the client machine. The most basic approach is that all such programs are executed with limited permissions. For example, they cannot write or delete files from the client machine. The piece of Java code which is sent over the Web is referred to as an *applet*. A special tag is introduced to include an applet in an HTML document. Here is an example:

```
<applet code=filename.class width=600 height = 600> </applet>
```

An applet does not have all the functions associated with a stand-alone Java application. Many of these limitations are due to security concerns. After all, an applet is a piece of code that you get from somewhere and execute on your machine. You want to have some control over what this piece of code can and cannot do. Unless you specifically permit it, all applets are executed on your machine as *untrusted*, meaning they have limited permission as to what they can do.

It is beyond the scope of this book to go into the details of the Java language. You are encouraged to consult one of the many reference books on the language. Information can also be found at the following on-line sites:

- A Directory and Registry of Java Resources (http://www.gamelan.com)

- Java: Programming for the Internet (http://www.javasoft.com/)

- comp.lang.java (Java Newsgroup)

- The Java Package Tutorial
  (http://v2ma09.gsfc.nasa.gov:2000/JavaPackages.html)

There is no doubt that Java gives a new dimension to Web application development. Rather than relying on the server and CGI to handle any processing or data manipulation, a browser can execute a complete application represented by an applet. Shortly after the release of Java, it became evident that in order for it to be seriously considered as an application development language, it had to support database operations. In March of 1996, Sun released the preliminary specifications for JDBC: A Java SQL API. JDBC provides a consistent mechanism for Java applications to connect to a database and perform database operations. It is modeled after the ODBC standard and offers many of the same features to a Java programmer. Unlike ODBC, which is a C interface, JDBC is a Java interface; in other words, it is optimized for the Java language. This section is a brief discussion of this specification in its preliminary form. During the writing of this book, the JDBC specification was still under public review. You are encouraged to download the latest version of the specification from Sun's Javasoft Web site.

JDBC implements a SQL level API. That is, it provides a mechanism for programmers to communicate with the database engine using SQL commands. This is a very low-level interface, but it provides a common denominator. In the future, higher-level abstractions can be built on top of it. JDBC requires that the database comply with at least ANSI SQL-2 Entry Level. An application is free to make more advanced SQL calls, but it should be prepared to accept an error message from a driver which does not support higher-level implementation of SQL.

The JDBC specification is divided into two distinct parts: JDBC API and JDBC Driver Interface. Their usage is shown in Figure 8-4.

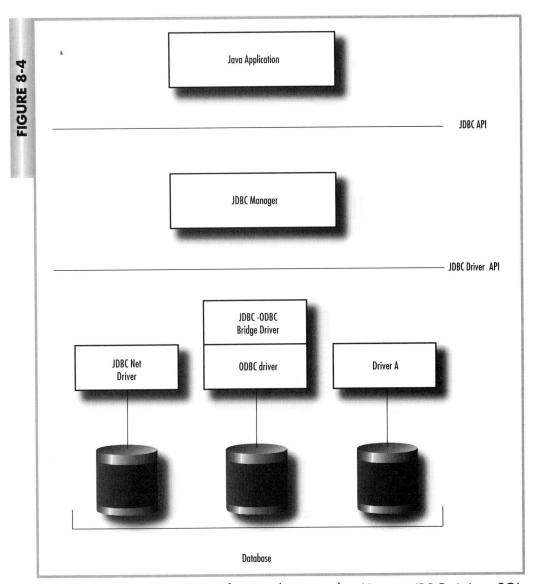

FIGURE 8-4

Java Application

JDBC API

JDBC Manager

JDBC Driver API

JDBC -ODBC
Bridge Driver

JDBC Net
Driver

ODBC driver

Driver A

Database

JDBC API and JDBC Driver Interface working together (Source: JDBC: A Java SQL API, Sun Microsystems)

JDBC API

The JDBC API is a set of abstract Java interfaces which provide the necessary means for an application to communicate with a database. This communication consists of

- opening a connection
- executing SQL statements
- processing the result

The primary abstract interfaces in the JDBC API are

- java.sql.Environment provides support for creation of connections to a database
- java.sql.Connection represents a connection to a particular database
- java.sql.Statement takes care of encapsulating SQL statements and their execution
- java.sql.ResultSet provides a mechanism to access the result of the SQL statement from the database

JDBC Driver Interface

The Driver Interface is the bridge between the JDBC API and the database API. It is through this bridge that Java can communicate with different databases in the same manner. The Driver Interface basically provides an implementation of the four interfaces required by the JDBC API. The driver can, in turn, be implemented on top of another middleware standard (such as ODBC), or it could provide a direct interface to the database. A third method, which is ideal for wide-area networks, is one in which the JDBC Driver Interface is built on top of a database network driver. The network driver would eliminate the need to have the database server on the same machine or even on the same network; the server can be on another continent. With such flexibility, the JDBC Driver Interface can communicate with almost any database engine as long as the engine offers an open API.

Application Usage

As with Java itself, JDBC can be used in two distinct environments. If the JDBC calls are made within an applet, then you can send an entire application over the network. The applet and the JDBC driver will communicate with their respective server components through two different channels. This is shown in Figure 8-5.

Such a configuration looks good on paper, but it presents a few challenges. For one thing, security instantly becomes a major issue. Applets are run on the client machine as *untrusted* by default. This limits their ability to open a network connection to talk to the database. A useful application would require more relaxed permissions than those associated with untrusted applets. Also, performance can be slow compared to local area networks.

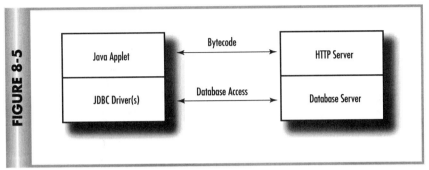

FIGURE 8-5

JDBC in Java applets (Source: JDBC: A Java SQL API, Sun Microsystems)

A second usage of JDBC would be within stand-alone Java applications. Such applications enjoy full privileges as any other application would on a machine, and so they can create network connections and perform file system operations as necessary. The application files can be downloaded from an HTTP server or distributed on a disk or CD-ROM. Such a configuration is depicted in Figure 8-6.

This configuration is gaining popularity as the backbone for Intranet installations in large, client-server-based companies.

Typically, a Java program retrieves a java.sql.Connection object using the java.sql.Environment.getConnection method. The argument passed to this method is a URL, which means the URL needs sufficient information to determine the type of database and driver required by the requested connection. The JDBC specification calls for URLs of the following form:

```
jdbc:<subprotocol>:<subname>
```

where *subprotocol* specifies the database connectivity mechanism desired. *Subname* depends on the value specified by subprotocol. The following URL requests a connection to the data source called *mydb* using the ODBC subprotocol:

```
jdbc:odbc:mydb
```

Once the connection is established, the next two phases of operations are sending SQL statements to the database and receiving some result set. The following code segment shows an example of how this can be accomplished:

```
java.sql.Statement sqlcmd = conn.createStatement();
ResultSet r = sqlcmdt.executeQuery("SELECT a, b FROM mytable");
while (r.next()) {
  int i = r.getInteger(1);
  String s = r.getVarChar(2);
  System.out.println("a = " + i + "b= " + s);
}
```

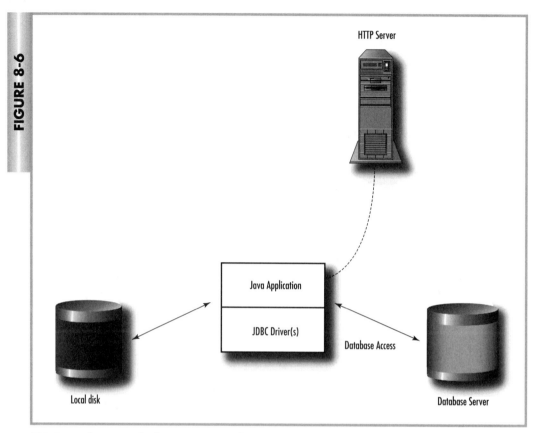

FIGURE 8-6

JDBC used in stand-alone Java applications (Source: JDBC: A Java SQL API, Sun Microsystems)

The variable sqlcmd contains the SQL statement we want to execute. This command is executed and its result set is stored in a variable called r, which is of the type ResultSet. The while loop goes through all the received rows and grabs the values associated with each column and stores them in appropriate variables. In this example, the values are immediately printed, but your application is free to do what it deems necessary with the values. JDBC supports queries made to stored procedures which have OUT or INPUT parameters. For details of how this is done, refer to the JDBC specifications.

Data Types

SQL has a number of data types, but not all of these data types are directly supported by Java. The designers of JDBC had to consider all the SQL data types and find an appropriate match in the Java data types. Table 8-2 shows the proposed mapping between the two sets.

Table 8-2 Mapping between SQL data types and Java data types

SQL	Java
CHAR	String
VARCHAR	String
LONGVARCHAR	java.io.InputStream
NUMERIC	java.sql.Numeric
DECIMAL	java.sql.Numeric
BIT	boolean
TINYINT	byte
SMALLINT	short
INTEGER	int
BIGINT	long
REAL	float
FLOAT	float
DOUBLE	double
BINARY	byte[]
VARBINARY	byte[]
LONGVARBINARY	java.sql.InputStream
DATE	java.sql.Date
TIME	java.sql.Time
TIMESTAMP	java.sql.Timestamp

Various GET methods are proposed to retrieve data of different types. Table 8-3 shows a listing of these methods along with the SQL data type they can retrieve. Most of the methods have built-in conversion routines and can actually retrieve data types other than the one shown the in the table. For example, the getReal method can accept data types of Integer, Numeric, Char, and a few more. A complete mapping of which data types are supported by which GET methods is included in the JDBC documentation distributed by Sun.

Table 8-3 GET methods and the data types they can retrieve

get Method	SQL data type
getTinyInt	TINYINT
getSmallInt	SMALLINT
getInteger	INTEGER
getBigInt	BIGINT
getFloat	FLOAT
getReal	REAL
getDouble	DOUBLE
getDecimal	DECIMAL
getNumeric	NUMERIC
getBit	BIT
getChar	CHAR
getVarChar	VARCHAR
getLongVarChar	LONGVARCHAR
getBinary	BINARY
getVarBinary	VARBINARY
getLongVarBinary	LONGVARBINARY
getDate	DATE
getTime	TIME
getTimeStamp	TIMESTAMP
getAsciiStream	LONGVARCHAR
getUnicodeStream	LONGVARCHAR
getBinaryStream	LONGVARBINARY
getObject	all SQL data types

The JDBC specification includes the definitions of the core java.sql interfaces and classes. These definitions are your definite resource to understanding JDBC and the interface it provides. You can find the definitions of the following interfaces in the specifications:

- java.sql.CallableStatement
- java.sql.Connection

- java.sql.Date
- java.sql.Driver
- java.sql.Environment
- java.sql.Numeric
- java.sql.PreparedStatement
- java.sql.ResultSet
- java.sql.Statement
- java.sql.SQLException
- java.sql.Time
- java.sql.Timestamp
- java.sql.Types

An Example

We conclude this discussion with a complete Java program which uses JDBC shown in Listing 8-11. The program makes a connection to an ODBC-compliant data source called mydb. After the connection is made, a simple SELECT statement is executed and the result set is retrieved. The program can do whatever is necessary with the result set. Finally, the connection is closed. This code segment, however simple, should give you a feel for how JDBC can be used in Java applications. JDBC provides a clean interface for database communication, an important consideration for any development language. Java's capabilities as an Internet language make it a prime nominee for the language of the future.

Listing 8-11 Sample Java program using JDBC

```
import java.net.URL;
import java.sql.*;
class select {
  public static void main(String argv[]) {
  try { // Create a URL specifying an ODBC data source name.
    String url = "jdbc:odbc:mydb";

    // Connect to the database
    Connection con = Environment.getConnection(url, "user", "");

    // Execute a SELECT statement
    Statement sqlcmd = con.createStatement();
    ResultSet r = sqlcmd.executeQuery("SELECT a, b, c, d, key FROM mytable");

    // Step through the result rows.
    System.out.println("Retreived result set:");
```

continued on next page

continued from previous page

```
      while (r.next()) {
        // get the values from the current row:
        int a = r.getInteger(1);
        Numeric b = r.getNumeric(2);
        char c[] = r.getVarChar(3).tocharArray();
        boolean d = r.getBit(4);
        String key = r.getVarChar(5);

        // do something with the result
      }
      sqlcmd.close();
      con.close();
    } catch (java.lang.Exception ex) {
      ex.printStackTrace(); }
    }
    }
  }
```

JavaScript

In this section, we switch gears and consider one of the more innovative additions to the Web environment. So far we have concentrated on server-side applications. We have shown how HTTP clients can display an entry form and transfer the data entered in the form to the HTTP server. The server executes a script (program) which conforms to a standard known as CGI. After execution is completed, the server sends the output produced by the script back to the browser. The main deficiency of this approach is lack of processing power on the client side. The client is nothing but a fill-out form. Your program will not know anything about the content of the form until it is submitted across the Internet to your server. For example, if the user entered the data in the wrong format, you would not be able to see the error until the form content had traveled across the network, which can be an expensive and lengthy operation. You would then have to send an error message across the network and present the user with the option to reenter the data in the correct format.

The idea behind client-side applications is to give the client some processing power. That is, let the client look at the data, examine it, and notify the user of any obvious errors (such as formatting errors) before the data is transmitted over the Net. This is a powerful concept and brings the Web very close to a more traditional client/server application environment. Aside from routine error checking, client-side applications can enhance the look and feel of your HTML-based user interface. The first shot at this idea came from Netscape Communications, Inc. with the release of version 2 of their browser. This browser supports a scripting language called JavaScript, an object-oriented language with commands embedded in an HTML document. As a result, when you send an HTML document across the Net, you also send the source code for the application you want executed by the browser. This is shown in Figure 8-7.

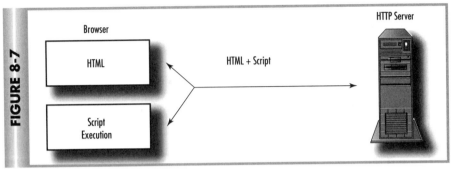

FIGURE 8-7

Browser

HTML

Script
Execution

HTML + Script

HTTP Server

Client-side applications

JavaScript vs. Java

The release of JavaScript coincided with the release of a new language called Java from Sun Microsystems. The two are not really related to each other. They were independent projects aiming to solve different problems. However, the two languages are similar in syntax and in their use of objects. JavaScript supports most of Java's expressions, data types, and basic constructs. Understanding one will undoubtedly help you understand the other. Actually, JavaScript used to be called LiveScript, but for whatever reason, the name was changed to JavaScript. Table 8-4 outlines a few of the main differences between Java and JavaScript.

Table 8-4 JavaScript vs. Java (Source: Netscape Communications, Inc.)

JavaScript	Java
Interpreted	Compiled
Object-based	Object-oriented
Code embedded in HTML	Applets a separate entity from HTML
loose typing	strong typing
dynamic binding	static binding

JavaScript is a great tool in Web application development. Unfortunately, it is not yet part of any standard. As a result, you need to be careful when using it. Fortunately, as you will see later, the way the language is incorporated into HTML makes browsers that do not understand JavaScript ignore it. Unlike frames, which include a noframe tag to deal with browsers which do not support it, a browser either does or does not support JavaScript. So it might be necessary to write error-checking code on the server side anyway, in case the error is not captured by a client that does not support JavaScript.

JavaScript is object-based, but not object-oriented. That is, it can deal with built-in objects and allows you to create new objects as extensions to those objects. JavaScript, however, does not allow you to define new classes based on inheritance. If you have worked with any object-oriented language, learning JavaScript should be a breeze. In short, a number of objects are available to you as a programmer. Some of the objects are specific to components of the browser and some are generic objects, like a string object. Table 8-5 is a list of objects available to JavaScript and the HTML tag used to create each one:

Table 8-5 JavaScript objects

JavaScript Object	Meaning / HTML tag
anchor	<a></a>
button	<input type="button">
checkbox	<input type="checkbox">
date	A generic object dealing with dates
document	The page shown on the browser
form	<form> </form>
frame	<frame> </frame>
hidden	<input type="hidden">
history	Contains information about the URLs visited by the client
link	Similar to the anchor object
location	Information about the current URL
math	A generic object dealing with mathematical functions
navigator	Information about the browser used
password	<input type="password">
radio	<input type="radio">
reset	<input type="reset">
select	<select> </select>
string	A generic object dealing with string and character functions
submit	<input type="submit">
text	<input type="text">
textarea	<textarea </textarea>
window	Information about the current window

You should immediately see the relationship between the objects and the components of an HTML form. For example, the <input type=password name=secret> is an HTML code which generates a text input box that can be used to capture a password entry from the user. In JavaScript, the text input box is considered an object and enjoys all the properties and methods associated with it.

Your program can manipulate this object by manipulating the properties and methods associated with the object. *Properties* are values associated with the objects. For example, a car can have a color property with red, blue, or any other color as its value. *Methods* are actions associated with the object. For example, a car can move, stop, or turn. JavaScripts mainly deal with objects and allow you tighter control over their behavior by providing an interface to the object's methods and properties. For example, the password object has the following properties:

- name: the name specified using the NAME option in the INPUT tag
- value: the value specified using the VALUE option in the INPUT tag

It also has the following methods which are explained later:

- focus
- blur
- select

In dealing with objects, JavaScript has a number of built-in functions for data manipulation, such as string or numeric functions. It also has the usual structural components for a language, such as loops and if-then statements. So it is very much like other programming languages. The only question remaining is how a JavaScript is executed. For example, a C program starts execution from the main() function, but how does JavaScript begin running? The answer lies in the event-driven programming model. This model fits well with graphical user interfaces and object-based languages. Simply put, a number of events are defined for each object. These events are

- Blur: A select, text, or textarea field on a form loses focus.
- Change: The value of a select, text, or textarea field on a form changes.
- Click: An object on the form is clicked on.
- Focus: A field receives input focus because of tabbing or a mouse click.
- Load: Browser has finished loading an HTML document. If the HTML document contains frames, the load event occurs when all the frames have finished loading.
- MouseOver: When the mouse pointer is on an object.
- Select: When the user selects part or all of a text in a textarea or a text input field.

● Submit: When the user submits a form.

● Unload: When the user leaves the document.

The object does nothing when it encounters one of those events unless you provide some code and associate that code with the particular event. For example, a common event for a button is when the user clicks on it. This clicking is an event. If the button is a submit button, the default behavior is to send the content of the form to the server. By providing your own code to handle the click event, you can override that behavior and replace it with a behavior that you want. Here is an example:

```
<input type="button" name="pushme" value="OK" onClick = "pushedOK()">
```

The onClick option specifies either a user-defined function or a JavaScript statement to be executed when the user clicks on the button called pushme. In the example, the function pushedOK() is executed.

JavaScript is an evolving language, so you can expect future revisions with the next release of the Netscape browser. Perhaps the best source for documentation is from the Netscape site at the following URL:

```
http://home.netscape.com/eng/mozilla/Gold/handbook/javascript/.
```

The documentation serves as the reference point for the different objects, their properties, and methods. It also includes some useful examples. Other recommended sources of information and examples are

● White Paper: Verifying Form Input with JavaScript
(`http://gmccomb.com/javascript/valid.htm`)

● JavaScript (`http://www.gamelan.com/pages/Gamelan.javascript.html`)

● JavaScript Resources: A Netscape 2.0 Enhanced Cheat Sheet
(`http://www.intercom.net/user/mecha/java.html`)

In case you want to get your hands dirty with JavaScript right away, the following short tutorial is provided. But this tutorial can by no means replace the extensive references from Netscape.

The first issue with JavaScript is harmlessly incorporating it into an HTML document. The *<script> </script>* tag pair allows you to denote the beginning and end of a block which includes JavaScript source code. Anything between these two tags is interpreted by the browser and must be valid JavaScript code, otherwise an error message is generated. It is best to enclose the actual code segment within the HTML comment tags (<-- -->). This way, a browser that does not support JavaScript will ignore the text of the code. Also, the best place to include the script tag is within the head tags for a document. The code is then read and verified (syntax-wise) when the page is first loaded. Because the code has been read, you can start associating events in the body of the HTML code with the JavaScript code segments.

In keeping with the above information, Listing 8-12 provides a simple JavaScript as it would appear within an HTML document:

Listing 8-12 A very simple JavaScript example

```
<html>
<head>
 <script language="JavaScript">
<--    function pushbutton() {
     alert("The button has been pushed!");
 } -->
 </script>
</head>
<body>
<form>
 <input type="button" name="mybutton" value="Click here" onclick="⇐
θpushbutton()">
 </form>
</body>
</html>
```

This simple HTML document contains a form with one object. This object is a button. Note the part of the button definition *onclick="pushbutton()."* This associates a JavaScript function (for example, pushbutton()) with an event (click). When the user clicks on the button, the function pushbutton() is executed. This function uses a predefined function called alert, which simply displays a message in an alert window to the user. As simple as the above few lines of code might seem, they demonstrate the soul of JavaScript as a programming language. A complex application would have more objects and more functions associated with the different events applicable to the objects. Try the above example on your browser. At least you will immediately know whether or not it supports JavaScripts. Figure 8-8 shows the HTML document as seen by the user. Figure 8-9 shows the screen after the button has been pushed.

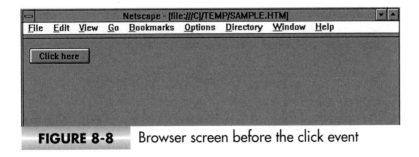

FIGURE 8-8   Browser screen before the click event

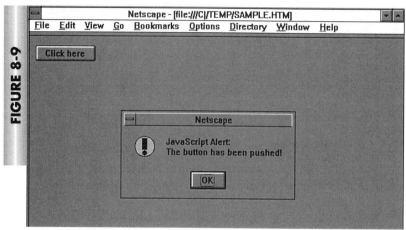

FIGURE 8-9

Browser screen after the click event

You can pass values to the JavaScript functions you call. The keyword, this, refers to the current object. In the sample code shown in Listing 8-13, this.value refers to the value property of the current object, which is the text input box. The function received this value as the variable STR, and it can use it within the body of the function.

Listing 8-13 JavaScript demonstrating passing values to functions

```
<html>
<head>
<script language="JavaScript">
<!--
 function getname(str) {
  alert("Greetings, "+ str+"!");
 }
-->
</script>
</head>
<body>
Please enter your name:
<form>
 <input type="text" name="name" onBlur="getname(this.value)" value="">
</form>
</body>
</html>
```

JavaScript is a powerful tool in application development. You should familiarize yourself with the language and use its features in your applications where you see fit. Do consider, however, that its features are meaningless to users who do not have a browser that supports JavaScript.

Visual Basic Script

During the writing of this book, Microsoft was developing another client-side language called Visual Basic Script and was planning a release for the first half of 1996. The latest information about this product and the corresponding documentation can be found at `http://www.microsoft.com/INTDEV/vbs/vbscript.htm`.

The concept behind Visual Basic Script is very similar to that of JavaScript, but Visual Basic Script has its root in the popular Visual Basic language. In fact, it is a direct subset of Visual Basic. Visual Basic Script enables developers to write Visual Basic code that is embedded in the HTML document. Although the exact tag name has not been finalized yet, it will most likely be the *<script> </script>* tag pairs. The following is a simple example provided by Microsoft in its draft documentation:

```
<Script>
Sub Command_click
Dim FlowerCount
For x = 1 to 10
   FlowerCount = FlowerCount + 2
Next
MyHTMLListBox.Text = FlowerCount
End Sub
</Script>
```

The above code is executed when a *click* event occurs on a button *command* (thus the function name Command_click) and the output is written to a text box called MyHTMLListBox. Note that the writing occurs by setting the Text property of the text box using the familiar dot notation.

Another benefit of Visual Basic Script, which applies only to clients running a form of the Microsoft Windows operating system, is OLE Automation. A Visual Basic Script can be used to manipulate both the browser and other applications on the desktop.

Although Visual Basic Script is at an early stage, it will be taken seriously when it hits the market. Its inherent ties to Microsoft products make it an ideal candidate for Intranet application development when you have some control over the client machines.

Summary

The CGI specification intentionally leaves the choice of the programming language up to the programmer. Almost any language can be used for CGI programming as long as it supports the CGI interface provided by the HTTP server and the API library provided by the database engine. Regardless of your choice, you should consider using some of the tools already developed for the language in which you write your CGI programs. All of these tools provide a mechanism to read the content of a submitted form and parse the *name=value* pairs. They will then allow you to assign the values to a variable of your choice which can be used elsewhere in the program.

When making your decision, consider the speed of compiled languages vs. their interpreted counterparts. Also, consider the overhead associated with the execution of your scripts. Depending on your application, the server might receive simultaneous requests for executing the same script. Plan ahead for such situations.

The Java programming language has emerged as the standard language for Internet application development. With Java an HTTP server serves not only an HTML document, but an entire Java application known as an applet. The Java code is then executed on the client machine. JDBC is a specification for connecting Java programs to database engines. It is similar to ODBC in function, but unlike ODBC, which has a C interface, JDBC has a Java interface. JDBC can be used in both stand-alone Java programs and in applets served over the Internet. As a result, it acts as a backbone for the installation of Intranet networks.

A relatively new class of languages is strictly client-based. The most prominent example is JavaScript. These languages provide limited processing power to the browser. As a result, the browser can perform tasks such as verification of the form contents. These languages are very simple and are object-based. Depending on an event associated with an object, a particular function or statement can be executed. The code for such programs is embedded within the HTML document. A second language of this kind is Visual Basic Script.

Questions

1. T/F: The CGI specification mandates that C be used as the programming language for all CGI scripts.

2. What are the three main functions performed by a typical CGI script?

3. How can a Java application perform database operations?

4. What are client-side applications?

5. Can you define new classes and objects in JavaScript?

6. Where does a JavaScript begin its execution?

Answers

1. False. The CGI specification intentionally leaves the choice of the programming language open.

2. Decode the form contents, perform database operations, and generate an HTML page as output.

3. By using the JDBC specification which is similar to ODBC.

4. These are scripting languages which are embedded in the HTML document. They provide some processing power to the browser displaying the HTML document.

5. JavaScript only allows you to define new classes based on existing classes.

6. There is no set place. JavaScript is event-driven. Depending on the occurrence of an event associated with an object, a particular function or statement can be executed.

9

Choosing the Right Tool

As with any development environment, you have your basic tools and another set of tools which perform at a higher level. Take, for example, the C language. The compiler can be invoked from the command prompt which, in turn, starts the linker, producing the executable. These tools are sufficient for creating an application. However your productivity can be increased if you have access to an integrated tool set such as Borland's compiler, which has incorporated into one package an editor, debugger, and tools for creating graphical elements of your interface. A similar situation exists in Web development. You can use the basic tools to create your application, or you can take advantage of some of the existing tools which may or may not ease the process. This chapter gives you an overview of some of the tools that exist today for creating Web database applications.

Overview

There are a number of software packages aimed at Web developers, and new products are being developed rapidly. These products take a variety of approaches to Web database development. Some concentrate on the CGI specifications and attempt to provide an easier develop-ment environment for CGI applications. Other tools are strictly for database interface. They act as middleware, allowing your application to communicate with a database engine. Yet another set of these tools provides a mechanism by which you can embed SQL commands within your HTML documents. This approach usually includes an addition to the HTTP server which handles the SQL commands and is shown in Figure 9-1.

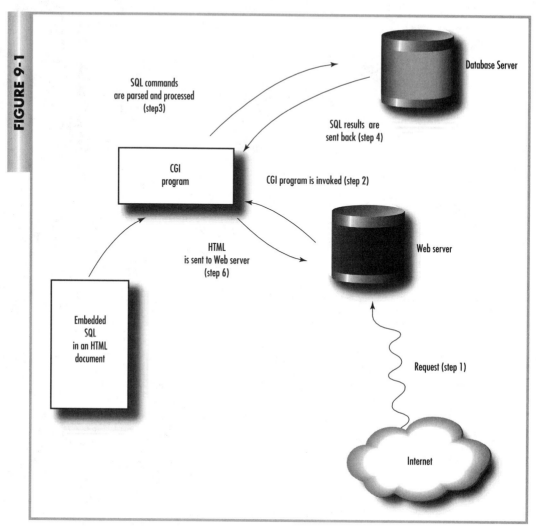

FIGURE 9-1

Embedded SQL in an HTML document

You saw a similar approach on the client side when we discussed JavaScript in Chapter 8, "Choosing a Programming Language." While the embedded JavaScript is interpreted by the browser, the embedded SQL commands are interpreted by the server. This approach seems to work well when the database vendor is providing both the database server and the HTTP server. In some cases, the design does not even include CGI. The two servers can communicate with each other directly as shown in Figure 9-2. Unlike JavaScript, there is no common standard for such an approach.

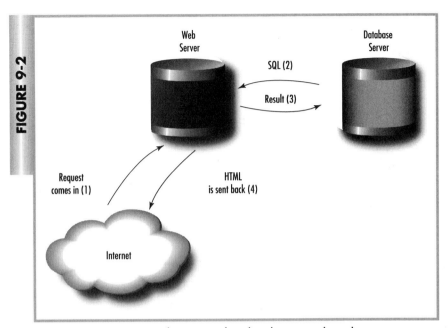

FIGURE 9-2

Direct communication between the database and Web servers

Finally, there is a new set of tools which use an object-oriented approach and treat both your database and your application as objects. The following is a review of a number of these packages. In each case, you are encouraged to visit the URL provided for up-to-date information. Most vendors allow you to test their product for a trial period.

Since some of the tools promise a complete application, you might be wondering why it is necessary to learn about HTML, CGI, and databases. It is necessary because your understanding of the basic concepts helps you choose the right tool and use it to its fullest potential. Also, it is likely that you will encounter some problems the tools cannot solve and will need to go back to the basics.

DB2WWW

Databases: IBM DB2

URL: `http://www.software.ibm.com/data/db2/db2wfac2.html`

This is a database connectivity tool for the IBM DB2 database product. The HTML forms and SQL queries are stored as macro files on the machine running the HTTP server. DB2WWW processes these macro files as it receives requests from Web browsers.

This product is intended for OS/2, Windows NT, Solaris, and AIX operating systems. Its SQL interface supports SELECT, INSERT, UPDATE, and DELETE commands. The main tool behind DB2WWW is a CGI program, which processes the content of an HTML form and sends SQL commands to a DB2 system specified in a DB2WWW Connection V1 application. This application consists of a macro file containing HTML input and report form definitions, SQL commands, and variable definitions. After performing the database operation, the DB2WWW Connection generates an HTML file which is sent back to the browser.

Data Security

Two types of user authentication are supported by DB2WWW. The DB2 database engine for OS/2 and AIX both support a userid login and password authentication mechanism. The valid user names are defined in the DB2WWW macro file. The HTTP server can also be configured to protect certain directories on the DB2 server. Depending on your server, you might be able to take advantage of S-HTTP and SSL standards which provide security for HTTP. These standards are discussed in Chapter 11.

dbCGI

Databases: Progress, Sybase, Oracle, Informix, Ingres, and ODBC

URL: `http://www.progress.com/webtools/webtools.html`

This tool uses embedded SQL commands in an HTML file to provide database connectivity. Documentation is provided for writing interface programs to other databases. Another popular aspect of dbCGI is its ability to support BLOB data that includes images, sound, and video, allowing you to incorporate multimedia into your applications.

In order to embed SQL commands in an HTML file, a unique tag is needed. dbCGI uses the *<sql></sql>* tag pair. The *<sql>* tag includes an option which is a SQL subcommand from the list shown in Table 9-1.

Table 9-1 dbCGI SQL subcommands

SQL subcommand	Task
init	Initialize the DBMS
uninit	Uninitialize the DBMS
connect	Connect to a database
disconnect	Disconnect from a database
query	Issue a SQL query to a connection

SQL subcommand	Task
execute	Issue an SQL command to a connection
format	Format the results of an SQL query
headings	Format the headings of an SQL query
error	Specify a format for errors from the database
valarg	Validate arguments received through the HTTP query string
valform	Validate a value received from a form

The HTML document also includes a number of escape characters which are used as placeholders and for formatting. They are

- %% substitutes to the "%" character.
- %# substitutes to a sequence number, unique per output record produced since starting dbCGI.
- %nd where *n* is a number starting at 1; substitutes to the value of the named column of the output record.
- %nh where *n* is a number starting at 1; substitutes to the heading of the named column of the output record.
- %na where *n* is a number starting at 1; substitutes to an argument from the HTTP query string (for example, the first *name=value* pair is denoted using %1a).
- %e substitutes to the current error message text (used in the SQL ERROR command).
- %c substitutes to the SQL command that caused the current error (used in the SQL ERROR command).
- %v substitutes to the value which failed validation (used in the SQL valarg and SQL valform commands).
- %{text%} generates an escaped representation of the enclosed for all non-alphanumeric characters.
- %n(text%) includes the enclosed text if the specified result column *n* is not null. *n* is a number starting at 1.
- %[!n1,n2,n3,...:text%] includes the text only if the values in the listed columns have not changed since the previous record. *n1*, *n2*, *n3*, and so on are column numbers starting at 1.

- %n[@*filename*%] stores the value of the named column *n* in the named file. This is usually used in conjunction with %$ and %# to create unique filenames. *n* is the column number of a BLOB or character column.

- %[*command*%] executes the named command.

- %[=*name*%] substitutes the value for the *name=value* pair.

The %[...%], %{...%}, and %(...%) sequences may all be nested.

Listing 9-1 shows a sample dbCGI file used for connecting to an Informix database. Note the sequences of *<sql></sql>* tags which perform the necessary actions. The query accesses all the columns from a table and prints a list of this information. Columns 7, 8, and 9 represent state, city, and zip code, respectively. Column 6 refers to an optional second address line which is displayed only if it has a value.

Listing 9-1 Structure of a dbCGI file

```
<TITLE>CorVu dbCGI for Informix</TITLE>
<sql init>
INFORMIXDIR=/usr/informix
SQLEXEC=/usr/informix/lib/sqlturbo
TBCONFIG=tbconfig
</sql>

<sql connect conn1>
DATABASE=stores
</sql>

<sql format>
%[!8:<H1>%8d</H1>%]
%[!7,8:<H2>%7d</H2>%]
%[!7,8,9:<H3>%9d</H3>%]
<H4>%4d</H4>
%3d %2d<BR>
%5d<BR>
%6(%6d<BR>%)
%10d<BR>
</sql>

<sql query conn1>
select *
from customer
order by date, city, zipcode
</sql>

<sql disconnect conn1>
</sql>

<sql uninit>
</sql>
```

DBperl

Databases: Oracle, mSQL, Ingres, Informix, Sybase, Empress, DB2, Quickbase, Interbase

URL: `http://www.hermetica.com/technologia/DBI/`

DBperl is a database access Application Programming Interface (API) for the Perl language. Since it uses a standard API set, you can change the back-end database with minimal modification to your code. The most notable change is in the connectivity part of your code, where you specify the database server to which you want to connect.

Genera

Databases: Sybase

URL: `http://gdbdoc.gdb.org/letovsky/genera/genera.html`

Genera is a gateway specific to the Sybase database system. It uses a proprietary syntax specified in a text file to link to a database. Genera can be used to both format SQL output and process queries by HTML forms. You will need Perl and Sybperl (discussed later in this chapter) to use Genera.

GSQL

Databases: Sybase, Oracle, Informix, ODBC

URL: `http://www.santel.lu/SANTEL/SOFT/gsql_new.html`

GSQL was one of the first packages developed specifically for addressing the problem of database connection to the Web. It uses PROC files to link the database components to HTML elements. PROC files allow for query specification and the formatting of query results. The package is composed of two main programs. The first is GSQL, which generates the necessary HTML tags to display a form. The second program is sqlmain, which connects to a database engine and performs the necessary operations. In a way, GSQL is a higher-level implementation of CGI.

The PROC File

The first step for using GSQL is to write a PROC file which maps components of the SQL string to HTML form elements. It also includes variable substitutions and a number of directives about the back-end program. The Table 9-2 describes the components of a PROC file.

Table 9-2 PROC file components

Component	Description
SQLPROG	file path specifies where the database back-end program is
DEFINE	*name=value* defines a name and associates it with the specified value
SUB/SHOW	command pairs are used to define variables and create widget mappings
SELECTLIST	what should appear in the SELECT clause
WHERELIST	what should appear in the WHERE clause
SORTLIST	how the output should be sorted

SHOW

Format: SHOW var TITLE "title" [WIDGETTYPE] [MENUOPTION]

Creates a widget for user entry or selection. A listing of WIDGETTYPEs is shown in Table 9-3.

Table 9-3 Valid WIDGETTYPEs

Widget	Description
BUTTON	creates a button widget
FIELD	creates a text-entry widget
PULLDOWN	creates a pulldown menu with SINGLE selection
SCROLL	creates a scroll menu with MULTIPLE selection
RADIO	creates a set of radio buttons (SINGLE selection)
CHECKBOX	creates a set of buttons (MULTIPLE selection)

MENUOPTION is available only for menu widgets (PULLDOWN, SCROLL, CHECK-BOX, RADIO). It may be

- A comma-separated list of menu items
- An EXEC command-generating output that will become menu items

Here are a couple of examples:

- SHOW menu1 TITLE "some states" SCROLL idaho, new york, hawaii;
- SHOW menu2 TITLE "my gif files" PULLDOWN EXEC (ls -1 *.gif);

SUB

Format: SUB var [LISTTYPE] AS sql-definition

Defines a local variable to represent an SQL query field or phrase. There are two types of variables:

- WHERELIST for variables associated with a phrase in the SQL query's WHERE clause

- SELECTLIST for variables associated with a phrase in the SQL query's SELECT clause

The following

```
SUB name SELECTLIST AS personnel..instructors.name;
```

creates a variable name that represents the database field personnel..instructors.name.
Similarly, the following

```
SUB name WHERELIST AS personnel..instructors.name like '$';
```

creates a variable name that represents the WHERE clause personnel..instructors.name like '$'.

Here, the $ sign is replaced by the input from the user.

EXEC

Format: EXEC *unix command*;

Executes a UNIX program and displays the results on the form. The UNIX commands are invoked using the SYSTEM() call. The following shows the processes running on the machine:

```
EXEC (ps);
```

TEXT

Format: TEXT any-HTML-text;

Displays any HTML text you specify. This allows for fine-tuning the way form elements are displayed.

HEADING

Format: HEADING any-HTML-text;

Displays a heading for the fill-out form. This heading will also be displayed in the query results page. Any valid HTML commands can be used here.

Writing the Database Back-End

The back-end is the program which actually connects to the database and processes the SQL query. GSQL invokes this program through a SYSTEM() call after the user has submitted the form. The back-end can be written in a number of languages, including C, Perl, and TCL. Using the *argc, argv* combination, the following is passed to the back-end program by GSQL:

- arg[0], the name of the executable (the back-end)
- arg[1], the SQL string
- arg[2], arg[3], the *name=value* pairs in the form "name value" (for example, SPORT Football)

Listing 9-2 shows the structure of a back-end program.

Listing 9-2 A sample GSQL back-end program

```c
#include <stdio.h>
#include <string.h>
main (ac,av) int ac; char**av;
{
  char * sqlstring = NULL;
  if (ac<3) exit(0);
  parseargs(ac,av);
  sqlstring = strdup(av[1]);
  execute_sql(sqlstring);
}
```

You only need to write the routine execute_sql(). Since you have access to the SQL command, you normally would pass the command to the database, retrieve the results, and print an output based on that result. Assuming you are using a Sybase database, Listing 9-3 shows how the above task can be accomplished.

Listing 9-3 A sample execute_sql() function

```c
int execute_sql (char *sqlstring) {

int i;
DBPROCESS *dbproc, *init_sybase;
char * app_getdefine();

/* -- setup environment, and init the database */
 putenv( app_getdefine("SYBASE_ENV"));
 dbproc = init_sybase ( app_getdefine("LOGIN"),
         app_getdefine("PASSWORD"));

/* -- execute the sql string */
 dbcmd (dbproc, sqlstring); /* send query to sybase */
 dbsqlexec (dbproc);

/* -- bind the results */
 nfields = dbnumcols (dbproc);
 for(i=0;i < nfields;i++) dbbind(dbproc, i+1, STRINGBIND, 0, results[i]);
```

```
/* -- retrieve each row, and print the results */
 while (dbnextrow(dbproc) != NO_MORE_ROWS) {
  for (i=0;i < nfields;i++) printf("%s ", results[i]);
  }
}
```

GSQL is written by Jason Ng at likkai@ncsa.uiuc.edu. The project was done at the National Center for Supercomputing Applications (NCSA) at the University of Illinois (Urbana-Champaign).

Informix CGI Interface Kit

Databases: Informix

URL: `http://www.informix.com/informix/dbweb/grail/freeware.html`

This is a database connectivity tool. A C library of function calls along with Informix's ESQL/C programming give programmers a minimal set of Web/database development tools. Currently, the kit requires INFORMIX-ESQL/C version 7.10.

According to Informix, the kit has been tested successfully on the Sun Solaris, Hewlett-Packard HP-UX, Silicon Graphics IRIX, and IBM AIX platforms.

Illustra, which is a relatively new subsidiary of Informix, is an object-relational database engine. It is expandable through a series of add-on data blades. One such data blade provides database connectivity to the Web. The engine allows for embedding SQL commands inside an HTML document, and the documentation indicates that the product can be used with minimal knowledge of CGI programming. Further information is available from `http://www.illustra.com`.

Ingres Tools Archive

Databases: Ingres

URL: `http://www.naiua.org/naiua-tools.html`

If you are using an Ingres database, you can use one of these tools to achieve connectivity between your database and your Web application. The first tool is ing-www-gsql, developed by Gordon Gallagher of King's College London. This tool provides an Ingres back-end procedure which, together with the GSQL system, allows WWW browsers to query Ingres databases.

ing-www-perl (developed by John Montald) is a similar tool but uses ingperl as its programming language. ingperl is an API library for accessing an Ingres database from a Perl program.

Mini SQL

Mini SQL (mSQL) is not a Web application development tool. It is actually a mini-database engine written in C. Its primary attraction is its low memory requirement, which makes it ideal as a back-end database engine for Web applications. It implements a subset of the ANSI SQL specification, which is sufficient for many applications.

The mSQL distribution includes the mSQL server, a C programming interface for client software, and several tools. There is a lot of user-contributed software available for mSQL, including interfaces to mSQL from Perl, TCL, REXX, Java, and Python. As of the writing of this book, Mini SQL 2.0 is under development and promises to handle larger queries and a larger subset of the ANSI SQL specification. Mini SQL was developed by Hughes Technologies Pty Ltd. Their Web page provides more information and links to some of the tools specifically designed for Web database development using Mini SQL. The URL is `http://Hughes.com.au/product/msql/`. There is also a JDBC-compliant driver for mSQL which is used in the application developed in Chapter 15 of this book.

ORALink

Databases: Oracle 7 Server for NT

URL: `http://oradb1.jinr.dubna.su/Software/ORALink/`

ORALink is a freeware product for Windows NT that works with Oracle 7 Server for NT. ORALink is basically a CGI application and is run by invoking the ORALink.exe file (under Windows NT the filenames are case-insensitive) by your HTTP server. There are some command line parameters you can specify:

- -d Debug mode provides you with a lot of debug output and can be used to track out the problem
- -s1 suppresses output of connect string
- -s2 suppresses output of copyright and build time stamp
- -s3 suppresses output of trailer
- -s4 suppresses output of rows processed count
- -s5 suppresses output of rows limit reached count

You can specify these parameters within the form tag as shown here:

```
<form action="/cgi-bin/oralink.exe?-ds1s2s3s4s5" method="POST">
```

The above statement will switch ORALink to debug mode and suppress all auxiliary output.

You will have to write the HTML file which includes the form, but within the form you can use ORALink commands and substitutions to achieve the desired results.

Commands

connect

Oracle connect string in form [username[/password[@dbpath]]].
   Example: <input name="connect"type="hidden"value="UnsecureName/UnsecurePassword">

title

HTML document title.
   Example: <input name="title" type="hidden" value="My query output">

sql

Any SQL statement or statements, separated by a semicolon.
   Example: <input name="sql" type="hidden" value="select id, salary from employers where salary > 120000">

background

Specifies the URL for an image to cover the background. The default is not to use a background image.

table_output

Specifies how the output should be presented. The possible values are

- *table,* which represents output via HTML <table> element
- *pre,* which represents output via HTML <pre> element
- *plain,* which represents output with no formatting

Example: <input name="table_output" type="hidden" value="table">

table_header

This command specifies whether table headers should be printed for the output. Its values are

- *on,* which prints the table header
- *off,* which does not print the table header

Example: <input name="table_header" type="hidden" value="off">

html

This command allows you to include HTML tags in your ORALink form. You can use it to enhance the look of your form or to make customization changes.

Example: <input name="html" type="hidden" value="<h2>VOTE RESULT, </h2> ">

file

Lets you append the content of a file to the output produced by ORALink.
Example: <input name="file" type="hidden" value="c:\http\docs\header.htm">

rec_limit

Limits how many records are included in the output. A negative value means there is no restriction.
Example: <input name="rec_limit" type="hidden" value="50">

Substitutions

Substitution tags are used by ORALink's interpreter. Any statements (except spaces) between left and right tags within the value option of an input tag are considered substituted. Similarly, any statements (except spaces) between left and right tags within the *name* option of an input tag are treated as substitutions. Substitutions are not case-sensitive.
Example: (assuming right substitution tag == left substitution tag == "::")
<input name="sql" type="hidden" value="select id, name, salary from employers where name like '%::Pattern::%'">
Enter employer name: <input size=30 type="text" name="::Pattern::" value="">

ORALink Utilities

ORALink comes with two utilities that help to configure the gateway and maintain internal accounts in your database. These utilities could be run on the same PC ORALink was installed on and by a person with administrator privileges. They are

- OLConfig, which is used to install, remove, and change settings of ORALink

- OLPasswd, which is used to add, delete, or change user account

OrayWWW

Databases: Oracle

URL: http://dozer.us.oracle.com:8080/sdk10/oraywww/

OrayWWW is an Oracle-specific gateway written in Oraperl. Oraperl is a flavor of Perl which supports database communication with an Oracle DBMS. It is very similar to Sybperl in function. Aside from a DBMS, Oracle has a Web server. If you use both, then you can bypass the CGI connectivity since the two are able to communicate with each other directly. Further information is available at http://www.oracle.com. Oracle is one of the few database vendors with its own Web server.

QDDB

QDDB stands for Quick and Dirty Database. It is a simple database engine that allows you to create relations, add tuples, modify tuples, delete tuples, and search for tuples in a fast and flexible way. QDDB revolves around the idea of a tuple tree, where tuples are stored and manipulated in an intuitive, pre-joined way.

QDDB supports the following search techniques: regular expressions, words and word ranges, numbers and numeric ranges, dates and date ranges. It is best used when your data is well-defined and you do not need a relational database engine. Because of its simplicity, QDDB is ideal for a CGI back-end where speed and efficient memory usage is a must. The entire package and some documentation can be downloaded from `ftp://ftp.ms.uky.edu/pub/unix/qddb/`.

VISIGATE

VISIGATE is a middleware product for Windows NT that connects to ODBC-compliant databases. By using asynchronous processing, VISIGATE can process multiple requests from Web browsers. It can also access multiple databases and can even be accessed from a single form. This product is built on the premise that it will support the largest number of databases possible. It enhances security by using a site-wide map file which hides the internal structure of the database tables from the end user. Application development using VISIGATE requires minimal, if any, HTML programming. Further information, along with a demo version of the product, can be downloaded from `http://prisys.com.au/lookfor/`.

web.sql

Databases: Sybase

URL: `http://www.sybase.com`

web.sql is Sybase's answer to Web database application development. This tool allows you to embed SQL statements and Perl scripts within an HTML document. Due to the fact that web.sql is directly linked to the HTTP server, it supports inline scripting. Such scripts are more efficient and execute faster than their CGI counterparts. web.sql is or can be supported on the following platforms:

- Sun Solaris (SPARC) 2.4
- Microsoft Windows NT 3.51 (Intel)
- SGI IRIX 5.3
- HP 9000/800 HP-UX 9.0
- IBM RS/6000 AIX 4.1.x

To use web.sql, you will need to have the Sybase System 10 or System 11 SQL Server running somewhere in your network. You will also need an HTTP server which supports CGI specification version 1.1 (almost all servers do). This tool will be a powerful utility if your development environment includes Sybase SQL Server and one of the supported platforms mentioned earlier.

HyperSTAR Web Developer's Kit

Databases: Sybase, Oracle, Informix, uniVerse, Ingres

URL: http://www.vmark.com/products/HyperStar

The Web Developer's Kit (WDK) is based upon the object-messaging middleware product HyperSTAR. It will work with any HTTP server which supports CGI. The WDK includes the following components:

- A visual query builder
- A C-language API
- A database-specific access server
- Documentation

HyperSTAR acts as middleware for all of the available information sources, regardless of location or hardware. HyperSTAR is a full-fledged development environment based on object technology.

NeXT WebObjects

Databases: Sybase, Oracle, Informix, DB/2

URL: http://www.next.com/WebObjects/

NeXT WebObjects is an object-oriented Web development platform that runs under Windows NT and various flavors of UNIX. The tool itself is database-independent and adds a dynamic HTML presentation layer to stored data.

According to the datasheet, WebObjects is "a server-based development environment for rapidly creating dynamic applications for the World Wide Web." A unique aspect of WebObjects is its ability to share the logic of your Web application and your data with other internal applications. It can use your database to generate the appropriate objects for their manipulation by the Web. In many cases, this means you will not need to rewrite your application to be used under the Web.

WebObjects is one of the few tools that supports the creation of Web applications containing Java applets. With Java applets, an entirely new set of sophisticated applications can be generated. WebObjects supports security standards such as SSL and SHTTP. It also includes built-in mechanisms to handle user authentication and operation under a network that uses firewalls.

WebObjects uses a three-tier architecture. These pieces include

- A graphic presentation layer based on the HTML forms
- The business logic of your application
- Data access

Such configuration is becoming increasingly popular since it allows you to share a piece of application logic or data with your internal (non-Web based) client/server applications. WebObjects is supported on Windows NT, HP-UX, Solaris, Digital UNIX, and NeXTSTEP.

O2Web

The O2 System is a fully modular object database system which integrates a database engine with a graphical programming environment. With O2DBAccess, an O2 application can manipulate information managed by any kind of SQL server. The O2 System is targeted for large-scale client/server development efforts. Further information is available from `http://www.o2tech.com`.

The O2 ODMG database system is a fully ODMG-compliant system and includes a database engine, a C++ programming interface, and an Object Query Language (OQL) query interface.

Oracle WebServer

The Oracle WebServer is Oracle's solution to Web and database integration. Designed specifically for the Oracle 7 database server, it supports standardized secure authentication mechanisms, encrypted data-streams, scalability, and support for numerous concurrent users. Dynamically generated HTML documents are created using PL/SQL, Oracle's procedural extension to SQL. The package includes three main components:

- Oracle Web Listener (HTTP Server)
- Oracle Web Agent (HTTP Client)
- Oracle 7 Workgroup Server (Database Engine Interface)

Oracle Web Server provides an environment for Web application development that is efficient and scalable. It can be used to create Intranet applications or external Web applications. For additional information about Oracle Web Server and demonstration software, visit `http://www.oracle.com/products/websystem/webserver/html/`.

Sapphire/Web

This is a graphical development tool which uses HTML forms as its user interface. A variety of database engines are supported, including Informix, Sybase, and Oracle servers. Sapphire/Web actually generates CGI programs in C or C++ which you can then customize to meet your needs.

As far as the developer is concerned, development using Sapphire/Web is similar to other tools made for the Windows or Motif environment. According to the product data sheet, the following steps are necessary for application development using Sapphire:

1. HTML forms and templates are created in your favorite HTML authoring tool.

2. You can then browse your application objects. These can be

   - Stored procedures in your database

   - Dynamic SQL functions

   - Executables

   - File (for read and write)

   - Objects available from object bridge (OLE, DSOM, Orbix, and so on)

3. After selecting an appropriate object Sapphire/Web, bring up a "Bind Editor" with appropriate arguments, results, and special editors.

4. Drag and drop from your HTML documents onto the Bind Editor. This *binds* HTML elements, such as a text input field or an option menu to arguments. It also binds the results of your query to appropriate HTML elements, such as an ordered list.

5. Conditional processing code can be added.

6. Finally, C or C++ code is generated to be used as a CGI program.

Additional information is available from `http://www.bluestone.com/products/sapphire/`.

Spider

Databases: Informix, Sybase, Oracle

URL: `http://www.w3spider.com/website/product.html`

Spider is another development tool targeted specifically for Web application development. It consists of two modules:

- Spider Development, which is a GUI-based Web/database interface development tool

- Spider Deployment, which executes applications

Supported platforms are SGI and Sun. According to the documentation, application development consists of the following steps:

1. Create an HTML form using any editor.

2. Select the action on the database: Query, Insert, Update, Delete, or Stored Procedure.

3. Define the SQL statement in the SQL editor.

4. Define the desired output, by dragging columns or tables from the output fields list.

5. Finally you can customize output, error handling, and security restrictions to meet your needs.

In the deployment phase, the Spider deployment module will dynamically generate the SQL as input to the database and HTML as output to the browser. Spider also supports Java.

SQLweb

SQLweb is an interactive server which provides full, dynamic database connectivity for Web applications. It is capable of performing the following database operations:

- Inserts
- Updates
- Deletes
- Queries
- Stored procedures

SQLweb runs under various flavors of UNIX and Windows NT. It supports most major database systems. Its latest information is available from `http://www.sqlweb.com/`.

A-XOrion

Databases: MS Access 2.0

URL: `http://www.clark.net/infouser/endidc.html`

A-XOrion is a CGI gateway that can access most brand-name PC databases. It runs under Windows 3.1/95/NT and requires MS Access 2.0. It supports the usual insert, update, and delete database operations.

ColdFusion

Databases: any ODBC-compliant database on Windows NT and 95

URL: `http://www.allaire.com/cfusion`

ColdFusion is actually a CGI program and achieves its objectives by mixing HTML tags and DBML (Database Markup Language) tags. As a result, there is no need for writing external CGI programs. Development of complete applications is supported by the ability to generate HTML pages on the fly. Among the many features of ColdFusion are the capabilities to

- Insert and update records in database tables with HTML forms
- Submit database queries that can then be used to dynamically generate Web pages
- Intermix the results of queries with HTML tags and text for complete control over how data is displayed and formatted
- Track users and customize their view of Web pages by using information about their browser, location, or other preferences
- Advanced data input and reporting features
- Validate form field entries as integer, floating point, date, or numeric range
- Make conditional statements (if...else branching) to dynamically customize output returned to users and decisions about queries submitted to the database
- Embed SQL statements in templates to specify queries. SQL statements may be dynamically customized using data from form submissions, URL query strings, and CGI environment variables, as well as the results returned from other queries.
- Execute multiple SQL queries and send SQL queries to multiple databases for each client request
- Supports Java and JavaScripts
- Supports Netscape cookies for state control

Instead of using plain HTML documents, ColdFusion uses templates which contain both HTML and DBML commands. ColdFusion parses the templates and executes the DBML commands. It then generates a page which includes only HTML tags and sends that to the browser. This can be summarized as follows:

1. When a user clicks on a form's submit button, the content of the form is submitted to the HTTP server.

2. The Web server opens a ColdFusion process, passing it the data submitted by the browser. It also specifies the appropriate template file to be used.

3. ColdFusion reads the data from the client and processes DBML commands used in the template, including the type of request to send to the database and the format that should be used to present information to the results page.

4. ColdFusion performs the necessary database operations using ODBC.

5. An HTML page is dynamically generated and sent to the browser.

The following example is taken from the documentation provided by ColdFusion. This template displays a list of products in a store.

```
Template (product.dbm)
    <DBQUERY NAME="Product" DATASOURCE="Store Database"
      SQL = " SELECT ProductName, Price FROM Products ">
    <HTML>
    <HEAD>
    <TITLE>Product List</TITLE>
    </HEAD>
    <BODY>
    <H1>Company X Products</H1>
    <P>
    <DBOUTPUT QUERY="Product">
    #ProductName# #DollarFormat(Price)# <BR>
    </DBOUTPUT>
    </BODY>
    </HTML>
```

Note how the *<DBQUERY>* tag specifies the SQL statement which forms the query. The result set from this query will be named *Product.*

The *<DBOUTPUT>* tag processes the results from the Product query. The variables enclosed by a # refer to the column names contained in the result set. The command DollarFormat places the numbers in the Price column in a standard dollar notation.

You can form a hyperlink to this template using the following URL:

```
http://www.company.com/cgi-shl/dbml.exe?Template=product.dbm
```

ColdFusion then generates an HTML document on the fly, which includes the result of the query.

DBML

You have already seen two DBML tags, namely *<DBQERY>* and *<DBOUTPUT>*.

The following is a description of additional DBML tags.

<DBINSERT>

Places data into a database without writing any SQL.

<DBUPDATE>

Updates data in a database without writing any SQL.

<DBIF... DBELSE>

Takes conditional action on the basis of query results or variables passed through URLs.

<DBMAIL>

Sends e-mail through SMTP. This function works like the DBOUTPUT function, except the record set is used to create e-mail messages instead of HTML documents.

<DBINCLUDE>

Embeds one template within another.

<DBSET>

Assigns variables within a template.

<DBCONTENT>

Sets the content type of the document. You could use this to deliver dynamic VRML (Virtual Reality Modeling Language) instead of HTML.

Compatibility and System Requirements

Since ColdFusion 1.5 employs the Common Gateway Interface (CGI), it can be used by a variety of Web servers. It also supports all standard Web server APIs, including the Internet Server API (ISAPI), the Netscape Server API (NSAPI), and the WebSite API (WSAPI).

ColdFusion has been tested for compatibility with the following servers:

- O'Reilly WebSite
- Netscape HTTPD
- Microsoft Internet Server
- Process Purveyor
- EMWAC HTTPS
- Internet Factory System
- Spry Web Server
- CSM Alibaba

DataRamp

Databases: any ODBC-compliant database

URL: http://dataramp.com

DataRamp is a tool for connecting to ODBC-compliant databases running on a remote machine. If your database engine is FoxPro, then your CGI program needs to communicate with it. This can be accomplished only if the FoxPro engine is running on the same machine as your HTTP server or on the same LAN. With DataRamp this location restriction is removed.

DataRamp is completely transparent to the application. The DataRamp client runs on Windows, Windows for Workgroups, Windows NT, and Windows 95. Free evaluation copies can be downloaded anonymously from the DataRamp Web site.

The DataRamp server acts as a Windows NT service. It listens for incoming requests from DataRamp clients and provides them with access to any ODBC data sources accessible to the server system. As for security, you can get a version of the server which uses RSA public-key encryption.

DB Gateway

Databases: FoxPro, MS Access

URL: `http://fcim1.csdc.com/DBGate`

DB Gateway is yet more middleware intended for linking the Web with databases. It is specifically designed to support Microsoft Access and FoxPro databases, but support for other databases is under development. It is actually a 32-bit Visual Basic application which runs as a server on an NT machine. Since all database interactions are handled directly by the program, no ODBC drivers are needed, removing an extra layer.

Submitted queries can be RQBE, internal Access, or external SQL files. The result sets can be raw tabular data or they can be exported to a reporting template that uses HTML-like tags to format the data. According to the documentation, the following is the DB Gateway process flow:

1. User submits an HTML form.

2. HTTP server starts the DB Gateway and passes to it the encoded form content.

3. DB Gateway uses the form content to build an appropriate query and submits it to the database.

4. DB Gateway receives the query result either in a raw tabular format or formatted using an external HTML report template.

5. The result is sent to the HTTP server, which is then sent to the browser.

dbWeb

dbWeb is a data-driven gateway between ODBC data sources and NT-based HTTP servers. Tools are provided to make the content of your ODBC-compliant database available over the Web with minimal CGI or HTML programming. Further information is available at `http://www.aspectse.com/Product/dbWeb/dbWeb.html`.

FoxWeb

Databases: FoxPro

URL: `http://www.foxweb.com`

As its name indicates, FoxWeb is a tool for connecting FoxPro databases to the Web. FoxWeb addresses the memory-consuming problem of starting several FoxPro applications by installing a number of native Visual FoxPro server instances that sit in the background waiting for a CGI call. Each CGI call starts an instance of a tiny executable written in C++, which then sends the request to the next available VFP server. Another advantage of this method is that the ODBC layer is bypassed, which boosts the speed. FoxWeb is designed to work under Windows 95 or NT. It works with any HTTP server that supports CGI 1.1.

R:WEB

R:WEB is an Internet version of the popular R:BASE application. It offers a Form Designer tool which allows the end user to create HTML forms and link them to a database. It is designed to run under Windows NT as a server. You will need R:BASE version 5.5 for Windows or higher for form and database design. The back-end database can be any database which R:BASE natively supports or any ODBC-compliant database. R:WEB acts as a CGI program to perform a query and generate an HTML output page. Additional information is available from `http://www.microrim.com/RBASE_Products/Software/RWeb.html`.

WebDBC

WebDBC is a Windows NT product that uses ODBC and CGI to access any ODBC-compliant database. It will be available for the Macintosh and Sparc Solaris platforms soon. Further information is available from `http://www.ndev.com/`.

WebBase

WebBase is an HTTP server with built-in database connectivity support. It runs under Windows 3.1/95/NT. SQL commands are embedded in the HTML document. Conditional branching is allowed in the form of if-else statements. Looping is also allowed so you can access records one at a time for processing. Additional information can be found at `http://www.webbase.com/`.

Tgate

Databases: Lotus Notes

URL: `http://www.shelby.com/pub/shelby/tgate.html`

Tgate provides connectivity between Lotus Notes databases and the Web. Currently it is available for Windows NT only. Full source code to TGate is included so you can extend the program to suit your particular needs. Tgate is written in Perl, and a Perl language interpreter is included. A Windows help file version of the Perl manual is also included.

PLWeb 2.04

PLWeb is not a database interface, but it is a useful tool for searching for textual information. It is a complete and powerful package with intelligent features such as:

- Natural language querying
- Relevance ranking of search results
- Dynamic concept discovery

PLWeb is based on the concept of distributed databases. When a client submits a search, the PLWeb engine searches multiple databases (local or remote) and generates a result set after contacting all the databases. The result set is a union of the information provided by each database. Since these actions are transparent to the user, it seems as if only one database had been searched.

PLWeb displays its output using a relevance-ranking mechanism, so the results that most likely meet the user's interest are shown first. Support is also provided for natural language and Boolean searching, so complex queries can be performed on the data. Another useful feature of PLWeb is concept searching which, coupled with a dynamic thesaurus, allows searching for *concepts* rather than keywords. This feature can be handy when a large collection of documents must be searched. PLWeb provides security mechanisms, an efficient indexing scheme (index size is approximately 35 percent of the data that is indexed), and full scalability.

Supported platforms are

- Sun SPARCstation - Solaris 2.3/2.4
- HP PA-RISC - HP-UX 9.05
- IBM RS/6000 - AIX 4.1
- SGI - IRIX 5.3
- DEC Alpha - OSF/1 (Digital UNIX 3.0)

PLWeb can search data stored in any of the following formats:

- ASCII in "PL Standard" format
- plain ASCII
- HTML
- Adobe Acrobat/PDF (HP and Solaris 2.3 only)

For a demonstration version and complete documentation, refer to `http://www.pls.com/products/web2dat.html`.

SWISH

SWISH stands for Simple Web Indexing System for Humans. With it, you can index directories of files and search the generated indexes. For example, you can index your e-mail directory and then search for all occurrences of "John Doe" in your e-mail files. Note that this is a two-step process. First the index needs to be generated, then it needs to be searched. The first task can be done weekly or biweekly, depending on your application.

As far as the Web is concerned, despite database connectivity there are still many applications in which a large amount of textual data (for example, office memos) needs to be searched. These applications can be developed using a database engine, by putting the text in a BLOB data field. Or, it can stay as it is and a search engine, such as SWISH, can be used to perform queries on it. SWISH is very simple in the way it indexes information and searches the indexes. It does not search for different versions of a word or do natural language processing. For some applications, SWISH might just be enough.

SWISH is written in C, so it is portable to many platforms. It has been tested on the following:

- SunOS 4.1.3
- Solaris 2.4
- BSDI 1.1
- IRIX 5.3/4
- OSF/1 2.0
- Linux 1.2.2/1.2.8
- AIX 3.2.5.

SWISH can be used in conjunction with a CGI program to provide a Web interface. It is executed like any other UNIX program from the shell. Here are the valid usage syntaxes:

- swish [-i dir file ...] [-c file] [-f file] [-l] [-v (num)]
- swish -w word1 word2 ... [-f file1 file2 ...] [-m num] [-t str]
- swish -M index1 index2 ... outputfile
- swish -D file
- swish -V

Complete documentation, along with examples, can be found at `http://www.eit.com/software/swish/`.

GLIMPSE

GLIMPSE (GLobal IMPlicit SEarch) is yet another search engine. Its trademarks are its speed and small index size. It also has a mechanism to search for misspelled words, making it an ideal tool for searching OCR documents which often have misspellings.

GLIMPSE is built on the UNIX tool agrep and supports many of the same options. A version of GLIMPSE built for specific use with HTTP servers is available. It is called GLIMPSE-HTTP and can be found at `http://glimpse.cs.arizona.edu:1994/ghttp/`. GLIMPSE has the ability to include or exclude files with certain extensions, so it is very easy to index your entire Web document directory. Source code for GLIMPSE is available at the above URL. There are also executables for the following platforms:

- Sparc Solaris
- Sparc Sun OS 4.1.1 and 4.1.3
- OSF/1 DEC Alpha
- Linux
- AIX
- SGI
- HPPA
- HP-mc68k
- RS6000
- freeBSD
- NeXTStep3 (on NeXT)

Excite for Web Servers

Excite is similar to the other search engines discussed so far. One of its unique features is its ability to perform concept-based queries instead of keyword queries. Using Excite requires minimal programming since it creates all the CGI programs and HTML files necessary to interface with the Web. It is specifically designed as a Web search engine.

Excite is supported by the following platforms:

- SunOS
- Solaris
- SGI Irix
- HP-UX
- IBM AIX
- BSDI
- Windows NT

It requires a minimum of 32 MB RAM and 5 MB for the search engine. You will also need disk space equal to approximately 40 percent of the size of your document collection for the index. Excite can index HTML and ASCII documents. Further information about Excite is available from `http://www.excite.com/`.

Sybperl 2.0

Databases: Sybase

`URL: http://www.sybase.com`

Sybperl is an extension to Perl for connecting to a Sybase database. It is written by Michael Peppler. It requires Perl 5.001 with patches 1a through 1m recommended. The distribution consists of three parts:

- Sybase::DBlib implements the Perl 5 version of the DB-Library API
- Sybase::Sybperl implements the Sybperl 1.0xx API, and is built on top of Sybase::DBlib.
- Sybase::CTlib implements a subset of the newer Client Library API

There are two methods for Sybperl to integrate itself with Perl. One method allows the Sybperl modules to load dynamically as they are required by the Perl script. This is similar in principle to how Dynamic Link Libraries (DLLs) function in the Windows operating system. The second method actually incorporates the Sybperl code with the Perl executable. Depending on your system, this could add as much as 1 MB to the size of your Perl interpreter.

A Point About Using the Dynamic Library

Recall that the HTTP server is responsible for spawning new processes to handle the CGI scripts. These scripts usually run under the ownership of a specific user with very limited privileges. If you choose to use the dynamic loading option with Sybperl, be sure that this user knows the appropriate path to the loadable modules during runtime. Otherwise, Sybperl fails to initialize and crashes the Perl program, causing a 5xx error to be generated by the HTTP server. This error is difficult to detect because when you run the script under your ownership, it will find the necessary modules since they are probably in your path.

In order to use Sybperl, follow the instructions in the README file which is included in the distribution package. Basically, you make some modifications to a configuration file and run the Makefile, which builds the library and the modules. A series of test modules are provided to check the package once you are done.

Documentation about the syntax and using the package can be found under the pod subdirectory in the distribution. The mailing list `sybperl-list@itf.ch` is established to discuss matters related to Sybperl. You can subscribe to this list by sending a message to `sybperl-list-request@itf.ch` with the word "subscribe" in the body. Sybperl's DB-Library module was used in previous chapters to demonstrate CGI applications.

dbedit

dbedit is a product of the Globewide Network Academy, whose Web server is located at `http://www.gnacademy.org/`. This package allows the user to create and edit database tables using the Web. dbedit works with the /rdb database system created by Revolutionary Software (`rdb@rsw.com`).

Unlike some of the other packages discussed in this chapter, dbedit is a CGI toolkit and does require Perl and HTML knowledge. It will take some of the routine tasks out of writing CGI scripts, but it still requires some programming. To use this package you must have a UNIX machine. The current version of dbedit is 0.9b4 and is available as a gzip'ed tar file from `http://www.gnacademy.org:8001/uu-gna/tech/dbedit/dbedit.html`.

Sibylla

Databases: Oracle, Informix, Sybase, BasicPlus, Ingres, Microsoft SQL Server, mSQL

Sibylla is an application development framework for Web-based database applications. It provides access, through the Internet or TCP/IP LAN, to data stored in a database, indexed HTML files, or any data managed by a server-side application.

Software developed with Sibylla is organized in simple modules which allow rapid application definition and prototyping together with simplicity in integrating external applications. These modules are written in the Tool Command Language (TCL). Due to the portability of TCL, Sibylla is available on many UNIX platforms, including

- SunOS
- Solaris
- HP-UX
- Ultrix
- AIX
- OSF1
- Dc/OSx Pyramid
- Linux
- VMS (available without the mSQL Module and the ODBC Module)

Sibylla version 2.0 is organized in four modules:

- WWW Module interacts with the HTTP server through CGI, performs URL manipulation and error handling, and activates server-side applications.
- SQL Module uses the msqltcl library from Hakan Soderstrom to access the mSQL database from Fiddich Technologies.
- BasisPlus Module is needed only for those applications which require interfacing with a BasisPlus database.
- ODBC Module lets you access every UNIX database supporting an ODBC interface. ODBC Module uses the ODBC driver from Visigenic Corporation.

The ODBC module provides the following functions to a Web application:

- Read and write access to SQL databases
- Creating and passing queries to databases
- Building reports by merging data from the different SQL databases and applications
- Data insert using data filled in an HTML form
- Displaying the database errors directly from a WWW client
- Writing Sibylla programs to automatically insert data in the database from a formatted ASCII file

Further information is available by e-mailing cotti@ariadne.it.

WebLib

WebLib is a tool built by NASA/GSFC which allows you to write a database interface (DBI) for each kind of database you want to query. The term database is used in a loose sense since it can refer to relational, object-oriented, or flat-file formats.

In WebLib, a search engine is called a *DBI*, or *database interface*, and is nothing more than an executable (written in any language you desire) which reads a query from the standard input and writes the results to the standard output. Both the input and output syntax are based on the *name=value* format. As a tool, WebLib provides specifications to write your own DBI for the database you use. It also provides you with a library of C utilities to assist you in DBI development. In a way, WebLib is different from the other tools discussed so far. It requires you to write the search engine component of your application, however, WebLib handles the rest.

Summary

Programmers always appreciate useful tools that help them with the application development process. Web developers are no exception. There is a wide variety of tools on the market today and many more emerging on a regular basis. These tools can be categorized into several classes. Some are basically CGI development tools. They take care of generating CGI scripts for an application. Since all HTTP servers support CGI, these tools work with any server.

A second group of tools shares the common theme of embedding SQL and database commands within the HTML document. These tools usually consist of a second server (in addition to the HTTP server) which parses the HTML document and performs the database operations. Such tools also include a reporting module where the query result can be formatted using HTML-like tags.

A third group of tools are not really database tools, but search engines for managing large static documents. These tools allow you to search a collection of HTML or ASCII documents. Usually these tools offer an indexer program that you must run in advance to generate proper indexes. A second component is actually the search engine which uses the indexes to search for a phrase or keywords in the collection. Sophisticated tools allow your search to include Boolean operators, natural language queries, and misspellings. CGI scripts are used to link these search engines to the Web.

Finally, a fourth class of tools is used only for connectivity. For example, Sybperl merely provides a link between a programming language (Perl) and a database (Sybase). These tools are important when you develop your own CGI applications. The majority of these tools act as middleware, which means they can connect to a number of databases.

Depending on your application and your environment, you might or might not choose to use one of these tools. However, it is nice to know about them and how they work. There might be just the right tool out there for your application that can save you valuable time.

10

The Final Applications

So far, we have discussed the individual components necessary to build a Web database interface. In this chapter, we put together the different pieces and discuss them as a whole. You will soon find out that the pieces can fit together in several different ways. Several different scenarios are discussed, along with their advantages and disadvantages. Also, several networking configurations are discussed since they relate to database security considerations.

Before you begin this chapter, be sure that you understand the individual components as they were described in previous chapters. Also review the Client/Server model described in Chapter 2.

Looking at the Overall Picture

Recall that there are four distinct components for interfacing a database to the WWW. These are

- HTTP client and server
- CGI program (your code)
- Database client and server
- Underlying network layers

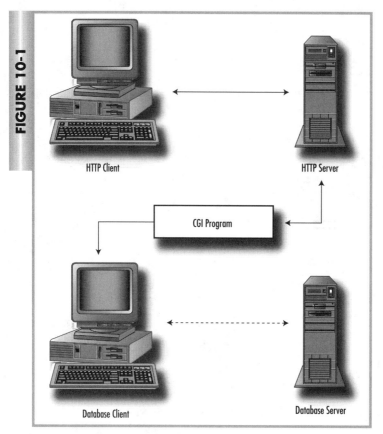

FIGURE 10-1

HTTP Client

HTTP Server

CGI Program

Database Client

Database Server

Communication among the components

Figure 10-1 shows the basic flow of information among these components. Note the dotted line between the database client and server. This indicates that you will not always have two distinct components for your database operation. For example, if your database is a FoxPro file, you can write to it directly. In other words, you do not really use a database server. On the other hand, if you are dealing with a larger system, your database server can reside on a different machine from the one running the HTTP server. Similarly, you could have a situation where the database resides on a mainframe computer and you have to find ways to establish a TCP/IP communication channel to the mainframe or middleware.

The above configuration is the basic model. Depending on your environment, you might have to use a variation. Some of these variations are used more often than others because of efficiency, cost, and other reasons. Some variations are not used simply because they do not make sense. You can think of the configuration as a puzzle where the pieces can fit together in several different ways; the art is to find the best way for your environment. For example, it is possible to have the WWW browser (HTTP client) and the database server on the same machine. By doing so, however, we are defeating the purpose of the client/server model. Figure 10-2 shows an example that uses Open Database Connectivity (ODBC) as middleware.

FIGURE 10-2

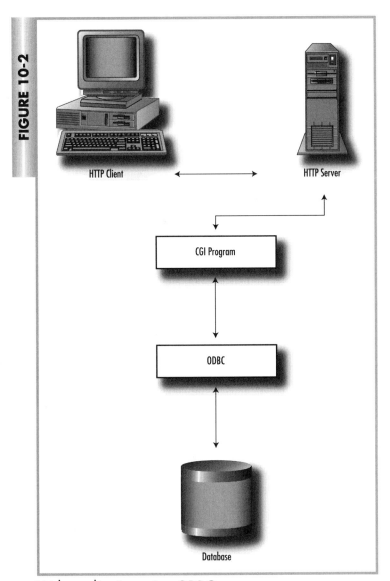

HTTP Client   HTTP Server

CGI Program

ODBC

Database

Web application using ODBC

In another configuration, you might use Java Database Connectivity (JDBC) and have a separate connection to the database, independent from the Web client. This is shown in Figure 10-3.

FIGURE 10-3

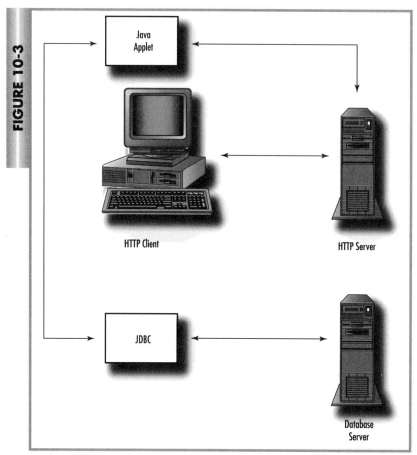

Web application using JDBC

Different configurations are possible. In secure environments, the architecture can get even more complicated since firewall machines can be used to separate the different components as needed. Talk to your network administrator and try to get an idea of how your Web application should be configured. Consider a single packet and trace its route. Consider the different machines it passes through, the different network hubs, and the different lines it must cross. In secure environments, make sure the network service you want to use is available on the machine. On some systems, services such as mail, telnet, and ftp are disabled due to security concerns. This information should give you a good idea of how best to configure your application. For example, if the connection between the database client and server is a slow one or the database server is running on a relatively slow machine, then purchasing extra memory for the Web server machine would not do much good. Understanding your configuration helps you design a better application overall. Remember, no matter how efficient and fast the individual components of your application are, it is usually the overall configuration that determines the usefulness of the application.

Networked Database Server

When you use a networked database model (for example, Oracle or Sybase) the database components of your Web application are fully integrated into the existing network. Any communication between the gateway program and the database must go through the network. To be more precise, the gateway program communicates to the database client on the same machine, and the database client communicates with the server over a network connection. This setup is illustrated in Figure 10-4.

This setup is very common in existing client/server situations where the database server resides on a *heavy-duty* machine all by itself. The server talks to its clients via a layer on top of the existing network layers, commonly known as the application layer or the database network layer. This is important since a busy network can mean a slow database.

Let's step through a typical communication path.

1. The user sits in front of machine 1, launches a browser, and points to a URL containing an order form. Through the Internet, machine 1 establishes a connection to the Web server residing on machine 2 and sends a request for the page containing the order form.

2. The Web server sends the form to the client, and the user can now fill out the form and submit it. The HTML page containing the order form might include some JavaScript code which the browser on machine 1 will execute.

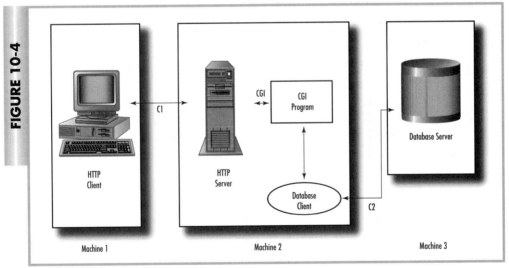

FIGURE 10-4

Networked database server

3. After submission of the form, the HTTP server takes control and the CGI interface transmits the data to the gateway program. Recall that this is the program you write.

4. This gateway program parses the data and makes calls to the database Application Programmer's Interface (API) to execute an INSERT statement. INSERT is an SQL statement for adding new data to a table. Your database might use another name for this command if it is not an SQL database server.

5. The APIs actually communicate to the database client on machine 2. The client transfers the information based on the database's protocol to the database server (machine 3) via the database network layer.

6. The database server on machine 3 executes the query and sends the result back to the database client on machine 2.

7. The database client in turn sends the result of the query to our gateway program, and our gateway program prints a "Thank you for your order" message to its standard output.

8. The output of the gateway program is sent back to the browser by the Web server through the Internet.

Note the two connections marked as *C1* and *C2*. They are both network connections, but they don't have to be on the same network. In other words, the HTTP network and the database network are independent of each other. For example, the HTTP network can run on TCP/IP, and the database network can run on Novel Netware or a Windows for Workgroups network. This can be useful, since you are separating your database from the TCP/IP network and, in doing so, you have provided some security (although this type of security is not sufficient for even a non-critical application). Another thing to note is that the connection between machine 2 and machine 3 can consist of several other machines, especially in situations where a firewall exists. This is shown in Figure 10-5.

You are likely to use this model if your database is relatively large and a true client/server database. Informix, Sybase, and Oracle are a few examples. In such a situation, chances are the database server resides on a machine maintained by a different group of administrators (DBAs) and perhaps in a different physical location than yours. You will need to be in close communication with the database administrator. Your application is providing another interface to the database engine. If the database is a mainframe application, there is the possibility that the data is not always up-to-date due to batch processing. There might be times when the database is not available for backup or other administrative duties. You need to take these occurrences into consideration as you develop your application.

FIGURE 10-5

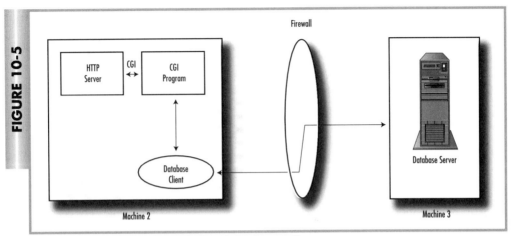

Connecting to a database behind the firewall

Another common problem—if you can call it a problem—with this configuration is that it provides access to mission-critical data. Some administrators set up a smaller database server that can be accessed by a Web application. At regular intervals, the content of this database can be copied to the main database. During this copy operation, several checks can be performed to assure the integrity of the database as a whole. This is shown in Figure 10-6.

You can offer this compromise solution to your database administrator. Sooner or later, people will accept the Web as a standard application interface and will lift the special restrictions and considerations.

Non-Networked Database Server

The non-networked database is useful for smaller organizations. In this case, the same machine (machine 2) handles the HTTP server and database server. The gateway program also resides on the same machine. This setup is shown in Figure 10-7. The obvious drawback of this setup is performance slowdown. Here we have one machine running two servers and executing a program on a regular basis. Depending on your applications, this configuration might or might not work for you. Also, notice we have eliminated the network connection for the database so we might get a performance boost.

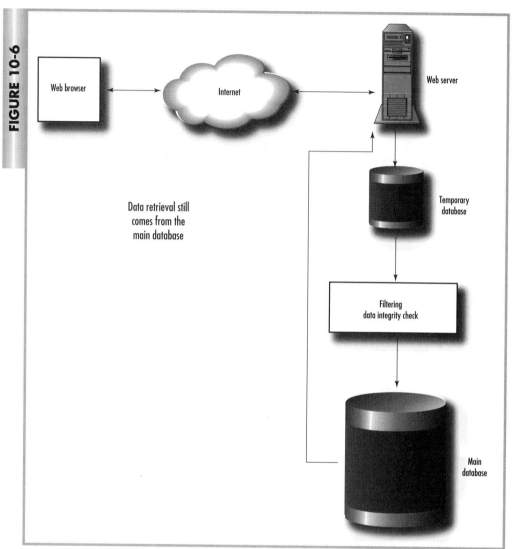

FIGURE 10-6

Temporary Web database

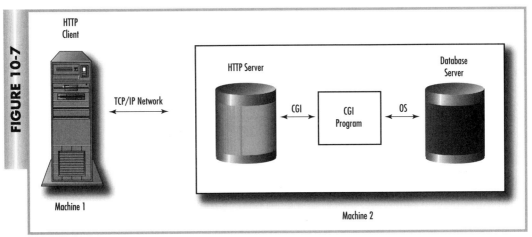

FIGURE 10-7

Non-networked database server

Let us walk through the communication path for this scenario.

1. The user points to a URL residing on the HTTP server, which is an on-line order form.

2. After filling out the form, the user submits it to the server, which in turn sends it to the gateway program.

3. The gateway program makes the necessary calls to the database API and receives a response from the database server. Since the server is on the same machine, no network communication occurs at this point. The communication between the CGI program and the database is operating system dependent.

4. Next, the gateway program sends a message to the HTTP server and the server transmits the message over the network to the HTTP client.

This configuration is very popular because of its simplicity. You need only one machine to act as your server machine, and you have to deal with only one network connection. If there is a slowdown of the network, the user will have to wait, but the server can go about processing other requests while waiting for a response from the database to the CGI program.

Another place where this type of configuration is useful is in a development environment. For example, if your application is written to comply with ODBC or JDBC, then the target database can be a small database on the same machine as the Web server. Later on, to move the application to a larger environment, all you need is to change the database driver (ODBC or JDBC) and replace it with one provided by a larger database such as Informix or Sybase. Your application can stay intact for the most part.

Finally, the price of this configuration is small, making it ideal for smaller businesses and organizations. You don't need complex networks on your side. All you need is a machine connected to the Internet. As for security, if the server machine is compromised, your database will be, too, since it is on the same machine. There definitely is a security risk associated with this configuration.

Networking Considerations

In conventional database programming, you can almost be sure the user will see any messages you put on the screen. In the world of WWW programming, however, this assumption is no longer valid. In any configuration, your gateway program talks to the HTTP server. It is the server that must transmit the message to the HTTP client residing on another machine. As a programmer, you are trusting the server to do its job, and that really is all you can do. If the server goes down or the network connection is disrupted, the user will never see the message you have sent (see Figure 10-8). There could also be a case where the server or the network is very busy and processing takes longer. By the time the server gets to process your request, the client is no longer listening.

You also have to take into account that your network connections can become a real bottleneck for your application. The Internet is a network of networks; therefore, you will

FIGURE 10-8

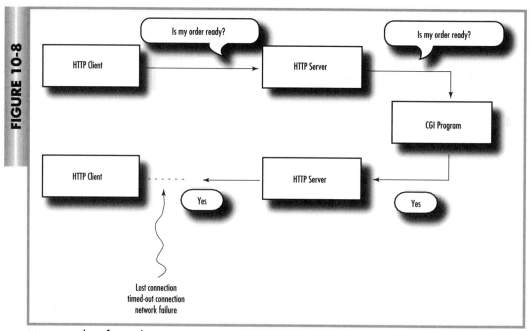

Message lost from the program

have HTTP clients from a variety of networks attempting to contact your server. Some connections are reliable and fast, some are not. Before you send a picture of a product to the client, it would be nice to at least warn the user that a large picture is coming their way. You don't want the user to stare at a blank browser screen not knowing what is happening. Try to eliminate or reduce the number of times this could occur in your application. For example, you can time each connection and classify it based on speed. Then you can send a message like, "It seems that you are residing on a slow network. Are you sure you want to see a picture of product X?" Most browsers offer the option of downloading a page without the pictures; however, not all users are aware of such features.

Determining the Client Software

Most CGI implementations convey the name of the client software and its version to the external program. They also provide information about what MIME types are accepted by the client. Under CGI/1.0 for UNIX, the environmental variable HTTP_USER_AGENT provides information about the browser. The general format is software/version. The HTTP_ACCEPT environmental variable lists the MIME types accepted by the browser. Each type is separated by commas. The format is type/subtype, type/subtype. By doing some of this work behind the scenes, you can improve your user interface substantially. Similar provisions are made available if you use NSAPI.

It is imperative that you have a basic understanding of your network. You should find out what happens to a packet after it leaves the Internet and enters your network. How many firewalls does it go through? How fast are the firewalls and how busy are they? How many routers and hubs are involved in your network? Similarly, you need to find out what happens to a packet after it leaves your HTTP server and before it enters the Internet.

You also will be dealing with a large variety of HTTP clients. Some support JavaScripts, some don't. Some support HTML 3.0 enhancements, some don't. Unless you are dealing with an Intranet application in which you have control over the clients and their configurations, your best bet is to equip your application to deal with different scenarios. You can use the environmental variables that are part of CGI specifications to get information about the browser. Some of the newer servers on the market have built-in capabilities to identify the browser for each request they receive. By now, you should have an idea about the function associated with each component and how the components fit together in an overall application. This leaves us with one more point to discuss: the CGI program.

How Does CGI Fit in the Picture?

The Common Gateway Interface (CGI) is a standard for interfacing external applications with information servers, such as HTTP servers. You can configure your HTTP server or your database server, but the CGI program is what you write. It is the heart of your Web application, and in it you perform all the functions necessary in your application. You need to write the CGI code with the Web environment in mind.

Since a CGI program is executable, it is basically the equivalent of letting the world run a program on your system, which causes security concerns for many system administrators. Chapter 11 deals with security issues related to CGI. A second point of concern is the overhead involved with CGI programs. An HTTP server might receive several requests in a short time period, each requiring the launch of a CGI program. In the same way that opening up several applications on your PC can slow it down or yield an "Out of memory" error, running multiple CGI programs can cause difficulties for your system.

The large overhead associated with CGI has prompted HTTP server vendors to come up with an alternative solution: server API. Many HTTP servers on the market also provide a set of API functions your program can call. They allow your program to communicate directly with the HTTP server with greatly reduced overhead. While CGI can be used with almost any language, server APIs are more restrictive. Also, there is not an accepted API for all servers, but CGI is universally supported by all HTTP servers. By using a server API, you will eliminate the security concerns associated with the CGI standard. Consider your environment and decide if a server API will work for you. Remember that you are restricting yourself somewhat as far as portability of your application is concerned, but in some cases it might be worth it.

CGI Program Communication with the Database

We discussed the interaction of the CGI program with the HTTP client in Chapter 5. Here we concentrate on the communication between the CGI program and the database. No matter what the database is, it provides a set of functions and statements so clients can communicate with it. Each database has its own API, although they all provide similar functions. A typical database transaction is shown in Figure 10-9.

All the usual considerations for a database application apply to Web-based programs. You just have the extra duty of dealing with Web protocols. For example, you still have to decide how to resolve the classic problem of two or more users attempting to modify the same data. Most database engines handle contention problems automatically by performing page locking, record locking, or some similar function. Familiarize yourself with how your database handles these situations.

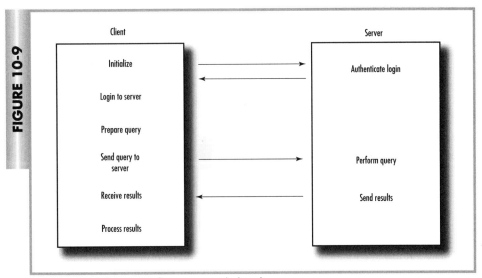

FIGURE 10-9

Transaction diagram for a typical database

The most common problem developers run into when they begin Web development is the stateless nature of HTTP, which means every form is treated independently by the HTTP server. The stateless nature of the protocol will prohibit you from developing any useful programs unless you provide continuity in your application by including extra variables. This is often done using the familiar **<input>** tag with the **type=hidden**. Suppose the user has entered a customer identification number in a form. You use that number to search the database and come up with a screen displaying the account history for that customer. Suppose the user then clicks on a particular transaction to get additional information. You have now lost the customer identification number and cannot search the database. To get around this problem, the initial form that accepted the customer identification number would generate the account history information plus the following:

```
<input type=hidden name=cust_id value=12345>
```

Now, the next form will have the customer identification number available to it as another *name=value* variable pair. The hidden type prevents the browser from displaying the value on the screen, but the user can see it by viewing the HTML source code. Don't use this technique to pass on confidential information such as passwords or credit card numbers. Figure 10-10 shows this technique. It is also used in Chapter 14 in the trouble reporting system application.

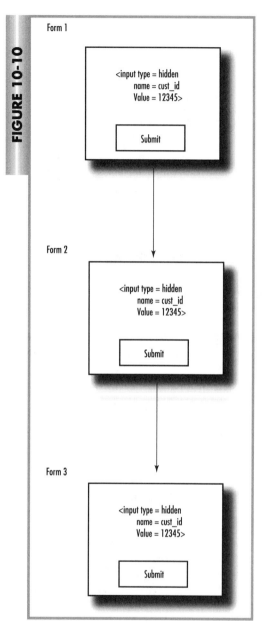

FIGURE 10-10

Using the hidden tag to pass
information to other forms

Netscape Cookies

Several methods exist for getting around the stateless nature of HTTP. One such method is Netscape Cookies. The idea is to store the state of the transaction on the client. When a Web server returns an HTTP object to the browser, it may include a piece of state information along with a list of URLs for which that state is valid. The client will store this information on its side. If the client sends a request pertaining to any of the stored URLs, it will also include the state information in the request. The object that holds the state information is called a cookie.

If your CGI program needs to store some state information on the client, it would send the following to the client:

```
Set-Cookie: name=value; expires=date
path=path; domain=domain_name; secure
```

The *name=value* pair is the state information that the server is asking the client to store. The *<expires>* tag indicates how long the cookie is valid for. If this attribute is not set, the cookie will expire when the user terminates the session. The doma in is used in matching URLs to those associated with cookies. This information, in conjunction with the PATH variable, is used to determine if any cookies are associated with a particular URL. The secure option assures that the cookie is transmitted only when a secure connection is in place.

If a URL matches a stored cookie on the client, then the client will send the following as part of its request:

```
Cookie: name=value; name=value; ...
```

which is a line containing the *name=value* pairs of all matching cookies.

You can find additional, up-to-date information about the cookies' specifications at the Netscape Web site. If you know the browser supports cookies, you should use this feature in your applications.

We conclude this section with Listing 10-1, a code segment in C that shows how a CGI program would complete its interaction with the database. This code segment assumes the database server resides on the same machine as the CGI program (non-networked database server). It is written using the Sybase DB-Library and heavily commented so you can follow the code.

Listing 10-1

```
/* Initialize DB-Library. */
if (dbinit() == FAIL)
    exit(ERREXIT);
```

continued on next page

continued from previous page

```
/* Install the user-supplied error-handling and message-handling
 * routines. They are defined at the bottom of this source file.
 */
dberrhandle((EHANDLEFUNC)err_handler);
dbmsghandle((MHANDLEFUNC)msg_handler);

/*
** Get a LOGINREC structure and fill it with the necessary
** login information.
*/

login = dblogin();
DBSETLUSER(login, USER);
DBSETLPWD(login, PASSWORD);
DBSETLAPP(login, "XYZ Company");

/*
** Get a DBPROCESS structure for communicating with SQL Server.
** A NULL servername defaults to the server specified by DSQUERY.
*/

dbproc = dbopen(login, NULL);

/*
** We are going to retrieve some information, from a table
** named "customer."
*/

/* First, put the commands into the command buffer. */
/* mzip is a variable set based on the user input from the fill-out form.

dbcmd(dbproc, "select name, address, phone from customer");
dbcmd(dbproc, " where zip = ");
dbcmd(dbproc, mzip);

/* Send the commands to SQL Server and start execution. */
dbsqlexec(dbproc);

/* Process each command until there are no more. */

while ((result_code = dbresults(dbproc)) != NO_MORE_RESULTS)
{
    if (result_code == SUCCEED)
      {
      /* Bind program variables. */

        dbbind(dbproc, 1, NTBSTRINGBIND, (DBINT)0, name);
        dbbind(dbproc, 2, NTBSTRINGBIND, (DBINT)0, address);
        dbbind(dbproc, 3, NTBSTRINGBIND, (DBINT)0, phone;
```

```
       /* Now print the rows, first specifying the MIME type*/
          printf("Content-type: text/html \n");
          while (dbnextrow(dbproc) != NO_MORE_ROWS)
          printf("%s %s %ld %s\n", name, address, phone);
       }
/* Close our connection and exit the program. */

dbexit();
exit(STDEXIT);
}
```

How It Works

In order to process a query, several steps are necessary. We first must initialize the DB-Library, which prepares it to process a transaction. We also specify the error-handling and message-handling routines. These steps are standard among most programs.

```
if (dbinit() == FAIL)
    exit(ERREXIT);

dberrhandle((EHANDLEFUNC)err_handler);
dbmsghandle((MHANDLEFUNC)msg_handler);
```

We now prepare to log in to the database. This involves creating a login structure and filling in the necessary information. For most applications, this information includes the login name and the password. It is usually a good idea to ask the user to enter that information every time. To keep this example simple, we hardcode this information. After we fill in the structure, we can use the **dbopen** function to log in to the database. This function returns a **dbproc** handle, which we will use in any subsequent communications with the server, very much like the file handle in a C or Perl program.

```
login = dblogin();
DBSETLUSER(login, USER);
DBSETLPWD(login, PASSWORD);
DBSETLAPP(login, "XYZ Company");

dbproc = dbopen(login, NULL);
```

Next, we create the query and send it to the server to be processed. In our case, we are asking the server to return all names, addresses, and phone numbers from the customer table that have a zip code equal to the value in variable mzip.

```
dbcmd(dbproc, "select name, address, phone from customer");
dbcmd(dbproc, " where zip = ");
dbcmd(dbproc, mzip);

dbsqlexec(dbproc);
```

The server processes our query and creates a result set. You can think of the result set as a grid containing the results of your query. This grid is basically a subset of your table that has matched your query. This concept is shown in Figure 10-11. We don't know how big this grid is, but we do know it is not larger than the original table.

FIGURE 10-11

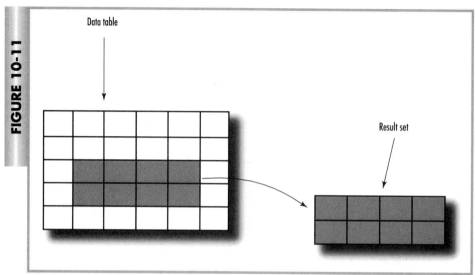

Data table

Result set

The concept of a result set

To process the result, we use a loop structure. The outer loop goes through each result set and the inner loop goes through each row within a result set. Since we sent only one query, we expect only one result set and only go through the outer loop once. If our query actually returns any data, we bind each column of the result set to the appropriate variable. Now we are ready to enter the inner loop. As long as there are rows left in our result set, we print their values. Note that the **dbnextrow(dbproc)** function takes care of retrieving the next row and putting the column values into appropriate variables as defined by the **dbbind** functions earlier. Also note the famous "Content-type: text/html \n\n" line, which is necessary before the HTTP client can display the results. Next, we close our connection and exit the program.

```
while ((result_code = dbresults(dbproc)) != NO_MORE_RESULTS)
{
    if (result_code == SUCCEED)
    {
        dbbind(dbproc, 1, NTBSTRINGBIND, (DBINT)0, name);
        dbbind(dbproc, 2, NTBSTRINGBIND, (DBINT)0, address);
        dbbind(dbproc, 3, NTBSTRINGBIND, (DBINT)0, phone;

        printf("Content-type: text/html \n\n");
        while (dbnextrow(dbproc) != NO_MORE_ROWS)
            printf("%s %s %ld %s\n", name, address, phone);
    }
}
dbexit();
exit(STDEXIT);
}
```

How Java Changes the Picture

The emergence of Java as *the* Internet programming language has introduced new ways of linking databases to the Web. Recall that an HTTP server can serve plain HTML documents, which are static, or it can execute a program that conforms to the CGI standard or the server's API. With Java, the server can also serve an entire application (or part of it). This application can establish a connection to a database using HTTP or its own independent communication channel (such as JDBC).

The ability to serve an application over the Net provides new venues for developers. Appendix C is a discussion of the Java language and its specifications. Figure 10-12 shows how Java enables an HTTP server to serve an application.

Java is a programming language like C or Pascal. Because it was developed as an Internet programming language, it has several unique features. A Java program can be executed on almost all platforms. Actually, the Java code is interpreted and not compiled like a C program. After you write your Java code, you compile it. The result of this compilation, however, is not an executable file, it is a special binary file called the *byte code*. This file contains the Java application. A Java interpreter is then used to execute (interpret) the byte code on a client machine.

How do you transfer a Java application over the Net? The most common method is through an applet. A Java program can be written in two modes: a stand-alone application and a Web application. Applets refer to Java programs written specifically for the Web. Recall how an image is embedded in an HTML document. The *<IMG>* tag is used. Upon seeing this tag, the browser knows an image needs to be received from the server and makes that request. Similarly, the *<APPLET>* tag is used to indicate the presence of a Java applet. The Java-capable browser understands this special tag and makes a request to the HTTP server for the byte code. After receiving the byte code, the browser begins executing the Java program. The program can use the HTML page as its output screen, or it can open up its own window.

Because the application code resides on the client, no inquiries to the server are needed. Java applications are all event-driven, which means you can capture events associated

Java application served by an HTTP server

with the objects in your application and perform appropriate code. You can tell immediately that the user has performed an action and will not have to wait for the action to be sent to the HTTP server and your CGI program.

The first question you should ask is: What happens to security? With Java, a server serves an application and the client machine executes it. What if the application is written to perform harmful functions on the client machine? The designers of Java were well aware of this fear and implemented several security measures, which are discussed in Chapter 11. Basically, an applet has limited authority for using system resources. The normal mode of operation is execution of an applet as an *untrusted* applet, which means the applet cannot write to the local file system, open up extra socket connections, and so on. In addition, several provisions which enhance security were made in the way the byte code is generated and executed.

JDBC is a standard that attempts to link Java to any database engine similar to ODBC. With JDBC, a Java applet can open up a connection to the database and maintain that connection. Your program no longer has to deal with the problems caused by the stateless nature of HTTP.

Another unique feature of Java is its ability to access resources over the Internet. For example, in C you can open a file on the local file system and perform some operations on it. With Java, you can open a file residing on a different network as seamlessly as you would open a file on your own network (assuming that you have the appropriate security permissions). As a result, Java is truly an Internet programming language.

Efforts are under way to develop a more efficient Java, replacing the byte code with a true compiled executable. Integrated development environments for Java are hitting the market gradually. With enhanced performance and increasing network connectivity, you should consider Java as you plan your database applications. Even if you are not ready to develop the entire application in Java, you could consider using Java to perform some of the functions offered by your program and gradually migrate the entire code to Java.

Summary

In this chapter, we basically put the pieces of the puzzle together and showed how they work with each other. The beauty of CGI is its open architecture, which is a result of the client/server model. For example, suppose you develop an application that uses an MS Access database but, at a later time, your database changes to Sybase. The only piece of the puzzle that needs to be changed is the Gateway program. Instead of using the MS Access API, it will have to use the Sybase API, which is not a huge modification.

We cannot emphasize enough the importance of a good network connection, especially if you are using a networked database server. Make a habit of tracing the dynamics of your application and see which connections are crucial. If you are writing a mission-critical application, you must have safeguards against slow or down networks.

Finally, the database API is your means of communicating with the database. Learn it well and determine the most efficient methods of accessing the data you need. If you are starting from step one and have to design the database, keep the purpose of the application and its operating environment in mind. If you have already been given a database, you must concentrate on making efficient use of your API calls.

Questions

1. Name the four basic components for interfacing a database to the WWW.

2. T/F: The database server communicates directly with the Gateway program in the *networked* database server configuration.

3. T/F: As a WWW programmer your main concern is the communication between the HTTP server and client.

4. What does CGI stand for?

5. Which component of the WWW causes security concerns the most?

6. What do you use to communicate to a database?

7. What are cookies?

Answers

1. HTTP client/server, Gateway program, database client/server, network layers

2. False. It must go through the database client first.

3. False. The Internet takes care of this part of the application.

4. Common Gateway Interface

5. CGI and the fact that a program gets executed on a server machine with input from the client.

6. The database's own API or middleware such as ODBC.

7. Cookies are the objects that hold the state information on the browser.

11

Security Issues

The increasing popularity of the Web as a business tool has raised some security concerns for both users and system administrators. Add a company database to the Web, and the concern is even greater. The Web is a network service, and in order to make it useful, it must be reachable by all the people who would potentially use the information. In some cases, these people might be company employees, or they might be anyone in world. You should quickly realize the foremost problem in computer security. It is a chicken-and-egg type of situation. You have to provide security, but at the same time you need to make sure that all *legitimate* users can gain access to your system.

This section gives you an overview of computer security as it applies to the Web environment. It discusses the implementation of several security methods. If you recall from Chapter 2, "The Internet and the World Wide Web," the OSI model divides a network service into seven layers. The immediate question becomes: Which layer is most suitable for implementing security mechanisms? As it turns out, security can be implemented in several layers, each with its own advantages and disadvantages.

Depending on your application, security might or might not be critical to you. Also, security implementations depend heavily on how the rest of your network is set up. The best implementations are those that consider the environment and come up with a solution for that particular environment.

The large amount of material available on computer security prohibits complete coverage in this book. For a more in-depth discussion, refer to a computer security text or the on-line resources mentioned throughout this chapter.

The Problem

World Wide Web security can be studied at several levels, with the most fundamental approach taken at the protocol level: HTTP. The key to the success of the HTTP protocol is its simplicity and open architecture. Such openness has made it available on a variety of platforms using different operating systems. As the technology matures, the World Wide Web is no longer viewed as a massive collection of documents. It is a complete interactive application interface, as reiterated throughout this book. Unfortunately, such openness does come at a price, which is compromising security.

The security threats from the World Wide Web can be categorized as follows:

- **Information leakage:** Confidential documents stored in the HTTP server falling into the hands of unauthorized individuals.

- **Illegitimate use:** Confidential information sent by the browser to the server (or vice versa) being intercepted. A good example is credit card information.

- **Integrity violation and denial of service:** Bugs that allow outsiders to execute commands on the server's host machine, enabling them to damage and modify the system.

- **Violation of server and network security:** Information about the Web server's host machine leaking through, giving unauthorized individuals access to data that may prompt them to break into the host, paving the way for all the attacks mentioned above.

Perhaps the best way to model security vulnerabilities of the HTTP protocol is to look at a typical HTTP transaction. Figure 11-1 shows the packet exchanges for the retrieval of an HTML document with at least one uncached inline image. The TCP packets are shown via arrows from the client to the server and vice versa.

First, the browser opens a TCP connection to the server based on the URL, and the server responds. The client must know that the responding server is really the server that the client intended to communicate with and not some other server acting as the legitimate server. Next, the browser sends the actual HTTP request for an HTML document. This request is made at the application level. The server accepts the request, reads the document from disk, and sends it to the client. The browser parses the HTML commands in the document and displays the file. Because HTTP is stateless, each request is made independently of the others. The browser once more opens a TCP connection and requests the data for the image that is part of the HTML document it just received. Note that this request does not have to be for an image. It could be a Java applet, an animation, or some other binary data. The server receives the request and sends the image back to the browser—without knowing that the request has come from the same browser that requested the HTML document.

Now that we have a low-level picture of the transaction activity, we can consider the problem at a higher level. Many companies are eager to complete financial transactions on-line (for example, mail-order catalogs). Let us examine such a transaction and consider its Web security issues. Suppose company XYZ sells a variety of clothing items using an on-line catalog. A customer uses a URL and accesses the home page for company XYZ. The very first issue is the customer's need to verify that the home page is indeed the official page for company XYZ. It is very important to verify who is on the other side of the wire, since the customer is going to send a credit card number over the Net and place an order. The process of making sure a server, a client, or a user is indeed the server, client, or user they purport to be

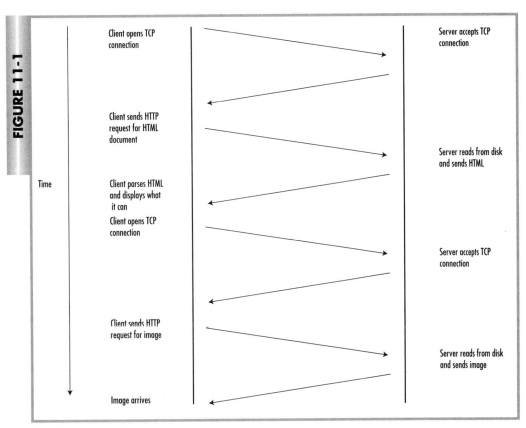

Packet exchanges for a typical HTTP transaction

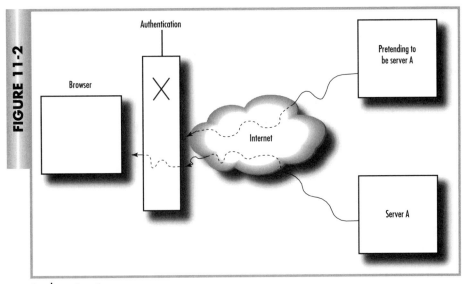

Authentication

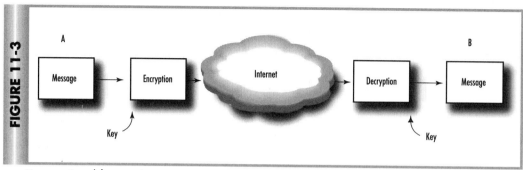

FIGURE 11-3

A

Message → Encryption

Key

Internet

Decryption → Message

B

Key

Encryption/decryption

is called *authentication*. As you will see, all security implementations have some built-in form of authentication. Also, authentication and in particular, user authentication, turns out to be the most difficult aspect of computer security. How can a machine sitting on the Net verify that it is communicating with a particular individual? The authentication process is shown in Figure 11-2.

After authentication, the customer must relay shipping and billing information to company XYZ's server in a secure manner. Since this information is enclosed in TCP/IP packets, it is subject to interception by a third party. Therefore, a secure method must be provided to transmit this information. The most common method is to use some form of an *encryption* algorithm so that the transmitted data can only be seen by legitimate users. Several encryption methods exist, each having its own mathematical foundation. At the application level, you should not be concerned with the mathematical details of the encryption algorithms. The encryption and decryption process occurs automatically, as shown in Figure 11-3.

Finally, company XYZ must send a confirmation back to the customer in a secure manner, a process subject to the same two problems discussed above.

So the problem boils down to two key components: authentication and secure transmission (encryption). Secure HTTP (S-HTTP) and Secure Socket Layer (SSL) are two of the more widely used security implementations. Both have been submitted for consideration as a standard. As you might expect, these methods require that both the server and the client perform additional functions related to security. As a Web developer you will not be dealing with the details of these implementations, but you should have a basic understanding of how they work. A good document summarizing Web security issues is found at `http://www.nortel.com/entrust/certificates/primer.html`.

S-HTTP

S-HTTP (Secure HTTP) was developed primarily in response to the growing involvement of businesses in the Internet. Its primary sponsor is CommerceNet, a coalition of businesses interested in developing the Internet for commercial uses. S-HTTP's main functions are user/

server authentication and secure transmission, the two basic elements needed for WWW security. Secure NCSA httpd is a reference implementation of S-HTTP and is available for most platforms. Information on this particular implementation can be found at `http://www.commerce.net/software/Shttpd/Docs/FAQ.html`. The server's security behavior is controlled through enhanced HTML document properties, local security configuration files, S-HTTP header directives, and server-side includes.

Security is included for all document transactions and Common Gateway Interface (CGI) programs. The server can be configured to perform in one of the following modes for all its transactions:

- **Sign:** This is similar to personal signatures on legal documents or checks. A signature is supposed to convey the authenticity of a document.

- **Encrypt:** Using a mathematical algorithm, the content of the document is converted to unreadable data. With the proper key, the decryption process can convert the unreadable data back to a readable form.

- **Sign and encrypt**

- **Neither sign nor encrypt**

Authentication

In the non-computer world, a person's signature or a company's stamp authenticates an item. In the computer world, digital signatures are used to certify document integrity. Needless to say, they work very similarly to the way normal signatures work. The server signs documents (or CGI program output) before they are sent to the client. The server can also verify the integrity of a query from a client by checking the digital signature of the query. S-HTTP uses a private/public key scheme based on the RSA algorithm. Its digital signature is a computed value called the Message Authentication Code (MAC). This code is the result of a key hash function which takes as its input the message text, the time (this is optional and would be used to prevent replay attack), and a shared secret between client and server. This function then generates the MAC as its output. This mechanism allows two parties to identify each other reliably in a transaction.

 ## What Is a Public/Private Key?

Several encryption/decryption algorithms are based on the idea of *public/private keys*. The RSA algorithm is no exception. The idea is best explained through an example. Consider two parties, A and B. Each party has its own private key known only to that party and no one else. Each party also has a public key that gets publicized to the world. When party A wants to send a document to party B, it signs it with its own private key and party B's public key. Since B's private key is the only key that can decrypt a document signed by B's public key, B is the only party that can decrypt the message. So the

continued on next page

continued from previous page

algorithm provides a mechanism to send data without worrying about it being intercepted by a third party. Furthermore, B will require usage of A's public key to decrypt the document. A document signed by A's private key can only be decrypted by A's public key. No other public key will work. As a result, B can be sure that the document was indeed sent and signed by A. Figure 11-4 shows this process.

FIGURE 11-4

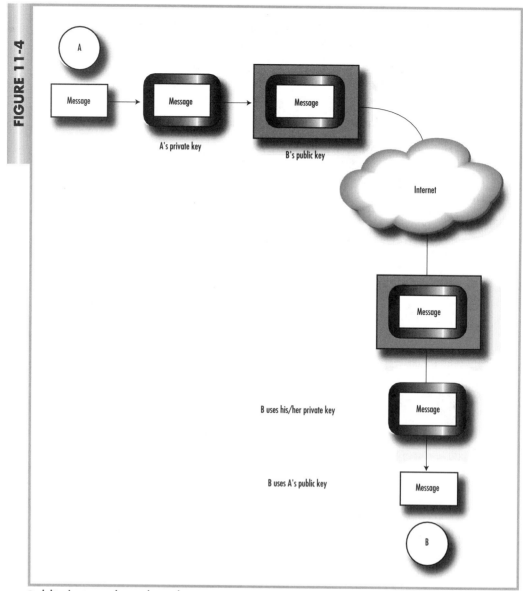

Public/private key algorithms

Replay Attacks

Depending on the algorithm used, decryption of a message can take years. As a result, attackers sometimes give up on decryption and use a replay attack. A *replay attack* consists of performing a certain number of actions known to produce a particular result. In the computer world, actions are presented by data, and so a replay attack often consists of presenting the same data to the server and hoping that it is accepted as legitimate data. To counter this type of attack, most implementations add a sequence number or a time stamp to a transaction. As a result, replay attacks always fail since no two transactions will have the same sequence number or time stamp.

Privacy

To ensure privacy, the HTTP server is capable of encrypting outbound messages and decrypting inbound messages. Both shared and public/private key schemes for encryption/decryption are supported. A *shared scheme* (Figure 11-5) involves only one key. Party B must somehow know the key before it can decrypt a message sent by party A. These schemes require less overhead and provide sufficient security in most cases. Several shared implementations exist, such as RC2, RC4, and DES. A mathematical treatment of these algorithms is beyond the scope of this book. For public/private keys, the RSA algorithm is used.

Regardless of the encryption method, an important issue is managing the different keys. After all, the keys are the heart of the security algorithms, and if they are compromised, the whole scheme is compromised. In S-HTTP, a server can have only one private key. This key, along with the matching public key, is stored in a database file on the local machine (the machine the Web server is running on). It is assumed that both physical and electronic access to this machine is limited. As an extra precaution, the database containing the keys is encrypted via a user-specified password.

HTTP Encapsulation

To ease transition, S-HTTP must be able to support the existing HTTP protocol. An S-HTTP message consists of a request or status line (as in HTTP), followed by a series of headers, followed by encapsulated content which can be an HTTP message, plain data, or another S-HTTP message.

The request line from the client should start with the S-HTTP protocol method, as in the following:

```
Secure * Secure-HTTP/1.1
```

Responses by the server should start with

```
Secure-HTTP/1.1 200 OK
```

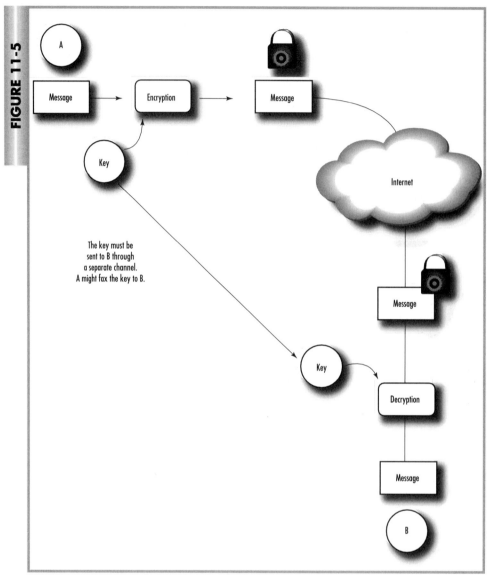

FIGURE 11-5

Shared (symmetric) key scheme

Several new header lines are defined for an S-HTTP message. Two of them are required. The first one is *Content-Privacy-Domain*, which exists merely to provide compatibility with PEM-based Secure HTTP systems. The two values defined by this header are *PEM* and *PKCS-7*. These are both standards for the format of a message. You can find the exact text of the standard on the Web. The second required header is *Content-Type*, and should read

```
Content-Type: application/http
```

which is consistent with HTTP specifications.

S-HTTP Header Lines

New header lines that go in the encapsulated content of the message and are protected are also introduced. These include

- **Security-Scheme:** The security scheme used in the current transaction.

- **Certificate-Info:** Providing the receiver with this information means he or she no longer has to retrieve this information explicitly or from a third party, which reduces overhead.

- **Key-Assign:** Indicates that the client wishes to bind a key to a symbolic name for later reference.

Negotiation

To add more flexibility to the secure environment, S-HTTP allows both parties to negotiate their needs and preferences regarding security parameters. The negotiation stage is very important. For example, a server can refuse to talk to a client if the client does not support any security mechanisms. This task is done at a *negotiation block*, a sequence of specifications each having four distinct parts:

- **Property:** The option being negotiated, such as encryption algorithm.

- **Value:** The value being discussed for the property, such as DES, RSA, or any other algorithm name.

- **Strength:** Degree of urgency for the preference. In other words, whether the option is required, optional, or refused. For example, a server might start by requiring a digital signature of a specified size. The larger the size of the signature, the more difficult it is to decrypt the message without knowing the key. If the client cannot accommodate the size requested by the server, the server might reduce its expectation and require a smaller size signature.

- **Direction:** The direction which is to be affected by the property. Valid values are during reception or origination (with respect to the negotiator).

Consider the following negotiation header:

```
SHTTP-Symmetric-Content-Algorithms: recv-optional=DES-CBC,RC4
```

implies that either the DES-CBC algorithm or the RC4 algorithm can be used for encryption.

S-HTTP defines a new protocol designator, `shttp`. A URL of the form `shttp://www.xyz.com` implies that the target server is S-HTTP capable and that a client capable of supporting S-HTTP is required to access the URL.

Vulnerabilities

S-HTTP offers a legitimate security scheme for the World Wide Web. Its encryption algorithms are sophisticated enough to ensure privacy and correct authentication. The optional time value can defeat ordinary replay attacks. However, since it implements security at the application level, lower-level attacks might succeed. That is, attacks through the TCP or IP level can occur without the application level ever finding out about them. There is also an underlying assumption that the Web system administrator has properly configured the machine and restricted unauthorized access to databases containing servers' private keys and public certificates.

SSL

Unlike S-HTTP, SSL (Secure Sockets Layer) is implemented at a lower layer in the OSI model. Therefore, it can be used to enhance security in not only HTTP, but in other protocols such as ftp, telnet, and NNTP. SSL includes provisions for both server and client authentication and encryption of data in transit. Netscape Corporation developed the scheme, and many vendors have endorsed it. SSL requires a reliable transport protocol (such as TCP) for data transmission and reception, which is always present in the case of HTTP and other application protocols. The latest version is SSL 3.0, which is available from the Netscape Web site.

Since SSL is implemented at a lower level than application protocols such as HTTP, it can encrypt the data and authenticate the sender before the application protocol sends or receives its first byte of data. This offers enhanced privacy compared with the other schemes. According to the specifications released by Netscape Corporation, the SSL protocol opens and maintains a *secure* channel through which higher level communication takes place. The secure channel has the following properties:

- **The channel is private.** Encryption is used for all messages after a handshake is used to define a secret key. Symmetric cryptography, such as DES and RC4, is used for data encryption.

- **The channel is authenticated.** The server always authenticates the clients, and the client can also authenticate the server. Asymmetric cryptography (public/private key) is used for authentication.

- **The channel is reliable.** Each message includes a message integrity check using a MAC. Secure hash functions, such as MD2 and MD5, are used for MAC computations.

The SSL protocol consists of two separate protocols (see Figure 11-6). On top of the reliable transport layer sits the *SSL Record Protocol*, which encapsulates all transmissions. On top of that is the *SSL Handshake Protocol*, which establishes security parameters through negotiations.

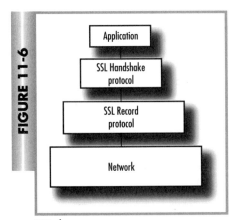

FIGURE 11-6

SSL layers

Unlike HTTP, an SSL session is stateful. The handshake protocol coordinates the states of the server and the client. The record layer receives data in blocks from higher layers. The record layer fragments the data into records of 2^{14} bytes or less and applies a compression algorithm to it if one is requested. Next, the data blocks are encrypted and readied for transmission.

During any SSL session, certain variables need to be defined. For example, the server needs to determine which version of SSL the browser supports and what encryption algorithm should be used. Such negotiations occur at the handshake layer dictated by the SSL handshake protocol. Authentication also occurs at this level. The handshake protocol is one of the more interesting components of SSL. It is also one of the more important parts of the security scheme. A summary of the protocol follows.

1. The browser transmits a `client hello` message. The exact form and content of the message is outlined in the SSL specification.

2. The server sends a `server hello` message in response. At this time, the above transaction has caused the following attributes to be agreed upon:

   - Protocol version (SSL 2.0 or 3.0)
   - Session ID (each SSL session has a unique ID)
   - Cipher suite (a list of the encryption/decryption algorithms supported by the client, sorted based on the client's first preference)
   - Compression method (a list of the compression methods supported by the client, sorted based on the client's first preference)
   - Two random numbers generated by the client and server

3. If the client must authenticate the server, the server will send its certificate. Additionally, a `server key exchange` message may be sent which is used for the exchange of keys for the agreed upon encryption algorithm.

4. After the server is authenticated, it may in turn request a certificate from the client.

5. The server transmits a `server hello done` message and awaits a response from the client.

6. If the client was asked to send a certificate, it does so now. If it has no certificate available, it must send a `no certificate` alert message. Next, the client key exchange message is sent to the server. The content of this message depends on the algorithm established by the `client hello` and `server hello` exchange.

7. If all has gone well by this time, the client sends a `change cipher spec` message, and the parameters that were agreed upon go into effect for this session. This is followed immediately by a `finished` message from the client.

8. The server sends its own `change cipher spec` message, which is followed by a `finished` message.

9. This ends the handshake between the client and the server.

Figure 11-7 is a summary of the handshake protocol. The different messages mentioned above are all in form structures in the C language. For details, refer to the SSL specification.

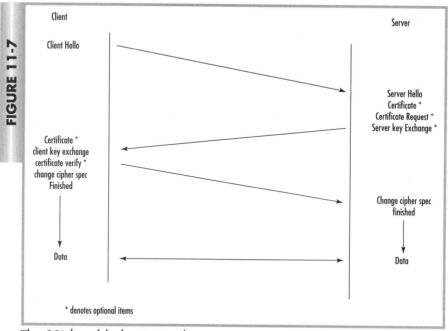

FIGURE 11-7

The SSL handshake protocol

What Are Certificates?

Certificates are an important part of the SSL protocol. With the introduction of Netscape Navigator 3.0 browser and the new servers, certificates will play a more important role in the authentication part of secure transmissions. A *certificate* is an electronic method of verifying the authenticity of a server. This lets the client verify that the server to which it has connected is indeed the correct server. When the server provides the client with a certificate, the client checks it against a list of certificates stored in its database. It also checks it against a list of certificate authorities in its database. A *certificate authority* is a third party that issues certificates to servers. If the browser trusts a certificate authority, it will trust any certificate that is signed by that certificate authority. One way to make sure only authorized users access your site is to distribute your site certificate to the users you want to use your site. Certificates have an expiration date after which they become invalid. Make sure all your clients receive a new certificate before theirs expires. You can contact one of the certificate authorities to receive a certificate for your site. This can usually be done through e-mail. Your Netscape browser comes with a list of site certificates and certificate authorities already in its database.

Vulnerabilities

The SSL protocol has been used since the early versions of the Netscape browser. It has proven to be an effective protocol that is expandable. The encryption schemes used (such as RSA) have been proven to be secure. An attractive feature of SSL is its implementation at a low level. As a result, the protocol can be used by other higher level applications. The Java language will have a secure transmission mode based on SSL. Sites that support SSL can be identified by the `shttp` prefix in their URL. Once you connect to a secure site, all your subsequent communication will be done in encrypted mode. With the popularity of SSL, you should make sure your Web server supports this protocol.

Securing Your Server

The HTTP server running on your machine is engaged in a live process. It listens to a particular port and performs actions based on the commands it receives. Usually these commands come from a legitimate browser pointing to your URL, but they could be coming from a person trying to gather information about your machine or attempting to break into your system. One of the most important steps you can take is to ensure that your HTTP server is installed properly and securely. Here are some of the things you should be aware of:

● The HTTP daemon spawns child processes to handle CGI scripts. Make sure that your CGI scripts are executed under ownership of a fake user such as *nobody* or *www*. This user should have very restricted access on your machine and minimal read/write privileges.

● All of your HTML documents and CGI programs should be writable only by the owner. Remove group or world write permissions from them.

● If your server has a directory in which it keeps logging information, make sure the directory is not writable, or even readable, by the world.

● If your server supports usernames and passwords for accessing documents, you can use it to restrict who can look at a particular page or execute a particular CGI program. NCSA HTTP provides a mechanism to do just that.

● When a URL points to a directory, most servers look for a file called `index.html` in the directory and send its content back to the client. In the absence of such a file, the directory listing is sent back to the client. Make sure all your directories contain an `index.html` file, even if it is just an empty file. This will prevent outsiders from looking at the content of your directories.

If your site uses a firewall, you will need to set up a *proxy server* to access sites outside of your domain. This is shown in Figure 11-8. When a browser sends a request, it does not directly communicate with your Web server. It must first go through a proxy server, which in turn sends the request to the actual HTTP server. Similarly, when a browser within your organization requests a document from a server outside your firewall, it makes that request first to the proxy server. Then the proxy server contacts the server and obtains the document.

Several proxy servers exist in the market, including one from Netscape and the CERN proxy server. You probably want to buy a proxy server that supports not only HTTP but other applications such as ftp and telnet, since they are all subject to the same restrictions as HTTP when used from behind the firewall. Aside from added security, proxy servers can also boost performance. A proxy server can cache the documents it has obtained. Therefore, if a number of users in your network request the same document, the proxy server must obtain it only once through the traffic of the Internet. Any subsequent requests do not have to go further than the proxy server. Note that proxy servers should not cache secure documents, for obvious reasons.

CGI Security

The CGI specification allows a browser to request that a particular program be executed on the server machine. The ability to execute a program on another machine sounds like and *is* a dangerous idea. If someone somehow put a copy of a harmful program in your

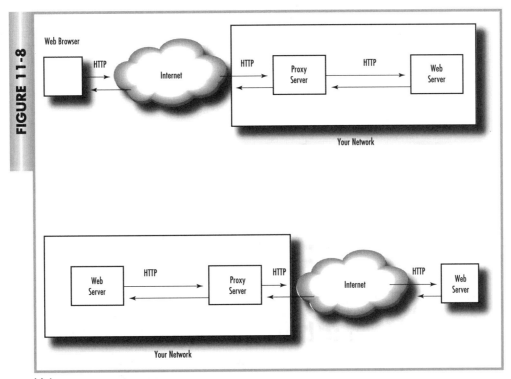

FIGURE 11-8

Using a proxy server

`cgi-bin` directory, then he or she could execute that program from anywhere, anytime, without logging onto the machine. Although this is an extreme case, CGI security is important and should be carefully considered.

Since database applications need to communicate with the database, security of your database engine also comes into play. Most database engines have an access control mechanism that allows you to specify which users can do what on a database. Use such a mechanism when you design your application, but don't rely solely on it. Security can and should be implemented at several levels.

Unless you have a good reason, a CGI script should not give out any information about the machine it is running on. If, for example, you put the **ps** command in your `cgi-bin` directory, it would show all the processes running on the server machine to the browser. Again, unless you have a good reason, avoid giving out such information.

Unless you are using JavaScript or some other client-side language, you cannot assume anything about what is entered in a text box. If you have declared a variable with a size of 10 characters, you might get 15 characters in the box. Most tools dynamically allocate memory and can deal with such issues, but you should be aware of them, especially when using a compiled language like C or C++.

In terms of security, it is extremely unwise to pass user input to a shell command without first checking it. Suppose you have an input box asking for the user's e-mail address. You then pass the content of the input box to the shell, asking it to execute the `sendmail` program like this:

```
/usr/lib/sendmail user-input
```

This will work fine if the `user-input` is a legitimate e-mail address. But what if the input is something like this?

```
john_doe@xyz.org; rm users.html
```

Now, the shell executes the `sendmail` program and sends an e-mail to `john_doe@xyz.org`. It sees a semicolon, which separates commands in a shell. So it tries to execute the next command, which is `rm users.html`!

There are many more issues regarding safe CGI programming. A good tutorial is available from `http://www.primus.com/staff/paulp/cgi-security`. If you use the Perl language for your CGI programs, consider using the taint checking option provided by the Perl interpreter. You can turn on taint checking by using the `-T` option when invoking Perl. Any variable that is set using data from outside your program, such as data from the environment and standard input, is flagged as tainted. These tainted variables cannot be used to affect anything outside of your program. For example, they cannot be used in SYSTEM(), EXEC(), or EVAL() function calls. Doing so will result in Perl exiting with a warning message. To untaint a tainted variable, you will need to perform an explicit *patent matching* operation on it. For example, if the variable `$phone` is used to store the value entered by the user in an HTML form, then it is tainted. To untaint it, we use the following line that eliminates all characters except numbers.

```
$phone =~ /[^\d]//g;
```

Java and Security

Languages such as Java also raise some security issues. With Java, the server sends an application to the client, and the client executes it. Again, a scary idea. Fortunately, the designers of Java have paid special attention to security issues and have incorporated many checks and balances. The most obvious is the inability of an applet to write to the file system or open up extra network connections unless it is authorized to do so. The default mode for running an applet is as an unauthorized applet.

Java addresses security concerns at several levels. The language itself is very robust. Without pointers, one of the greatest causes of bugs in C programs has been eliminated. Also, pointers were used by a malicious program to write to areas of memory and cause unwanted results. Java classes and their variables and methods are designated as private or public, thus limiting their scope. When a byte code is executed, checks are done to make sure it has not been tampered with. The byte code verifier is responsible for this task. Figure 11-9 shows a diagram of the different stages of Java code from the Java white paper published by Sun Microsystems.

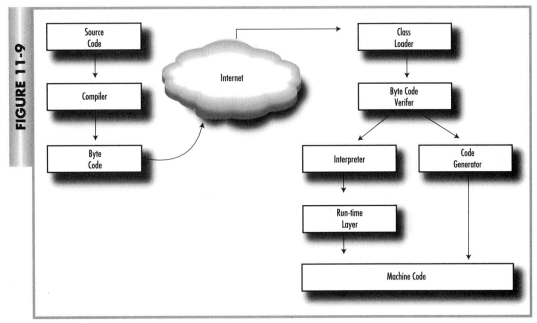

FIGURE 11-9

Java code stages

Despite all the precautions, security holes in the Java language itself and browsers that support it have been found. Researchers at Princeton University found several flaws in the security implementation of Java and have summarized their findings in a paper available from `http://www.cs.princeton.edu/~ddean/java`. The Java language is still evolving, and as implementations are developed, new security holes will be found.

Other Issues

The mechanisms shown above are useful when both the client and the server wish to perform a secure transmission and have the capabilities to support such transmission. There are some other areas where security concerns have risen. For example, when your browser accesses a Web page, the HTTP server logs that access. It also receives some information about the browser, which usually includes

- The name and version of the browser
- The IP address of the browser machine
- The operating system of the browser machine
- The types of documents (content-type) which your browser will accept
- Your user name (if available)

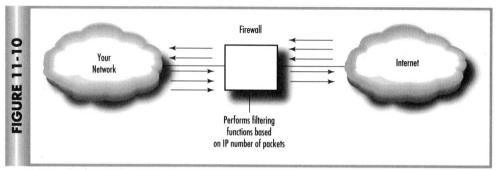

FIGURE 11-10

A simple firewall

As you can see, this is a lot of information and certainly is sufficient for a hacker to at least attempt a break-in. In short, be aware of information that you give out to the public on a routine basis. If you use a proxy server, which makes the actual request to the external Web sites, the above information becomes secondhand and less useful to an intruder.

Firewalls are the most common method for keeping outsiders away from your network. There are too many details to mention in this book, but basically a simple firewall is a machine running special software. This machine sits between your network and the Internet. It filters all packets your network receives or sends based on some rules. For example, you can say, "reject all packets from host with IP number xxx.xxx.xxx.xxx." This example is shown in Figure 11-10. Firewalls can be very sophisticated. A good reference is *Firewalls and Internet Security* by William R. Cheswick and Steven M. Bellovin.

Summary

When developing applications, security should always be given fair consideration. Web applications are even more security conscious because of their accessibility. Unlike a traditional client/server application used by employees of a company, a Web application can potentially be used by a global audience. Since the Web application is connected to your database, you want to be especially careful to protect the integrity and security of your database.

Since the OSI model divides the network into layers, Web security can be implemented at several layers. When you install a firewall, you deal with security at the transport level and the Internet level by filtering out packets based on their IP address. This is a very low-level mechanism, but it ensures that all layers on top can operate in a secure space. The drawback is that the client and the server must support this low-level security mechanism.

Web security measures have also been implemented at the application level. These mechanisms enhance the existing HTTP protocol, which is an application layer protocol, and have added security mechanisms.

The two basic security issues are verification of legitimate users (*authentication*) and transmission of information in a secure manner (*encryption*). Any Web security measure must include support for these two parts.

Finally, there are steps you can take when writing your CGI program to assure it is executed with proper permission and not prone to attacks by outsiders. There are also server configuration parameters you can set to enhance security of your server, but these parameters seem to be different from server to server.

Questions

1. What are the two basic security mechanisms necessary for a secure Web transaction?

2. What sets SSL apart from other Web security implementations?

3. What is a replay attack and how can it be prevented?

4. Who should execute CGI scripts?

5. How is privacy compromised on the Web?

Answers

1. Authentication and encryption.

2. SSL implements security at a much lower level (socket level), ensuring that all higher levels enjoy a secure channel for transmission.

3. A replay attack occurs when an intruder listens to a legitimate communication and tries to replay it, expecting the receiver to act similarly. It is usually prevented by including a time stamp or a life-time value in each communication so that it cannot be used again.

4. A fake user like *nobody* or *www* with very limited access on the system.

5. All HTTP requests by browsers are logged in the server, including the IP number, the version of the browser being used, and some other information. You are constantly giving out this information.

12

Maintaining Your Application

As a developer, you are well aware that finishing up an application does not get you off the hook. Applications must be maintained, and Web applications are no different. The term *maintenance* is used in a generic sense here and includes common tasks such as debugging, modifying the application, adding new features, making structural changes, and keeping the application suitable for the operating environment.

Web applications offer some challenging maintenance issues for developers used to traditional application development cycles. For one thing, Web applications are heavily dependent on smooth operations of Local and Wide Area Networks (LANs and WANs). You cannot easily trace a slow operation to a portion of your code. In addition, different parts of your application could reside on different machines. The prime example is the database engine, which will most likely reside on a different machine for larger applications. This chapter concerns itself with maintenance issues related to Web applications. Of course, all standard maintenance techniques and software engineering issues from non-Web development environments still apply.

Documentation

Having correct and helpful documentation around for your application is extremely important, regardless of whether you or someone else is responsible for maintaining it. A Web application can very easily become complex due to the relatively large number of components it contains. Providing documentation at different levels is also important, as discussed in the following sections.

Network Connections

You should have a map of your network connections as they relate to your application. Some refer to this map as the *application architecture*. If your application is accessible by anyone in the outside world, your map should show what happens from your point of connection to the Internet, as shown in Figure 12-1. If your application will be deployed in an intranet, you need to concern yourself with the details of how your intranet is set up. This is shown in Figure 12-2.

Your map should include at least the following information about the different machines:

- **Network name:** This is the name by which the network knows this machine. Some machines might not have a name for security reasons.

- **IP number:** The IP number is assigned to the machine by your network administrator. This is handy if you need to access the machine remotely.

- **Operating system and version:** It is always nice to know the type of system you are dealing with.

- **System administrator:** Who to contact with regards to that machine.

- **Component of your application running on the machine:** For example, database server or firewall.

- **Component's effect on the operation of the application:** For example, your application probably will not function at all if the database server goes down, but it might be able to partially function if your multimedia file server is not operating.

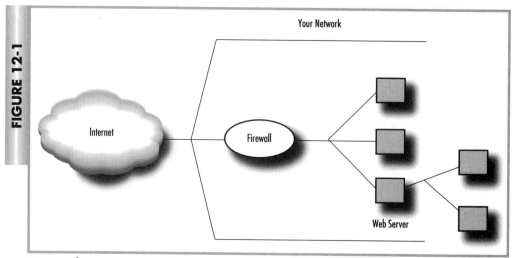

FIGURE 12-1

Scope of an Internet application

FIGURE 12-2

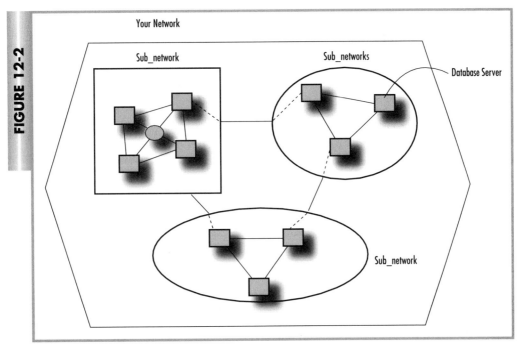

Scope of an intranet application

Figure 12-3 shows a sample network map for the application discussed in Chapter 13. Note that at a glance, you can gain an overall understanding of how the application functions and what the key components are. Of course, creating the map is one challenge and keeping it up-to-date is another. Depending on your organization, such maps might change rather quickly. Be sure you update your maps.

Security Documentation

Somewhere along the line you will get a question about the security of your application from management or clients (or, if you are lucky, both). If your organization has a security officer, seek his or her assistance in preparing security documentation. This documentation should show the security mechanisms used in your application and how they prevent different types of attacks.

For example, if your application includes a login screen, you should mention it and provide information as to how the login and password are verified. If you use Secure Socket Layer (SSL), encrypted transmissions, public or private keys, database access control, or any other security-related components, this document should mention it.

FIGURE 12-3

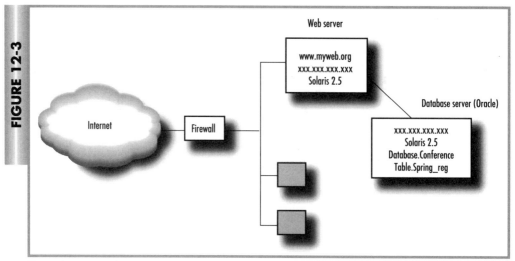

Sample network map

Basically, your document should address the following:

- How the application guards against unauthorized users
- How the application guards against network spoofing
- What happens if the security is compromised

Discussion of these issues can be at different levels. For example, you can protect against unauthorized entries by using a firewall which filters packets based on their IP address. This implementation occurs at the network level. You can also use login and password verification to achieve a similar goal, but at the application level.

A security document can be handy in cases where your application has been subject to an attack. It will help you discover weak points and guard against them. If you use firewalls, your documentation should reflect that and the role they play in your application. At a minimum, it should mention what parts of the network are separated by a particular firewall and what criteria the firewall uses to perform its filtering operations.

Application Documentation

This type of documentation contains notes about your code. If you use CGI or server API to communicate with the server, chances are your code is divided among a number of different files. A flowchart or similar tool is a practical way to visualize the interaction among the pieces. Each program uses variables from the submitted form (*name=value* pairs), some of which might be hidden and carry state information. These variables can be classified based on their criticality and input origin.

Sometimes a particular variable needs to be entered by the user before the program can continue. For example, for an order-verification system the user might be asked to enter an order number. If that number is not entered, the program has nothing to search the database with and should terminate with an appropriate error message. Conversely, there is some information in a form that can be left blank and the CGI program will still continue. Examples are survey questions with optional information, such as name and address of the participant. The logic behind most of these programs would not require that optional parameters be filled. Depending on the language and tool you use, such empty variables can be assigned different values, but the most popular one is NULL, or the number 0, for numeric fields.

The second classification deals with how the values are originated. Most variables, of course, are set based on the input from the user. Some variables, however, are set by the program for internal housekeeping. An example would be a connection number which is passed onto each CGI program invocation. This gives the programmer an artificial way of keeping track of states in a stateless protocol such as HTTP. Most such variables are stored using the *hidden* option in an *<input>* tag and are not visible to the user. You would expect errors or improper formats in user-entered variables, but not in the ones generated by the program itself.

The application documentation should also include information about the database engine(s) used and how you established those connections. For example, you should include what database and what version you are using. If you are using middleware, then that information should be documented. Other useful information includes database connectivity (network or non-networked), any required maintenance operations that the database administrator must perform, and any potential limitations on the database (such as size, number of tables, and number of columns within a table).

Performance Monitoring

One of the easiest ways to find weak areas of your code is by monitoring the performance of the application. There are a number of tools available to help you in this task. Again, such monitoring can be done at several levels:

- Network level
- Web server level
- Database server level

There are electrical devices that can monitor your network traffic and can help network engineers with placement of new routers, gateways, and bridges. Although your application is not directly concerned with these statistics, they do affect its overall performance. So you might want to ask your network administrator for such figures and numbers.

Your Web server either comes equipped with the ability to generate logs with different levels of detail or supports a third-party package. A list of such programs is presented in Chapter 5. Logs can easily become a maze of information. You need to develop a feel for what information is important to your assessment of the application. Logs can tell you what programs are used more than others and with what frequency. Logs are also a good place to check when users encounter errors. Basic messages such as "malformed headers" are documented in the logs so you know where the error occurred. Finally, logs are good for security purposes since all requests to the Web server are recorded.

The Web server is where CGI programs are executed. Web servers are capable of launching multiple instances of the same CGI program. Depending on the program, this can consume a considerable amount of memory. Web server logs should give you an idea about memory and disk requirements for the HTTP server. You might be able to enhance the performance of the Web server, and therefore your application, with additional physical or virtual memory, a faster network card, or additional cache. If you use server API the overhead is reduced considerably, but you still face some of the same issues.

Your database engine has its own logs for its own operations. Aside from routine database maintenance information, such as free disk space, free log space, and index sizes, database logs could record instances of malformed SQL submissions. In many instances, your Web application generates an SQL statement based on the input from the user and submits it to the database. Unless you perform rigorous validation checks on the SQL statement, it could cause the database to generate an error. Most of these errors are caused by wrong data types (for example, typing a string where a number is expected). Another common error is submission of complex or large SQL statements that overfill the database engine's buffer. Learn whether your database has logging capability and use it if it can help you pinpoint errors and bugs.

A final warning about logs is to not overuse them. Logs are very helpful, but when you overdo it, they become bottlenecks. Sophisticated database engines usually have an auditing feature which, when turned on, will record everything that happens in the database. For a medium-sized operation, these logs could take up hundreds of megabytes of disk space. Also, writing these logs takes time away from processing user requests, so there is also a performance issue with maintaining detailed logs. While it is acceptable to keep detailed logs for a limited period to help debug an application or capture a hacker, overdoing it does have consequences that may or may not be appropriate for your operation.

Common Bugs

Since Web applications are in a class of their own, they have their own bugs. Here is a list of some of the most common errors in Web applications:

1. A CGI program does not print the content type of the page it generates. As a result, the browser cannot display the output. Remember, the HTTP server simply sends the output of a CGI program back to the browser. The first line of this output must contain something like the following:

```
Content-type: text/html
```

If such a line does not exist, the browser displays an error to the user. This same error occurs when the CGI program crashes or terminates unexpectedly. When this happens, the program may not get to the part that displays the content type.

2. The *name=value* pairs are defined in the HTML form. When you try to access the same names in a program and assign their values to appropriate variables, be sure the names are identical. If you are using CGI-LIB with Perl and the specified name does not have a corresponding name in the HTML form, a blank value is

assigned to the variable. No error message is generated at this stage. You may get an error message later when you try to use this blank value in an SQL statement or another part of your code. With the C language most tools assign a NULL value, but that strictly depends on the tool.

3. Your application will need to talk to the database. This communication can lead to errors. Make sure you know the database API, its syntax, and usage. Check your database logs to see if an error was recorded. It could be that your CGI program is functioning properly, but the error is caused by the database.

4. Web servers have designated directories where CGI scripts can reside. If you are going to put your scripts in a different directory than the default, you must be sure that the server knows about it. This can usually be done in the HTTP server's configuration files.

5. Make sure you test your application with more than one browser. This can help you evaluate your application from two access points, in other words, the two browsers. You might want to use a low-end browser (such as Lynx) to see how your pages look with browsers that don't support certain features such as JavaScripts or frames.

6. Multiple selection menus seem to always cause problems. Remember that each *name=value* pair is separated by the & character. In a multiple selection menu, the individual selections are delimited using the & character.

7. Your CGI program runs as a process owned by a user you specify in the HTTP server's configuration files. Usually this is a special user called webuser or nobody. New Web developers seem to forget this fact. When they run a CGI program in their UNIX shell, it functions fine, but it fails when run from the Web server. This is because the users of the two processes are different, and a file or directory permission setting is probably causing the problem. For example, while your user name has write access to a particular directory, the webuser or nobody does not.

8. Firewalls and special gateways can add complexity to your program. Simulate all the connections that you need before writing code. If you need to communicate with a database engine that is behind a firewall, test a sample program first before including the code in your main Web application.

9. Caching is a process of storing heavily used items in a place where they can be retrieved quickly. The concept is used in designing microprocessors to Web servers. Most Web clients maintain a cache. Proxy servers do the same on the server side. If you've changed your code and still see the same result after running it, check the cache. Sometimes you need to reload the document, and sometimes it is best to simply clear the cache altogether.

10. Programs that use dynamic libraries need to know where those libraries are. This information is usually retrieved from an environmental variable or a PATH variable. When you log in to your machine, the code may function properly because the proper variables are set under your environment. When the same code executes under the Web, it may fail because the variables are not set under the Web environment. This problem applies particularly to database clients.

Expanding Your Application

A successful deployment usually means that your clients want additions and enhancements to the application. With Web applications, this process is somewhat simplified since your application is developed in distinct pieces from the start. Users invoke different CGI scripts and browse through different HTML files via a point-and-click interface. Expansion usually means adding another hyperlink or button to a page and writing the corresponding CGI programs for that portion of the application.

A new CGI script can be directly invoked by specifying its URL. It might be tempting to do your development work in the same directory where your working application resides, since users will not know that your new CGI script exists until you provide a link to it. This generally is not a good habit. The production version and the development version of your application should be on different servers or at least different port numbers if you use the same server. This reduces the risk of users accidentally running a development version of your code or problems with the development version interfering with the production version.

Expansion does not always occur at the application level. Your database might have to change. If you have used a middleware program such as ODBC, then this should not be a problem. Your application speaks ODBC, and ODBC communicates with the database. If the database is changed, then a new ODBC driver needs to be installed. Your application should still work fine. The same goes for other middleware standards, such as JDBC for Java.

Since your application probably generates SQL statements, and SQL statements contain field names and table names, you should make sure that the naming of the database objects remains the same when you change the database engine. If this is not possible, examine your code and make the necessary changes.

What if the Web server changes? The changes depend on whether you used CGI or a server-specific API library. A new HTTP server might not support a different server's API, so your code needs to be changed. Applications that use CGI should continue working without any need for modifications. Performance under a new server is something you should monitor so you can make necessary changes. Also, be sure the new server's configuration files have the same information as the old server. This way, your security settings, aliases, and directory designations stay the same. Creating a new server usually means a new directory must be set up on the file system to include all the server-related files. Be sure that the permissions on these directories are identical to those on the old server, so all applications that write to a particular directory continue to work.

Networking changes usually are of no concern to you except in cases where an increase or decrease in application performance is imminent. Mirror servers can be set up to handle high traffic and route it to the least busy server. These are, however, networking decisions and not application decisions. If such expansion is necessary, your networking documentation will come in handy to make sure firewalls and other network-related components of your application will work as expected under the new network. From a protocol-level point of view, your application runs on any network that supports TCP/IP. The Internet runs based on TCP/IP, and all the browsers run TCP/IP. That is how you can have a global audience instantly.

Finally, it is possible that your platform might completely change. For example, your environment might change from a UNIX machine to Windows NT or vice versa. This is the most complicated migration and expansion scenario. Your most imminent problem is compiling all your CGI scripts on the new operating system. If you use an interpretive language, you must find an appropriate interpreter for the new machine. After the CGI scripts have been migrated, you need to establish a connection among the scripts, the Web server, and the database server. This process is entirely dependent on the type of servers and how they migrate to a new environment. If you use the same servers, you probably don't have to make many changes. If you use a new database server or a new HTTP server, your migration task might be more difficult.

Summary

Any successful application development cycle includes a maintenance phase. This is where the application is enhanced and new revisions are released. For a successful maintenance phase you need to know how your application works, how it is performing given the environmental constraints, and how you can make it better.

It is imperative that you have correct and informative documentation about your application. It should contain information about the networking environment on which your application is deployed, security considerations, and comments about the code itself and its operation. This documentation can be useful for both maintaining the application and adding new features.

You should develop methods to monitor how your application is performing. Logs generated by the HTTP server, the operating system, and the database server can be helpful. You might want to consider using a third-party package that organizes the data included in logs and presents useful summaries of system performance. Logs are also an effective method for tracking the security status of your application.

When Web applications are developed using distinct components, expansion is not difficult. Expansion might involve changing the database engine, the HTTP server, the network, or the operating system. Of the four, the last one is the most difficult since it could involve the recompilation of code under a new environment.

Questions

1. What are the three types of documentation for a Web application?

2. If a router is changed in your organization, which documentation class must be updated?

3. Who is the owner of processes under which CGI scripts are executed?

4. Why is specification of content type is important?

5. What information should you expect from monitoring your network?

6. What information should you expect from monitoring your Web server?

Answers

1. Network documentation, security documentation, and application documentation.

2. Routers are network components, so the networking documentation must reflect this change.

3. The user is specified in the HTTP server's configuration files. It is usually a fake user with minimal permissions.

4. A client (browser) needs to know the content type of a page before it can display it. When a CGI script fails to specify the content type (either due to an oversight by the programmer or because the program crashes), the browser cannot display the message and generates an error.

5. Monitoring network traffic can help you determine where most requests are coming from and how responsive your server is to these requests.

6. Monitoring the Web server can tell you which CGI scripts are frequently accessed and how fast they are executed.

PART III: Sample Applications

13

Conference Registration System

One of the most common Web applications is data collection. The Web attracts a large audience. It is easy to get some input from members of that audience as long as they can type or select items from menus. Usually what happens is the data gets stored in a database that can be analyzed later or merged with the data in the company's main database. These types of applications are easy to create since no update or delete operations are needed.

Specifications

In this chapter, a simple conference registration system is developed. The actual registration probably will occur by phone or postal mail, since not all payment methods can be processed on-line. The application allows interested users to enter information about themselves, such as name, address, and phone number. It also allows the users to select one of the registration packages from a radio button menu. Finally, the users are asked how they heard about the conference. This information is validated and stored in a database which is used to print mailings for registration packets.

Environment

This is a very simple Web application. You have seen all the elements of such an application in previous chapters. If this is your first application, it might take some time as you configure your system. Remember, you only have to do this once; after proper setup, you are on your way to developing many more applications. In this example, the CGI program is written in Perl 5. The back-end database is Sybase System 10, and Sybperl is used to establish communication between the CGI script and the database. It is very easy to replace the back-end with another database. The same is true about the CGI script language. Since no special enhancements are used, any browser can run this application. If the collected information is confidential, then some security measures should be taken, such as using SSL, as discussed in Chapter 11, "Security Issues." However, for this application, no special security provisions are made.

Listing 13-1 is the SQL code used to generate the table for data storage.

Listing 13-1 SQL code for the conference registration system

```
use conference
go

create table register
(c_fname    char(30)    null,
 c_lname    char(30)    null,
 c_add1     char(40)    null,
 c_add2     char(40)    null,
 c_city     char(30)    null,
 c_state    char(2)    null,
 c_zip     char(15)    null,
 c_phone    char(15)    null,
 c_fax     char(15)    null,
 c_email    char(30)    null,
 c_package  char(1)    null,
 c_ad      char(1)    null),
go

grant select, insert, update on register to public
go

print 'created table register'
go
```

CGI Program

The first part of the application is the HTML form itself. By now you should be familiar with the HTML elements and how they are used in a form. Listing 13-2 is the HTML code for this application. Figure 13-1 shows the screen capture of the entry form.

Listing 13-2 HTML code for the registration system

```
<header>
<title>Conference Registration System</title>
</header>

<BODY>
<H2>Registration for XYZ Conference </H2>

Please fill out the following form. A registration packet will be sent to ⇐
you immediately.

Note that all <B>bold-faced</B> fields must be completed.
<HR>
<FORM METHOD="POST" ACTION="/cgi-bin/register.pl">

<b>First Name:</b> <INPUT TYPE="text" NAME="c_fname" SIZE=30 MAXLENGTH=30>
<p>
<b>Last Name:</b> <INPUT TYPE="text" NAME="c_lname" SIZE=30 MAXLENGTH=30>
<P>
<b>Address 1:</b> <INPUT TYPE="text" NAME="c_add1" SIZE=40 MAXLENGTH=40>
<P>
Address 2: <INPUT TYPE="text" NAME="c_add2" SIZE=40 MAXLENGTH=40>
<P>
<b>City:</b> <INPUT TYPE="text" NAME="c_city" SIZE=30 MAXLENGTH=30>
<P>
<b>State:</b> <INPUT TYPE="text" NAME="c_state" SIZE=2 MAXLENGTH=2>
<P>
<b>Zip:</b> <INPUT TYPE="text" NAME="c_zip" SIZE=15 MAXLENGTH=15>
<P>
Phone: <INPUT TYPE="date" NAME="c_phone" SIZE=15 MAXLENGTH=15>
<P>
Fax: <INPUT TYPE="text" NAME="c_fax" SIZE=15 MAXLENGTH=15>
<P>
Email: <INPUT TYPE="text" NAME="c_email" SIZE=30 MAXLENGTH=30>
<P>
Package:
<uL>
<LI> <INPUT TYPE="radio" NAME="c_package" VALUE="a"> Package A
<LI> <INPUT TYPE="radio" NAME="c_package" VALUE="b"> Package B
<LI> <INPUT TYPE="radio" NAME="c_package" VALUE="c"> Package C
</uL>
<P>
How did you hear about the conference:
<uL>
<LI> <INPUT TYPE="radio" NAME="c_ad" VALUE="a"> Direct Mail
<LI> <INPUT TYPE="radio" NAME="c_ad" VALUE="b"> Associate
<LI> <INPUT TYPE="radio" NAME="c_ad" VALUE="c"> Journal
<LI> <INPUT TYPE="radio" NAME="c_ad" VALUE="d"> Other
</uL>
<P>
```

continued on next page

continued from previous page

```
<input type="reset" value="Clear"> <input type="submit" value="Register"> <p>
</FORM>
<HR>

</BODY>
```

As always, a CGI script is needed to process the form and store the information in the database. Regardless of the back-end database and the language used, the script must do some initialization work, such as setting up a communication channel and specifying the database and table to be used. Next, the script will check the values of the data fields to be sure they are not blank. The script cannot decide that a last name is misspelled, for example, but it can catch a submission without a last name. Finally, the script will store this information in the database and perform the necessary house-cleaning activities.

Listing 13-3 shows such a script written in Perl 5. The code is commented, but there isn't anything in the listing that we have not discussed before.

Listing 13-3 Perl script to process the registration form

```
#!/usr/local/bin/perl

require "cgi-lib.pl";

# Read in all the variables set by the form
```

Conference registration system

```
&ReadParse(*input);
$mc_fname = $input{'c_fname'});
$mc_lname = $input{'c_lname'});
$mc_add1 = $input{'c_add1'});
$mc_add2 = $input{'c_add2'});
$mc_city = $input{'c_city'});
$mc_state = $input{'c_state'});
$mc_zip = $input{'c_zip'});
$mc_phone = $input{'c_phone'});
$mc_fax = $input{'c_fax'});
$mc_email = $input{'c_email'});
$mc_package = $input{'c_package'});
$mc_ad = $input{'c_ad'});

# Print the header
print &PrintHeader;

# Check that they have entered all the required data

if (($mc_fname eq "") || ($mc_lname eq "") || ($mc_add1 eq "") ||
    ($mc_add2 eq "") || ($mc_city eq "") || ($mc_state eq "") ||
    ($mc_zip eq "")) {
            printf("<br>");
            printf("<strong> Your registration cannot be processed as is.⇐
Please make sure all the required fields are filled properly.</strong>");
        print "<p>";
        print "Please use the <i>Back</i> button to complete the form.\n";
}
else { # data is OK

        use Sybase::DBlib;
        $dbh = Sybase::DBlib->dblogin('conf_user', '123', 'DB_SERVER', 'REG');
        $dbh->dbuse('conference');

        $sqlcmd = "insert into reg (c_fname, c_lname, c_add1, c_add2, c_city, ⇐
        c_state, c_zip, c_phone, c_fax, c_email, c_package, c_ad) ";
        $sqlcmd = $sqlcmd . "values (";
        $sqlcmd = $sqlcmd . "\"" . $mc_fname . "\",";
        $sqlcmd = $sqlcmd . "\"" . $mc_lname . "\",";
        $sqlcmd = $sqlcmd . "\"" . $mc_add1 . "\",";
        $sqlcmd = $sqlcmd . "\"" . $mc_add2 . "\",";
        $sqlcmd = $sqlcmd . "\"" . $mc_city . "\",";
        $sqlcmd = $sqlcmd . "\"" . $mc_state. "\",";
        $sqlcmd = $sqlcmd . "\"" . $mc_zip. "\",";
        $sqlcmd = $sqlcmd . "\"" . $mc_phone . "\",";
        $sqlcmd = $sqlcmd . "\"" . $mc_fax . "\",";
        $sqlcmd = $sqlcmd . "\"" . $mc_email . "\",";
        $sqlcmd = $sqlcmd . "\"" . $mc_package . "\",";
        $sqlcmd = $sqlcmd . "\"" . $mc_ad . "\",";
        $sqlcmd = $sqlcmd . "\"" . $mc_fax . "\",";
        $sqlcmd = $sqlcmd . "\"" . $mc_email"\")";
```

continued on next page

continued from previous page

```
$dbh->dbcmd($sqlcmd . "\n");
$dbh->dbsqlexec;
```

- print "<strong> Thank you.</strong> Your registration has been ⇐ submitted. You should receive your packet shortly in the mail. ";

}

As mentioned before, setting up the environment for your first application might take some time. The following is a checklist that might help you with debugging your application.

- **Make sure the Web server is indeed running.** On UNIX platforms, the ps command will show you if the process is running. In Windows NT or Windows 95, depending on the Web server, look for an icon or a process name in the task window.

- **Make sure the Web server is responding to requests correctly.** Use a URL of the form http://*domain_name,* where *domain_name* is the name of the machine running your Web server. If all is set up correctly, you should get a page, as most servers have a default page stored in their htdocs directory. If you don't get anything, place a sample HTML page in the htdocs directory and try again.

- **The above test shows only that the server can handle requests for static HTML pages.** You must also test its ability to run a script. Again, most servers come with sample scripts that run using CGI. They might display information such as date and time. Try the server with such a script. The most likely place you'll find these scripts is in the cgi-bin directory.

- **Make sure the CGI script has execution permission.** Also check that this permission is extended to the user running your Web server. Most often, the script runs fine when you invoke it from the operating system because it executes with you as its owner. The same script fails when executed from the Web because the permissions are not set up correctly.

- **Make sure the PATH and any other necessary environmental variables are set correctly.** Most database servers look at a particular environmental variable for version information, server name, and other pertinent information. You need to make sure that such variables are set properly and that they are available to the Web process.

- **Check the permissions on the database and the tables you are accessing.** It is a good idea to manually perform some of the SQL commands your application will perform on the database. Most databases offer a terminal interface from which you can type SQL commands. By doing this, you can immediately catch syntax errors in your SQL, permission problems, and many other database-specific problems.

● **Check the spelling of the *name=value* pairs in your HTML forms and the variables you use in your CGI script.** For example, Sybperl uses the construct in {'*name*'} to retrieve the value associated with the key *name*. Be sure the two match exactly.

14

Trouble Reporting System

In this chapter, an application is developed to track hardware and software trouble reports. The application is meant to be used in an Intranet with a small organization. However, it is very scalable and can be expanded to accommodate larger user bases.

Specifications

The program has three main functions for performing the following tasks:

- **Problem reporting:** Allows a user to report a problem. The user can see the existing problems, and hopefully, one problem will not be reported multiple times.

- **Problem resolution:** The system administrator can browse through the problems and specify solutions, which can be sent via e-mail to the user who reported the problem.

- **Problem lookup:** A user can browse through problems to see if a solution for his or her problem exists. A system administrator can look through problems for repeating patterns.

Each trouble report has a case number associated with it. The case number is generated based on the current time and is unique for each reported problem. There is also a flag which indicates the status of the problem. Possible values are

- **Reported:** The problem has been reported and is waiting for a solution.
- **Resolved:** The problem has been resolved, and the user has been notified.

The lookup facility and the problem resolution module allow for several types of searches. They are

- **Find all trouble reports:** A list is generated containing all the trouble reports in the database. The user can jump to a specific one by clicking on it.
- **Find based on date:** All trouble reports whose entry dates fall within a specified range are retrieved from the database.
- **Find by machine name:** All trouble reports associated with a particular machine are retrieved from the database.
- **Find all unresolved reports:** Trouble reports with an unresolved status are retrieved from the database.

Environment

The CGI scripts are written using Perl 5, and a connection to a Sybase back-end is established using SybPerl. The HTTP server used is NCSA's httpd 1.5. The look of the application is enhanced if the browser can support frames; however, the application is still usable if the browser does not support frames.

The SQL statement for generating the table used in the application is shown in Listing 14-1. Note that only one table is used in the database.

Listing 14-1 SQL to generate the table used in the application

```
use trouble
go

if exists (select * from trouble.dbo.sysobjects
where name = "trp")
begin
drop table trp
end
go

create table trp
(tr_reporter        char(30)        null,
tr_email            char(50)        null,
tr_date             datetime        null,
tr_time             char(20)        null,
tr_mach_name        char(30)        null,
```

```
tr_mach_type        char(10)        null,
tr_b_desc           char(100)       null,
tr_f_desc           text            null,
casenum             char(15)        null,
fix_person          char(30)        null,
fix_soln            text            null,
fix_date            datetime        null,
status              char(30)        null,
notes               text            null)
go

grant select, insert, update on trp to public
go

print 'created table trp'
go
```

CGI Program

Figure 14-1 shows the flow of the application. The starting point is a CGI script which contacts the database, retrieves a list of unresolved trouble reports, and displays them. After that, depending on the function chosen by the user, an HTML form is displayed. These are static HTML files and are not generated on the fly. Some of them include frames. After that, the remaining screens are generated dynamically by the Perl scripts.

Main Screen

Listing 14-2 shows the Perl code used to generate the main screen of the Trouble Reporting Facility. The code basically prints out some header information. It then connects to the database and searches for all unresolved cases. It displays them in a tabular format. Finally, it presents the user with three hyperlinks, each launching a separate module of the program.

Listing 14-2 Main screen code

```
#!/usr/local/bin/perl

require "cgi-lib.pl";
print &PrintHeader;

print "<head>\n";
print "<title>Trouble Reporting Facility</title>\n";
print "</head>\n";

print "<BODY>\n";
print "<H2>Trouble Reporting Facility </H2>\n";
print "<H3> XYZ Company </H3>\n";
```

continued on next page

continued from previous page

```
        print "A list of the current problems is shown below. If your problem has ⇐
        been reported, please do not re-report it. Thank you.\n";
        print "<HR>\n";

        use Sybase::DBlib;
        $dbh = Sybase::DBlib->dblogin('trp_user', '123', 'DB_SERVER', 'TRP');
        $dbh->dbuse('trouble');

        $sqlcmd = "select tr_date, tr_time, tr_mach_name, tr_b_desc ";
        $sqlcmd = $sqlcmd . "from trp ";
        $sqlcmd = $sqlcmd . "where trp.status = \"reported\"";

        # print $sqlcmd . "\n";

        print "<TABLE BORDER WIDTH=\"100%\"> \n";
        print " <TR> \n";
        print " <TH width=\"10%\">Date</TH> <TH width=\"10%\">Time</TH> ⇐
        <TH width=\"20%\">Machine</TH> <TH width=\"60%\">Description</TH> \n";
        print " </TR> \n";

        $dbh->dbcmd($sqlcmd . "\n");
        $dbh->dbsqlexec;
        $dbh->dbresults;

        if ($status = $dbh->DBROWS) {
            while (@data = $dbh->dbnextrow) {
                print "  <TR> \n";
                print "  <TD>" . substr($data[0],0,11). " </TD> <TD>$data[1]</TD> ⇐
         <TD>$data[2]</TD> <TD>$data[3]</TD> \n";
                print "  </TR> \n";
            }
        }
        else {
                print "  <TR> \n";
                print "  <TD>No outstanding problems exist</TD> \n";
                print "  </TR> \n";
        }

        print "</TABLE> \n";

        print "<hr>\n";
        print "<p>\n";

        print "To <strong>report</strong> a problem, please click ⇐
        <A HREF=\"/TrRep/tr_form.html\">here.</A>\n";
        print "<p>\n";
        print "To <strong>resolve</strong> a problem, please click <A
        HREF=\"/TrRep/sol_form.html\">here.</A>\n";
        print "<p>\n";
        print "To <strong>browse</strong> a problem, please click <A
        HREF=\"/TrRep/sol_form2.html\">here.</A>\n";
        print "<p>\n";
```

```
print "Last update 1/12/96";
print "<hr>";
print "<address>";
print "For comments:";
print "<A HREF=\"mailto:mohseni\@ameslab.gov\">mohseni\@ameslab.gov</A>";
print "</address>";
print "<hr>";
print "</BODY>\n";
```

Figure 14-2 shows the output of the above code.

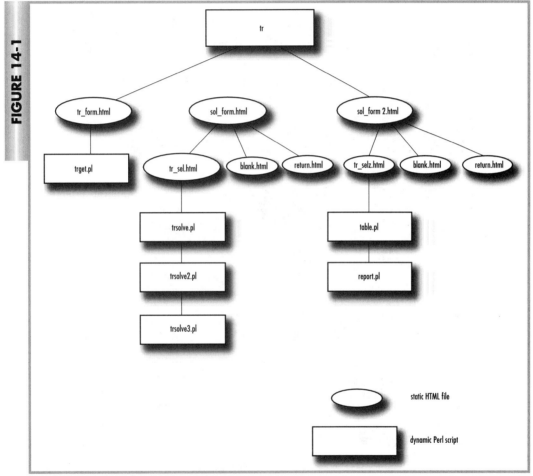

Application flow for the Trouble Reporting System

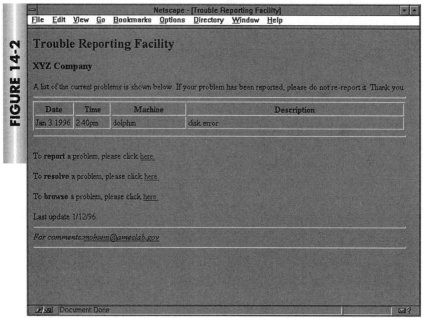

Trouble reporting main screen

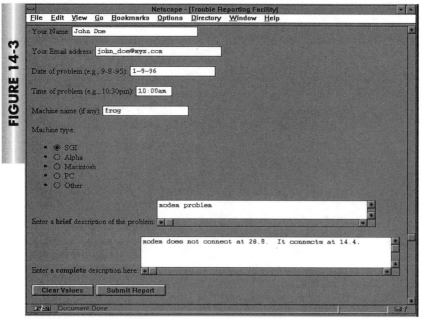

Trouble reporting data entry screen

Reporting a Problem

This module is responsible for collecting and storing information about a new problem.
It is composed of two files:

- An HTML file that contains the form to be used

- A Perl script to process the content of the submitted form

Figure 14-3 shows the data entry screen, and Listing 14-3 gives the HTML code.

Listing 14-3 HTML code to generate the data collection form

```
<head>
<title>Trouble Reporting Facility</title>
</head>

<BODY>
<H2>Trouble Reporting Facility </H2>
<H3> XYZ Company </H3>

Please use the following form to report a hardware or software problem.

Note that <B>all</B> fields must be completed.
<HR>
<FORM METHOD="POST" ACTION="/cgi-bin/TrRep/trget.pl">

Your Name: <INPUT TYPE="text" NAME="tr_reporter" SIZE=30 MAXLENGTH=30>
<P>
Your Email address: <INPUT TYPE="text" NAME="tr_email" SIZE=30 MAXLENGTH=30>
<P>
Date of problem (e.g., 9-8-95): <INPUT TYPE="date" NAME="tr_date"⇐
MAXLENGTH=10>
<P>
Time of problem (e.g., 10:30pm): <INPUT TYPE="text" NAME="tr_time" ⇐
SIZE=8 MAXLENGTH=8>
<P>
Machine name (if any): <INPUT TYPE="text" NAME="tr_mach_name"⇐
SIZE=20 MAXLENGTH=20>
<P>
Machine type:
<uL>
<LI> <INPUT TYPE="radio" NAME="tr_mach_type" VALUE="SGI"> SGI
<LI> <INPUT TYPE="radio" NAME="tr_mach_type" VALUE="Alpha"> Alpha
<LI> <INPUT TYPE="radio" NAME="tr_mach_type" VALUE="Mac"> Macintosh
<LI> <INPUT TYPE="radio" NAME="tr_mach_type" VALUE="PC"> PC
<LI> <INPUT TYPE="radio" NAME="tr_mach_type" VALUE="Other"> Other
</uL>
<P>
Enter a <STRONG>brief</STRONG> description of the problem: <TEXTAREA ⇐
NAME="tr_b_desc" ROWS=2 COLS=50></TEXTAREA>
```

continued on next page

continued from previous page

```
<P>
Enter a <STRONG>complete</STRONG> description here: <TEXTAREA ⇐
NAME="tr_f_desc" ROWS=4 COLS=60></TEXTAREA>
<P>
<input type="reset" value="Clear Values"> <input type="submit" value="Submit ⇐
Report"> <p>
</FORM>
<HR>

</BODY>
```

Once the user has entered all the data, the content of the form is submitted to a Perl script for processing. This script is shown in Listing 14-4.

Listing 14-4 Perl script to process information about a problem

```
#!/usr/local/bin/perl

require "cgi-lib.pl";

MAIN:
{
# Read in all the variables set by the form
    &ReadParse(*input);

    $mtr_reporter = $input{'tr_reporter'};
    $mtr_email = $input{'tr_email'};
    $mtr_date = $input{'tr_date'};
    $mtr_time = $input{'tr_time'};
    $mtr_mach_name = $input{'tr_mach_name'};
    $mtr_mach_type = $input{'tr_mach_type'};
    $mtr_b_desc = $input{'tr_b_desc'};
    $mtr_f_desc = $input{'tr_f_desc'};

# Print the header
    print &PrintHeader;

# Check that they have entered all the data

    if (($mtr_reporter eq "")  || ($mtr_email eq "") || ($mtr_date eq "") ||
        ($mtr_b_desc eq "")   || ($mtr_f_desc eq "")) {
        printf("<br>");
        printf("<strong>  Your report cannot be processed as is.  Please make ⇐
sure all the fields are filled properly.</strong>");
        print "<p>";
        print "Please use the <i>Back</i> button to complete the form.\n";
#        print "<a href=\"tr_form.html>Go Back</a> \n";
    }
    else {
```

```
# Generate a case number
      $mtr_casenum = sprintf("%lx", time);
      $_ = $mtr_casenum;
      tr/a-z/A-Z/;
      $mtr_casenum = $_;

# Now we can insert the data into the database

      use Sybase::DBlib;
      $dbh = Sybase::DBlib->dblogin('trp_user', '123', 'DB_SERVER', 'TRP');

      $dbh->dbuse('track');

      $sqlcmd = "insert into trp (tr_reporter, tr_email, tr_date, tr_time, ";
      $sqlcmd = $sqlcmd . "tr_mach_name, tr_mach_type, tr_b_desc, ⇐
tr_f_desc, ";
      $sqlcmd = $sqlcmd . "casenum, status) ";
      $sqlcmd = $sqlcmd . "values (";
      $sqlcmd = $sqlcmd . "\"" . $mtr_reporter . "\",";
      $sqlcmd = $sqlcmd . "\"" . $mtr_email . "\",";
      $sqlcmd = $sqlcmd . "\"" . $mtr_date . "\",";
      $sqlcmd = $sqlcmd . "\"" . $mtr_time . "\",";
      $sqlcmd = $sqlcmd . "\"" . $mtr_mach_name . "\",";
      $sqlcmd = $sqlcmd . "\"" . $mtr_mach_type . "\",";
      $sqlcmd = $sqlcmd . "\"" . $mtr_b_desc . "\",";
      $sqlcmd = $sqlcmd . "\"" . $mtr_f_desc . "\",";
      $sqlcmd = $sqlcmd . "\"" . $mtr_casenum . "\",";
      $sqlcmd = $sqlcmd . "\"" . "reported" . "\")";

# print $sqlcmd . "\n";

      $dbh->dbcmd($sqlcmd . "\n");
      $dbh->dbsqlexec;

      print "<strong> Thank you.</strong>  The trouble report has been ⇐
entered into the database.
Someone will contact you at the email address ";
      print "<strong>" . $mtr_email . "</strong>";
      print "<p>";
      print "Your case number for this trouble report is: ";
      print "<strong>" . $mtr_casenum . "</strong>";
       print "<hr>\n\n<a href=http://shemp.tip.ameslab.gov/cgi-bin/TrRep/tr ⇐
target=_top><IMG SRC=\"/TrRep/back.gif\" HSPACE=5 VSPACE=0 ALIGN=Left
       WIDTH=30 HEIGHT=30 BORDER=1>Return to trouble reporting facility</a>";
        }
}
```

Assuming the user has entered all the data correctly, the screen in Figure 14-4 appears, confirming the result and also providing the user with a case number for feature references.

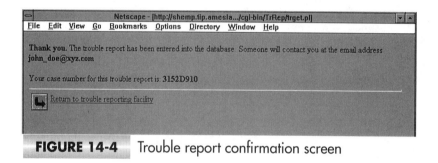

FIGURE 14-4 Trouble report confirmation screen

Problem Resolution

This module allows a technician or a system administrator to respond to a particular reported problem. The response will be e-mailed to the address specified at the time of reporting. Once again, the module begins by providing a form written in HTML. The HTML code uses frames as shown in Listing 14-5. The frame has three parts:

- The selection form
- A blank frameset
- A frameset allowing the user to return to the main screen

Listing 14-5 Problem Resolution Frame

```
<frameset rows=45%,48%,7%>
 <frame src=/TrRep/tr_sel.html name=select_type>
 <frame src=blank.html name=table>
 <frame src=/TrRep/return.html>
 <noframes>
<H1>You must have a browser that supports forms to <a ⇐
href="TrRep/tr_sel.html">view this document</a> correctly.</H1>
 </noframes>
</frameset>
```

Without a browser that supports frames, the user receives an appropriate message, but the application continues to work.

The first frameset allows the user to select trouble reports based on specific criteria. The code for the HTML file is shown in Listing 14-6. It is basically a set of radio buttons, each indicating a particular selection type.

Listing 14-6 Form to display trouble selection criteria

```
<head>
<title>Trouble Reporting Facility</title>
</head>
<BODY>
<H2>Trouble Reporting Facility </H2>
<H3> XYZ Company </H3>

<FORM  METHOD="POST" ACTION="/cgi-bin/TrRep/trsolve.pl" target=table>
<BR><INPUT TYPE="radio" NAME="query" VALUE="listall">Find all trouble reports
<BR><INPUT TYPE="radio" NAME="query" VALUE="date">Find based on date
    <INPUT MAXLENGTH=2 SIZE=2 NAME="month1">/<INPUT MAXLENGTH=2 SIZE=2 ⇐
NAME="day1">/<INPUT MAXLENGTH=2 SIZE=2 NAME="year1"> TO
    <INPUT MAXLENGTH=2 SIZE=2 NAME="month2">/<INPUT MAXLENGTH=2 SIZE=2 ⇐
NAME="day2">/<INPUT MAXLENGTH=2 SIZE=2 NAME="year2">
<BR><INPUT TYPE="radio" NAME="query" VALUE="machine">Find by machine name
    <INPUT NAME="machine">
<BR><INPUT TYPE="radio" NAME="query" VALUE="unresolved">Find all ⇐
unresolved trouble reports
<P>
<INPUT TYPE=submit VALUE="Find" >
<INPUT TYPE=reset VALUE="Reset">
</P>
</FORM>
</BODY>
```

The resulting screen output is shown in Figure 14-5.

Every form must have a corresponding CGI script. Listing 14-7 shows this script. The script is responsible for determining which retrieval method the user has selected. It is also responsible for performing an appropriate query on the database to retrieve the information.

FIGURE 14-5

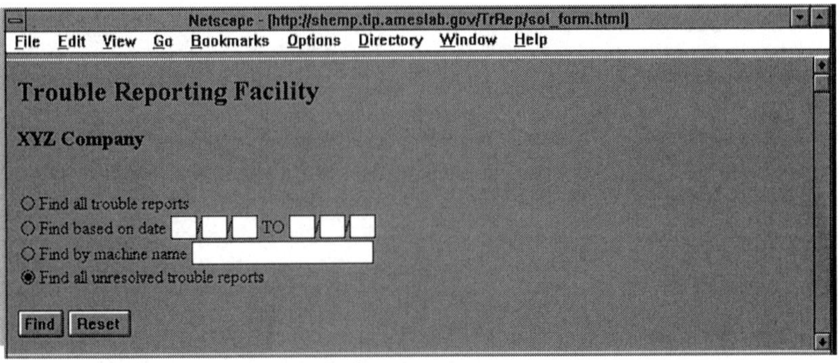

Initial stage of problem resolution screen

Listing 14-7 CGI script for the trouble resolution module

```perl
#!/usr/local/bin/perl

require "cgi-lib.pl";
print &PrintHeader;
print "<head>\n";
print "<title> Trouble Reporting Facility</title>\n";
print "</head>\n";
print "<BODY>";

# Read all variables set by form
&ReadParse(*input);
($m_check = $input{'query'});

use Sybase::DBlib;
$dbh = Sybase::DBlib->dblogin('trp_user', '123', 'DB_SERVER', 'TRP');
$dbh->dbuse('trouble');

if ($m_check eq 'listall')
{
        $sqlcmd = "select casenum, tr_date, tr_time, tr_mach_name, tr_b_desc ";
        $sqlcmd = $sqlcmd . "from trp \n";
        $sqlcmd = $sqlcmd . "order by trp.casenum ";
}

if ($m_check eq "date")
{
        $m_mm1 = $input{'month1'};
        $m_dd1 = $input{'day1'};
        $m_yy1 = $input{'year1'};
        $m_mm2 = $input{'month2'};
        $m_dd2 = $input{'day2'};
        $m_yy2 = $input{'year2'};
        $m_firstdate =  $m_mm1 . "-" . $m_dd1 . "-" . $m_yy1 ;
        $m_seconddate =  $m_mm2 . "-" . $m_dd2 . "-" . $m_yy2 ;
        $sqlcmd = "select casenum, tr_date, tr_time, tr_mach_name, tr_b_desc ⇐
\n";
        $sqlcmd = $sqlcmd . "from trp \n";
        $sqlcmd = $sqlcmd . "where tr_date BETWEEN \"$m_firstdate\" AND ⇐
\"$m_seconddate\" \n";
        $sqlcmd = $sqlcmd . "order by trp.tr_date \n";
}

if ($m_check eq "machine")
{
        ($m_machine = $input{'machine'});
        $sqlcmd = "select casenum, tr_date, tr_time, tr_mach_name, tr_b_desc ⇐
\n";
        $sqlcmd = $sqlcmd . "from trp \n";
        $sqlcmd = $sqlcmd . "where trp.tr_mach_name = \"$m_machine\" \n";
        $sqlcmd = $sqlcmd . "order by trp.tr_date \n";
}
```

```
if ($m_check eq "unresolved")
{
        ($m_unresolved= $input{'unresolved'});
        $sqlcmd = "select casenum, tr_date, tr_time, tr_mach_name, tr_b_desc ⇐
\n";
        $sqlcmd = $sqlcmd . "from trp \n";
        $sqlcmd = $sqlcmd . "where trp.status = \"reported\"";
}

print "<TABLE BORDER WIDTH=\"100%\"> \n";
print " <TR> \n";
print " <TH width=\"20%\">Case Number</TH> <TH width=\"10%\">Date</TH> <TH ⇐
width=\"10%\">Time</TH> <TH width=\"20%\">Machine</TH>
        <TH width=\"40%\">Description</TH>\n";
print " </TR> \n";


$dbh->dbcmd($sqlcmd . "\n");
$dbh->dbsqlexec;
$dbh->dbresults;

if ($status = $dbh->DBROWS) {
    while (@data = $dbh->dbnextrow) {
        print "  <TR> \n";
        print "  <TD><A  HREF=\"/cgi-
bin/TrRep/trsolve2.pl?tr_casenum=$data[0]\" TARGET=_top>$data[0]</a></TD> ⇐
<TD>" . substr($data[1],0,12). " </TD><TD>$data[2]</TD>
</TD><TD>$data[3]</TD><TD>$data[4]</TD>\n";
        print "  </TR> \n";
    }
}
else {
        print "  <TR> \n";
        print "  <TD>No outstanding problems exist</TD> \n";
        print "  </TR> \n";
}

print "</TABLE> \n";
print "<hr>";
print "<p>";
print "</BODY>\n";
```

Note how a target value is specified for the form. This will redirect the output of the form to appear in the second frameset, as shown in Figure 14-6.

So far, the user has been able to select trouble reports based on set criteria and view the result in tabular form. The next stage is to select one of the trouble reports and see the specific information about it as contained in the database. The user can then add a solution for the trouble report. To facilitate this interaction, each case number is hyperlinked. By clicking on the hyperlink, the user invokes a Perl script which searches the database based on the case number and retrieves the data. The user can add his or her name and offer a solution to the problem. Information about the reporter of the problem is shown statically and cannot be modified.

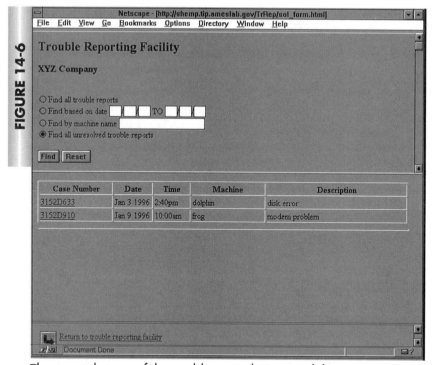

FIGURE 14-6

The second stage of the problem resolution module

Listing 14-8 is the script invoked when a case number is clicked. Figure 14-7 is the resulting screen.

Listing 14-8 Script to search the database based on a case number

```perl
#!/usr/local/bin/perl

require "cgi-lib.pl";

# Read in all the variables set by the form
&ReadParse(*input);
$mtr_casenum = $input{'tr_casenum'};
print &PrintHeader;

# get the data matching the case number

use Sybase::DBlib;
$dbh = Sybase::DBlib->dblogin('trp_user', '123', 'DB_SERVER', 'TRP');

$dbh->dbuse('trouble');

$sqlcmd = "select tr_date, tr_time, tr_reporter, tr_email, ";
```

```
$sqlcmd = $sqlcmd . "tr_mach_name, tr_mach_type, tr_b_desc, tr_f_desc, ";
$sqlcmd = $sqlcmd . "fix_person, fix_date, fix_soln, notes, status\n";
$sqlcmd = $sqlcmd . "from trp \n";
$sqlcmd = $sqlcmd . "where trp.casenum = \"$mtr_casenum\" \n";

$dbh->dbcmd($sqlcmd . "\n");
$dbh->dbsqlexec;
$dbh->dbresults;

if ($status = $dbh->DBROWS) {
    while (@data = $dbh->dbnextrow)
    {
        $mtr_date = substr($data[0], 0, 11);
        $mtr_time = $data[1];
        $mtr_reporter = $data[2];
        $mtr_email = $data[3];
        $mtr_mach_name = $data[4];
        $mtr_mach_type = $data[5];
        $mtr_b_desc = $data[6];
        $mtr_f_desc = $data[7];
        $mtr_fix_person = $data[8];
        $mtr_fix_date =  substr($data[9], 0, 11);
        $mtr_fix_soln = $data[10];
        $mtr_notes = $data[11];
        $mtr_status = $data[12];

    }
}

print "<h2>case #: $mtr_casenum</h2> ";
print "<b>name:</b> $mtr_reporter <br>";
print "<b>email:</b> $mtr_email <br>";
print "<b>date:</b> $mtr_date <br>";
print "<b>time:</b> $mtr_time <br>";
print "<b>machine name:</b> $mtr_mach_name <br>";
print "<b>machine type:</b> $mtr_mach_type <br>";
print "<b>Brief desc:</b> $mtr_b_desc <br>";
print "<b>Full desc:</b> $mtr_f_desc <br>";
print "<b>Status:</b> $mtr_status <br>";

print "<P> \n";
print "<FORM METHOD=\"POST\" ACTION=\"/cgi-bin/TrRep/trsolve3.pl\"> \n";
print "<INPUT TYPE=\"hidden\" NAME=\"tr_casenum\" VALUE= \"$mtr_casenum\"> ⇐
<br>";
print "Your Name: <INPUT TYPE=\"text\" NAME=\"tr_fix_person\" VALUE = ⇐
\"$mtr_fix_person\" SIZE=30 MAXLENGTH=30> \n";
print "<P> \n";
print "today's date: <INPUT TYPE=\"text\" NAME=\"tr_fix_date\" VALUE = ⇐
\"$mtr_fix_date\" SIZE=12 MAXLENGTH=12> \n";
print "<P> \n";
print "Solution: <br><TEXTAREA NAME=\"tr_fix_soln\" ROWS=5 ⇐
COLS=50>$mtr_fix_soln</TEXTAREA> \n";
print "<P> \n";
```

continued on next page

continued from previous page

```
print "Notes and comments: <br><TEXTAREA NAME=\"tr_notes\" ROWS=5 ⇐
COLS=50>$mtr_notes</TEXTAREA> \n";
print "<P> \n";
print "<input type=\"reset\" value=\"Clear Values\"> <input type=\"submit\" ⇐
value=\"Submit Report\"> <p> \n";
print "</FORM>\n";
}
```

The last stage is to process the content of the form, save the data in the database, and present the user with an appropriate messsage. This script is also responsible for e-mailing the original reporter with the solution. Listing 14-9 is the CGI script.

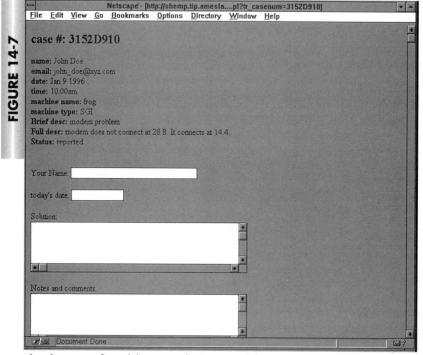

FIGURE 14-7

case #: 3152D910

name: John Doe
email: john_doe@xyz.com
date: Jan 9 1996
time: 10:00am
machine name: frog
machine type: SGI
Brief desc: modem problem
Full desc: modem does not connect at 28.8. It connects at 14.4.
Status: reported

Your Name:

today's date:

Solution:

Notes and comments:

Third stage of problem resolution module

Listing 14-9 CGI script to store data and notify the reporter via e-mail

```perl
#!/usr/local/bin/perl
require "cgi-lib.pl";
# Read in all the variables set by the form
&ReadParse(*input);
$mtr_casenum = $input{'tr_casenum'};
$mtr_fix_person = $input{'tr_fix_person'};
$mtr_fix_date = $input{'tr_fix_date'};
$mtr_fix_soln = $input{'tr_fix_soln'};
$mtr_notes = $input{'tr_notes'};

print &PrintHeader;


# Now we can insert the data into the database

use Sybase::DBlib;
$dbh = Sybase::DBlib->dblogin('trp_user', '123', 'DB_SERVER', 'TRP');

$dbh->dbuse('trouble');
$sqlcmd = "update trp \n";
$sqlcmd = $sqlcmd . "set fix_person = \"$mtr_fix_person\", ";
$sqlcmd = $sqlcmd . "fix_date = \"$mtr_fix_date\", ";
$sqlcmd = $sqlcmd . "fix_soln = \"$mtr_fix_soln\", ";
$sqlcmd = $sqlcmd . "status = \"resolved\", ";
$sqlcmd = $sqlcmd . "notes = \"$mtr_notes\" ";
$sqlcmd = $sqlcmd . "where casenum = \"$mtr_casenum\"";

$dbh->dbcmd($sqlcmd . "\n");
$dbh->dbsqlexec;

print "<b>Your solution has been recorded to the database.  The person ⇐
filing the report has been notified via e-mail. </b>";
print "<hr>";
 print "<a href=/cgi-bin/TrRep/tr target=_top><IMG SRC=\"/TrRep/back.gif\" ⇐
HSPACE=5 VSPACE=0 ALIGN=Left WIDTH=30 HEIGHT=30 BORDER=1>Return to trouble ⇐
reporting facility</a><hr>";

# Now get the person's e-mail address and information that is needed to ⇐
e-mail them.

$sqlcmd = "select tr_date, tr_time, tr_reporter, tr_email, ";
$sqlcmd = $sqlcmd . "tr_mach_name, tr_mach_type, tr_b_desc, tr_f_desc, ";
$sqlcmd = $sqlcmd . "fix_person, fix_date, fix_soln, notes, status\n";
$sqlcmd = $sqlcmd . "from trp \n";
$sqlcmd = $sqlcmd . "where trp.casenum = \"$mtr_casenum\"";

$dbh->dbcmd($sqlcmd . "\n");
$dbh->dbsqlexec;
$dbh->dbresults;
if ($status = $dbh->DBROWS)
```

continued on next page

continued from previous page

```
{
    while (@data = $dbh->dbnextrow)
    {
      $mtr_date = substr($data[0], 0, 11);
      $mtr_time = $data[1];
      $mtr_reporter = $data[2];
      $mtr_email = $data[3];
      $mtr_mach_name = $data[4];
      $mtr_mach_type = $data[5];
      $mtr_b_desc = $data[6];
      $mtr_f_desc = $data[7];
      $mtr_fix_person = $data[8];
      $mtr_fix_date =  substr($data[9], 0, 11);
      $mtr_fix_soln = $data[10];
      $mtr_notes = $data[11];
      $mtr_status = $data[12];
    }
}

# the following line makes sure the email address only contains
# alphanumeric characters and the @ character. Since this argument
# is passed to the mail process, we need to safeguard against
# intruders
$mtr_email ~= s/[^\w\@]//g;

# Mailing the information to the person that reported the problem.
open(MAIL,"|mail $mtr_email");
print MAIL "$mtr_reporter:\nThis e-mail is the Trouble Reporting Facility of ⇐
XYZ Company.\n";
print MAIL "Your report is as follows:\n\n\nCase #:$mtr_casenum\n\nName: ⇐
$mtr_reporter\n\nE-mail: $mtr_email\n\n";
print MAIL "Date: $mtr_date\n\nTime: $mtr_time\n\nMachine\nname: ⇐
$mtr_mach_name\n\nMachine\ntype: $mtr_mach_type \n";
print MAIL "\nBrief desc: $mtr_b_desc\n\nFull desc: $mtr_f_desc\n\nStatus: ⇐
$mtr_status \n\n\n\n\n";
print MAIL "Solution\nreporter: $mtr_fix_person\n\nSolution\ndate: ⇐
$mtr_fix_date\n\nSolution: $mtr_fix_soln\n\n";
print MAIL "Notes and\ncomments: $mtr_notes\n\n\n\nThank you for your ⇐
time,\nTrouble Reporting Facility.\n";

close(MAIL);
```

Figure 14-8 is the final screen for this module.

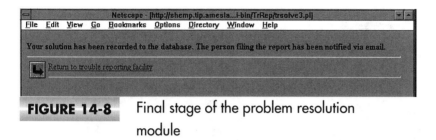

FIGURE 14-8   Final stage of the problem resolution
module

Problem Lookup

The last module is provided as a browsing tool to let either users or system administrators look through problems. Users might be able to find a solution to a problem that has already been reported by someone else. System administrators can find trouble patterns and other administrative information. This module does not do anything new; all of the functions have been used previously by other modules.

The first screen shown in Figure 14-9 gives the same selection radio buttons as the problem resolution module. This is implemented in a frame with the code shown in Listing 14-10.

Listing 14-10 HTML code for the lookup module

```
<frameset rows=45%,48%,7%>
 <frame src=/TrRep/tr_sel2.html name=select_type>
 <frame src=/TrRep/blank.html name=table>
 <frame src=/TrRep/return.html>
 <noframes>
<H1>You must have a browser that supports frames to <a ⇐
href="/TrRep/tr_sel2.html">view this document</a> correctly.</H1>
 </noframes>
</frameset>
```

Once again, three framesets are used in the frame. The second and third ones are identical to the problem resolution module. The code for the first frameset is shown in Listing 14-11.

FIGURE 14-9

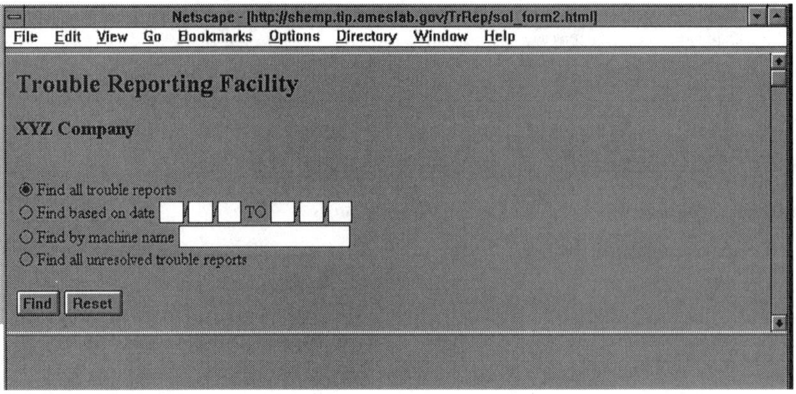

Entry screen for the problem lookup module

Listing 14-11 HTML code for the first frameset in the lookup module

```
<head>
<title>Trouble Reporting Facility</title>
</head>
<BODY>
<H2>Trouble Reporting Facility </H2>
<H3> XYZ Company </H3>

<FORM  METHOD="POST" ACTION="/cgi-bin/TrRep/table.pl " target=select_type>
<BR><INPUT TYPE="radio" NAME="query" VALUE="listall">Find all trouble reports
<BR><INPUT TYPE="radio" NAME="query" VALUE="date">Find based on date
<INPUT MAXLENGTH=2 SIZE=2 NAME="month1">/<INPUT MAXLENGTH=2 SIZE=2 ⇐
NAME="day1">/<INPUT MAXLENGTH=2 SIZE=2 NAME="year1"> TO
     <INPUT MAXLENGTH=2 SIZE=2 NAME="month2">/<INPUT MAXLENGTH=2 SIZE=2 ⇐
NAME="day2">/<INPUT MAXLENGTH=2 SIZE=2 NAME="year2">
<BR><INPUT TYPE="radio" NAME="query" VALUE="machine">Find by machine name
     <INPUT NAME="machine">
<BR><INPUT TYPE="radio" NAME="query" VALUE="unresolved">Find all unresolved ⇐
trouble reports
<P>
<INPUT TYPE=submit VALUE="Find" >
<INPUT TYPE=reset VALUE="Reset">
</P></FORM></BODY>
```

The CGI script in Listing 14-12 is responsible for handling the selection form and producing the data in a tabular format. Each case number is hyperlinked, so clicking on the number displays the information associated with that case number in the bottom frameset. This will allow the user to look at different trouble reports based on his/her case numbers.

Listing 14-12 CGI script to retrieve all reports based on a particular selection

```perl
#!/usr/local/bin/perl

require "cgi-lib.pl";
print &PrintHeader;

print "<head>\n";
print "<title>Trouble Reporting Facility</title>\n";
print "</head>\n";

print "<BODY>";

# Read all veriables set by form
&ReadParse(*input);
($m_check = $input{'query'});

use Sybase::DBlib;
$dbh = Sybase::DBlib->dblogin('trp_user', '123', 'DB_SERVER', 'TRP');
$dbh->dbuse('trouble');

if ($m_check eq 'listall')
{
        $sqlcmd = "select casenum, tr_date, tr_time, tr_mach_name, tr_b_desc ";
        $sqlcmd = $sqlcmd . "from trp \n";
        $sqlcmd = $sqlcmd . "order by trp.casenum ";
}

if ($m_check eq "date")
{
        ($m_mm1 = $input{'month1'});
        ($m_dd1 = $input{'day1'});
        ($m_yy1 = $input{'year1'});
        ($m_mm2 = $input{'month2'});
        ($m_dd2 = $input{'day2'});
        ($m_yy2 = $input{'year2'});
        $m_firstdate =  $m_mm1 . "-" . $m_dd1 . "-" . $m_yy1 ;
        $m_seconddate =  $m_mm2 . "-" . $m_dd2 . "-" . $m_yy2 ;
        $sqlcmd = "select casenum, tr_date, tr_time, tr_mach_name, tr_b_desc ⇐
\n";
        $sqlcmd = $sqlcmd . "from trp \n";
        $sqlcmd = $sqlcmd . "where tr_date BETWEEN \"$m_firstdate\" AND ⇐
\"$m_seconddate\" \n";
        $sqlcmd = $sqlcmd . "order by trp.tr_date \n";
}

if ($m_check eq "machine")
{
        ($m_machine = $input{'machine'});
        $sqlcmd = "select casenum, tr_date, tr_time, tr_mach_name, tr_b_desc ⇐
\n";
```

continued on next page

continued from previous page

```
        $sqlcmd = $sqlcmd . "from trp \n";
        $sqlcmd = $sqlcmd . "where trp.tr_mach_name = \"$m_machine\" \n";
        $sqlcmd = $sqlcmd . "order by trp.tr_date \n";
}

if ($m_check eq "unresolved")
{
        ($m_unresolved= $input{'unresolved'});
        $sqlcmd = "select casenum, tr_date, tr_time, tr_mach_name, tr_b_desc ⇐
\n";
        $sqlcmd = $sqlcmd . "from trp \n";
        $sqlcmd = $sqlcmd . "where trp.status = \"reported\"";
}

print "<TABLE BORDER WIDTH=\"100%\"> \n";
print " <TR> \n";
print " <TH width=\"20%\">Case Number</TH> <TH width=\"10%\">Date</TH> <TH ⇐
width=\"10%\">Time</TH> <TH width=\"20%\">Machine</TH>
        <TH width=\"40%\">Description</TH>\n";
print " </TR> \n";

$dbh->dbcmd($sqlcmd . "\n");
$dbh->dbsqlexec;
$dbh->dbresults;

if ($status = $dbh->DBROWS) {
    while (@data = $dbh->dbnextrow) {
      print "  <TR> \n";
      print "  <TD><A  HREF=\"/cgi-bin/TrRep/report.pl?tr_casenum=$data[0]\"
TARGET=table>$data[0]</a></TD> <TD>" . substr($data[1],0,12). " </TD> ⇐
<TD>$data[2]</TD> <TD>$data[3]</TD> <TD>$data[4]</TD>\n";
      print "  </TR> \n";
    }
}
else {
        print "  <TR> \n";
        print "  <TD>No outstanding problems exist</TD> \n";
        print "  </TR> \n";
}

print "</TABLE> \n";
print "<hr>";
print "<p>";
print "</BODY>\n";
```

Figure 14-10 shows the screen generated by the above script.

Listing 14-13 is the CGI script invoked after the user clicks on a case number hyperlink. It basically searches the database using the case number and paints a screen showing the result of the query.

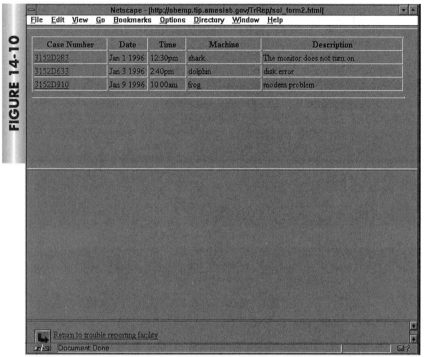

FIGURE 14-10

Listing of troubles

Listing 14-13 CGI script to retrieve information about a report specified by a case number

```perl
#!/usr/local/bin/perl
require "cgi-lib.pl";
# Read in all the variables set by the form
&ReadParse(*input);
$mtr_casenum = $input{'tr_casenum'};
print &PrintHeader;

# get the data matching the case number
use Sybase::DBlib;
$dbh = Sybase::DBlib->dblogin('trp_user', '123', 'DB_SERVER', 'TRP');
$dbh->dbuse('trouble');

$sqlcmd = "select tr_date, tr_time, tr_reporter, tr_email, ";
$sqlcmd = $sqlcmd . "tr_mach_name, tr_mach_type, tr_b_desc, tr_f_desc, ";
$sqlcmd = $sqlcmd . "fix_person, fix_date, fix_soln, notes, status\n";
$sqlcmd = $sqlcmd . "from trp \n";
$sqlcmd = $sqlcmd . "where trp.casenum = \"$mtr_casenum\" \n";

#    print $sqlcmd;
```

continued on next page

continued from previous page

```
$dbh->dbcmd($sqlcmd . "\n");
$dbh->dbsqlexec;
$dbh->dbresults;

if ($status = $dbh->DBROWS) {
    while (@data = $dbh->dbnextrow)
    {
        $mtr_date = substr($data[0], 0, 11);
        $mtr_time = $data[1];
        $mtr_reporter = $data[2];
        $mtr_email = $data[3];
        $mtr_mach_name = $data[4];
        $mtr_mach_type = $data[5];
        $mtr_b_desc = $data[6];
        $mtr_f_desc = $data[7];
        $mtr_fix_person = $data[8];
        $mtr_fix_date =  substr($data[9], 0, 11);
        $mtr_fix_soln = $data[10];
        $mtr_notes = $data[11];
        $mtr_status = $data[12];
    }
}

print "<h2>case #: $mtr_casenum</h2> ";
print "<b>name:</b> $mtr_reporter <br>";
print "<b>email:</b> $mtr_email <br>";
print "<b>date:</b> $mtr_date <br>";
print "<b>time:</b> $mtr_time <br>";
print "<b>machine name:</b> $mtr_mach_name <br>";
print "<b>machine type:</b> $mtr_mach_type <br>";
print "<b>Brief desc:</b> $mtr_b_desc <br>";
print "<b>Full desc:</b> $mtr_f_desc <br>";
print "<b>Status:</b> $mtr_status <br>";
print "<HR><H3>Solution reporter:  $mtr_fix_person</H3>";
print "<B>Solution date:</B>  $mtr_fix_date<BR>";
print "<HR><H1>Solution:</H1>";
print "<B>$mtr_fix_soln</B>";
print "<HR><H1>Notes and comments:</H1>";
print "<B>$mtr_notes</B><HR>";
```

Figure 14-11 shows the screen displaying information about a case number.

This application shows many of the basic elements of a complete Web application. You can immediately understand the limitations caused by lack of a continuous protocol. Each time the user clicks on a link, information about the previous state is lost unless you explicitly carry that information to the next module.

You can enhance this application by adding some JavaScript code which reduces some of the overhead associated with checking user input on the server side. Another issue brought to life by this application is security. A direct write to the database is not advisable for all environments. You might want to allow writing to a temporary database, then move the data to the main database on a routine basis.

FIGURE 14-11

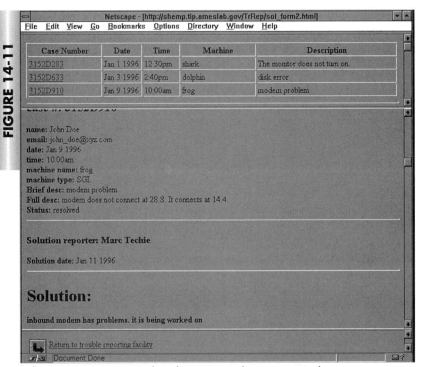

Case Number	Date	Time	Machine	Description
3152D283	Jan 1 1996	12:30pm	shark	The monitor does not turn on.
3152D633	Jan 3 1996	2:40pm	dolphin	disk error
3152D910	Jan 9 1996	10:00am	frog	modem problem

name: John Doe
email: john_doe@xyz.com
date: Jan 9 1996
time: 10:00am
machine name: frog
machine type: SGI
Brief desc: modem problem
Full desc: modem does not connect at 28.8. It connects at 14.4.
Status: resolved

Solution reporter: Marc Techie

Solution date: Jan 11 1996

Solution:

inbound modem has problems. it is being worked on

Return to trouble reporting facility

Document Done

Information associated with a particular case number

Finally, you should appreciate the need for proper documentation of your application. You can see that as the application becomes more complex, it becomes harder to keep track of the scripts, the HTML files, and how they interact.

15
Using the JDBC

In this chapter, a simple order entry form is created using Java and its database interface (JDBC). As you will see, this method of Web database application development offers many innovative ways for improving the friendliness and efficiency of an application. The most notable distinction between an application developed based on CGI and its Java counterpart is the ability to respond to user events. With Java, all user actions can be tracked, and your program can respond to them immediately—*without* consulting the Web server. This feature is used in a simple shipping application developed in this chapter. The shipping rate field is updated automatically based on the entered zip code. The user does not have to click on a submit button.

To use the example in this chapter, you will need the following:

- Java Developer's Kit
- JDBC Library
- A Java-enabled browser such as Netscape
- A JDBC-compliant database

The way the application is set up is somewhat different than what you are used to. Try to understand the overall architecture and see why it makes sense based on what you know about Java. You will soon appreciate the new possibilities that Java brings to the world of Web database development.

Specification

The goal is to develop a very simple order entry form using Java. The form includes a number of text boxes to collect information such as the name, address, and phone number of the customer. Using event-trapping techniques, after the insertion of the zip code the program automatically contacts the database and retrieves an appropriate shipping rate based on the zip code. It then displays the shipping rate in the appropriate text field. At the end, the user can save the form to the database, clear the form, or exit the program.

The program will be developed using nothing but Java. No CGI components are allowed. The communication between the Java program (applet) and the database will occur using JDBC. The program should make no assumption about the back-end database. In other words, you should be able to change the database engine and have the program still run, simply by pointing to the new engine.

Environment

The application was developed using Java Developer's Kit version 1 on a Sun workstation running Solaris 4.2. The HTTP server was NCSA's httpd 1.5. The back-end database was mSQL (mini-SQL) available from `http://hughes.com.au/product/msql/`. It is a simple and light database engine which supports a subset of the SQL standard.

Version 0.65 of JDBC was used and is available from `http://splash.javasoft.com/jdbc/`.

The mSQL JDBC driver used is available from `http://www.minmet.uq.oz.au/msql-java/index.html`.

Figure 15-1 shows the architecture of the application. The database engine must run on the same machine that runs the HTTP server. The applet is served to the browser, then executed on the local machine. Using the URL format specified by JDBC (`jdbc:msql://hostname/database_name`), the applet connects to the database engine.

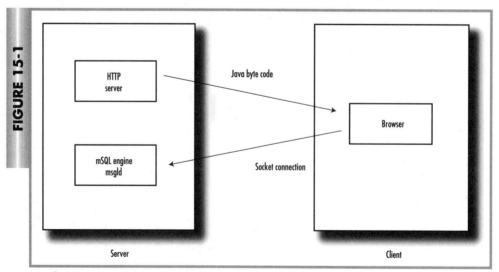

FIGURE 15-1

Application environment

Java Program

The Java code consists of three main parts:

- **The TitlePanel class:** Takes care of drawing a title for the application.

- **The OrderPanel class:** Manages the text fields, accepts input from the user, and establishes a connection to the database to retrieve the shipping rate based on the zip code.

- **The ButtonPanel class:** Draws the buttons (Save, Clear, Exit) and executes the appropriate code segment based on which button has been pressed.

Before discussing the code, the database and its tables should be discussed. Two tables are used in the application. The orders table stores all the information about an order. The rates table contains the shipping rates and the corresponding zip codes. For simplicity, only the first digit of the zip code is considered when determining the shipping rate.

Listing 15-1 shows the SQL statement used to create the two tables. The \g command indicates to the mSQL engine that the preceding command should be executed. It is not part of SQL.

Listing 15-1 SQL statements for creating orders and rates tables

```
CREATE TABLE orders (
 fname char(20),
 lname char(20),
 address char(30),
 city char(15),
 state char(2),
 zip char(10),
 phone char(15),
 sh char(4)
)
\g

CREATE TABLE rates (
 zip char(10),
 rate real
)
\g
```

Listing 15-2 shows the SQL commands used to populate the rates table. Once again, the first number is the first digit of the zip code, and the second number is the shipping rate in dollars.

Listing 15-2 Values for the rates table

```
INSERT INTO rates (zip, rate)
VALUES ('1', 4.00)
\g
INSERT INTO rates (zip, rate)
VALUES ('2', 4.25)
\g
INSERT INTO rates (zip, rate)
VALUES ('3', 3.75)
\g
INSERT INTO rates (zip, rate)
VALUES ('4', 4.00)
\g
INSERT INTO rates (zip, rate)
VALUES ('5', 4.50)
\g
INSERT INTO rates (zip, rate)
VALUES ('6', 3.50)
\g
INSERT INTO rates (zip, rate)
VALUES ('7', 4.00)
\g
INSERT INTO rates (zip, rate)
VALUES ('8', 4.75)
\g
INSERT INTO rates (zip, rate)
VALUES ('9', 5.00)
\g
INSERT INTO rates (zip, rate)
VALUES ('0', 4.25)
\g
```

The entire Java program is shown in Listing 15-3. The code is somewhat long, but it is very modularized and should be easy to follow.

Listing 15-3 Order form Java code

```
import java.awt.*;
import java.io.*;
import java.net.URL;
import java.applet.Applet;
import java.sql.*;
import imaginary.sql.*;

public class OrderForm extends java.applet.Applet {

    public int appletHeight = 200;
    public int appletWidth = 200;

    public final static Color TITLECOLOR = Color.white;

    public final static String FNAME = "First Name";
```

```
    public final static String LNAME = "Last Name";
    public final static String ADDRESS = "Address";
    public final static String CITY = "City";
    public final static String STATE = "State";
    public final static String ZIP = "Zip";
    public final static String PHONE = "Phone";
    public final static String SH = "S&H";
    public final static String SAVE = "Save";
    public final static String CLEAR = "Clear";
    public final static String EXIT = "Exit";

    public final static Font TITLEFONT = new Font("Dialog", Font.BOLD, 14);
    public final static Font BUTTONFONT = new Font("Dialog", Font.BOLD, 12);

    public String fName, lName, address, city, state, zip, phone;

    public TitlePanel titlePanel;
    public OrderPanel orderPanel;
    public ButtonPanel buttonPanel;

    public void init() {
        setLayout(new BorderLayout());

        titlePanel = new TitlePanel(this);
        add("North", titlePanel);

        orderPanel = new OrderPanel(this);
        add("Center", orderPanel);

        buttonPanel = new ButtonPanel(this);
        add("South", buttonPanel);

        layout();
        resize(appletWidth, appletHeight);
        repaint();
    }

    public void start() {
        resize(appletWidth, appletHeight);
        layout();
        repaint();
    }
}


class TitlePanel extends java.awt.Label {
        OrderForm applet;

    public TitlePanel(OrderForm applet) {
        this.applet = applet;
        setBackground(OrderForm.TITLECOLOR);
        repaint();
```

continued on next page

continued from previous page

```
        }

    public void paint (Graphics g) {
        String s;
        s = "Simple Order Entry Form with Database Connectivity";
        g.setColor(Color.black);
        g.setFont(OrderForm.TITLEFONT);
        g.drawString(s, 20,20);
    }
}


class OrderPanel extends java.awt.Panel {
        OrderForm applet;

        Label fnameLabel;
        Label lnameLabel;
        Label addressLabel;
        Label cityLabel;
        Label stateLabel;
        Label zipLabel;
        Label phoneLabel;
        Label shLabel;
        TextField fnameTextF;
        TextField lnameTextF;
        TextField addressTextF;
        TextField cityTextF;
        TextField stateTextF;
        TextField zipTextF;
        TextField phoneTextF;
        TextField shTextF;


        public OrderPanel(OrderForm applet) {
                this.applet = applet;

                setLayout(new GridLayout(8,2));

        fnameLabel = new Label(OrderForm.FNAME);
        lnameLabel = new Label(OrderForm.LNAME);
        addressLabel = new Label(OrderForm.ADDRESS);
        cityLabel = new Label(OrderForm.CITY);
        stateLabel = new Label(OrderForm.STATE);
        zipLabel = new Label(OrderForm.ZIP);
        phoneLabel = new Label(OrderForm.PHONE);
        shLabel = new Label(OrderForm.SH);

        fnameTextF = new TextField(20);
        lnameTextF = new TextField(20);
        addressTextF = new TextField(30);
        cityTextF = new TextField(15);
        stateTextF = new TextField(2);
```

```
            zipTextF = new TextField(10);
            phoneTextF = new TextField(15);
            shTextF = new TextField(4);

                    add(fnameLabel);
                    add(fnameTextF);
                    add(lnameLabel);
                    add(lnameTextF);
                    add(addressLabel);
                    add(addressTextF);
                    add(cityLabel);
                    add(cityTextF);
                    add(stateLabel);
                    add(stateTextF);
                    add(zipLabel);
                    add(zipTextF);
                    add(phoneLabel);
                    add(phoneTextF);
                    add(shLabel);
                    add(shTextF);
        }

        public boolean handleEvent(Event e) {
          if (e.target instanceof TextField && e.target.equals(zipTextF)
         && e.id == Event.LOST_FOCUS) {
                    get_rate();
          }
          return super.handleEvent(e);
        }

        void get_rate() {
          try {
                    new imaginary.sql.iMsqlDriver();
                    String url = "jdbc:msql://domain_name:4333/order_db";
            String rate_num = new String(applet.orderPanel.zipTextF.getText().sub-
string(0,1));

                    String query = new String("select rate from rates where zip like
" + "'" + rate_num + "%'");

                    Connection con = DriverManager.getConnection(url, "", "");
                      Statement stmt = con.createStatement();

                    System.out.println(query);

                    ResultSet rs = stmt.executeQuery(query);

                    String str = new String("temp");
                    while (rs.next()) {
                     str = rs.getChar(1);
                    }
            applet.orderPanel.shTextF.setText(str);
```

continued on next page

continued from previous page

```
                stmt.close();
                con.close();
        }
        catch ( Exception e) {
                e.printStackTrace();
           }
         }

        public void update(Graphics g) {
                paint(g);
        }
}


class ButtonPanel extends java.awt.Panel {
        OrderForm applet;
        Button saveButton;
        Button clearButton;
        Button exitButton;

        public ButtonPanel (OrderForm applet) {
                this.applet = applet;
                setLayout(new GridLayout(1,3));

                saveButton = new Button();
                saveButton.setFont(OrderForm.BUTTONFONT);
                saveButton.setLabel(OrderForm.SAVE);

                clearButton = new Button();
                clearButton.setFont(OrderForm.BUTTONFONT);
                clearButton.setLabel(OrderForm.CLEAR);

                exitButton = new Button();
                exitButton.setFont(OrderForm.BUTTONFONT);
                exitButton.setLabel(OrderForm.EXIT);

                add(saveButton);
                add(clearButton);
                add(exitButton);

                repaint();
        }

        public boolean action(Event e, Object o) {
          boolean status = false;
          if (e.target instanceof Button &&
        (saveButton.getLabel().equals((String)o))) {
                save();
          } else if (e.target instanceof Button &&
        (clearButton.getLabel().equals((String)o))) {
                clear();
          } else if (e.target instanceof Button &&
```

```
        (exitButton.getLabel().equals((String)o))) {
            mexit();
      }
      return status;
    }

    void save() {
      try {
            new imaginary.sql.iMsqlDriver();
            String url = "jdbc:msql://domain_name:4333/order_db";
            String query = new String("INSERT INTO orders VALUES (");

            Connection con = DriverManager.getConnection(url, "", "");
            Statement stmt = con.createStatement();

    query = query.concat("'");
    query = query.concat(applet.orderPanel.fnameTextF.getText());
    query = query.concat("', ");
    query = query.concat("'");
    query = query.concat(applet.orderPanel.lnameTextF.getText());
    query = query.concat("', ");
    query = query.concat("'");
    query = query.concat(applet.orderPanel.addressTextF.getText());
    query = query.concat("', ");
    query = query.concat("'");
    query = query.concat(applet.orderPanel.cityTextF.getText());
    query = query.concat("', ");
    query = query.concat("'");
    query = query.concat(applet.orderPanel.stateTextF.getText());
    query = query.concat("', ");
    query = query.concat("'");
    query = query.concat(applet.orderPanel.zipTextF.getText());
    query = query.concat("', ");
    query = query.concat("'");
    query = query.concat(applet.orderPanel.phoneTextF.getText());
    query = query.concat("', ");
    query = query.concat("'");
    query = query.concat(applet.orderPanel.shTextF.getText());
    query = query.concat("')");
            System.out.println(query);

            ResultSet rs = stmt.executeQuery(query);
            stmt.close();
            con.close();
}
catch ( Exception e) {
            e.printStackTrace();
      }

      repaint();
    }

    void clear() {
```

continued on next page

continued from previous page

```
                        applet.orderPanel.fnameTextF.setText("");
                        applet.orderPanel.lnameTextF.setText("");
                        applet.orderPanel.addressTextF.setText("");
                        applet.orderPanel.cityTextF.setText("");
                        applet.orderPanel.stateTextF.setText("");
                        applet.orderPanel.zipTextF.setText("");
                        applet.orderPanel.phoneTextF.setText("");
                        applet.orderPanel.shTextF.setText("");
            }

        void mexit() {
        applet.stop();
        }
}
```

When you first run the application, your browser should display something similar to
Figure 15-2. The exact layout depends on your platform and the window manager you are
running.

Rather than going through the code line by line, only the major parts and those
specifically related to JDBC are discussed. The following two lines include the packages
related to JDBC.

```
import java.sql.*;
import imaginary.sql.*;
```

FIGURE 15-2

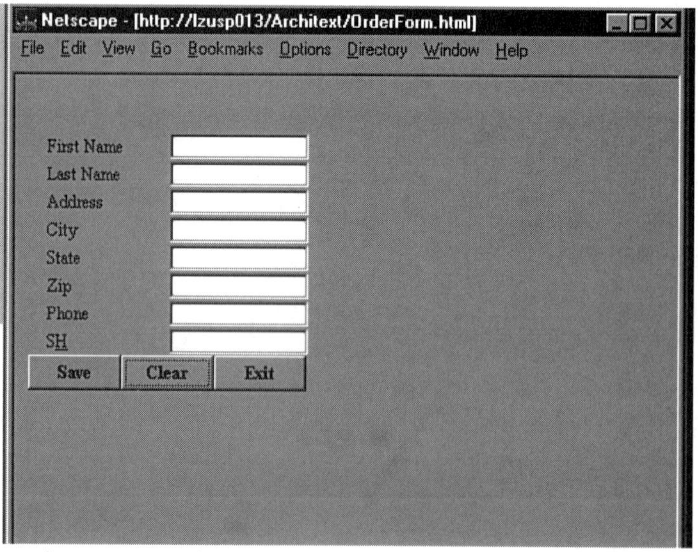

Order entry application

The first is the JDBC package and the second is the JDBC driver specific to the database, which in this case is the mSQL database. If you get errors about JDBC functions used in your program, these two lines are the first place to check. Also, be sure that your CLASS-PATH environmental variable points to appropriate directories which contain these packages.

Next, the application itself is introduced using the following class declaration:

```
public class OrderForm extends java.applet.Applet
```

The first thing you should notice is that the application is an extension of the applet class rather than a standalone Java program. This is very important since, by default, most browsers treat Java applets as *untrusted*, prohibiting them from performing certain functions which could be considered security hazards. One of these functions is the ability to open a socket connection on which JDBC depends. In order to run this applet, you must set the options of your browser to treat the applet as *trusted*.

After declaring some constants, the three main classes which compose the OrderForm class are declared. They correspond to the different parts of the screen. First is the TitlePanel, next is the OrderPanel, and last is the ButtonPanel. Each part is initialized in the init() method of the OrderForm class. This is the first method executed by the applet and a good place to perform main initializations.

The TitlePanel calls the paint() method in its constructor. In turn, the paint() method is overridden. In this method, a title string is drawn on the top part of the screen as determined by the coordinates 20, 20 in pixels.

The OrderPanel takes care of displaying all the text boxes for data entry. It also is responsible for updating the shipping rate text box after a zip code has been entered. In order to determine when the zip code has been entered, an event handler routine is defined for this class as shown below:

```
public boolean handleEvent(Event e) {
  if (e.target instanceof TextField && e.target.equals(zipTextF)
&& e.id == Event.LOST_FOCUS) {
      get_rate();
  }
  return super.handleEvent(e);
}
```

Any event that occurs within this class goes through the event handler. In the event handler, the event is checked to see if it is

- caused by a TextField object

- caused by the zipTextF object in particular

- indicating a LOST_FOCUS event

If all three of the above conditions are met, it means that the user has entered a zip code and has left the zip code text box. The get_rate() function is called under this condition. Otherwise, the events are handled as before. Figure 15-3 shows the application screen after the get_rate() function has finished execution. Note how the shipping rate field is filled in automatically.

FIGURE 15-3

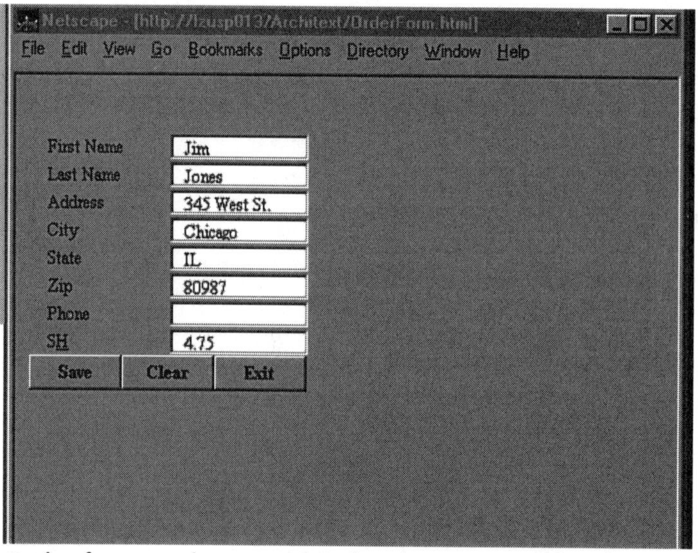

Order form application after the shipping rate has been
retrieved

The get_rate() function includes the JDBC code. It is shown here again.

```
void get_rate() {
  try {
    new imaginary.sql.iMsqlDriver();
    String url = "jdbc:msql://domain_name:4333/order_db";
    String rate_num = new
      String(applet.orderPanel.zipTextF.getText().substring(0,1));

    String query = new String("select rate from rates where zip like "
      + "'" + rate_num + "%'");

    Connection con = DriverManager.getConnection(url, "", "");
    Statement stmt = con.createStatement();

    System.out.println(query);

    ResultSet rs = stmt.executeQuery(query);

    String str = new String("temp");
    while (rs.next()) {
     str = rs.getChar(1);
    }
    applet.orderPanel.shTextF.setText(str);
    stmt.close();
    con.close();
  }
```

```
  catch ( Exception e) {
    printStackTrace();
  }
}
```

Note that the main body of the function is contained within a try-catch block to capture run-time errors. The *try-catch block* is an important feature of the Java language which helps in development of robust applications. You should consult a Java reference book for a discussion of this feature. The resulting StackTrace should lead you to the line causing the error. The most common problem is lack of a connection to the database. Make sure you have set up your environment correctly and the database is accessible from other clients. After establishing a connection, a string is formed containing a SELECT query and is submitted to the database. The RS.NEXT() method continues retrieving rows in a result set from the database. In this case, only one row will be returned for each query, since only one rate is specified for the first digit of each zip code. After retrieving the rate, it is placed on the text box labeled S&H, and the connection is terminated.

The ButtonPanel has a similar structure. The event handler checks to see which button was pressed and executes the appropriate method. The save button causes another communication with the database, during which the data is saved in the database via an INSERT statement. Note that mSQL uses single quotes to enclose a string. Double quotes will cause an error.

After you get the applet to run, experiment with the code. Change the queries or the data types and see the results (or errors). You will develop an appreciation for how Java enhances an application that was either impossible or very cumbersome in the traditional CGI environment. Think about some of the security issues related to Java and compare them with those related to CGI. Also note that Java applications require the transfer of the Java byte codes across the Net to the client machine. In the example shown above, this was not a big deal since the application was small, but for larger applications, the transfer time can be a major performance bottleneck.

16

Real World Applications

Congratulations! You have come a long way. Still, you might want to take a look at some finished applications before diving into designing your own. This chapter covers a number of Web databases in production use today. Obviously, it is not possible to disclose their exact architecture and design, but you can see some of the principles discussed throughout the book and gain some insight as to how you would implement your own Web database application. After reading about it, you are encouraged to visit the site and gain some firsthand experience.

Federal Express

`http://www.fedex.com/track_it.html`

Federal Express was one of the first companies to put a Web database out for public use. The query screen is simple (see Figure 16-1). An input box shows where the user can enter an Airbill Tracking Number. In addition, a single selection menu designates the destination country.

FIGURE 16-1

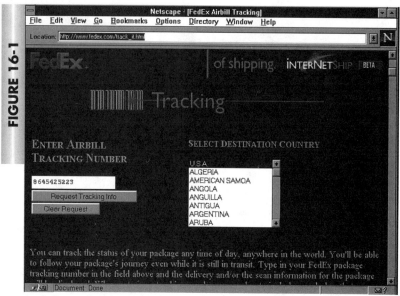

Airbill Tracking application

The *<form>* tag is shown below:

```
<FORM METHOD="GET" ACTION="http://www.fedex.com/cgi-bin/track_it">
```

Note that the GET method is used, and the CGI script responsible for handling the form input is track_it. This script generates an HTML page containing information about the Airbill Tracking Number (see Figure 16-2).

There is no reason to keep track of the state of the application, since the design calls for a one-step transaction. Each additional query of the database is treated independently from the others. On the response page, you can see the *name=value* pairs which are appended to the CGI script name.

American Airlines

http://www.amrcorp.com

American Airlines also has a Web database which allows for a partial query of their flight information database. In Figure 16-3, the query method assumes the user knows the flight number and the date of the flight. Note that the page is generated by a CGI script (fltInfo.cgi). This is convenient because the items in the Flight Date menu change based on the date. Rather than hard coding the dates in a static HTML file and changing them daily, the script generates the page. Therefore, it can automatically adjust the dates.

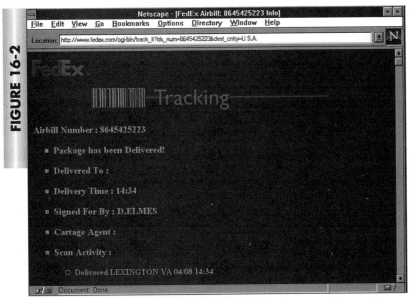

Output of the Airbill Tracking application

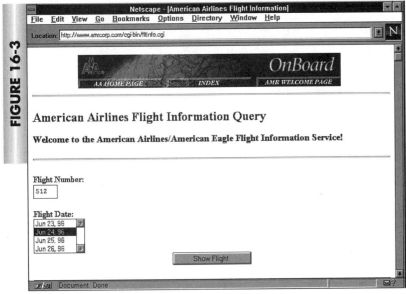

Flight Information system

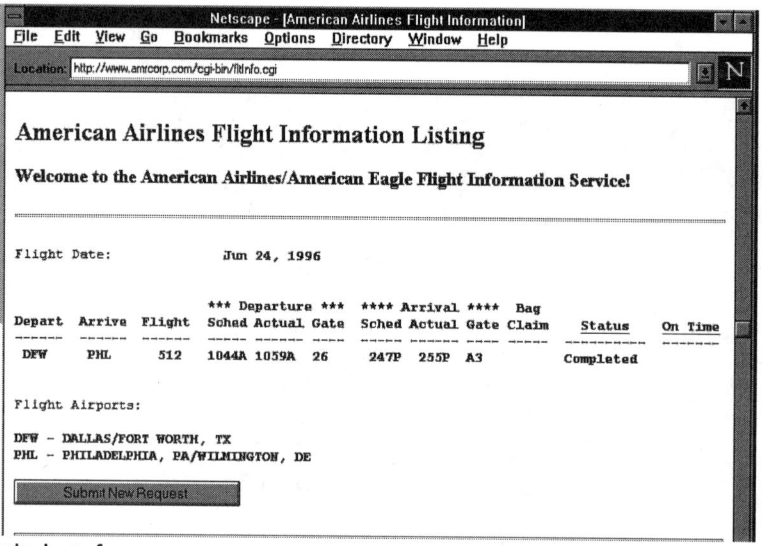

FIGURE 16-4

Flight Information output

The output of the script (see Figure 16-4) is some text information about the flight. Like the Federal Express application, the transaction occurs in one step so there is no need to keep track of states.

Another interesting point about this CGI script is that the same script is used to generate the input page and the output page. An internal flag such as an <input type=hidden> tag can be used to tell the script which screen to produce.

Switchboard

http://www2.switchboard.com

This Web database is slightly more complex because it has more input fields and must do some state keeping. Figure 16-5 shows a sample input screen.

Note that the screen is generated by a CGI script. The buttons on the bottom of the screen allow the user to switch to a different query form easily. For the discussion, we use the module dealing with businesses (see Figure 16-6). Note that the script name has not changed, but the *name=value* pair passed to it has changed. It is now BUS in place of MG. This might seem strange at first, since the *name=value* pair only has the name. The value part is left blank. This is perfectly legal, however. The script checks for a particular name among the *name=value* pairs passed to it. If the script finds the name, it tries to grab its corresponding value. If it doesn't find the name, it must assign a predetermined value, such as NULL, to it. As long as the values in the two cases are different, the name without a value can be used as a flag which instructs the script to perform different actions or paint different screens.

Switchboard screen for finding a person

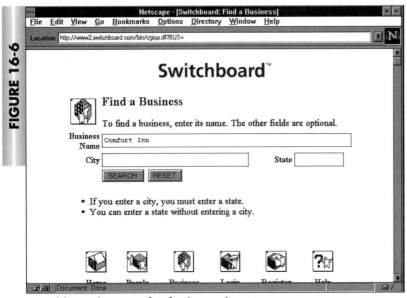

Switchboard screen for finding a business

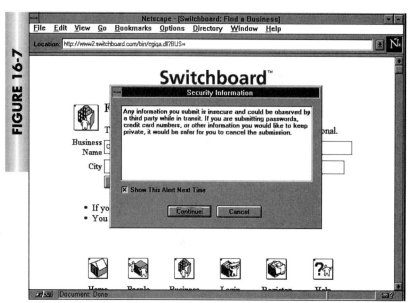

Security warning from Netscape browser

After you submit the form, the Netscape browser informs you that the communication channel through which the form information was submitted is insecure and asks for approval to continue (see Figure 16-7). Unless the HTTP server is a secure server, you will not be able to send the information securely. We will look at some secure examples later in this chapter.

Finally, the result of your query is printed as shown in Figure 16-8. You should pay special attention to the three hyperlinks: Next Page, Modify Search, and New Search. By placing the cursor on any one of them, you can see the URL to which the hyperlink points. If your browser does not support this feature, you should look at the source code of the page to see the URL to which they point. Here is what you would see:

- **New Search:** The hyperlink executes the original CGI script, which paints the input screen. It starts an entirely new and independent search.

- **Modify Search:** This hyperlink takes you back to the input screen while preserving the values you have already entered in the input boxes. Note that the *name=value* pair passed to the script includes L=Comfort%20Inn. The %20 indicates there is a space between the two words. The user can now fill in some other boxes or modify the value in the Business Name box. The important point is that as far as the server is concerned, the next query is independent from any of the previous ones (no states). By passing on the values already filled in by the user, the program gives the impression that a continuous session dedicated to the user is in place.

Next Page: This link makes a request to the server for more results based on the previous query. The URL looks something like: `http://www2.switchboard.com/bin/cgiqa.dll?SK=OEOOFF0008000000C9A9313D0A13A4EF&SR=&NN=8&L=comfort%20inn&BUS=`. This action does not require another search by the database. The search should occur once. The search merely requests that the server send additional results its way. This requires the server to have some idea about the state of the transaction. The server needs to know which search results were sent to the client in the first place, so it can send additional results from the same search. We have already discussed several methods to implement state tracking, such as Cookies and hidden text boxes. This particular CGI script seems to be using some ID number to keep track of the different result sets returned by the database.

StockMaster

`http://www.stockmaster.com`

As you already know, CGI scripts are not restricted to producing text as their output. StockMaster uses CGI scripts to draw a graph for the value of a particular stock and its trading volume. The input screen is very simple and well designed (see Figure 16-9).

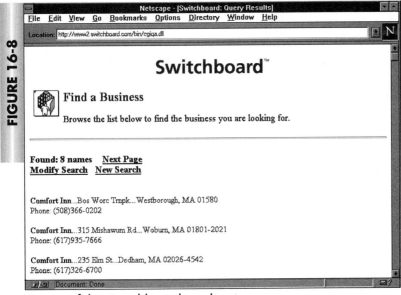

FIGURE 16-8

Output of the Switchboard application

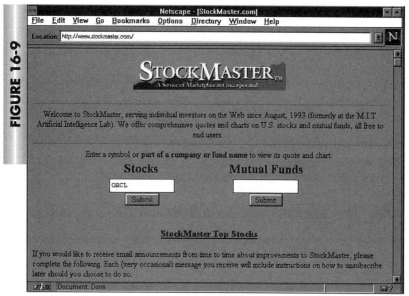

FIGURE 16-9

StockMaster input screen

After entering the symbol for a stock or mutual fund, the CGI script generates an HTML page that includes the images of the graphs (see Figure 16-10). The new page has a form that allows the user to enter another stock symbol which repeats the cycle. The page also includes another form (remember it is possible to have more than one form in an HTML page, as long as each form has its own submit button). This second form is responsible for collecting data on how you think the stock will do in the future. This latter part is not shown in the figure due to space constraints.

The point about the StockMaster application that should be emphasized is that the output of a CGI script can be any data format. You need to be careful not to send binary data to a browser when it is not able to interpret and display that data. Also, be sure that the proper MIME type is specified before you begin to send binary data.

University of Missouri Course Catalog

http://www.iru.missouri.edu/courses.html

The Course Catalog application from the University of Missouri is another good example of a Web database. Implementation notes about the system point out that an Oracle back-end is used as the database, along with Oracle's own Web interface. Figure 16-11 shows the main screen where a particular keyword is entered in the input box. This keyword is used to search the course catalog. Note that the HTML file is static.

Output of the StockMaster program

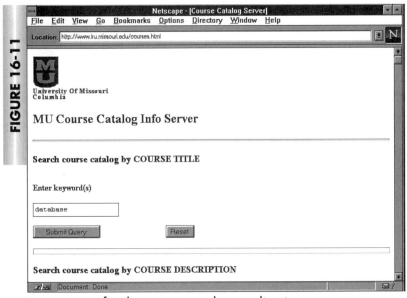

Input screen for the course catalog application

The word *database* is used for demonstration purposes. After searching the course database, a list of course titles in which the word *database* appears is printed out, as shown in Figure 16-12. Note that each course is hyperlinked, which means additional information can be obtained by clicking on it.

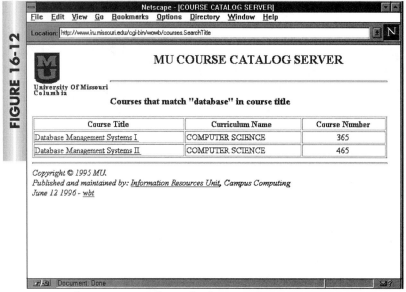

Listing of courses matching the keyword

Figure 16-13 shows the detailed information about the Database Management Systems I course. Note the *name=value* pairs that are passed to the CGI script. They are responsible for instructing the script as to what action(s) are desired. The tabular formatting and bold titles for the different fields make the output easy to read and understand.

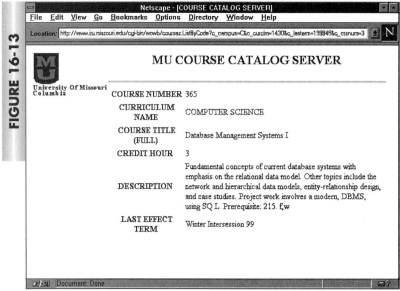

Detailed course description

The Wall Street Journal

`http://wsj.com`

It is very likely that you will need to validate your users in your application. This is usually done via a user name and a password in traditional client/server applications. Web applications are no different and offer many forms of implementation. Figure 16-14 shows a login verification screen used by the Interactive Edition of *The Wall Street Journal*. Note that the screen is generated by a CGI script called login. Two *name=value* pairs are passed onto the script. The input boxes are ordinary text input boxes as part of HTML tags. The Sign On button is used to submit the information to the server.

FIGURE 16-14

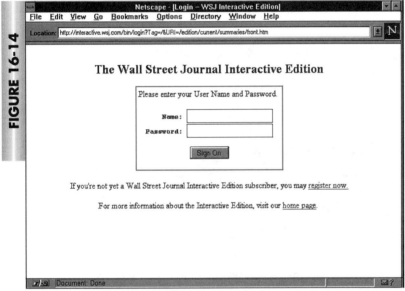

Login screen for *The Wall Street Journal*

Once the user name and password are submitted, they are processed and matched against a database. If a match is found, the next screen will be pages of the newspaper. If no match is found, an error message appears. Bookmarking the newspaper page will not do any good since the page is dynamic and the server won't serve it to you unless you come in through the login screen. This is a popular method of providing login verification among applications. The CGI script does the verification. The trick is to be sure that the user cannot directly enter the page that appears after successful verification and bypass the verification system.

Lombard

http://www.lombard.com/PACenter

This example shows another method of user verification, used by the Lombard Web site. The Web server is actually responsible for asking the browser to use a pop-up window (see Figure 16-15) to get the user name and password. Many Web servers offer this feature using different implementations. Normally, you would designate a particular HTML file or a directory as secure. Any time the Web server needs to serve a secure document, it will ask for user verification. The pop-up window appears once during a session, which means that by entering correct information once, the user will not see the pop-up window again. Entering an incorrect username and password will take you to an error page generated by the Web server. Investigate the security features of your Web server, then decide if this verification method is suitable to your environment.

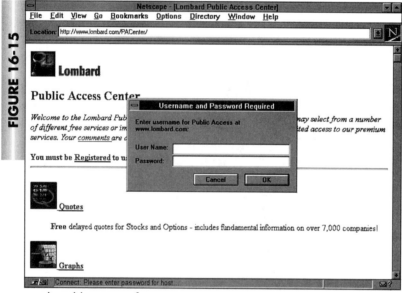

FIGURE 16-15

Lombard login verification

Wells Fargo

http://banking.wellsfargo.com

The example shown in Figure 16-16 is another login verification screen. It is included for two reasons. First, note that this service is provided by a bank. When more banks feel safe on the Web, we will see another explosion in on-line monetary transactions like shopping. The Web seems like an ideal place for this type of activity, but concerns over security have slowed progress. It is a matter of time before people will feel safe doing business on the Web.

The second reason for including this example is its usage of secure transmission. Note that the URL starts with https and not plain http. This tells us that the server is a secure server and has successfully established a secure socket channel with the browser. Also, you can see the key in the lower left of the Netscape browser window is intact, which visually indicates the existence of a secure channel. Of course, other browsers will have different means of conveying the same message.

With a secure channel, the information entered in the input boxes will be transferred to the CGI script in encrypted form, which is desirable since one of the input boxes contains a Social Security number. By using a secure server on your site, you show your concern for security. That will boost customer confidence. You will also make your own application more robust and less prone to hackers. You should definitely invest in a secure Web server if you intend to perform monetary transactions over the Web.

Patient Record Database

`http://kayak.npac.syr.edu:2020/work/Main.html`

The example shown in Figure 16-17 demonstrates how complex Web database applications can become. The application is written by researchers at the Northeast Parallel Architectures Center of Syracuse University. By using frames and JavaScript, the authors have added an effective user interface to their database. The Netscape browser 2.02 which is used throughout this book does not allow you to directly look at the source code of an individual

FIGURE 16-16

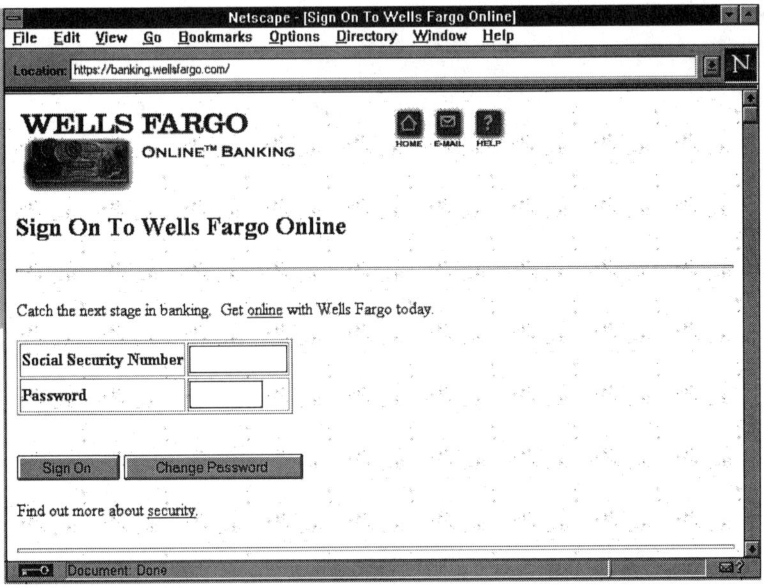

Wells Fargo secure login screen

frameset. You have to load each frameset separately before you can view the source. You will find many lines of JavaScript code which allow the application to perform some processing of user input without contacting the server. Note that this work is experimental and might not be available at all times.

Selecting a patient name and clicking the search button at the top of the screen retrieves the patient's record and displays it in the center frameset. Note that one of the information pieces stored is a picture of the patient. Once the patient data is loaded by the browser, you click on any of the categories on the right to jump to the particular section of the record you want. This is shown in Figure 16-18, but you are strongly encouraged to connect to the site and examine it for yourself. All elements of this application have been discussed in the previous chapters. This example shows that the Web can be used as an effective means to provide a powerful user interface to very complex databases.

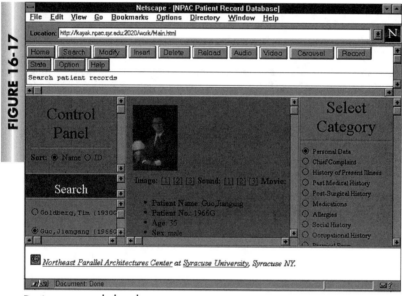

FIGURE 16-17

Patient record database

Live Java Graphs

http://gserver.grads.vt.edu/cgi-bin/wowtgd/hr.showDeptj

The example shown in Figure 16-19 is from a Web site at Virginia Tech University. It shows how Java can be used to generate graphs on the fly from a database. While this book is being written, the JDBC specification was still under review, and there weren't many public Java database interfaces. This particular application uses CGI to establish an applet-to-database connection.

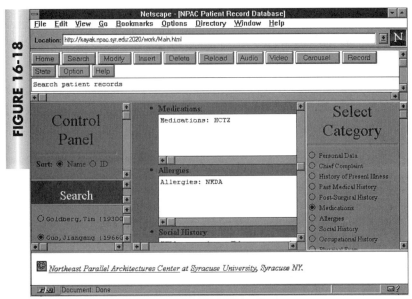

Browsing through the patient record information

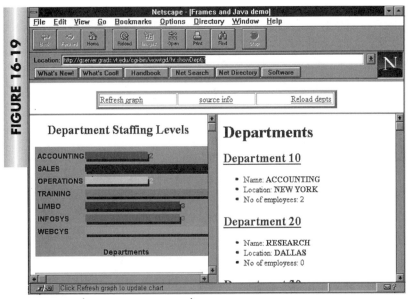

Live graphs using Java applets

This applet is contained in a frameset and integrated into the Web page. It does not directly interact with the user. In other words, if you put your mouse button on it and click away, nothing happens. As JDBC gains popularity, the same applet can turn into a live application. It can accept user input and respond to different events. The applet would also have a direct link to the database. All of this assumes that the Web browser grants the necessary permissions to the applet. You can consult the source code information about how the applet was written.

17
New Technologies

The computer industry is one of the most dynamic fields in the world. The Internet and World Wide Web are no exceptions. Every day new products are introduced to the market. The constant flow of new technologies is part of what makes the computer industry so exciting. It also makes writing a book on the topic somewhat challenging.

This chapter introduces some of the new technologies affecting Web databases and the Internet. It's easy to get overwhelmed with current technology, without even looking at what the future holds. However, your applications need to have a decent life expectancy in order to be successful. An awareness of where the technology you're using is headed will help you create cutting-edge applications that remain useful even as the technology changes. So instead of being intimidated by the developments in the computer industry, just jump in. You'll be amazed at how much you can learn in just one day. And when you want more, there's an infinite source of information right at your fingertips on the Web.

Internet Architecture

The Internet itself will be subject to some changes in the near future. The Internet Protocol uses the IP numbering system to address all machines in the network of networks. The original design did not anticipate such a growth in the number of computers. Recall that an *IP number* is composed of four parts, each containing a number ranging from 0 to 255. A machine is uniquely identified by all four parts of an IP number. For example, a machine could have an IP address of 145.123.32.45. At first glance, it seems that the numbering scheme can address more than 4 billion computers (255^4). You must, however, remember that masking is used to divide the address space into smaller pieces which are then allocated to individual networks. A site could be assigned the IP number of 123.145.*.*. This will give the site control of about 65,000 addresses which it must manage. The site could only have 5,000 computers needing IP addresses, but it has 65,000 addresses assigned to it. With this addressing scheme, much of the address space goes unused. Several alternatives, including a larger IP address space, have been introduced. It is only a matter of time before their utilization becomes a reality. You can learn more about IP Next Generation at `http://playground.sun.com/pub/ipng/html/ipng-main.html/`.

The IP addressing scheme is only part of the main Internet architecture. Several others areas have shown deficiencies which must eventually be addressed. One such area is the HTTP protocol itself. The HTTP/1.1 proposal addresses some of the shortcomings of the current protocol. Information is available from `http://www.w3.org/pub/WWW/Protocols`.

Application Servers

With the emergence of Java and Active X technologies, a relatively new architecture has also shown some growth. An application server sits between the Web server and a database as shown in Figure 17-1. The application server maintains an open connection to the database at all times. A CGI program or a program using the Server API communicates with the application server, and the application server actually performs a query on the database, retrieves the result, and sends it to the program. Such an architecture allows the design to concentrate on the application itself.

Another variation of the above architecture holds promise for Java applications and inter-object communication. This is shown in Figure 17-2. Here, the Web server sends information (an applet) to the browser. The applet is then able to establish a connection to the application server and grab the components it needs. It can also communicate with the database through the application gateway.

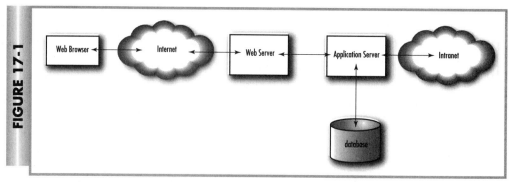

FIGURE 17-1

A typical application server

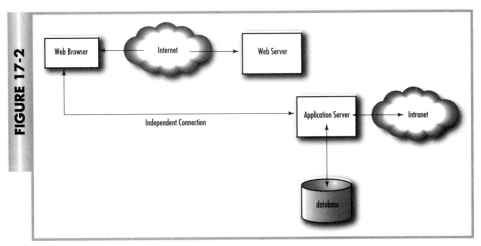

FIGURE 17-2

Application server architecture using Java or Active X technology

Java

Java is certainly a promising player in the Web application development world. However, several advances are necessary to make it a major player. The first is performance. Benchmarks consistently rank Java considerably slower than compiled languages such as C or C++. This will soon change as Java compilers and operating systems are developed.

Although the Java language addresses security extensively, implementations of the Java virtual machine continue to harbor security holes. So far, the industry has kept an open ear to these issues and has tried to correct problems as they are reported. By keeping this attitude, the technology will continue to evolve and improve.

Java's need for database connectivity is answered by the Java Database Connectivity (JDBC) API. It will be some time before most databases begin to support JDBC. Performance and security issues remain an open question in this area. However, as Java's support for multimedia applications increases, so will its popularity.

Networking

Advances in networking will play a great role in how widespread the Web will become. Although many large organizations enjoy high-speed networks and high-speed connections to Internet backbones, many people still connect to the Internet through a phone line using a modem. This speed of data transfer is not sufficient to take full advantage of some of the multimedia capabilities of the Web, such as audio, animation, and real-time videos. Streaming techniques are used to address some of these issues, but they do not replace a high-speed network connection. Several technologies, including ISDN and high-speed cable modems, seem to be emerging to meet this need. The trend to connect more computers to the network will continue, and along with it, the trend to increase the speed of those connections.

Security

The Web has a lot of potential for business use; however, that potential has yet to flourish. New advances in security such as SSL, site certificates, personal certificates, digital identifications, and electronic money promise to open up this aspect of the Web. While the industry has concentrated on the technical advances of computer security, it has neglected the end users. Using sophisticated encryption, a credit card number transmitted over the Net is much safer than when it is commnicated over the phone to a clerk. So why do people continue to use their credit cards over the phone and not on the Net? The reason could be that people simply are not used to doing business over the Net. With time, as technology and security improve, on-line shopping could be as common as a trip to the mall and a lot more convenient.

Meanwhile, as a developer, you can help educate your users about security and how it applies to your applications. New features of Microsoft Explorer 3.0 and Netscape Navigator 3.0 have enhanced security and, at the same time, made many of the technical details transparent to the casual user. There are several companies at the forefront of using enhanced security to offer services to customers. Cybercash (`http://www.cybercash.com`) offers an Internet payment service which encourages commerce over the Net. First Virtual (`http://www.fv.com`) is another player in the development of Internet payment systems.

Databases

The database market has been growing. Databases are the most popular tool for storing and retrieving information in an orderly manner. Traditionally, relational databases have struggled with binary data types such as pictures and videos. They have attempted to handle such data using the *blob* data type, which is basically a generic binary format. This approach simply has not been effective. A new wave is object-oriented and object-relational database engines. They treat data types, such as videos, like an object and associate the appropriate retrieval and search methods with that object. It does not make sense to search a database of pictures based on text, but it makes sense to perform a search based on color or other photographic attributes unique to the picture data type.

Web pages can be stored in a such a database, eliminating the need for keeping HTML and other files in complex flat file systems. Illustra (an Informix subsidiary) has made great progress on that front. Other database vendors will most likely enter this market in the near future.

Active X Controls

Microsoft enjoys a huge market share in the world of operating systems. The technology behind Active X controls is very promising. Formerly known as OLE controls or OCX controls, Active X controls allow one application (such as a Web browser) to use packaged functionality offered by other programs. Hundreds of Active X controls are available, offering anything from simple timers to sophisticated spreadsheets. Active X promises to be an integral part of Internet Explorer 3.0, bridging Windows desktop applications and the Web.

Active X controls, along with Netscape plug-ins and Java applets, offer distinct approaches to Web application development. Each has some unique features. Perhaps all three can live and prosper, but if history is a precedent, one will emerge as the winner.

Network PC

Larry Ellison of Oracle is a strong proponent of network PCs. These small, inexpensive machines are also known as PC appliances. They promise to offer an easy, inexpensive way for people to connect to the Web and run applications. Without huge processing power, network PCs count on the server to which they are connected to perform most of the work. They encourage a server-based approach to computing. Some versions will have built-in chips to run Java applications, so they can act as smart clients. They also will probably be much more specialized than a typical PC.

Another player in this area is Inferno from Lucent Technologies. Inferno is a network operating system with its own programming language, called Limbo. Some people see a lot of promise in this type of machine, and some dismiss the idea as a shift to the old mainframe world. Regardless, network PCs are likely to allow more people to become familiarized with the Web, the Internet, and the services they offer. Once users are comfortable, they might move to a traditional PC if needed.

Appendix A: HTML Quick Reference

HTML is the language of the Web. It is a markup language used to create Web pages. The original specifications were very limited. For example, they did not support tables, frames, or even tags for placement of images on the page. Many enhancements have been made to the standard, which as of the writing of this book, stands at version 2.0. The following is a very simple guide to some of the more widely used features of HTML. The user is strongly encouraged to check on-line sources for the latest revisions of the standard.

General Structure of an HTML Document

All HTML documents follow the same basic structure. Tags are used to delimit the different parts of a document. The following is the basic structure when a page does not use frames:

```
<html>
     <head>
      header tags
     </head>

     <body>
      body tags
     </body>
</html>
```

Header Tags

HTML supports a number of tags that are specific to the header area of the document, which is the area between the *<head> </head>* tag pairs. The most common is the title tag.

Example

```
<title> How to write a good HTML document </title>
```

Another tag is the base tag. It is used to indicate the URL of the current document which helps browsers resolve relative hypertext links within the document. The syntax is

```
<base href=URL>
```

where URL is the URL for the current document.

Body Tags

The remaining tags are intended to be used within the *<body></body>* tag pairs. They make up the actual content of the document.

Heading Tags

Six levels of heading styles are specified in HTML. Each heading tag presents the enclosed text in a distinct format and style.

Example

```
<H1>This is an example of a level 1 heading</H1>
<H2>This is an example of a level 2 heading</H2>
<H3>This is an example of a level 3 heading</H3>
<H4>This is an example of a level 4 heading</H4>
<H5>This is an example of a level 5 heading</H5>
<H6>This is an example of a level 6 heading</H6>
```

The way different heading styles are presented depends on the browser. An output for the above markup is shown in Figure A-1.

Paragraph Tag

The paragraph tag encloses text to be marked as a paragraph. The closing tag (written as *</p>*) is optional.

Example

```
<P>This is the text of a third paragraph.</P>
```

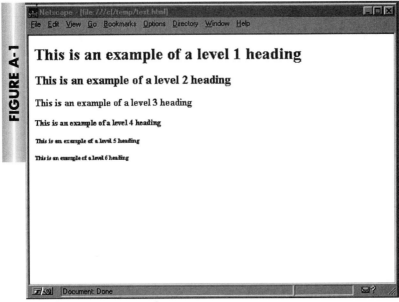

FIGURE A-1

Heading tags example

Preformatted Text

Preformatted text tags surround text that needs to retain its formatting characteristics. Normally, spaces, tabs, and other whitespace are ignored.

Example

```
<PRE>
You can begin a new line without the use of a paragraph tag.
This is a new line. Here is something
                    Here is nothing
Note that something is aligned with nothing!
</PRE>
```

The result of this markup is shown in Figure A-2.

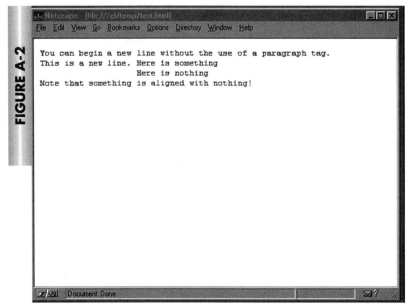

Preformatted text example

Line Break

The line break tag simply denotes the start of a new line of text.

Example

```
This is a line break demo. We break the line here <br>
and here<br>
and twice here <br><br>
This is the end.
```

The result of this markup is shown in Figure A-3.

Block Quotation

Text enclosed within the block quotation tag pair is set to stand out as a block of quoted text, similar to what might appear in a literary work.

Example

```
<BLOCKQUOTE>
This is a block quote example.
</BLOCKQUOTE>
```

The result of this markup is shown in Figure A-4.

FIGURE A-3

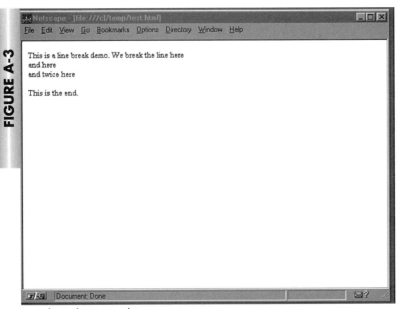

Line break example

FIGURE A-4

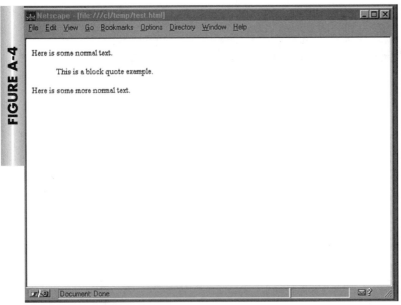

Block quotation example

Comments

You can use the comments tag to insert comments into your HTML markup that won't show up on your Web page.

Example

```
<!-- your comments -->
```

Unordered Lists

The unordered list tag is used to create a list of bulleted items. It also allows for nested lists.

Example

```
<ul>
<li> First list item
<li> Second list item
<li> Third list item
</ul>
```

The result of this markup is shown in Figure A-5.

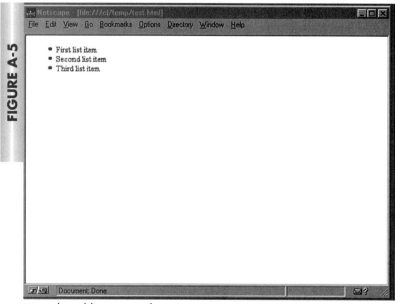

FIGURE A-5

Unordered list example

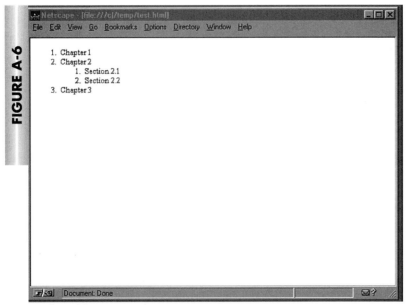

FIGURE A-6

Ordered list example

Ordered Lists

The ordered list tag is used to create numbered lists. Nesting is allowed.

Example

```
<ol>
<li> Chapter 1
<li> Chapter 2
<ol>
<li> Section 2.1
<li> Section 2.2
</ol>
<li> Chapter 3
</ol>
```

The result of this markup is shown in Figure A-6.

Menu Lists

The menu list tag is similar to the ordered list tag, but the spacing is a bit different.

Example

```
<menu>
<li> First menu item
<li> Second menu item
<li> Third menu item
</menu>
```

Definition List

The definition list tag is used to show a list of definitions or term explanations.

Example

```
<DL>
<DT> Term 1 <DD> Definition for term 1.
<DT> Term 2 <DD> Definition for term 2.
</DL>
```

The result of this markup is shown in Figure A-7.

Compact Definition List

The compact definition list tag is the same as the definition list tag, but the items are presented in a more compact format.

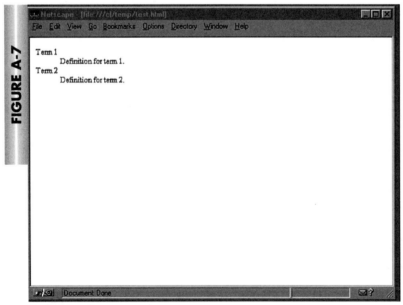

FIGURE A-7

Definition list example

FIGURE A-8

Compact definition list example

Example

```
<DL COMPACT>
<DT> Term <DD> Definition for term 1 in compact form.
<DT> Term <DD> Definition for term 2 in compact form.
</DL>
```

The result of this markup is shown in Figure A-8.

Character Formatting

The following are character formatting tag pairs:

Italics: <i></i>

Underline: <u></u>

Bold: <strong></strong>

Bold: <b> </b>

Italics: <em></em>

Anchors

The anchors tag makes the Web a surfing tool by creating a link to another document.

Example

```
<a HREF="http://sun.java.com"> Java</a>
```

You can also create a link to a specific part of a document by identifying the specific part with a unique name.

Example

```
<a NAME="part3"> Part 3</a>
```

You can then make a reference to that specific part by including the name as part of the reference.

Example

```
<a HREF="http://servername/hello.html#part3">Part 3</a>
```

Images

The images tag allows for inclusion of images in an HTML page.

Example

```
<img src="filename / URL">
<img src="image.gif" align=alignment type>
```

Alignment type is one of the following:

- Top
- Bottom
- Middle

Special Characters

The special characters tag lets you display any character by including its decimal ASCII code after an ampersand in the HTML markup. Also, the following codes are valid:

- < displays <
- > displays for >
- & displays &

Tables

Tables allow for a more strict arrangement of items on a page. Tables will be part of the new HTML standard when it comes out. The entire table is enclosed in the *<table>* tag. An optional BORDER parameter can be specified to draw a border around the table. Each row is enclosed within a *<TR></TR>* tag pair, and each cell within a row is enclosed in the *<TD></TD>* tag pair.

Example

```
<TABLE BORDER>
<TR>
      <TD>R1C1</TD>  <TD>R1C2</TD>  <TD>R1C3</TD>
</TR>
<TR>
      <TD>R1C1</TD>  <TD>R2C2</TD>  <TD>R2C3</TD>
</TR>
</TABLE>
```

The result of this markup is shown in Figure A-9.

Frames

The frames tag allows the client to display more than one document at a time. Frames also offers the capability of freezing panes. Frames is not part of the current HTML standard.

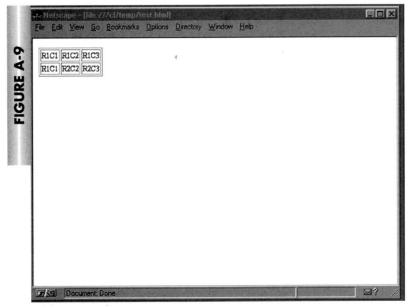

FIGURE A-9

Table example

Example

```
<html>
    <head>
    </head>

    <frameset rows="100, 200">
        <frame src=URL>
        <frame src=URL>
    </frameset>
</html>
```

Frame sizes can be specified with absolute values (size in pixels) or as percentages. There is a third type which allows fractional specification of the frame sizes.

The following attributes can be specified for a frame:

- **SCROLLING:** This attribute can have the values *yes*, *no*, and *auto*. It specifies whether scrollbars should be attached to the frame box.

- **NORESIZE:** The presence of this flag prohibits the user from resizing the frame box.

- **NAME:** The value for this attribute is a unique name which can be used to create a link to the frame from other documents or the same document. This is similar to the NAME attribute in the *<href>* tag.

The *<noframes>* tag dictates how an HTML page that uses frames should be displayed on a browser that does not support frames.

Appendix B: HTML Style Guide

There is no universally *good* way to write prose or poetry. Similarly, there is no universally accepted style for writing HTML documents. However, there are certain guidelines that can enhance the usefulness of your document and make it more presentable to readers. This appendix covers some of these guidelines.

1. Use a consistent presentation style

The way a document looks has an enormous effect on its power to present information. Perhaps the most important element in a document is consistency. HTML has made great strides in creating documents with a consistent presentation style. Let us consider a simple example. Suppose you want to write a report using a word processor. To create consistent headings, you use a particular heading style throughout your document. This heading style is defined by specifying font size, font type, and other pertinent information. Your document retains its look as you move it to other machines, provided the other machines have the same font.

In HTML, things are a bit different. As you might recall, the *<H1></H1>* tag pair never defines anything about the way a level 1 heading should be displayed. It does not specify the font to be used or its size. The presentation style is left up to the client. Different browsers can display the text marked as a level 1 heading in completely different ways. As the author of an HTML document, you do not have as much control over the cosmetic aspects as you do when using a word processor. This is perhaps the biggest and most important adjustment users must make when developing HTML documents.

HTML is filled with tags similar to the heading tags, and HTML 3 promises to add even more. Consider the *<strong></strong>* tag pair. Although most browsers display text enclosed within these tags using a boldface type, there is no specification that says they must. Once again, the presentation is left up to the client.

You should take advantage of such open-ended tags and try to use them in your documents. Even though HTML 3 might introduce tags that allow direct modification of fonts and sizes, you should be careful when using them. If you do, then you dictate to the client how you want your document to display. When you are dealing with a world audience such as Internet users, you want as much flexibility as possible. Let the client decide.

2. Be careful when using nonstandard HTML tags

Web documents are accessible from all over the world. People using different machines with different graphics and processing capabilities will visit your page. You want to maximize the size of your audience, and you want everyone to be impressed by your creation. If this is your goal, be careful when using nonstandard HTML tags and extensions. There is nothing worse than looking at a document that does not display correctly because of nonstandard extensions. It may discourage some people and appear to others that they are being excluded.

If you use nonstandard tags, always offer an alternative version for "less-privileged" users and make sure they know it exists. A simple link such as *alternate version* will do. You can also use the CGI information about the client software to see what capabilities it has. Always remember that not everyone uses the same browser you do.

3. Make your documents look credible

Make your documents look credible by stamping them with a date. Also, sign your documents or indicate who has written the page or is maintaining it. A document, as informative as it might be, does not look credible when it is not dated or signed. Also, keep in mind that many people use the information provided on Web pages as reference material. In order to compose a comprehensive bibliography, these users need to include the author's name for the pages they reference. Even if you don't consider your pages research material, sign and date them. The World Wide Web is a means to exchange information, and in many cases, the *freshness* of the information is information itself. You can use the *<address>* tag to sign your documents.

4. Organize your document

HTML provides a variety of tags to help you organize your document. Use them. If you can enhance your presentation by breaking the content into outline form, then by all means do it. That is why the heading tags were invented. It is much easier to figure out a text's subject by looking at headings rather than reading a bunch of words. In large documents, you might want to take advantage of the *<href>* tag and create links to the different sections of your document from a table of contents. This method of organization not only helps the reader jump to a section of interest, but also eliminates the need to download the entire document when only a certain portion interests him or her. As with any document, solid and logical organization can help the overall presentation and effectiveness of your document.

5. Enhance readability of your document

Aside from the overall organization of your document, try to make the smaller sections more readable. Take advantage of the tags for creating bulleted lists or numbered lists. Use the paragraph tag to break your document at logical points. Use the tags *<em>* and *<strong>*

to emphasize certain words that play a special role in helping the reader better understand the information you are providing.

6. Create meaningful links

HTML allows you to create links to other documents. The link concept is not new, but previously it was not used as extensively as it is today. Make your links meaningful and informative. It is easy to get carried away and create documents that include almost as many links as there are words on the page. Most of the time, such documents are ineffective and turn off readers. Try to create a general focus for your page and create links that support that focus. For example, if you are writing a page about common problems with an automobile engine, then your links should be related to engines and their problems. Don't have a link to a page that discusses an unrelated aspect of automobiles.

7. Carefully choose the words indicating a link

Links are marked differently than the rest of the document. Most browsers display the links in a different color or use some other visual effect. As a result, the words making up the link stand out in a document. You should choose good words as links. Avoid using weak links such as, "Click here to learn more about our offerings." Instead, use something like, "Learn more about our offerings."

The word *here* does not really say anything about the topic of the link. However, the word *offerings* gives users a very good idea about where they are headed.

8. Be aware of the sources of your links

If you have links to documents on other servers, check and see who the author is and whether the page will remain at its present location. You don't want to have a link to a page whose address has changed and will give the user an error message. If the link is to a major company, chances are the URL will be valid for a while. Smaller sites tend to change more often. You might want to consider using a utility package that automatically checks the links within your page to determine if they point to valid locations. These software packages will not determine if the valid location is the specific site you anticipated. There are instances when the site name stays valid, but it is now owned by a different organization. This might create some surprise visits for your audience. Also, the site to which you are linking might offer a mailing list pointing out its new features and updates.

9. Pictures and their effectiveness

A picture is worth a thousand words. This old cliché has been proved right for centuries, but in the context of the World Wide Web, it has some problems holding its ground. There are millions of Web surfers who have relatively slow connections or might be using terminals that don't support graphics. When you put a large picture on your page, these users might not have the patience to wait until the picture is downloaded onto their machine. As a result, your one-thousand-word picture ends up saying nothing at all! Consider such users when you incorporate images into your pages. You might want to create a link to the image, rather than including the image itself on the page. If you do this, make sure you describe exactly what the image is and how large it is. This way, the user can determine whether it is worth his or her time to download the picture.

Imagemaps offer the same dilemma. Always offer a text-only alternative to the imagemap and try to store it in a different page. Make sure you let users know they can use a different address to get to the text-only page. Imagemaps are nice and make your pages look professional, but if the user can't see it or has a slow connection, they become more of a nuisance than a useful tool.

10. Proofread your documents

Always check the content of your page for accuracy, spelling errors, and so on—before you put it on your Web server. Your Web page speaks for you and gives others an impression about you and your organization. It is annoying to see a careless spelling error on the welcome page. Before you put your page on the server, have someone else look at it, preferably with a different browser than yours. Always check your pages. Don't use the *Under Construction* sign as an excuse.

11. Write good HTML code

As you might have discovered, some HTML tags are not required. For example, most browsers won't complain if you don't include the *<html></html>* tags to denote that the document is an HTML document. They assume that it is. Despite this, you should get into the habit of including such tags in your document. HTML and the Web are evolving and, though it is unlikly, these tags could become mandatory. However, if it happens, you will already be ahead of the game and your pages will still look the same. Try to conform to the standards as much as possible; there is probably a good reason that a certain tag is written into the standard. Though the presence of certain tags might not have any visual effect on your document, it could in the future. Also, for your own benefit, make your HTML code readable by including spaces and indentations. It will be easier for you to edit your document later.

12. Always plan ahead

As you create Web pages, keep in mind that your pages might be moved to a different server or a different machine. There are a few things you may consider to make this migration smoother. The most important are filenames and their paths. For example, in DOS or Windows 3.x, filenames are limited to 8 characters and a 3-letter extension. This will create problems if you try to move pages created under a UNIX environment to a PC running Windows 3.x. When you move a directory tree to another location, remember that some of the virtual paths specified in your HTML code or in your external programs may no longer work. Check your links after such a move.

Appendix C: Java Quick Reference

Java has experienced explosive growth since its birth in early 1996. The rising popularity of the Internet and computer networking created an immediate need for a network-based language. Traditional client/server languages just didn't seem to fit the new Internet paradigm. Java came out at just the right time and promised many things. Aside from being a robust programming language, it also addressed issues such as accessing network resources, security, and software development concerns. But Java did not stop there. It went a step further and introduced the concept of *applets*, Java codes executed within the realm of the World Wide Web. Traditionally servers were known to serve data, but with an applet the server is serving out an application. All of this brought about new architectures and ideas. The Internet was expanded into private Intranets which could take advantage of this new architecture.

There are many fine references and tutorials about the Java language both on-line and in print. This appendix in no way attempts to serve as a complete reference to Java. It merely provides an overview of the language, how it is used in the context of the Web, and its connectivity to databases.

What Is Java Like?

One way to describe a new idea is to list its similarities to other well-known ideas. Java is a programming language just like C, C++, and Perl. It is actually more like C++ because it is an object-oriented language. Its syntax is very similar to C and C++. You will learn more about the actual language later in this appendix. An added advantage of Java is its ability to run many different platforms. However, the language really doesn't run on different platforms; rather the Java environment enables multiple platform support. Without getting into the details, here is a summary of how this works.

In a language such as C, when you compile the program it is translated into object code (machine code) by the compiler. It is also linked with some libraries from which an executable code is generated. This executable code can be run only on the machine for which it was compiled. Take an executable program from Windows 95 and try running it under Solaris. It just won't work. For years the computer industry tried to surmount this problem and failed. A software vendor with a good product had to develop the same program under different platforms and stay up-to-date with changes under each platform. This is not an impossible task, and many vendors have done it. For example, Oracle database engines run on many different platforms.

With Java, things change a bit. When you compile a Java program, no machine code is generated. What is generated is a *virtual* machine code commonly referred to as *byte code*. Think of a byte code as something that runs on any machine under a very special circumstance: the machine has the proper environment for it. That special environment is Java. You can take a Java byte code to any platform that supports Java. Type in `java filename` and the program will execute. Figures C-1 and C-2 depict the two different environments discussed above.

So how does the Java environment run on different platforms? Actually it doesn't run on all platforms—Windows 3.x does not support Java, nor does DOS. But many other operating systems do, hence the astronomical growth of Java. Although the process of porting the Java environment to different platforms is tedious, many vendors have recognized its importance and dedicated resources for its accomplishment. Gambling that it wouldn't be long before Java applications were flooding the market, vendors got their platforms ready to run it.

It is only fair to mention that the idea behind a virtual machine and byte codes is not new. Some mainframe computers used (and still use!) similar concepts in their architecture. Java added a new twist by incorporating the idea into an object-oriented language and associating it with the World Wide Web.

Writing in Java

As with any language, before you can write Java code you will need the compiler and a Java interpreter. Java has now been ported to many platforms. A simple search of the Web should point you to the site from which you can download the Developer's Kit. This kit contains everything you need to start coding. You might also consider purchasing an Integrated Development Environment for Java. The kit you obtain includes a number of programs and perhaps some documentation. The three main components are discussed below.

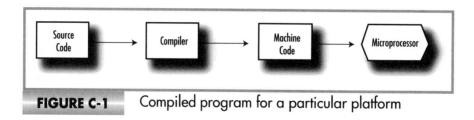

FIGURE C-1 Compiled program for a particular platform

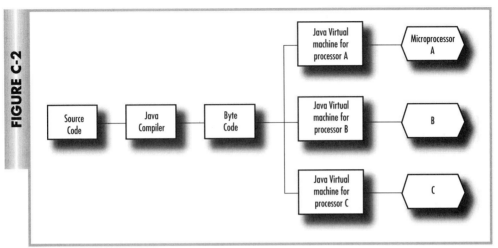

FIGURE C-2

How Java achieves multiple platform support

javac

This is the compiler. Some people object to the use of the term *compiler* because in Java, no object code is generated (remember, in Java the end product is byte code). This program takes in the name of the file containing the Java program and generates a file with the same name but with the .class extension which is the byte code. You will probably need to set the environmental variable CLASSPATH to where Java classes are stored. Consult the documentation that comes with your kit to properly set this variable.

java

Once you have a file with the .class extension, you can give it to anyone and they can execute it on any machine that supports Java. All they have to do is type `java filename`.

You can think of the Java program as the house of Java. A byte code by itself cannot do much, but under the shelter of the Java program, it is executed and performs a task. In other words, only the Java program knows how to make sense and interpret the byte code.

appletviewer

Although the Java program executes stand-alone Java applications, applets are not executed this way. Applets are executed within the realm of the Web. The reference to an applet is actually embedded in an HTML file using the *<applet></applet>* tag pair. To view your applet, make an HTML file and put the proper reference in it. You can then run the `appletviewer` program and pass the name of the HTML file as a parameter to view the applet. Alternatively, you can use a browser that supports Java to view an applet; there are usually problems, however, with reloading a modified applet in a browser. Also, the time to restart a browser is considerably higher than starting the `appletviewer`.

The Java Developer's Kit also contains a debugger and some other utilities.

The Java Language

The Java language is similar to C++. A complete language specification can be found at `http://java.sun.com`.

Table C-1 lists the keywords in Java. You should not use any of them to name your own classes or variables.

Table C-1 Reserved keywords in Java

Keywords				
abstract	do	implements	package	throw
boolean	double	import	private	throws
break	else	inner	protected	transient
byte	extends	instanceof	public	try
case	final	int	rest	var
cast	finally	interface	return	void
catch	float	long	short	volatile
char	for	native	static	while
class	future	new	super	
const	generic	null	switch	
continue	goto	operator	synchronized	
default	if	outer	this	

The way integers, real numbers, characters, and strings are represented in Java is identical to that of C or C++. Java uses the same operators as C and C++ and adds a few more.

Data Types

There are four data types in Java:

- Primitive
- Class
- Interface
- Array

Primitive

The primitive data types are the simple data types which you normally use in all your codes. They are listed in Table C-2.

Table C-2 Java primitive data types

type	size	range
byte	8-bit integer	(-256, 255)
short	16-bit integer	(-32768, 32767)
int	32-bit integer	(-2147483648, 2147483647)
long	64-bit integer	(-9223372036854775808, 9223372036854775807)
float	32-bit floating point number	
double	64-bit floating point number	
char	character type	
boolean	valid values are *true* and *false*	

Class

Classes are the heart of object-oriented languages. A class contains some variables and some methods to manipulate the variables. A class variable can hold a reference to any instance of the class. The keyword new is used to instantiate a class variable.

Interface

Java supports multiple-inheritance with interfaces. An interface dictates how one class interacts with another class. As you get into more advanced programming situations, you will appreciate the need for interfaces and how they help you create classes with multiple parents.

Array

Arrays are collections of variables similar to those used in C or C++. You can have arrays of arrays (multi-dimensional arrays).

Program Structure

Java uses a hierarchical approach to code structure. At the lowest level you have the individual classes along with their variables and methods. At the highest level you have packages, which are collections of classes. The `import` keyword is used to incorporate the content of a package into the current code. There is also a naming convention proposed by Sun Microsystems for the packages.

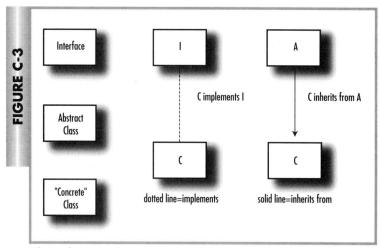

FIGURE C-3

Class diagram conventions

Within methods, the usual loop structures and decision-making constructs (if-then, case statements) are all supported in a syntax very similar to that of the C language.

Java Packages

The Java language includes some fundamental classes and methods that are foundations for more advanced code. To help familiarize you with these packages, class diagrams are included in this appendix. Figure C-3 shows the conventions used in the diagrams. More specialized packages, such as JDBC for database connectivity, are based on the fundamental classes described.

applet

The applet package contains the methods necessary to create an applet, which is run within a Web browser. To view your application, you will need either the appletviewer program or a Web browser. The applet package includes support for images, animation, and audio. Applications to be viewed as applets use the following basic structure:

```
import java.applet.Applet
public class MyApplet extends Applet
{
  public void init()
  {
  // initialization statements
  }
  public void paint (Graphics g)
  {
  // what should be drawn in a paint event
  }
```

```
// any other methods that need to be overridden
}
```

Figure C-4 shows the class diagram for the applet class.

awt

The Abstract Windows Toolkit is your roadway to creating graphical user interfaces for your applications. It contains common elements such as menus, buttons, lists, and radio boxes. It also handles fonts and drawing functions. Java's awt uses the concept of layouts to force a particular arrangement of graphical elements. Normally, you would choose a particular layout, assign the elements to it, and leave the arrangement up to its internal routines. However, you could have stricter control over the elements by using very primitive layouts or overriding some of the methods your own layout uses. The package also contains numerous functions that will return some information (such as color or location) about a particular element.

Figures C-5 and C-6 show the class diagram for the awt package.

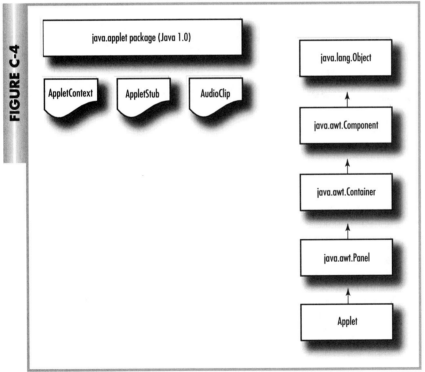

FIGURE C-4

Applet class diagram

FIGURE C-5

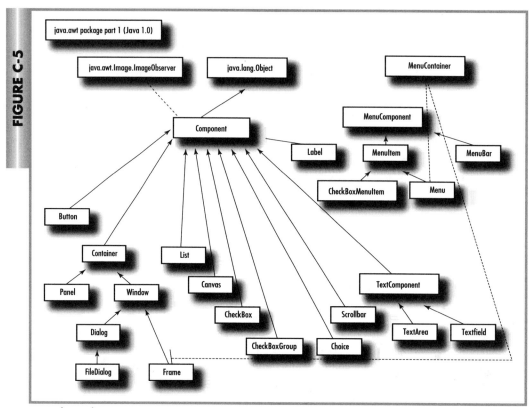

awt class diagram (part 1)

awt.image

Java handles images with the awt.image package. While the package is not very sophisticated, it can greatly enhance your applications. Three main interfaces are included in this package. They are

- **ImageConsumer:** This interface is used by ImageProducer to deliver image data to objects requesting it.

- **ImageProducer:** This interface is used by ImageConsumer to request information about the image from objects creating it.

- **ImageObserver:** This interface provides an asynchronous callback method that may be used to update objects interested in displaying images.

Figure C-7 shows the class diagram for the awt.image package.

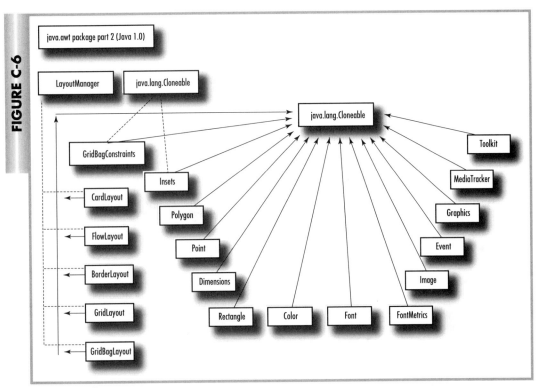

awt class diagram (part 2)

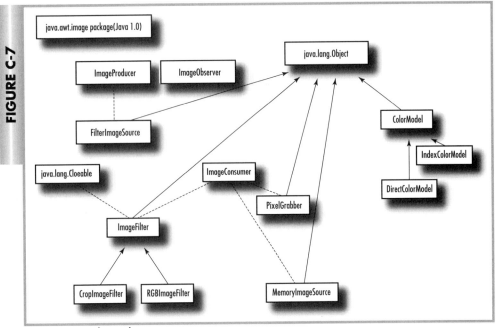

awt.image class diagram

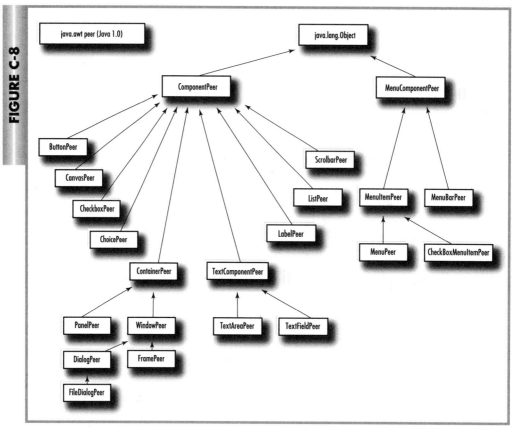

FIGURE C-8

awt.peer class diagram

awt.peer

This package is the internal implementation for the awt package. Normally, you would not directly deal with this package. Figure C-8 shows its class diagram.

io

The io (input/output) package is your doorway to outside resources. You use the methods in this package to print messages to the terminal, a file, or a printer. Similarly, input from standard input is read through this channel. Support is provided for reading and writing from/to text and binary files. Figure C-9 shows the class diagram for this package.

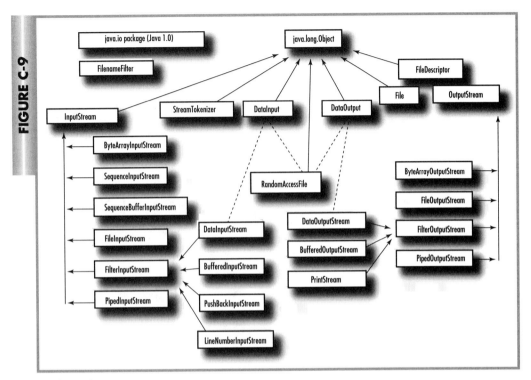

FIGURE C-9

io class diagram

lang

The lang package contains the necessary methods for manipulating the primitive data types of Java, such as character and integers. This package also performs the important task of thread creation and operation. If you write a multi-threaded application, you will definitely need the routines in this package. Java's error capturing, which is also a part of this package, is done through exceptions. Figure C-10 is the class diagram for this important package.

net

Recall that one of the unique features of Java is its ability to access network resources in a native manner. This is possible for the most part through the net package. Networking operations are done using the familiar socket operations. However, with the addition of error-handling capabilities, the operations are somewhat smoother in Java. Also, they fit very nicely with the usual input/output operations. Java applications can access data using their URL (if applicable), making Java a truly *connected* language. Figure C-11 shows a class diagram for this package.

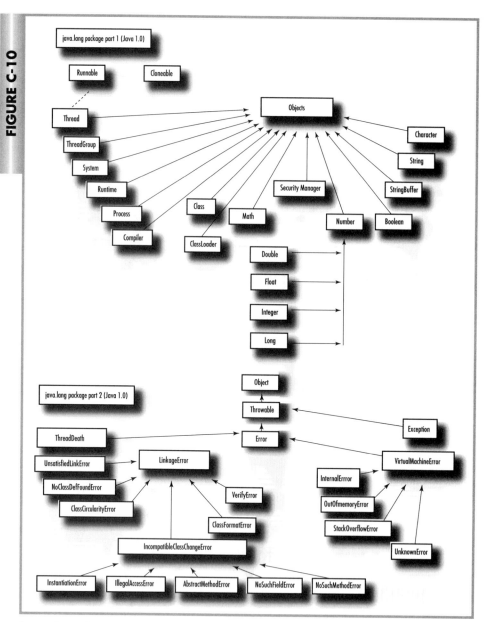

FIGURE C-10

lang class diagram

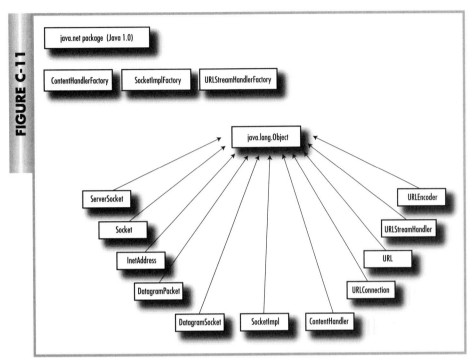

FIGURE C-11

net class diagram

util

The utilities package is the extra treat you get for using Java. It contains very useful routines that are usually provided by third-party libraries in the cases of C and C++. Examples include support for stacks, vectors, random number generators, hash tables, and date functions. Figure C-12 shows the class diagram for the util package.

As Java grows in popularity, many more third-party packages will arrive on the market, each addressing the needs of a particular application. In Chapter 8 of this book we discussed the JDBC package, which provides a uniform mean of data connectivity for Java applications. When you examine the package closely, you will see that it is based entirely on the fundamental packages mentioned above. This is why you should make yourself very comfortable with these packages and how they can be used in an application. The rest of your Java programming experience will grow from them.

FIGURE C-12

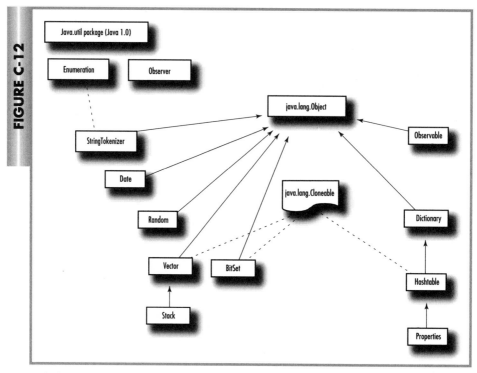

util class diagram

Appendix D: SQL Quick Reference

Structured Query Language (SQL) is the standard language used to search relational databases. This language has been around for a long time and has evolved over the years. SQL was created to standardize the way we look for data in a database. It is not a traditional programming language like C or Pascal. It includes a number of keywords and a consistent syntax to facilitate creation and manipulation of database components such as tables, indexes, fields, and so on.

Many excellent texts have been written on SQL and database principles. Also, there are many tools that create much of the SQL code for you with a graphical user interface. This appendix is a quick reference to some of the more important SQL commands and their syntax. The syntax is based on Sybase's Transact-SQL, but it should also run on other databases. You should always consult the SQL manual that comes with your database for the syntax and any additional features your database might have added to standard SQL.

To Create a Table

One of the most basic elements of a database is the table. Tables can be independent or related to other tables. You can create tables using the following syntax:

```
create table table_name
(column_name datatype {identity | null | not null},
...)
```

The arguments **table_name** and **column_name** must meet the requirements for an identifier in your database. The **datatype** argument is a standard SQL datatype or one offered by your database. Here is an example for creating a table that holds students' names and grades.

```
create table grades
(name     char(50)  not null,
 grade    char(2)   not null)
```

By using the non-null clause, we are requiring the user to enter data for these fields. For example, a student name with no grade does not mean anything in our database definition.

To Create an Index

Indexes speed up the query process. They are most useful when you know how you will be searching a database and creating one based on that information. For example, if you plan on searching a customer database by phone numbers, create an index based on the column that stores phone numbers. Databases have a variety of indexing schemes, and each one is good for a specific class of queries. You will usually decide on the indexing scheme during the database design stage. Here is the basic syntax for creating an index:

```
create index index_name
on table_name(column_name, ...)
```

For example, to create an index based on phone numbers you would use something like the following:

```
create index phone_idx
on customer (phone_num)
```

To Alter the Structure of an Existing Table

Throughout the life of a database, you will need to change the structure of its tables. These changes can range from modifying a column name to changing the relations among columns in different tables. The alter command helps you with such changes. Here is the basic syntax, although most databases have added many more options.

```
alter table table_name
add column_name datatype
```

Suppose you have a customer table and now want to add a column to store e-mail addresses. Here is the command you would issue:

```
alter table customer
add email char(60)
```

To Remove a Data Object (such as a Table or an Index)

To keep your database dynamic, you might need to remove a table or an index when it is no longer in use. Most database objects can be removed using the drop command like this:

```
drop data_object_name
```

To Perform a Query

Most of your SQL commands will be query statements. The way you search a database depends on many factors, including the structure, indexes, and column types. Most databases have an optimizer which translates your query statement to an alternate form for efficiency purposes. The general syntax is shown below:

```
select [all | distinct] field list
[into table name]
[from table name]
[where predicate]
[group by expression]
[order by column(s)]
```

[where predicate]

The where clause is the place the selection criteria is specified. Varied formats are used for the predicate, but they all follow one of these forms:

- Field name operation expression

- Field name operation field name

In the first form, the criteria checks the value of a field and compares it to an expression (for example, emp_id = 235). In the second form, the values of two fields are compared (for example, employee.emp_id = timesheet.emp_id). Depending on the data types of the values being compared, several operations can be performed. They include

- **=** checks for equality

- **!=** checks for inequality

- **>** checks if the left-hand side is greater than the right-hand side (also **>=**)

- **<** checks if the left-hand side is less than the right-hand side (also **<=**)

- **[not] between** checks if the left-hand side is (is not) within a certain range

- **[not] in** checks if the left-hand side is (is not) a member of a specified set

- **[not] like** checks if the left-hand side is (is not) a substring of the right-hand side

- **is [not] null** checks if the left-hand side is (is not) a null value

The _ character stands for any single character, and the % character stands for any combination of characters. For example, `employee.lname like "Jo%"` would match **Jones** and **Johnson**.

Complex predicates can be created using the keywords <AND>, <OR>, and <NOT>. They allow for checking multiple criteria sets using Boolean expressions. For example, to check for time cards in a range of dates, we can use timesheet.ts_date > "1/1/96" and timesheet.ts_date < "1/3/96" as the predicate.

The following retrieves the names of customers who live in Chicago and prints the them in alphabetical order:

```
select name
from customer
where city = "Chicago"
order by name
```

To Insert Data into a Table

As you populate your database, use the **insert** command to add new data. If you use a migration tool, the SQL commands are created for you by the tool. Make sure you have sufficient space before inserting large amounts of data into your database. The basic syntax is shown below:

```
insert [into] table [(column(s))]
values ( expression(s))
```

To add a student and his or her grade to the database, you would use something like the following:

```
insert into students (name, grade)
values ("John Smith", "B")
```

To Delete Data from a Table

The **delete** command is just the opposite of the **insert** command. It removes data from a table based on the criteria you specify. The basic syntax is

```
DELETE from table_name
where search_condition
```

To remove all students who have received a NC (not complete) grade, issue the following:

```
delete from students
where grade = "NC"
```

To Change Data in a Table

You can also modify the data in a table. You specify the column you want to change and the search criteria that limits your change to one or more records. Here is the basic syntax:

```
UPDATE table_name
SET col_name1 = expression,
    col_name2 = expression, ...
where search_condition
```

To change the grades of all students from B to A, issue the following:

```
update students
SET grade = "A"
where grade = "B"
```

To Switch to a Specific Database

Your project might use more than one database. The following is how you specify which database you want to use:

```
use database_name
```

Aggregate Functions

SQL has a number of aggregate functions that are helpful when generating reports or when you want an overall picture of the data. Most databases have added many more functions to the list; you should definitely consult your database manuals for information about using them. Often, these functions can significantly reduce the number of lines of code you have to write. Table D-1 lists some of the more widely used aggregate functions.

Table D-1 SQL's most commonly used aggregate functions

Function	Meaning
sum(expression)	Produces a summation of the expression
avg(expression)	Produces an average of the expression
count(expression)	Produces a simple count of the expression
count(*)	Produces a count of the number of rows
max(expression)	Calculates the maximum value out of the list
min(expression)	Calculates the minimum value out of the list

In all of the functions listed in Table D-1, **expression** is any valid SQL expression. It can be a combination of two or more columns, another SQL function, or just a simple column.

Appendix E: Perl Quick Reference

Perl is a popular interpreted language on UNIX workstations. It has been ported to Windows NT and MacOS. It follows a C-like dialect and has an Open feature that allows it to expand and include specialized libraries. Perl is simple, yet very powerful. These two characteristics have made Perl a popular language for developing CGI applications. The following is a quick reference to the language and its syntax. You will find many similarities between Perl and C. This is not a tutorial on Perl; it is merely a quick reference. For tutorials, introductory material, or a complete reference on Perl consult *Learning Perl*, by Randal L. Schwartz, published by O'Reilly & Associates, Inc.

Command Line Options

Perl is itself a program. It is similar to the UNIX command shells. The following is a summary of the command line options for the Perl program:

- **a** turns on autosplit mode when used with -n or -p. Splits to @F.

- **c** checks syntax of script but does not execute.

- **d** runs the script under control of the debugger. You may use '-de 0' to directly jump into the debugger.

- **D** *<number>* sets debugging flags.

- **e** *<commandline>* enters a single line of script. Multiple -e commands may be given to build up a multiline script.

- **F** *<regexp>* specifies a regular expression to split on if -a is in effect.

- **i** *<ext>* files processed by the <\,> construct are to be edited in place.

- **I** *<dir>* with **-P** tells the C preprocessor where to look for include files. The directory is prepended to @INC.

- **l** [*<octnum>*] enables automatic line ending processing, for example, -l013.

- **n** assumes an input loop around the script. Lines are not printed.

- **p** assumes an input loop around the script. Lines are printed.

- **P** runs the C preprocessor on the script before compilation by Perl.

- **s** interprets "-xxx" on the command line as switches and sets the corresponding variables $xxx in the script.

- **S** uses the PATH environment variable to search for the script.

- **T** forces taint checking.

- **u** dumps the core after compiling the script. To be used with the undump program (where available).

- **U** allows Perl to perform unsafe operations.

- **v** prints the version and patch level of your Perl executable.

- **w** prints warnings about possible spelling errors and other error-prone constructs in the script.

- **x** [*<dir>*] extracts the Perl program from the input stream. If *<dir>* is specified, Perl switches to this directory before running the program.

Data Types

As with any programming language, Perl has a number of data types, which are discussed below.

Scalar Data

Scalar data types are the simplest data that Perl works with. A *scalar* is either a number or a string, as shown below:

- **Numbers:** 123, 123.4, 7E-10, 0xAC (hex), 0564 (octal).

- **Strings:** When enclosed in single quotes, the string is interpreted exactly as it is written. There is no interpretation of variables or escape characters except \' and \\ (for example, 'Hello'). When enclosed in double quotes, the string is interpreted, meaning variable names will be replaced by their variables and escape sequences will be allowed (as in "Hello $fname\n").

Escape Characters

Escape characters allow you to specify special characters. Table E-1 shows a partial list.

Table E-1 Escape characters

Escape character	Meaning
\n	Newline
\t	Tab
\r	Return
\f	Formfeed
\\	Backslash
\b	Backspace
\"	Double quote
\a	Bell
\e	Escape character
\033	An octal ASCII value
\xAB	A hex ASCII value
\l and \u	Lowercase/uppercase the next character that follows
\L and \U	Lowercase/uppercase all characters that follow until an \E is encountered
\E	Terminates \L or \U

Variables

A scalar variable holds a single scalar value. Unlike C, the same scalar variable can hold a number, string, or character. Scalar variable names must begin with a dollar sign. The actual name must meet the following criteria:

- The first character must be a letter
- The name can include letters, numbers, and underscores
- Variable names are case-sensitive

$name, $name2, and $name_2 are all valid scalar variables. $8name or $name^3 is not valid.

Arrays

Aside from the simple scalar types, Perl has the ability to store arrays and list data. The literal representation of an array is a list of comma-separated values enclosed in parentheses. This is how you would explicitly define array elements within a Perl program. Here are a few examples:

- (1,2,3) defines a numerical array with three elements: 1, 2, and 3.

- () defines an empty array.

- ("hello", 55.5) defines an array with two elements: the string "hello" and the number 55.5.

- (1..4) is the same as (1,2,3,4).

Array Variables

Array variables hold a single array value. Note than an array value is made out of zero or more scalar values. The same rules for scalar variables apply to array variables, with one exception: The array variable name must begin with the @ character.

- name = ("John", "Kelli") assigns the specified array to the array variable @name.

- name2 = @name assigns the content of array @name to @name2. In other words it, performs a copy operation.

Access to Individual Elements

It is often necessary to perform an operation on the individual elements of an array or simply retrieve the individual elements. Perl is very much like C in this respect. Consider the following assignment:

```
@score = (90, 87, 80, 92)
The first element of the array @score can be accessed by using the following
construct: $score[0]
```

$score[0] refers to the first element, which is the number 90. $score[1] refers to the second element, which is 87, and so on.

You can assign a different value to the first element of the array like this:

```
$score[0] = 100
```

The following syntax might at first look odd, but it is legal and useful.

```
$var_name = @array_name
```

At first it might seem that assigning an array to a scalar variable should be an illegal operation, but this actually takes the length of the array (number of elements in the array) and assigns it to the variable name. So it is actually a valid and useful operation. Perl is filled with little things like that.

Associative Arrays

An associative array is similar to a normal array because it is a collection of scalar values. The difference, however, is in the way these elements are indexed. Unlike a normal array which uses non-negative integers as its index, an associative array uses arbitrary scalars which are called *keys*. The assignment syntax is

```
$array_name{key} = value
```

For example, the following creates a key called *John* and assigns to it the value *Ford Mustang*.

```
$car {"John"} = "Ford Mustang";
```

You can use associative arrays to create multiple keys and assign a value to each one. You can then retrieve the value for each key. This should sound familiar to you since this is how CGI specification passes the content of a form to a program (as in *name=value* pairs).

Operators

It would be a waste to have data types if you could not do anything to them. Perl has its share of operators that let you manipulate the variables in your program. Table E-2 contains a list of most operators.

Table E-2 Perl's operators

Operator	Meaning
**	Exponentiation
+ - * /	Addition, subtraction, multiplication, division
%	Modulo division
& | ^	Bitwise AND, bitwise OR, bitwise exclusive OR
>> <<	Bitwise shift right, bitwise shift left
|| &&	Logical OR, logical AND
.	Concatenation of two strings

All of the above operators can be combined with the assignment operator. The following two operations are identical:

```
$a = $a + 3
$a += 3
```

Table E-3 is a list of some additional operators:

Table E-3 Additional Perl operators

Operator	Meaning
->	Dereference operator
! ~	Negation (unary), bitwise complement (unary)
++ --	Auto-increment, auto-decrement
== !=	Numeric equality, inequality
eq ne	String equality, inequality
< >	Numeric less than, greater than
lt gt	String less than, greater than
<= >=	Numeric less (greater) than or equal to
le ge	String less (greater) than or equal to
=~ !~	Search pattern, substitution, or translation (negated)
..	Range operator or list constructor
? :	Ternary if-then-else operator
,	Comma operator, also list element separator

Precedence and Associativity

Any language specification includes a section which describes what should happen in ambiguous cases. For example, if we have an expression like 8+6*2, should we perform the addition operation or the multiplication operation first?

Table E-4 lists the associativity and precedence of operators, from lowest to highest. Any given operator has precedence over all operators above it. When two operators appear at the same level, the rules of associativity act as a tie breaker.

Table E-4 Associativity and precedence of operators

Associativity	Operator
none	The "list" operator
left	,
right	+=, -=, *=, /+ (and other assignment operators)
right	?:
none	..

Associativity	Operator
left	||
left	&&
left	| ^
left	&
none	== != <=> eq ne cmp
none	< <= > >= lt le gt ge
none	-r and other file operators
left	<< >>
left	+ - .
left	* / % x (string repetition)
left	=~ !~
right	**
right	! ~ -
none	++ --

Statements

In Perl, every statement is an expression, optionally followed by a modifier and terminated with a semicolon. The semicolon may be omitted if the statement is the final one in a block. The following are valid:

- expr1 if expr2;
- expr1 until expr2;
- expr1 || expr2;
- expr1 ? expr2 : expr3;

Control Structures

Several control structures to regulate the flow of a program are offered by the Perl language. They are very similar to what C offers. A block of statements is enclosed by opening and closing braces ({}). These blocks are used within a control structure, such as a loop, to set aside a set of commands. The following is a description of the control structures:

if-else

To make a decision at runtime and execute an appropriate block of code, the if-else structure is used. The syntax is

```
if (expr) block [ [ elsif (expr) BLOCK ... ] else block ]
```

Here is an example:

```
if ($a == 5) {
        $j = 8;
} elsif ($a == 6) {
        $j = 2;
} else {
        $j = 3;
        $k = 3;
}
```

Note that the keyword is elsif and not elseif as you might expect. The condition specified within the parentheses must evaluate to a true or false value.

Perl also has an unless structure whose syntax is

```
unless (expr) block [ else block ]
```

The keyword unless replaces if and negates the condition specified. The following two statements are equivalent:

```
unless ($a == 5) {
        print "a is not 5";
}
if ($a != 5) {
        print "a is not 5";
}
```

while/until Loop

To perform a loop, you can use a while or an until statement:

- [label:] while (expr) block [continue block]
- [label:] until (expr) block [continue block]

For example:

```
while ($a < 10) {
        $a++;
        print $a . "\n";
}
```

A while loop begins looping when the expression within the parentheses evaluates to true and stops looping when this expression evaluates to false. You can use an until loop, which does exactly the opposite of the while loop. It begins looping when the expression in the parentheses is false and stops looping when that expression evaluates to a true value.

for Loop

A for loop is usually used when you know the beginning and ending condition and want to iterate through the values in between. The syntax is

```
[ label: ] for ( [ expr ] ; [ expr ] ; [ expr ] ) block
```

Here is an example:
```
for ($a = 1; $a < 11; $a++) {
    print "$a \n";
}
```

This example iterates through the values 1 to 10 for the variable $a and prints each one.

foreach Loop

The final looping structure is the foreach loop. This construct is useful when you need to traverse a list of values and assign each of them to a scalar variable one at a time. The syntax is

```
[ label: ] foreach var (array) block
```

Suppose you have an array of exam scores and you want to give 5 bonus points to all students. The following code segment does this.

```
@score = (67, 90, 87, 70, 75)
foreach $single_score (@score) {
    $single_score = $single_score + 5;
}
```

Now the score array contains the values 72, 95, 92, 75, and 80.

Other Control Constructs

Perl has a few other control constructs. Some are used more widely than others. The following is a list of them:

- goto [*label*] continues execution at the specified label.
- last [*label*] immediately exits the loop in question.
- next [*label*] starts the next iteration of the loop.
- redo [*label*] restarts the loop without evaluating the conditional again.

There is a second variety of the while and until loops which delays the evaluation of the conditional expression until after the first iteration is completed. Their syntaxes are

- do block while expr;
- do block until expr;

Subroutines

Perl allows you to define your own functions (also called *subroutines*). There are two parts to this process: You first declare and define your function, and then you call your function.

A function is defined using the keyword sub with the following syntax:

```
sub sub_name {
     block
}
```

Unlike other names in Perl, the name of a subroutine in its definition is not preceded by another character, such as $ or @; it is just a plain name. Function definitions can appear anywhere in the Perl program. Functions can return values just like C functions. The return value is implicitly stated as the value of the last expression evaluated within the body of a function. This value can be a scalar or an array. This concept is clearly illustrated in a later example.

You can also pass arguments to functions. The way it is done might seem a bit strange, but you will get used to it. Basically, each function has a special variable $_ which is local to that function. This variable is an array whose elements are the arguments passed on to the function. Let's go through an example which defines a function that adds its two arguments and returns the sum. Here is the function definition:

```
sub sum_two {
     local($sum);
     $sum = $_[0] + $_[1];
$sum;
}
```

Note the use of the keyword *local* which creates a variable local to the current subroutine. Also, note that the variable $sum is the last statement in the function block, so its value is returned by the function. We invoke the function with something like:

```
print &sum_two(5,6);   #prints 11
```

Note that the name of the function is preceded by an ampersand. The arguments to the function are separated by commas.

A collection of functions can be stored in a package, which gives you a way to organize your collection of functions based on their functionality. SybPerl is one such package.

Built-In Functions

Perl comes equipped with a wealth of built-in functions. The following discusses some of the more common ones. The reader is encouraged to consult a Perl reference book.

Arithmetic Functions

As their name suggests, these are math-related functions. Table E-5 is a listing of some of the more common arithmetic functions.

Table E-5 Perl's arithmetic functions

Function	Meaning
abs (*expression*)	Returns the absolute value of the specified expression.
atan2 (*y, x*)	Returns the arctangent of y/x (in the range -π to π).
cos (*expression*)	Returns the cosine of the specified expression.
exp (*expression*)	Returns e to the power of the specified expression.
int (*expression*)	Returns the integer portion of the specified expression.
log (*expression*)	Returns the natural logarithm of the specified expression.
rand [(*expression*)]	Returns a random fractional number between 0 and the value of the expression. If the expression is not specified, the random number will be a value between 0 and 1.
sin (*expression*)	Returns the sine of the specified expression.
sqrt (*expression*)	Returns the square root of the specified expression.
srand [(*expression*)]	Sets the random number seed for the rand function.
time	Returns the number of seconds since January 1, 1970.

Conversion Functions

There is a series of functions that allow you to change the way a value is presented. For example, the number 10 can be presented as A in hexadecimal notation. The conversion functions are listed in Table E-6.

Table E-6 Conversion functions

Function	Meaning
chr (*expression*)	Returns the character represented by the expression.
hex (*expression*)	Returns the decimal value of a hexadecimal expression.
oct (*expression*)	Returns the decimal value of an octal expression.
gmtime (*expression*)	Converts a time as returned by the time function to a 9-element array (0:$sec, 1:$min, 2:$hour, 3:$mday, 4:$mon, 5:$year, 6:$wday, 7:$yday, 8:$isdst) with the time analyzed for the Greenwich time zone. $mon is between 0 and 11; $wday is between 0 and 6.
ord (*expression*)	Returns the ASCII value of the first character of the expression.

String Functions

One of Perl's strong points is its string-handling capability. Table E-7 is a list of some of the string functions provided by Perl.

Table E-7 Perl's string functions

Function	Name
chop (*list*)	Chops off the last character on all elements of the list.
crypt (*plaintext, key*)	Encrypts a string using the specified key.
eval (*expression*)	The specified expression is executed like a Perl program. The returned value is the value of the last expression evaluated.
index (*str, substr* [, *offset*])	Returns the position of *substr* in *str* at or after *offset*. If the substring is not found, returns -1.
rindex (*str, substr* [, *offset*])	Returns the position of the last *substr* in *str* at or before *offset*.
substr (*expression, offset*[, *len*])	Extracts a substring out of the expression and returns it. If *offset* is negative, counts from the end of the string.
length (*expression*)	Returns the length in characters of the value of the specified expression.
lc (*expression*)	Returns a lowercase version of the expression.
uc (*expression*)	Returns an uppercase version of the expression.

Array and List Functions

These functions deal strictly with arrays and lists. They are listed in Table E-8.

Table E-8 Array and list functions

Function	Meaning
delete $array_name{*key*}	Deletes the specified key from the associative array.
exists (*expression*)	Checks for existence of the specified expression as a key in an associative array.
join (*expression, list*)	Joins the elements of the list into one single string using the expression as the delimiter for the different fields. The string is then returned.
keys (%*array_name*)	Returns an array of all the keys in the named associative array.
pop (@*array*)	Pops off and returns the last value of the specified array.
push (@*array, list*)	Pushes the values of the list onto the end of the specified array.

Function	Meaning
reverse (*list*)	In scalar context, returns the first element of the list with bytes in reverse order. In array context, returns the list in reverse order.
scalar (@*array*)	Returns the number of elements in the array.
scalar (%*array*)	Returns true if the associative array has elements defined.
shift [@*array*]	Removes the first element of the array and returns it. It shortens the array by one element and moves the remaining elements down. If @array is omitted, it shifts @ARGV in main and @_ in subroutines.
sort ([*subroutine,*] *list*)	Sorts the list and returns the sorted array. If a subroutine is specified, it uses it for sorting purposes. The subroutine should return a value less than zero, zero, or greater than zero, depending on how the elements should be sorted.
splice (@*array, offset* [, *length* [, *list*]])	Removes the elements of @array specified by *offset* and *length*, and replaces them with *list* (if specified). The removed elements are returned.
split ([*pattern* [, (*expression*) [, *limit*]]])	Splits a given string into an array of strings and returns it. The maximum number of fields into which the string should be split is set by *limit*. If *pattern* is omitted, splits on whitespace.
unshift (@*array, list*)	Adds the list to the front of the array and returns the number of elements in the newly formed array.
values (%*array*)	Returns an array consisting of all the values of the named associative array.

Regular Expressions

One of the trademarks of Perl is its ability to handle regular expressions. This ability gives Perl an edge over other languages because it allows it to parse and manipulate complex regular expressions.

A *regular expression* is a search pattern. The more ways you can specify the search pattern, the more powerful the regular expression. Here is a summary of how these search patterns are formed.

- Each character matches itself, unless it is one of the special characters +?.*^$()[]. The special meaning of these characters can be escaped using a '\'.

- Matches an arbitrary character.

- (...) groups a series of pattern elements.

- ^ matches the beginning of the line.

- $ matches the end of the line.

- [...] denotes a class of characters to match. [^...] negates the class.

- (...|...|...) matches one of the given alternatives.

- (?# text) Comment.

You can quantify the entire pattern or a subpattern when searching. Table E-9 lists the valid quantifiers.

Table E-9 Valid quantifiers for searching

Quantifier	Meaning
+	Matches the preceding pattern element one or more times.
?	Matches zero or one time.
*	Matches zero or more times.
{n,m}	Matches a minimum of n and a maximum of m times. {n} means exactly n times; {n,} means at least n times.

Aside from removing the special meaning from special characters, the "\" character gives special meaning to most alphanumeric characters.

- \w matches alphanumeric, including "_"; \W matches non-alphanumeric.

- \s matches whitespace; \S matches non-whitespace.

- \d matches numeric; \D matches non-numeric.

- \A matches the beginning of the string; \Z matches the end.

- \b matches word boundaries; \B matches non-boundaries.

Using Regular Expressions

The preceding discussion gives you information you need to form complex regular expressions. The remaining question is how they are used within a Perl program. A common way to use regular expressions is with the =~ operator, which allows you to search an expression based on a regular expression. Here is an example:

```
$a = "Good morning";
$a =~ /^Go/;  # true
```

The above line searches for the string "Go" at the beginning of the expression specified on the left side of the operator (for example, $a). Since this pattern is found, the expression has a true value. Such searches can be found within the conditional part of loops and if-else statements. Table E-10 lists the options available with the =~ operator:

Table E-10 Options available with the =~ operator

Option	Meaning
g	Matches as many times as possible
i	Searches in a case-insensitive manner
o	Interpolates variables only once
m	Treats the string as multiple lines
s	Treats the string as a single line
x	Allows for regular expression extensions

Another way you can use regular expression is as a substitution pattern using the syntax:

```
$variable =~ s/pattern/replacement/
```

This searches $variable for the specified *pattern* and, when found, replaces it with *replacement.* To substitute all occurrences of *pattern,* use the g modifier.

Finally, the tr operator allows a substitution based on characters rather than strings. Here is the syntax:

```
$variable =~ tr/searchlist/replacementlist/ [ c ] [ d ] [ s ]
```

This switches all occurrences of the characters found in the search list with the corresponding character in the replacement list. It returns the number of characters replaced. Optional modifiers are

- **c** complements the *searchlist.*

- **d** deletes all characters found in *searchlist* that do not have a corresponding character in *replacementlist.*

- **s** squeezes all sequences of characters translated into the same target character into one occurrence.

File Test Operators

Perl has a set of operators specifically designed to test some aspect of a file or directory. These operators are in the form of -x, where x is a letter specifying the property to be tested. So for example, you can use a statement like the following to test for the existence of a file:

```
$a = "/etc/hosts";
if (-e $a) {
        print "/etc/hosts exists";
}
```

In this case, the operand for the -e operator is a filename. It could also be a filehandle (discussed in the next section). In the absence of an argument, $_ is used. The operators are listed in Table E-11:

Table E-11 Perl's file test operators

Operator	Meaning
-r -w -x	File is readable/writable/executable by effective uid/gid.
-R -W -X	File is readable/writable/executable by real uid/gid.
-o -O	File is owned by effective/real uid.
-e -z	File exists and has zero size.
-s	File exists and has non-zero size. Returns the size.
-f -d	File is a plain file; file is a directory.
-l -S -p	File is a symbolic link, a socket, a named pipe.
-b -c	File is a block/character special file.
-u -g -k	File has setuid/setgid/sticky bit set.
-t	Tests if filehandle (STDIN by default) is opened to a terminal.
T -B	File is a text/non-text (binary) file.
-M -A -C	File modification/access/inode change time which is measured in days.

File Operations

There are many file/directory operations which are usually done at a shell prompt. Sometimes, it is necessary to perform these tasks from within a program. Perl has a number of functions for this purpose. All of the functions discussed in this section perform an operation on a list of files and return the number of files on which the operation was successfully performed. The functions are listed in Table E-12.

Table E-12 Perl's functions for file operations

Function	Meaning
chmod *array*	Changes the permissions of a list of files. The first element of the list must be the numerical mode to which the permissions must change.
chown *array*	Changes the owner and group of a set of files. The first two elements of the array must be the numerical uid and gid.
truncate *file, size*	Truncates the specified file to size. *file* may be a filename or a filehandle.
link *oldfile, newfile*	Creates a new filename linked to the old filename.
lstat *file*	Like stat, but does not traverse a final symbolic link.
mkdir *dir, mode*	Creates a directory with the given permissions.
readlink (*expression*)	Returns the value of a symbolic link.
rename *oldname, newnam*	Changes the name of a file (like mv).
rmdir *filename*	Deletes an empty directory.
stat *file*	Returns a 13-element array (0:$dev, 1:$ino, 2:$mode, 3:$nlink, 4:$uid, 5:$gid, 6:$rdev, 7:$size, 8:$atime, 9:$mtime, 10:$ctime, 11:$blksize, 12:$blocks). Returns a null list if the stat fails.
symlink *oldfile, newfile*	Creates a symbolic link from the old filename to the new filename.
unlink *array*	Deletes a list of files.
utime *array*	Changes the access and modification times. The first two elements of the array must be the numerical access and modification times.

Input/Output

Any language must talk to the outside world. In Perl, the entire fleet of input/output operations depends on the existence of a filehandle. A filehandle can be the handle returned by the open function, a predefined filehandle such as STDIN or STDOUT, or a scalar variable whose value is a valid filehandle.

Once we have a valid filehandle, the following can be used to read some data from the file into a program variable:

```
variable = <filehandle>
```

If the variable is a scalar one, then a single line is read from the file specified by the file-handle and stored in the variable. If the variable is an array, then the entire file specified by the filehandle is read and assigned to the variable.

<> reads from the input stream formed by the files specified in @ARGV or standard input if no arguments were supplied.

Table E-13 lists the functions provided by Perl to facilitate input/output operations.

Table E-13 Functions to facilitate input/output operations

Function	Meaning
binmode *filehandle*	Arranges for the file specified by filehandle to be read or written in *binary* mode as opposed to text mode.
close *filehandle*	Closes the file associated with the filehandle.
eof *filehandle*	Returns 1 if the next read will return an end of file or if the file has not been opened.
eof	Returns the eof status for the last file read.
fcntl *filehandle, function, $var*	Implements the fcntl function. This function has nonstandard return values. See your UNIX manual for details.
fileno *filehandle*	Returns the file descriptor for a given file.
flock *filehandle, operation*	Calls flock on the file.
getc [*filehandle*]	Yields the next character from the file (similar to getc() in C), or "" on end of file. If filehandle is omitted, reads from STDIN.
ioctl *filehandle, function, $var*	Performs ioctl on the file. This function has nonstandard return values. See your UNIX manual for details.
open *filehandle* [, *filename*]	Opens a file and associates it with *filehandle*. If filename is omitted, the scalar variable of the same name as the filehandle must contain the file-name.

Table E-14 Lists the filename conventions that apply when opening a file.

Convention	Meaning
"file"	Opens a file for input.
">file"	Opens a file for output, creating it if necessary.
">>file"	Opens a file in append mode.
"+>file"	Opens a file with read/write access.

Convention	Meaning
"	command"	Opens a pipe to command.
"cmd	"	Opens a pipe from command.
pipe *readhandle, writehandle*	Returns a pair of connected pipes.
print [*filehandle*] [*array*]	Prints the elements of the specified array to the target specified by the *filehandle*. If filehandle is omitted, the output is directed to the standard output.
read *filehandle, $var, length* [, *offset*]	Reads a specified number of binary bytes from the file into the variable. The number of bytes read is indicated by the *length* parameters. Returns number of bytes actually read.
seek *filehandle, position, whence*	Positions the file to location designated by the second and third parameters. The second parameter is an offset which is interpreted in conjunction with the third parameter. If the third parameter is zero, then the second parameter selects a new absolute position for the next read or write to the file.
select [*filehandle*]	Returns the currently selected filehandle. Sets the current default filehandle for output operations if filehandle is supplied.
sprintf *format, array*	Returns a string formatted by (almost all of) the normal printf conventions.
sysread *filehandle, $var, length* [, *offset*]	Reads *length* bytes into *$var* at *offset*.
syswrite *filehandle, scalar, length* [, *offset*]	Writes *length* bytes from scalar at *offset*.
tell [*filehandle*]	Returns the current file position for the file. If filehandle is omitted, assumes the file which was last read.

Directory Reading Routines

Some of the same types of operations for files need to be performed on directories. For example, your program might need to list all the files in a particular directory and perform an operation on each file listed there.

 A Word of Caution

Directory operations only work if your UNIX flavor supports the *readdir* library function.

Table E-15 is a list of these operations:

Table E-15 Perl filename conventions for directories

Operation	Meaning
closedir *dirhandle*	Closes a directory opened by opendir.
opendir *dirhandle, dirname*	Opens a directory on the handle specified.
readdir *dirhandle*	Returns the next entry (or an array of entries) in the directory.
rewinddir *dirhandle*	Positions the directory at the beginning.
seekdir *dirhandle, pos*	Sets position for readdir on the directory.
telldir *dirhandl*	Returns the postion in the directory.

System Functions

System functions are those that directly interact with the operating system. They let your program manage processes and perform general *system-level* functions. Using some of these functions requires familiarity with the UNIX operating system and process management. Table E-16 lists the system functions.

Table E-16 Perl's system functions

Function	Meaning
alarm *expr*	Schedules a SIGALRM to be delivered after *expr* seconds.
chdir [*expression*]	Changes the working directory to the one specified by *expression*.
chroot *filename*	Changes the root directory for the process and all of its children.
die [*string*]	Prints the specified string to STDERR and exits with the current value of $! (errno).
exec *string*	Executes the system command specified in the string. The process does not return.
exit [*expression*]	Exits immediately with the value of (*expression*). Default is zero.
fork	Does a fork system call. Returns the child pid to the parent process and zero to the child process.
getlogin	Returns the current login name.
getpgrp [*pid*]	Returns the process group for process *pid* (0, or omitted, means the current process).

Function	Meaning
getppid	Returns the process id of the parent process.
getpriority *which, who*	Returns the current priority for a process, process group, or user.
kill *array*	Sends a signal to a list of processes specified in the array. The first element of the array must be the signal to send.
setpgrp *pid, pgrp*	Sets the process group for the pid (0 = current process).
setpriority *which, who, prio*	Sets the current priority for a process, process group, or a user.
sleep [*expression*]	Causes the script to sleep for *expression* seconds, or forever, if no *expression* is specified. Returns the number of seconds actually slept.
syscall *array*	Calls the system call specified in the first element of the array and passes the rest of the array elements as arguments.
system *array*	Same as exec *array*, except that a fork is performed first, and the parent process waits for the child process to complete its task and return.
time	Returns a 4-element array (0:$user, 1:$system, 2:$cuser, 3:$csystem) giving the user and system times, in seconds, for this process and the children of this process.
umask [*expression*]	Sets the umask for the process and returns the old one. If *expression* is omitted, returns current umask value.
wait	Waits for a child process to terminate and returns the pid of the terminated process (-1 if none).
warn [*string*]	Prints the message on STDERR like die, but does not exit.

Networking

If your UNIX flavor supports networking as specified in Berkeley BSD UNIX, then your Perl program can be used as your networking software. Perl offers all the low-level functions needed to perform socket-to-socket or datagram-type network operations; they are listed in Table E-17. To use these functions effectively you need to be familiar with socket programming. There are many sources of information in books, articles, and on-line resources.

Table E-17 Perl functions to perform socket-to-socket or datagram type network operations

Function	Meaning
accept *newsocket, genericsocket*	Accepts a new socket.
bind *socket, name*	Binds the name to the socket.
connect *socket, name*	Connects the name to the socket.
getpeername *socket*	Returns the socket address of the other end of the socket.
getsockname *socket*	Returns the name of the socket.
getsockopt *socket, level, optname*	Returns the socket options.
listen *socket, queue_size*	Starts listening on the specified socket using the queue size.
recv *socket, scalar, length, flags*	Receives a message on the socket.
send *socket, msg, FLAGS* [, *to*]	Sends a message on the socket.
setsockopt *socket, level, optname, optval*	Sets the requested socket option.
shutdown *socket, how*	Shuts down a socket.
socket *socket, domain, type, protocol*	Creates a socket in domain with type and protocol specified.
socketpair *socket1, socket2, domain, type, protocol*	Same as socket, but creates a pair of bidirectional sockets.

Information from System Files

Table E-18 lists the functions that allow your Perl program to retrieve information from a number of UNIX system files, such as /etc/passwd, /etc/group, and others. The return value for all of these functions is an array.

Table E-18 Functions to retrieve information from UNIX system files

Function	Meaning
passwd	Returns ($name, $passwd, $uid, $gid, $quota, $comment, $gcos, $dir, $shell).
endpwent	Ends lookup processing.
getpwent	Gets next user information.

Function	Meaning
getpwnam name	Gets information by name.
getpwuid uid	Gets information by user ID.
setpwent	Resets lookup processing.
group	Returns ($name, $passwd, $gid, $members).
endgrent	Ends lookup processing.
getgrgid gid	Gets group information by group ID.
getgrnam name	Gets group information by name.
getgrent	Gets next group information.
setgrent	Resets lookup processing.
hosts	Returns ($name, $aliases, $addrtype, $length, @addrs).
endhostent	Ends lookup processing.
gethostbyaddr *addr*, *addrtype*	Gets information by IP address.
gethostbyname name	Gets information by host name.
gethostent	Gets next host information.
sethostent *stayopen*	Resets lookup processing.
networks	Returns ($name, $aliases, $addrtype, $net).
endnetent	Ends lookup processing.
getnetbyaddr *addr*, *typ*	Gets network information by address and type.
getnetbyname *name*	Gets network information by network name.
getnetent	Gets next network information.
setnetent *stayopen*	Resets lookup processing.
services	Returns ($name, $aliases, $port, $proto).
endservent	Ends lookup processing.
getservbyname *name*, *proto*	Gets service information by service name.
getservbyport *port*, *prot*	Gets service information by service port.
getservent	Gets next service information.
setservent *stayopen*	Resets lookup processing.

continued on next page

continued from previous page

Function	Meaning
protocols	Returns ($name, $aliases, $proto).
endprotoent	Ends lookup processing.
getprotobyname *name*	Gets protocol information by protocol name.
getprotobynumber *number*	Gets protocol information by protocol number.
getprotoent	Gets next protocol information.
setprotoent *stayopen*	Resets lookup processing.

Special Variables

You have already seen some of the special variables in Perl, such as $_. The following is a list of all such variables set by the Perl interpreter. They are all global variables.

- $_ is the default input and pattern-searching space.

- $. is the current input line number of the last filehandle read. $/ The input record separator. Default is the newline character.

- $, is the output field separator for the print operator.

- $" is the separator which joins elements of arrays interpolated in strings.

- $ is the output record separator for the print operator.

- $? is the status returned by the last command, pipe, or system operator.

- $] is the Perl version number, for example, 5.001.

- $; is the subscript separator for multidimensional array emulation. Default is "034."

- $! If used in a numeric context, yields the current value of errno. If used in a string context, yields the corresponding error string.

- $@ is the Perl error message from the last eval or do *expression* command.

- $: is the set of characters after which a string may be broken to fill continuation fields (starting with "^") in a format.

- $0 is the name of the file containing the Perl script being executed.

- $$ is the process number of the Perl interpreter running the current script.

- $< is the real user ID of this process.

- $> is the effective user ID of this process.

- $(is the real group ID of this process.
- $) is the effective group ID of this process.
- $^A is the accumulator for formline and write operations.
- $^D is the debug flags as passed to Perl using "-D."
- $^F is the highest system file descriptor, ordinarily 2.
- $^L is the formfeed character used in formats.
- $^P is the internal debugging flag.
- $^T is the time (as delivered by time) when the program started.
- $^W is the value of the `-w' option as passed to Perl.
- $^X is the name by which this Perl interpreter was invoked.
- $% is the current page number of the currently selected output channel.
- $= is the page length of the current output channel. Default is 60 lines.
- $- is the number of lines remaining on the page.
- $~ is the name of the current report format.
- $^ is the name of the current top-of-page format.
- $ If set to nonzero, forces a flush after every write or print on the output channel currently selected. Default is 0.
- $ARGV is the name of the current file when reading from <>.

Special Arrays

As with special scalar variables, there are a number of predefined arrays used by Perl. Without further comments, here is the list of these special arrays.

- @ARGV contains the command line arguments for the script (not including the command name).
- @EXPORT names the methods a package exports by default.
- @EXPORT_OK names the methods a package can export upon explicit request.
- @INC contains the list of places to look for Perl scripts to be evaluated by the do filename and require commands.
- @ISA is a list of base classes of a package.
- @_ is a parameter array for subroutines. Also used by split if not in array context.

- %ENV contains the current environment.
- %INC is a list of files that have been included with require or do.
- %OVERLOAD can be used to overload operators in a package.
- %SIG is used to set signal handlers for various signals.

Environment Variables

Perl uses the following environment variables:

- HOME is used if chdir has no argument.
- LOGDIR is used if chdir has no argument and HOME is not set.
- PATH is used in executing subprocesses and in finding the Perl script if -S is used.
- PERL5LIB is a colon-separated list of directories to look in for Perl library files before looking in the standard library and the current directory.
- PERL5DB is the command to get the debugger code.
- PERLLIB is used instead of PERL5LIB if the latter is not defined.

The Perl Debugger

The Perl symbolic debugger is invoked with `perl -d`. Its command-line options are:

- h prints out a help message.
- T prints a stack trace.
- s single steps.
- n single steps around subroutine call.
- RET repeats last s or n.
- r returns from the current subroutine.
- c [line] continues (until line, or another breakpoint, or exit).
- p (expression) prints expr.
- l [range] lists a range of lines. Range may be a number, start—end, start+amount, or a subroutine name. If omitted, lists next window.
- - lists previous window.
- w lists window around current line.

- f file switches to file and starts listing it.

- l sub lists the named subroutine.

- S lists the names of all subroutines.

- /pattern/ searches forward for pattern.

- ?pattern? searches backward for pattern.

- b [line [condition]] sets breakpoint at line, default: current line.

- b subname [condition] sets breakpoint at the subroutine.

- d [line] deletes breakpoint at the given line.

- D deletes all breakpoints.

- L lists lines that have breakpoints or actions.

- a line command sets an action for line.

- A deletes all line actions.

- < command sets an action to be executed before every debugger prompt.

- > command sets an action to be executed before every s, c, or n command.

- V [package [vars]] lists all variables in a package. Default package is main.

- X [vars] like V, but assumes the current package.

- ! [[-]number] re-executes a command. Default is the previous command.

- H [-number] displays the last -number commands of more than one letter.

- t toggles trace mode.

- = [alias value] sets alias, or lists current aliases.

- q quits the debugger.

- command executes command as a Perl statement.

Appendix F:
On-Line Resources

In this appendix, we have tried to list all the on-line references made in this book. A bookmark file is included on the companion CD-ROM. Due to the dynamic nature of the Web, some of these URLs might no longer be valid.

General Internet

The Web Developer's Virtual Library
http://www.stars.com/

Network Wizards. Internet Surveys and Data
http://www.nw.com/

Domain Registration for the American Region and the Rest of the World
http://www.internic.net

Domain Registration for Europe
http://www.ripe.net

Domain Registration for the Asian-Pacific Region
http://www.apnic.net

Imagemaps and HTML Authoring Tools

Mac-ImageMap
http://weyl.zib-berlin.de/imagemap/Mac-ImageMap.html

MapTHIS!
http://galadriel.ecaetc.ohio-state.edu/tc/mt/

mapedit
http://www.boutell.com/mapedit/

Imagemaps Standards
http://www.hway.com/ihip/cside.html

HTML Assistant
http://fox.nstn.ca/~harawitz/index.html

WebForms
http://www.q-d.com/wf.html

Standards and Specifications

HTTP Specifications
http://www.w3.org/hypertext/WWW/Protocols/HTTP/HTTP2.html

DOS CGI
http://www.achilles.net/~john/cgi-dos

MIME Frequently Asked Questions
http://www.cis.ohio-state.edu/hypertext/faq/usenet/mail/mime-faq/top.html

Representation of Non-ASCII Text in Internet Message Headers
http://www.cis.ohio-state.edu:82/rfc/rfc1342.html

SQL Standard
http://www.jcc.com/sql_stnd.html

Web Servers

NCSA HTTP Server
http://hoohoo.ncsa.uiuc.edu/

Netscape Web Server
http://www.netscape.com

Windows HTTP
http://www.city.net/win-httpd/

Website HTTP Server
http://website.ora.com/

Mac HTTP
http://www.starnine.com/machttp/machttpsoft.html

Mac Web Resources

AppleScripts
http://www.scriptweb.com/scriptweb/books/books_new.html

Macintosh WWW Resources
http://www.comvista.com/net/www/WWWDirectory.html

Ian's Mac Web Tools
http://trinculo.educ.sfu.ca/tools.html

ACS Mac Pages
http://www.ualr.edu/doc/mac/mac_home.html

The Well Connected Mac
http://www.macfaq.com/

Databases

Oracle
http://www.oracle.com

Sybase
http://www.sybase.com

MS SQL Server
http://www.microsoft/SQL/default.html

Informix
http://www.informix.com

FoxPro
http://www.microsoft.com/FoxPro/

MS Access
http://www.microsoft.com/MSAccess/

Filemaker Pro
http://www.claris.com/

Paradox
http://www.borland.com

Server Log Tools

Getstats
http://www.eit.com/software/getstats/getstats.html

WWWstat
http://www.ics.uci.edu/WebSoft/wwwstat/

Wusage
http://www.boutell.com/wusage

Webstat
http://arpp1.carleton.ca/machttp/doc/util/stats/webstat.html

WebReporter
http://www.openmarket.com/products/webreport.html

CGI Tools

cgic
http://www.boutell.com/cgic/

LIBCGI
http://wsk.eit.com/wsk/dist/doc/libcgi/libcgi.html

CGIHTML
http://hcs.harvard.edu/~eekim/web/cgihtml/

CGI++
http://sweetbay.will.uiuc.edu/cgi++

Perl FAQ
http://www.cis.ohio-state.edu:80/text/faq/usenet/perl-faq/top.html

Perl 5 Documentation
http://www.metronet.com/0/perlinfo/perl5/manual/perl.html

Perl Newsgroup
news:comp.lang.perl

Perl Sources and Binaries
http://www.metronet.com/1/perlinfo/source

MacPerl
ftp://sra.co.jp/pub/lang/perl/MacPerl/

Perl 386 for DOS
ftp://ftp.ee.umanitoba.ca/pub/msdos/perl/

cgi-lib
http://www.bio.cam.ac.uk/web/form.html

TCL and CGI Programming
http://hplyot.obspm.fr/~dl/wwwtools.html

The TCL/TK Project at Sun Microsystems Laboratories
http://www.sunlabs.com:80/research/tcl/

The Santa Cruz Operation
http://www.sco.com/Technology/tcl/Tcl.html

An Index of TCL Resources, by Wade Holst
http://web.cs.ualberta.ca/~wade/Auto/Tcl.html

A Brief Introduction to TCL and TK
http://http2.brunel.ac.uk:8080/~csstddm/TCL2/TCL2.html

Teacher Hypertools for TCL and TK, by David Svoboda
http://www.ece.cmu.edu/afs/ece/usr/svoboda/www/th/homepage.html

Un-CGI
http://www.hyperion.com/~koreth/uncgi.html

Visual Basic in CGI
http://website.ora.com/devcorner/db-src/index.html

PowerSoft's FTP Site
http://www.powersoft.com/custserv/pwrs_ftp.html

PowerCerv's Sampler Site
http://www.powercerv.com/index.html

Ventana's Own Software Archive
http://www.vmedia.com/alternate/vvc/onlcomp/powerbuilder/software.html

Java and JavaScripts

A Directory and Registry of Java Resources
http://www.gamelan.com

Java: Programming for the Internet
http://www.javasoft.com/

Java Newsgroup
comp.lang.java

The Java Package Tutorial
http://v2ma09.gsfc.nasa.gov:2000/JavaPackages.html

JavaScript
http://home.netscape.com/comprod/products/navigator/version_2.0/script/script_info/lsintro.html

White Paper: Verifying Form Input with JavaScript
http://gmccomb.com/javascript/valid.html

JavaScript
http://www.gamelan.com/Gamelan.javascript.html

JavaScript Resources: A Netscape 2.0 Enhanced Cheat Sheet
http://www.intercom.net/user/mecha/java.html

VBScript
http://www.microsoft.com/INTDEV/vbs/vbscript.html

Security

SSL
http://www.netscape.com/newsref/std/SSL.html

Web Security
http://www.nortel.com/entrust/certificates/primer.html

HTTP Security Group of W3C
http://www.w3.org/hypertext/WWW/Security/Overview.html

CGI Security
http://www.primus.com/staff/paulp/cgi-security

Appendix G: GNU GPL and LGPL

GNU General Public License Version 2, June 1991

Preamble

The licenses for most software are designed to take away your freedom to share and change it. By contrast, the GNU General Public License is intended to guarantee your freedom to share and change free software—to make sure the software is free for all its users. This General Public License applies to most of the Free Software Foundation's software and to any other program whose authors commit to using it. (Some other Free Software Foundation software is covered by the GNU Library General Public License instead.) You can apply it to your programs, too.

When we speak of free software, we are referring to freedom, not price. Our General Public Licenses are designed to make sure that you have the freedom to distribute copies of free software (and charge for this service if you wish), that you receive source code or can get it if you want it, that you can change the software or use pieces of it in new free programs; and that you know you can do these things.

To protect your rights, we need to make restrictions that forbid anyone to deny you these rights or to ask you to surrender the rights. These restrictions translate to certain responsibilities for you if you distribute copies of the software, or if you modify it.

For example, if you distribute copies of such a program, whether gratis or for a fee, you must give the recipients all the rights that you have. You must make sure that they, too, receive or can get the source code. And you must show them these terms so they know their rights.

We protect your rights with two steps: (1) copyright the software, and (2) offer you this license which gives you legal permission to copy, distribute and/or modify the software.

Also, for each author's protection and ours, we want to make certain that everyone understands that there is no warranty for this free software. If the software is modified by someone else and passed on, we want its recipients to know that what they have is not the original, so that any problems introduced by others will not reflect on the original authors' reputations.

Finally, any free program is threatened constantly by software patents. We wish to avoid the danger that redistributors of a free program will individually obtain patent licenses, in effect making the program proprietary. To prevent this, we have made it clear that any patent must be licensed for everyone's free use or not licensed at all.

The precise terms and conditions for copying, distribution and modification follow.

Terms and Conditions for Copying, Distribution and Modification

0. This License applies to any program or other work which contains a notice placed by the copyright holder saying it may be distributed under the terms of this General Public License. The "Program", below, refers to any such program or work, and a "work based on the Program" means either the Program or any derivative work under copyright law: that is to say, a work containing the Program or a portion of it, either verbatim or with modifications and/or translated into another language. (Hereinafter, translation is included without limitation in the term "modification".) Each licensee is addressed as "you". Activities other than copying, distribution and modification are not covered by this License; they are outside its scope. The act of running the Program is not restricted, and the output from the Program is covered only if its contents constitute a work based on the Program (independent of having been made by running the Program). Whether that is true depends on what the Program does.

1. You may copy and distribute verbatim copies of the Program's source code as you receive it, in any medium, provided that you conspicuously and appropriately publish on each copy an appropriate copyright notice and disclaimer of warranty; keep intact all the notices that refer to this License and to the absence of any warranty; and give any other recipients of the Program a copy of this License along with the Program. You may charge a fee for the physical act of transferring a copy, and you may at your option offer warranty protection in exchange for a fee.

2. You may modify your copy or copies of the Program or any portion of it, thus forming a work based on the Program, and copy and distribute such modifications or work under the terms of Section 1 above, provided that you also meet all of these conditions:

   a. You must cause the modified files to carry prominent notices stating that you changed the files and the date of any change.

   b. You must cause any work that you distribute or publish, that in whole or in part contains or is derived from the Program or any part thereof, to be licensed as a whole at no charge to all third parties under the terms of this License.

   c. If the modified program normally reads commands interactively when run, you must cause it, when started running for such interactive use in the most ordinary way, to print or display an announcement including an appropriate copyright notice and a notice that there is no warranty (or else, saying that you provide a warranty) and that users may redistribute the program under these conditions, and telling the user how to view a copy of this License. (Exception: if the Program itself is interactive but does not normally print such an announcement, your work based on the Program is not required to print an announcement.)

These requirements apply to the modified work as a whole. If identifiable sections of that work are not derived from the Program, and can be reasonably considered independent and separate works in themselves, then this License, and its terms, do not apply to those sections when you distribute them as separate works. But when you distribute the same sections as part of a whole which is a work based on the Program, the distribution of the whole must be on the terms of this License, whose permissions for other licensees extend to the entire whole, and thus to each and every part regardless of who wrote it. Thus, it is not the intent of this section to claim rights or contest your rights to work written entirely by you; rather, the intent is to exercise the right to control the distribution of derivative or collective works based on the Program. In addition, mere aggregation of another work not based on the Program with the Program (or with a work based on the Program) on a volume of a storage or distribution medium does not bring the other work under the scope of this License.

3. You may copy and distribute the Program (or a work based on it, under Section 2) in object code or executable form under the terms of Sections 1 and 2 above provided that you also do one of the following:

   a. Accompany it with the complete corresponding machine-readable source code, which must be distributed under the terms of Sections 1 and 2 above on a medium customarily used for software interchange; or,

   b. Accompany it with a written offer, valid for at least three years, to give any third party, for a charge no more than your cost of physically performing source distribution, a complete machine-readable copy of the corresponding source code, to be distributed under the terms of Sections 1 and 2 above on a medium customarily used for software interchange; or,

   c. Accompany it with the information you received as to the offer to distribute corresponding source code. (This alternative is allowed only for noncommercial distribution and only if you received the program in object code or executable form with such an offer, in accord with Subsection b above.)

The source code for a work means the preferred form of the work for making modifications to it. For an executable work, complete source code means all the source code for all modules it contains, plus any associated interface definition files, plus the scripts used to control compilation and installation of the executable. However, as a special exception, the source code distributed need not include anything that is normally distributed (in either source or binary form) with the major components (compiler, kernel, and so on) of the operating system on which the executable runs, unless that component itself accompanies the executable.

If distribution of executable or object code is made by offering access to copy from a designated place, then offering equivalent access to copy the source code from the same place counts as distribution of the source code, even though third parties are not compelled to copy the source along with the object code.

4. You may not copy, modify, sublicense, or distribute the Program except as express-ly provided under this License. Any attempt otherwise to copy, modify, sublicense or distribute the Program is void, and will automatically terminate your rights under this License. However, parties who have received copies, or rights, from you under this License will not have their licenses terminated so long as such parties remain in full compliance.

5. You are not required to accept this License, since you have not signed it. However, nothing else grants you permission to modify or distribute the Program or its deriva-tive works. These actions are prohibited by law if you do not accept this License. Therefore, by modifying or distributing the Program (or any work based on the Program), you indicate your acceptance of this License to do so, and all its terms and conditions for copying, distributing or modifying the Program or works based on it.

6. Each time you redistribute the Program (or any work based on the Program), the recipient automatically receives a license from the original licensor to copy, distrib-ute or modify the Program subject to these terms and conditions. You may not impose any further restrictions on the recipients' exercise of the rights granted here-in. You are not responsible for enforcing compliance by third parties to this License.

7. If, as a consequence of a court judgment or allegation of patent infringement or for any other reason (not limited to patent issues), conditions are imposed on you (whether by court order, agreement or otherwise) that contradict the conditions of this License, they do not excuse you from the conditions of this License. If you can-not distribute so as to satisfy simultaneously your obligations under this License and any other pertinent obligations, then as a consequence you may not distribute the Program at all. For example, if a patent license would not permit royalty-free redis-tribution of the Program by all those who receive copies directly or indirectly through you, then the only way you could satisfy both it and this License would be to refrain entirely from distribution of the Program.

If any portion of this section is held invalid or unenforceable under any particular circumstance, the balance of the section is intended to apply and the section as a whole is intended to apply in other circumstances.

It is not the purpose of this section to induce you to infringe any patents or other property right claims or to contest validity of any such claims; this section has the sole purpose of protecting the integrity of the free software distribution system, which is implemented by public license practices. Many people have made generous contributions to the wide range of software distributed through that system in reliance on consistent application of that system; it is up to the author/donor to decide if he or she is willing to distribute software through any other system and a licensee cannot impose that choice. This section is intended to make thoroughly clear what is believed to be a consequence of the rest of this License.

8. If the distribution and/or use of the Program is restricted in certain countries either by patents or by copyrighted interfaces, the original copyright holder who places the Program under this License may add an explicit geographical distribution limitation excluding those countries, so that distribution is permitted only in or among countries not thus excluded. In such case, this License incorporates the limitation as if written in the body of this License.

9. The Free Software Foundation may publish revised and/or new versions of the General Public License from time to time. Such new versions will be similar in spirit to the present version, but may differ in detail to address new problems or concerns. Each version is given a distinguishing version number. If the Program specifies a version number of this License which applies to it and "any later version," you have the option of following the terms and conditions either of that version or of any later version published by the Free Software Foundation. If the Program does not specify a version number of this License, you may choose any version ever published by the Free Software Foundation.

10. If you wish to incorporate parts of the Program into other free programs whose distribution conditions are different, write to the author to ask for permission. For software which is copyrighted by the Free Software Foundation, write to the Free Software Foundation; we sometimes make exceptions for this. Our decision will be guided by the two goals of preserving the free status of all derivatives of our free software and of promoting the sharing and reuse of software generally.

No Warranty

11. BECAUSE THE PROGRAM IS LICENSED FREE OF CHARGE, THERE IS NO WARRANTY FOR THE PROGRAM, TO THE EXTENT PERMITTED BY APPLICABLE LAW. EXCEPT WHEN OTHERWISE STATED IN WRITING THE COPYRIGHT HOLDERS AND/OR OTHER PARTIES PROVIDE THE PROGRAM "AS IS" WITHOUT WARRANTY OF ANY KIND, EITHER EXPRESSED OR IMPLIED, INCLUDING, BUT NOT LIMITED TO, THE IMPLIED WARRANTIES OF MERCHANTABILITY AND FITNESS FOR A PARTICULAR PURPOSE. THE ENTIRE RISK AS TO THE QUALITY AND PERFORMANCE OF THE PROGRAM IS WITH YOU. SHOULD THE PROGRAM PROVE DEFECTIVE, YOU ASSUME THE COST OF ALL NECESSARY SERVICING, REPAIR, OR CORRECTION.

12. IN NO EVENT UNLESS REQUIRED BY APPLICABLE LAW OR AGREED TO IN WRITING WILL ANY COPYRIGHT HOLDER, OR ANY OTHER PARTY WHO MAY

MODIFY AND/OR REDISTRIBUTE THE PROGRAM AS PERMITTED ABOVE, BE LIABLE TO YOU FOR DAMAGES, INCLUDING ANY GENERAL, SPECIAL, INCIDENTAL OR CONSEQUENTIAL DAMAGES ARISING OUT OF THE USE OR INABILITY TO USE THE PROGRAM (INCLUDING BUT NOT LIMITED TO LOSS OF DATA OR DATA BEING RENDERED INACCURATE OR LOSSES SUSTAINED BY YOU OR THIRD PARTIES OR A FAILURE OF THE PROGRAM TO OPERATE WITH ANY OTHER PROGRAMS), EVEN IF SUCH HOLDER OR OTHER PARTY HAS BEEN ADVISED OF THE POSSIBILITY OF SUCH DAMAGES.

END OF TERMS AND CONDITIONS

Appendix: How to Apply These Terms to Your New Programs

If you develop a new program, and you want it to be of the greatest possible use to the public, the best way to achieve this is to make it free software that everyone can redistribute and change under these terms.

To do so, attach the following notices to the program. It is safest to attach them to the start of each source file to most effectively convey the exclusion of warranty, and each file should have at least the "copyright" line and a pointer to where the full notice is found.

```
one line to give the program's name and an idea of what it does.
Copyright (C) 19yy  name of author

This program is free software; you can redistribute it and/or modify it under
the terms of the GNU General Public License as published by the Free Software
Foundation; either version 2 of the License, or (at your option) any later
version.

This program is distributed in the hope that it will be useful, but WITHOUT
ANY WARRANTY; without even the implied warranty of MERCHANTABILITY or FITNESS
FOR A PARTICULAR PURPOSE. See the GNU General Public License for more details.

You should have received a copy of the GNU General Public License along with
this program; if not, write to the Free Software Foundation, Inc., 675 Mass
Ave, Cambridge, MA 02139, USA.
```

Also, add information on how to contact you by electronic and paper mail.

If the program is interactive, make it output a short notice like this when it starts in an interactive mode:

```
Gnomovision version 69, Copyright (C) 19yy name of author
Gnomovision comes with ABSOLUTELY NO WARRANTY; for details type 'show w'.
This is free software, and you are welcome to redistribute it under certain
conditions; type 'show c' for details.
```

The hypothetical commands 'show w' and 'show c' should show the appropriate parts of the General Public License. Of course, the commands you use may be called something other than 'show w' and 'show c'; they could even be mouse-clicks or menu items—whatever suits your program.

You should also get your employer (if you work as a programmer) or your school, if any, to sign a "copyright disclaimer" for the program, if necessary. Here is a sample; alter the names:

```
Yoyodyne, Inc., hereby disclaims all copyright interest in the program
'Gnomovision' (which makes passes at compilers) written by James Hacker.

signature of Ty Coon, 1 April 1989
Ty Coon, President of Vice
```

This General Public License does not permit incorporating your program into proprietary programs. If your program is a subroutine library, you may consider it more useful to permit linking proprietary applications with the library. If this is what you want to do, use the GNU Library General Public License instead of this License.

GNU Library General Public License Version 2, June 1991

```
Copyright (C) 1991 Free Software Foundation, Inc.
675 Mass Ave, Cambridge, MA 02139, USA

Everyone is permitted to copy and distribute verbatim copies of this license
document, but changing it is not allowed.

[This is the first released version of the library GPL.  It is numbered 2
because it goes with version 2 of the ordinary GPL.]
```

Preamble

The licenses for most software are designed to take away your freedom to share and change it. By contrast, the GNU General Public Licenses are intended to guarantee your freedom to share and change free software—to make sure the software is free for all its users.

This license, the Library General Public License, applies to some specially designated Free Software Foundation software, and to any other libraries whose authors decide to use it. You can use it for your libraries, too.

When we speak of free software, we are referring to freedom, not price. Our General Public Licenses are designed to make sure that you have the freedom to distribute copies of free software (and charge for this service if you wish), that you receive source code or can get it if you want it, that you can change the software or use pieces of it in new free programs; and that you know you can do these things.

To protect your rights, we need to make restrictions that forbid anyone to deny you these rights or to ask you to surrender the rights. These restrictions translate to certain responsibilities for you if you distribute copies of the library, or if you modify it.

For example, if you distribute copies of the library, whether gratis or for a fee, you must give the recipients all the rights that we gave you. You must make sure that they, too, receive or can get the source code. If you link a program with the library, you must provide complete object files to the recipients so that they can relink them with the library, after making changes to the library and recompiling it. And you must show them these terms so they know their rights.

Our method of protecting your rights has two steps: (1) copyright the library, and (2) offer you this license which gives you legal permission to copy, distribute and/or modify the library.

Also, for each distributor's protection, we want to make certain that everyone understands that there is no warranty for this free library. If the library is modified by someone else and passed on, we want its recipients to know that what they have is not the original version, so that any problems introduced by others will not reflect on the original authors' reputations.

Finally, any free program is threatened constantly by software patents. We wish to avoid the danger that companies distributing free software will individually obtain patent licenses, thus in effect transforming the program into proprietary software. To prevent this, we have made it clear that any patent must be licensed for everyone's free use or not licensed at all.

Most GNU software, including some libraries, is covered by the ordinary GNU General Public License, which was designed for utility programs. This license, the GNU Library General Public License, applies to certain designated libraries. This license is quite different from the ordinary one; be sure to read it in full, and don't assume that anything in it is the same as in the ordinary license.

The reason we have a separate public license for some libraries is that they blur the distinction we usually make between modifying or adding to a program and simply using it. Linking a program with a library, without changing the library, is in some sense simply using the library, and is analogous to running a utility program or application program. However, in a textual and legal sense, the linked executable is a combined work, a derivative of the original library, and the ordinary General Public License treats it as such.

Because of this blurred distinction, using the ordinary General Public License for libraries did not effectively promote software sharing, because most developers did not use the libraries. We concluded that weaker conditions might promote sharing better.

However, unrestricted linking of non-free programs would deprive the users of those programs of all benefit from the free status of the libraries themselves. This Library General Public License is intended to permit developers of non-free programs to use free libraries, while preserving your freedom as a user of such programs to change the free libraries that are incorporated in them. (We have not seen how to achieve this as regards changes in header files, but we have achieved it as regards changes in the actual functions of the Library.) The hope is that this will lead to faster development of free libraries.

The precise terms and conditions for copying, distribution, and modification follow. Pay close attention to the difference between a "work based on the library" and a "work that uses the library". The former contains code derived from the library, while the latter only works together with the library.

Note that it is possible for a library to be covered by the ordinary General Public License rather than by this special one.

Terms and Conditions for Copying, Distribution and Modification

1. This License Agreement applies to any software library which contains a notice placed by the copyright holder or other authorized party saying it may be distributed under the terms of this Library General Public License (also called "this License"). Each licensee is addressed as "you". A "library" means a collection of software functions and/or data prepared so as to be conveniently linked with application programs (which use some of those functions and data) to form executables. The "Library", below, refers to any such software library or work which has been distributed under these terms. A "work based on the Library" means either the Library or any derivative work under copyright law: that is to say, a work containing the Library or a portion of it, either verbatim or with modifications and/or translated straightforwardly into another language. (Hereinafter, translation is included without limitation in the term "modification".) "Source code" for a work means the preferred form of the work for making modifications to it. For a library, complete source code means all the source code for all modules it contains, plus any associated interface definition files, plus the scripts used to control compilation and installation of the library. Activities other than copying, distribution, and modification are not covered by this License; they are outside its scope. The act of running a program using the Library is not restricted, and output from such a program is covered only if its contents constitute a work based on the Library (independent of the use of the Library in a tool for writing it). Whether that is true depends on what the Library does and what the program that uses the Library does.

2. You may copy and distribute verbatim copies of the Library's complete source code as you receive it, in any medium, provided that you conspicuously and appropriately publish on each copy an appropriate copyright notice and disclaimer of warranty; keep intact all the notices that refer to this License and to the absence of any warranty; and distribute a copy of this License along with the Library. You may charge a fee for the physical act of transferring a copy, and you may at your option offer warranty protection in exchange for a fee.

3. You may modify your copy or copies of the Library or any portion of it, thus forming a work based on the Library, and copy and distribute such modifications or work under the terms of Section 1 above, provided that you also meet all of these conditions:

    1. The modified work must itself be a software library.

    2. You must cause the files modified to carry prominent notices stating that you changed the files and the date of any change.

3. You must cause the whole of the work to be licensed at no charge to all third parties under the terms of this License.

4. If a facility in the modified Library refers to a function or a table of data to be supplied by an application program that uses the facility, other than as an argument passed when the facility is invoked, then you must make a good faith effort to ensure that, in the event an application does not supply such function or table, the facility still operates, and performs whatever part of its purpose remains meaningful. (For example, a function in a library to compute square roots has a purpose that is entirely well-defined independent of the application. Therefore, Subsection 2d requires that any application-supplied function or table used by this function must be optional: if the application does not supply it, the square root function must still compute square roots.)

These requirements apply to the modified work as a whole. If identifiable sections of that work are not derived from the Library, and can be reasonably considered independent and separate works in themselves, then this License, and its terms, do not apply to those sections when you distribute them as separate works. But when you distribute the same sections as part of a whole which is a work based on the Library, the distribution of the whole must be on the terms of this License, whose permissions for other licensees extend to the entire whole, and thus to each and every part regardless of who wrote it. Thus, it is not the intent of this section to claim rights or contest your rights to work written entirely by you; rather, the intent is to exercise the right to control the distribution of derivative or collective works based on the Library. In addition, mere aggregation of another work not based on the Library with the Library (or with a work based on the Library) on a volume of a storage or distribution medium does not bring the other work under the scope of this License.

4. You may opt to apply the terms of the ordinary GNU General Public License instead of this License to a given copy of the Library. To do this, you must alter all the notices that refer to this License, so that they refer to the ordinary GNU General Public License, version 2, instead of to this License. (If a newer version than version 2 of the ordinary GNU General Public License has appeared, then you can specify that version instead if you wish.) Do not make any other change in these notices. Once this change is made in a given copy, it is irreversible for that copy, so the ordinary GNU General Public License applies to all subsequent copies and derivative works made from that copy. This option is useful when you wish to copy part of the code of the Library into a program that is not a library.

5. You may copy and distribute the Library (or a portion or derivative of it, under Section 2) in object code or executable form under the terms of Sections 1 and 2 above provided that you accompany it with the complete corresponding machine-readable source code, which must be distributed under the terms of Sections 1 and 2 above on a medium customarily used for software interchange. If distribution of object code is made by offering access to copy from a designated place, then

offering equivalent access to copy the source code from the same place satisfies the requirement to distribute the source code, even though third parties are not compelled to copy the source along with the object code.

6. A program that contains no derivative of any portion of the Library, but is designed to work with the Library by being compiled or linked with it, is called a "work that uses the Library". Such a work, in isolation, is not a derivative work of the Library, and therefore falls outside the scope of this License. However, linking a "work that uses the Library" with the Library creates an executable that is a derivative of the Library (because it contains portions of the Library), rather than a "work that uses the library". The executable is therefore covered by this License. Section 6 states terms for distribution of such executables. When a "work that uses the Library" uses material from a header file that is part of the Library, the object code for the work may be a derivative work of the Library even though the source code is not. Whether this is true is especially significant if the work can be linked without the Library, or if the work is itself a library. The threshold for this to be true is not precisely defined by law. If such an object file uses only numerical parameters, data structure layouts and accessors, and small macros and small inline functions (ten lines or less in length), then the use of the object file is unrestricted, regardless of whether it is legally a derivative work. (Executables containing this object code plus portions of the Library will still fall under Section 6.) Otherwise, if the work is a derivative of the Library, you may distribute the object code for the work under the terms of Section 6. Any executables containing that work also fall under Section 6, whether or not they are linked directly with the Library itself.

7. As an exception to the Sections above, you may also compile or link a "work that uses the Library" with the Library to produce a work containing portions of the Library, and distribute that work under terms of your choice, provided that the terms permit modification of the work for the customer's own use and reverse engineering for debugging such modifications. You must give prominent notice with each copy of the work that the Library is used in it and that the Library and its use are covered by this License. You must supply a copy of this License. If the work during execution displays copyright notices, you must include the copyright notice for the Library among them, as well as a reference directing the user to the copy of this License. Also, you must do one of these things:

   1. Accompany the work with the complete corresponding machine- readable source code for the Library including whatever changes were used in the work (which must be distributed under Sections 1 and 2 above); and, if the work is an executable linked with the Library, with the complete machine-readable "work that uses the Library", as object code and/or source code, so that the user can modify the Library and then relink to produce a modified executable containing the modified Library. (It is understood that the user who changes the contents of definitions files in the Library will not necessarily be able to recompile the application to use the modified definitions.)

2. Accompany the work with a written offer, valid for at least three years, to give the same user the materials specified in Subsection 6a, above, for a charge no more than the cost of performing this distribution.

3. If distribution of the work is made by offering access to copy from a designated place, offer equivalent access to copy the above specified materials from the same place.

4. Verify that the user has already received a copy of these materials or that you have already sent this user a copy.

For an executable, the required form of the "work that uses the Library" must include any data and utility programs needed for reproducing the executable from it. However, as a special exception, the source code distributed need not include anything that is normally distributed (in either source or binary form) with the major components (compiler, kernel, and so on) of the operating system on which the executable runs, unless that component itself accompanies the executable. It may happen that this requirement contradicts the license restrictions of other proprietary libraries that do not normally accompany the operating system. Such a contradiction means you cannot use both them and the Library together in an executable that you distribute.

8. You may place library facilities that are a work based on the Library side-by-side in a single library together with other library facilities not covered by this License, and distribute such a combined library, provided that the separate distribution of the work based on the Library and of the other library facilities is otherwise permitted, and provided that you do these two things:

1. Accompany the combined library with a copy of the same work based on the Library, uncombined with any other library facilities. This must be distributed under the terms of the Sections above.

2. Give prominent notice with the combined library of the fact that part of it is a work based on the Library, and explaining where to find the accompanying uncombined form of the same work.

9. You may not copy, modify, sublicense, link with, or distribute the Library except as expressly provided under this License. Any attempt otherwise to copy, modify, sublicense, link with, or distribute the Library is void, and will automatically terminate your rights under this License. However, parties who have received copies, or rights, from you under this License will not have their licenses terminated as long as such parties remain in full compliance.

10. You are not required to accept this License, since you have not signed it. However, nothing else grants you permission to modify or distribute the Library or its derivative works. These actions are prohibited by law if you do not accept this License. Therefore, by modifying or distributing the Library (or any work based on the Library), you indicate your acceptance of this License to do so, and all its terms and conditions for copying, distributing, or modifying the Library or works based on it.

11. Each time you redistribute the Library (or any work based on the Library), the recipient automatically receives a license from the original licensor to copy, distribute, link with or modify the Library subject to these terms and conditions. You may not impose any further restrictions on the recipients' exercise of the rights granted herein. You are not responsible for enforcing compliance by third parties to this License.

12. If, as a consequence of a court judgment or allegation of patent infringement or for any other reason (not limited to patent issues), conditions are imposed on you (whether by court order, agreement or otherwise) that contradict the conditions of this License, they do not excuse you from the conditions of this License. If you cannot distribute so as to satisfy simultaneously your obligations under this License and any other pertinent obligations, then as a consequence you may not distribute the Library at all. For example, if a patent license would not permit royalty-free redistribution of the Library by all those who receive copies directly or indirectly through you, then the only way you could satisfy both it and this License would be to refrain entirely from distribution of the Library. If any portion of this section is held invalid or unenforceable under any particular circumstance, the balance of the section is intended to apply, and the section as a whole is intended to apply in other circumstances. It is not the purpose of this section to induce you to infringe any patents or other property right claims or to contest validity of any such claims; this section has the sole purpose of protecting the integrity of the free software distribution system which is implemented by public license practices. Many people have made generous contributions to the wide range of software distributed through that system in reliance on consistent application of that system; it is up to the author/donor to decide if he or she is willing to distribute software through any other system and a licensee cannot impose that choice. This section is intended to make thoroughly clear what is believed to be a consequence of the rest of this License.

13. If the distribution and/or use of the Library is restricted in certain countries either by patents or by copyrighted interfaces, the original copyright holder who places the Library under this License may add an explicit geographical distribution limitation excluding those countries, so that distribution is permitted only in or among countries not thus excluded. In such case, this License incorporates the limitation as if written in the body of this License.

14. The Free Software Foundation may publish revised and/or new versions of the Library General Public License from time to time. Such new versions will be similar in spirit to the present version, but may differ in detail to address new problems or concerns. Each version is given a distinguishing version number. If the Library specifies a version number of this License which applies to it and "any later version", you have the option of following the terms and conditions either of that version or of any later version published by the Free Software Foundation. If the Library does not specify a license version number, you may choose any version ever published by the Free Software Foundation.

15. If you wish to incorporate parts of the Library into other free programs whose distribution conditions are incompatible with these, write to the author to ask for permission. For software which is copyrighted by the Free Software Foundation, write to the Free Software Foundation; we sometimes make exceptions for this. Our decision will be guided by the two goals of preserving the free status of all derivatives of our free software and of promoting the sharing and reuse of software generally.

No Warranty

16. BECAUSE THE LIBRARY IS LICENSED FREE OF CHARGE, THERE IS NO WARRANTY FOR THE LIBRARY, TO THE EXTENT PERMITTED BY APPLICABLE LAW. EXCEPT WHEN OTHERWISE STATED IN WRITING THE COPYRIGHT HOLDERS AND/OR OTHER PARTIES PROVIDE THE LIBRARY "AS IS" WITHOUT WARRANTY OF ANY KIND, EITHER EXPRESSED OR IMPLIED, INCLUDING, BUT NOT LIMITED TO, THE IMPLIED WARRANTIES OF MERCHANTABILITY AND FITNESS FOR A PARTICULAR PURPOSE. THE ENTIRE RISK AS TO THE QUALITY AND PERFORMANCE OF THE LIBRARY IS WITH YOU. SHOULD THE LIBRARY PROVE DEFECTIVE, YOU ASSUME THE COST OF ALL NECESSARY SERVICING, REPAIR OR CORRECTION.

17. IN NO EVENT UNLESS REQUIRED BY APPLICABLE LAW OR AGREED TO IN WRITING WILL ANY COPYRIGHT HOLDER, OR ANY OTHER PARTY WHO MAY MODIFY AND/OR REDISTRIBUTE THE LIBRARY AS PERMITTED ABOVE, BE LIABLE TO YOU FOR DAMAGES, INCLUDING ANY GENERAL, SPECIAL, INCIDENTAL OR CONSEQUENTIAL DAMAGES ARISING OUT OF THE USE OR INABILITY TO USE THE LIBRARY (INCLUDING BUT NOT LIMITED TO LOSS OF DATA OR DATA BEING RENDERED INACCURATE OR LOSSES SUSTAINED BY YOU OR THIRD PARTIES OR A FAILURE OF THE LIBRARY TO OPERATE WITH ANY OTHER SOFTWARE), EVEN IF SUCH HOLDER OR OTHER PARTY HAS BEEN ADVISED OF THE POSSIBILITY OF SUCH DAMAGES.

END OF TERMS AND CONDITIONS

How to Apply These Terms to Your New Libraries

If you develop a new library, and you want it to be of the greatest possible use to the public, we recommend making it free software that everyone can redistribute and change. You can do so by permitting redistribution under these terms (or, alternatively, under the terms of the ordinary General Public License).

To apply these terms, attach the following notices to the library. It is safest to attach them to the start of each source file to most effectively convey the exclusion of warranty; and each file should have at least the "copyright" line and a pointer to where the full notice is found.

```
one line to give the library's name and an idea of what it does.
Copyright (C) year  name of author
```

```
This library is free software; you can redistribute it and/or modify it under
the terms of the GNU Library General Public License as published by the Free
Software Foundation; either version 2 of the License, or (at your option) any
later version.

This library is distributed in the hope that it will be useful, but WITHOUT
ANY WARRANTY; without even the implied warranty of MERCHANTABILITY or FITNESS
FOR A PARTICULAR PURPOSE. See the GNU Library General Public License for more
details.

You should have received a copy of the GNU Library General Public License
along with this library; if not, write to the Free Software Foundation, Inc.,
675 Mass Ave, Cambridge, MA 02139, USA.
```

Also, add information on how to contact you by electronic and paper mail.

You should also get your employer (if you work as a programmer) or your school, if any, to sign a "copyright disclaimer" for the library, if necessary. Here is a sample; alter the names:

```
Yoyodyne, Inc., hereby disclaims all copyright interest in the library 'Frob'
(a library for tweaking knobs) written by James Random Hacker.

signature of Ty Coon, 1 April 1990
Ty Coon, President of Vice
```

That's all there is to it!

Index

M-O

P-R

Books have a substantial influence on the destruction of the forests of the Earth. For example, it takes 17 trees to produce one ton of paper. A first printing of 30,000 copies of a typical 480-page book consumes 108,000 pounds of paper, which will require 918 trees!

Waite Group Press™ is against the clear-cutting of forests and supports refor-estation of the Pacific Northwest of the United States and Canada, where most of this paper comes from. As a publisher with several hundred thousand books sold each year, we feel an obligation to give back to the planet. We will therefore support organizations that seek to preserve the forests of planet Earth.

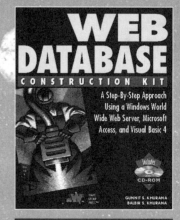

LIMITED WARRANTY

The following warranties shall be effective for 90 days from the date of purchase: (i) The Waite Group, Inc. warrants the enclosed disk to be free of defects in materials and workmanship under normal use; and (ii) The Waite Group, Inc. warrants that the programs, unless modified by the purchaser, will substantially perform the functions described in the documentation provided by The Waite Group, Inc. when operated on the designated hardware and operating system. The Waite Group, Inc. does not warrant that the programs will meet purchaser's requirements or that operation of a program will be uninterrupted or error-free. The program warranty does not cover any program that has been altered or changed in any way by anyone other than The Waite Group, Inc. The Waite Group, Inc. is not responsible for problems caused by changes in the operating characteristics of computer hardware or computer operating systems that are made after the release of the programs, nor for problems in the interaction of the programs with each other or other software.

THESE WARRANTIES ARE EXCLUSIVE AND IN LIEU OF ALL OTHER WARRANTIES OF MERCHANTABILITY OR FITNESS FOR A PARTICULAR PURPOSE OR OF ANY OTHER WARRANTY, WHETHER EXPRESS OR IMPLIED.

EXCLUSIVE REMEDY

The Waite Group, Inc. will replace any defective disk without charge if the defective disk is returned to The Waite Group, Inc. within 90 days from date of purchase.

This is Purchaser's sole and exclusive remedy for any breach of warranty or claim for contract, tort, or damages.

LIMITATION OF LIABILITY

THE WAITE GROUP, INC. AND THE AUTHORS OF THE PROGRAMS SHALL NOT IN ANY CASE BE LIABLE FOR SPECIAL, INCIDENTAL, CONSEQUENTIAL, INDIRECT, OR OTHER SIMILAR DAMAGES ARISING FROM ANY BREACH OF THESE WARRANTIES EVEN IF THE WAITE GROUP, INC. OR ITS AGENT HAS BEEN ADVISED OF THE POSSIBILITY OF SUCH DAMAGES.

THE LIABILITY FOR DAMAGES OF THE WAITE GROUP, INC. AND THE AUTHORS OF THE PROGRAMS UNDER THIS AGREEMENT SHALL IN NO EVENT EXCEED THE PURCHASE PRICE PAID.

COMPLETE AGREEMENT

This Agreement constitutes the complete agreement between The Waite Group, Inc. and the authors of the programs, and you, the purchaser.

Some states do not allow the exclusion or limitation of implied warranties or liability for incidental or consequential damages, so the above exclusions or limitations may not apply to you. This limited warranty gives you specific legal rights; you may have others, which vary from state to state.

SATISFACTION REPORT CARD

Please fill out this card if you wish to know of future updates to
***Web Database Primer Plus,* or to receive our catalog.**

First Name: _____ **Last Name:** _____

Street Address: _____

City: _____ **State:** _____ **Zip:** _____

E-mail Address _____

Daytime Telephone: (   ) _____

Date product was acquired: Month _____ **Day** _____ **Year** _____ **Your Occupation:** _____

Overall, how would you rate *Web Database Primer Plus?*
- ☐ Excellent ☐ Very Good ☐ Good
- ☐ Fair ☐ Below Average ☐ Poor

What did you like MOST about this book? _____
_____
_____

What did you like LEAST about this book? _____
_____
_____

Please describe any problems you may have encountered with installing or using the disk: _____
_____

How did you use this book (problem-solver, tutorial, reference...)?
_____

What is your level of computer expertise?
- ☐ New ☐ Dabbler ☐ Hacker
- ☐ Power User ☐ Programmer ☐ Experienced Professional

What computer languages are you familiar with? _____
_____

Please describe your computer hardware:
Computer _____ Hard disk _____
5.25" disk drives _____ 3.5" disk drives _____
Video card _____ Monitor _____
Printer _____ Peripherals _____
Sound Board _____ CD-ROM_____

Where did you buy this book?
- ☐ Bookstore (name): _____
- ☐ Discount store (name): _____
- ☐ Computer store (name): _____
- ☐ Catalog (name): _____
- ☐ Direct from WGP   ☐ Other _____

What price did you pay for this book? _____

What influenced your purchase of this book?
- ☐ Recommendation ☐ Advertisement
- ☐ Magazine review ☐ Store display
- ☐ Mailing ☐ Book's format
- ☐ Reputation of Waite Group Press ☐ Other

How many computer books do you buy each year? _____

How many other Waite Group books do you own? _____

What is your favorite Waite Group book? _____
_____

Is there any program or subject you would like to see Waite Group Press cover in a similar approach? _____
_____

Additional comments? _____
_____
_____

Please send to: **Waite Group Press**
200 Tamal Plaza
Corte Madera, CA 94925

☐ **Check here for a free Waite Group catalog**

BEFORE YOU OPEN THE DISK OR CD-ROM PACKAGE ON THE FACING PAGE, CAREFULLY READ THE LICENSE AGREEMENT.

Opening this package indicates that you agree to abide by the license agreement found in the back of this book. If you do not agree with it, promptly return the unopened disk package (including the related book) to the place you obtained them for a refund.